GRANDMOTHER'S SCHOLAR.

The Art of
KNITTING

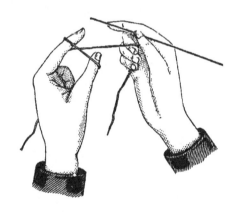

DOVER PUBLICATIONS, INC.
MINEOLA, NEW YORK

Bibliographical Note

This Dover edition, first published in 2016, is an unabridged republication of the work originally published by The Butterick Publishing Co., London and New York, in 1892.

Library of Congress Cataloging-in-Publication Data

The art of knitting. — Dover edition.
    pages cm.
    Reprint of: New York : The Butterick Publishing Co., 1892.
    ISBN-13: 978-0-486-80311-1
    ISBN-10: 0-486-80311-2
    1. Knitting. 2. Knitting—Patterns.

TT820.A78 2016
746.43'2—dc23

2015030864

Manufactured in the United States by LSC Communications
80311202   2016
www.doverpublications.com

INTRODUCTION.

———•———

IN PRESENTING our patrons this book upon THE ART OF KNITTING, in response to their continuous demand for such a work, we take especial pride in announcing that it is the most complete of its kind, and the only one devoted wholly to the occupation or pastime of Knitting ever published. As it is intended for a companion-pamphlet to our publication upon THE ART OF CROCHETING, it has been prepared upon the same basis— that is, the very first rudiments of the work are carefully described and illustrated, so that the amateur may acquire correctness and celerity in personally beginning and developing the art of Knitting, and with little difficulty soon keep pace with an expert in the work.

The secret of the success of any undertaking is—first, complete mastery of details from the very first preliminaries; second, sufficient perseverance to grasp and conquer difficulties through a knowledge of detail, thus bringing harmonious results from puzzling or complicated conditions.

The same foundation of success is incorporated in the ART OF KNITTING. We give you the first principles and many designs from the simple to the intricate, each accompanied by correct instructions whose signs and symbols are fully explained at the beginning of the collection. Given these, the persevering knitter can, with little difficulty, develop in a perfect manner every article described or suggested in THE ART OF KNITTING. But "patience" must be "a virtue" belonging to every knitter, whether it be a gift of nature or a matter of cultivation and discipline.

We have endeavored to present the best of everything in the way of designs, and have spared neither time nor expense, nor the virtue we recommend, in selecting and properly preparing the collection, and feel, therefore, a justifiable gratification in the result—a sentiment the purchasers of THE ART OF KNITTING cannot but experience, once they are in possession of the book and begin to follow its instructions.

THE BUTTERICK PUBLISHING CO. [Limited],

7, 9 AND 11 WEST 13TH STREET, NEW YORK.

CONTENTS.

The Art of Knitting.

ABBREVIATIONS USED IN KNITTING.

k.—Knit plain.
p.—Purl, or as is often called, seam.
pl.—Plain knitting.
n.—Narrow.
k 2 to.—Knit 2 together. Same as n.
th o or o.—Throw the thread over the needle.
Make one.—Make a stitch thus: Throw the thread in front of the needle and knit the next stitch in the ordinary manner. (In the next row or round this throw-over, or put-over as it is frequently called, is used as a stitch.) Or, knit one and purl one out of a stitch.
To Knit Crossed.—Insert needle in the back of the stitch and knit as usual.

sl.—Slip a stitch from the left needle to the right needle without knitting it.
sl. and b.—Slip and bind. Slip one stitch, knit the next; pass the slipped stitch over the knit stitch as in binding off work.
To Bind or Cast off.—Either slip or knit the first stitch; knit the next; pass the first or slipped stitch over the second, and repeat as far as directed.
Row.—Knitting once across the work when but two needles are used.
Round.—Knitting once around the work when four or more needles are used, as in a sock or stocking.
Repeat.—This means to work designated rows, rounds or portions of work as many times as designated.

☞ * Stars or asterisks mean, as mentioned wherever they occur, that the details given between them are to be repeated as many times as directed before going on with those details which follow the next star. As an example: * K 2, p l, th o, and repeat twice more from * (or last *) means that you are to knit as follows: k 2, p l, th o; k 2, p l, th o; k 2, p l, th o, thus repeating the k 2, p l, th o, twice after knitting it the first time, making it three times in all before proceeding with the next part of the direction.

GENERAL DIRECTIONS FOR KNITTING.

Most amateur knitters, and many experts, confess to an inability to follow the instructions and

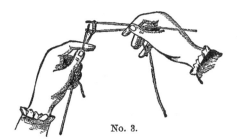

No. 1.

No. 2.

knitting designs published in various books and periodicals for their benefit. This is the result of a lack of perseverance on the part of the knitter, and is also often due to the different abbreviations used by different publishers of such work. A mastery of any set of abbreviations will overcome the main difficulty; then, if the instructions are correct, the development of the design will be

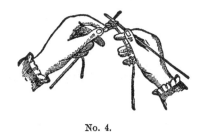

No. 3.

No. 4.

Nos. 1, 2, 3 and 4.—Details for Casting on Stitches with Two Needles.

comparatively easy. We therefore urge those who purchase this manual, to become familiar with the abbreviations given above before beginning any of the designs presented on the following pages; for much time has been spent to render them plain and correctly adapt them to the accompanying instructions.

Casting On Stitches.

As every other task or pleasure has a beginning,

so has knitting. The foundation, materials in hand, is, "casting on stitches," for which we give several methods, as follows:

Of the two or three methods of casting on stitches, the one best adapted to garments or articles where an elastic edge is desired, is developed with a single thread or yarn and two needles. It is conducted as follows:

First Method.

Make a loop in the yarn or thread and slip it onto a needle. (See No. 1.)

Next slip the second needle into the loop, (see No. 2.) throw the yarn around it, draw it through (see No. 3.) and slip the loop thus formed onto the left-hand needle, thrusting the latter needle through it from the front to the back. Put the right-hand needle into the second loop (see No. 4,) make another loop as at No. 3, and slip it onto the left-hand needle. Repeat in this manner until you have as many stitches as required.

Second Method. (With One Needle.)

Hold the end of the yarn under the third and fourth fingers of the left-hand. With the right (which also holds the needle) bring the yarn from under the left thumb up over it and also over the first finger of the left hand, then downward under the finger and up over the thumb; (see No. 5). Then pass the point of the needle under the crossing up back of that

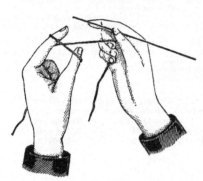

No. 5.

portion of the yarn that is brought down from the first finger (see No. 6), draw it forward toward the left, grasp the crossing with the thumb and finger (see No. 7), throw the yarn over the needle with the right hand (which holds the yarn as in regular knitting) draw a loop through, slip the yarn off the left first finger and draw it down to knot the loop or stitch on the needle. Then arrange the yarn over the left hand again and make another loop or stitch in the same way. Repeat until you have the required number of stitches on the needle.

Third Method.

Same as second except that the yarn which passes over the left hand is

Plain Knitting.

Having cast on the requisite number of stitches, thrust the right-hand needle into the first stitch; throw the thread around its point, draw it through to form a loop or stitch; repeat this movement for the next and all the stitches on the left-hand needle. In knitting a sock or stocking repeat along each needle in regular order, round and round.

Fancy Knitting.

This is done according to special instructions given stitch by stitch, but the details include only foundation principles, such as knitting plain, seaming or purling, widening, narrowing, etc., etc.

Seaming or Purling.

"Seam" and "purl" are different names for the same movement. Every knitter knows how to

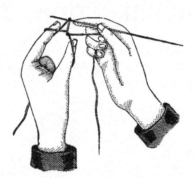 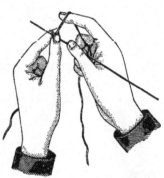

No. 6.   No. 7.

Nos. 5, 6 and 7.—Details for Casting on Stitches with One Needle.

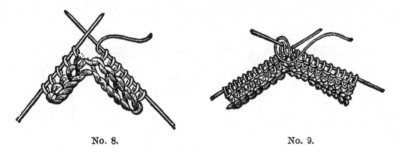

No. 8.   No. 9.

Nos. 8 and 9.—Method of Seaming or "Purling."

"seam a stitch." To purl a stitch means exactly the same thing. For those who are not proficient in knitting as yet, we explain as follows: To "seam" or "purl," throw the thread from its usual position at the back of the work in front of the right-hand needle (see No. 8); then insert the point of the latter under the next stitch thrusting it through from the *right* toward the *left* instead of the way usual in knitting plain; this will bring the right-hand needle in front of the left one instead of back of it as in plain knitting; now throw the thread around the right-hand needle by the same movement as the one used in plain knitting (see No. 9), and draw the loop *backward* instead of forward. Seam or purl as many stitches as required, and then throw the yarn back of the needle into its ordinary position. The front of the work is the side next to the knitter; the back, the side away from her.

doubled, the end being held, with the yarn itself, to begin the casting, the same as in the beginning of the Second Method. The yarn is held single in the right hand and unwinds from the ball. The length of the doubled portion must, necessarily be a matter of guess-work, depending upon the size of the article to be knit. The doubled thread or yarn makes a very firm edge for stockings and socks, or any garments that are to be subjected to continuous service.

METHODS OF WIDENING OR INCREASING.

Widening by throwing the thread in front of the needle between stitches makes a tiny opening that is objectionable, except in fancy patterns. In plain knitting it is best to widen by knitting a plain and a purled stitch out of the same loop without slipping the loop until both are made; or, by knitting one out of the front and one out of the back of the same loop or stitch in the same manner; or, by taking up and knitting, as a stitch, the bar of thread between the two needles. Where two stitches are to be made by throwing the thread, it must pass in front of the needle, over it and to the front again. The general direction for this is, "thread over twice." In working back, to complete the two new stitches knit the first throw-over like an ordinary stitch, but in knitting the second you must put the needle into the back loop of the stitch instead of the front. In widening or increasing three stitches, the same plan must be observed, by knitting from the back of the second and third throw-overs. In increasing by throwing the thread, the following is another method: Pass the right needle through a loop in the ordinary manner, throw the thread twice around it and draw the two throw-overs through together as if they were one. This is practically the same as throwing the thread over the needle twice between stitches, and the throw-overs are knit off in the same manner.

TO WIDEN WHEN PURLING.

The thread, being already in front of the needle, must be wound once entirely around it.

METHODS OF NARROWING OR DECREASING.

The most generally used method of narrowing is to "knit two together." To do this slip the point of the right-hand needle in the ordinary manner under *two* stitches at once, and then throw the thread over and draw the loop through both as if they were one. This method may also be used by putting the needle through the *back* of two stitches instead of through the *front;* this will make them lie more flatly than by the other method and will form a regular chain. Another method is to slip one, knit one, and pass the slipped stitch over the knitted one. This narrows by one stitch. To narrow two stitches: Slip one, knit two together and pass the slipped stitch over the two knitted stitches. Three stitches may be narrowed upon the same principle.

TO NARROW WHEN PURLING.

Purl two together; or, purl one, put it back on the left-hand needle and then draw the next stitch beyond over it, drop the drawn stitch off the needle, and then slip the first stitch back on the right needle. Or, two stitches may be purled from the back, by throwing the thread forward in the usual way and taking up the two stitches by slipping the point of the right needle under them from the *left* side toward the *right*, and bringing the right-hand needle over the left one in the usual way.

EDGE STITCHES.

The stitch at each end of a row in knitting is called the edge stitch. It is generally disposed of so as to keep the edge straight or even, but is not spoken of as an edge stitch in instructions.

THE FIRST STITCH.

Always slip the first stitch in knitting and knit the last, unless special instructions for disposing of them are given. This will make a more even edge. A chain-edge for stripes is formed by slipping the first and purling the last stitch.

STITCHES UNINTENTIONALLY DROPPED.

Either ravel your work back to the dropped stitch and then restore it and the others to the needle, or, if it has slipped down for a number of rows, take a crochet hook and carefully chain it up through all the lines until the needle is reached.

TO FASTEN TWO THREADS TOGETHER.

Lap the ends of the threads for a short distance and knit a few stitches with both at the same time. This will prevent a knot and make the work firm and smooth.

TO JOIN OR BIND TOGETHER.

Knit as far across the row as directed—generally to the middle. Then fold the work so as to bring the two needles side by side. Take an extra needle, put it through the first or end stitch on the needle next to you, then through the corresponding stitch on the other needle; knit the two together as one stitch. Knit in this way across the two needles, break off the yarn and fasten.

DOUBLE KNITTING.

The two sides of double knitting look alike and can be lifted apart. The work is done as follows: Cast on an even number of stitches. Bring the thread in front, slip one stitch inserting the needle as if for purling, put the thread back and knit one stitch. Repeat to the end of the row. The second row is like the first, except that you *knit* the *slipped* stitches and *slip* the *knitted* ones.

RIB KNITTING.

This is made by purling and knitting alternately a like number of stitches. The most general rib is made by knitting two and purling two, across or around the work. When the ribbing is done on two needles, in working every other time across, the stitches that were *knitted* must be *purled*, and those that were *purled* must be *knitted*.

PATENT KNITTING.

This method is frequently used in knitting children's underwear. It is worked as follows: * Throw the wool forward, slip one, knit two together, and repeat from * across or around the work. In knitting on two needles, work back in the same way.

FANCY STITCHES AND DESIGNS IN KNITTING.

KNOTTED STITCH.

No. 1.—Cast on any number of stitches required.

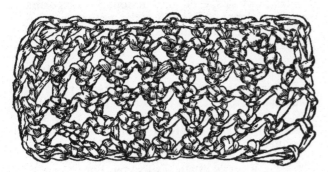

No. 1.—KNOTTED STITCH.

First row.—Th o twice, k 1, and repeat across the row.

Second row.—* K 1; out of the two put-overs (th o twice) p 1, k 1. Now pass the 1st and 2nd stitches on the left hand needle over the 3rd; then repeat these details from the *, and continue repeating in this way to the end of the row. These two rows complete the pattern.

DESIGN FOR KNITTING SHAWLS, FASCINATORS, CLOUDS, ETC.

No. 2.—Cast on an even number of stitches and knit across plain, using No. 4 or 6 needles.

First row.—Knit plain.

Second row.—Slip 1, k 1, * wool in front of the needle, insert needle under 3 stitches and knit as 1; repeat from * to the end of the row, and knit the last stitch.

Third row.—Knit 2, * knit 1 out of the put-over thread, purl 1, knit 1, and repeat from *.

Fourth, Fifth and Sixth rows.—Knit plain.

Repeat from 2nd row for all the work.

CANE-WORK DESIGN.

No. 3.—Use four needles. (The design may also be knitted on two needles by making 1 stitch in every 4th purled row to take the place of the last put-over in the preceding row).

Cast on any number of stitches divisible by 4.

First row.—Th o, k 1, th o, k 3 and repeat across the row.

Second, Fourth, Sixth, Eighth and Tenth rows.—Purl.

Third row.—* K 3, th o, sl 1, k 2 together, pass the slipped stitch over, th o and repeat from * (or beginning of the row) across the work.

Fifth row.—* Th o, sl 1, k 2 together, pass slipped stitch over, th o, k 3 and repeat from * across the work.

Seventh row.—Same as third.

Ninth row.—Same as fifth.

Tenth row.—Purl as directed and then repeat from third row for the next section of the work.

This is a favorite design for the fronts of stockings and is generally made about three inches wide, and may extend from the toe as high as desired.

DESIGN IN KNITTING.

(No Illustration.)

This stitch is suitable for clouds, shawls, etc. Split zephyr wool and No. 4 or 6 needles are used in knitting the design. Bone or wooden needles may be used if the work is desired very open. Cast on an even number of stitches, and knit a plain row.

First row.—Knit plain.

Second row.—Slip 1, knit 1, * th o, knit 3 together, *; repeat from star to star to the end of the row; knit last stitch plain.

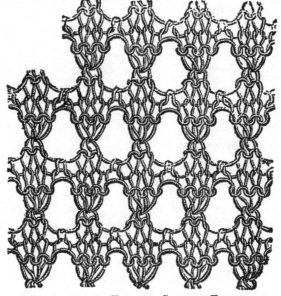

No. 2.—DESIGN FOR KNITTING SHAWLS, FASCINATORS, CLOUDS, ETC.

Third row.—Knit 2; * where the thread was put over in last row, knit 1 stitch plain, and seam 1; then knit 1, *; repeat from star to star to end of row.

Fourth row.—Plain.

Fifth and Sixth rows.—Plain; repeat from 2nd row.

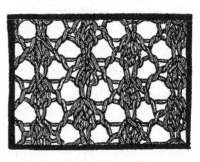

No. 3.—CANE-WORK DESIGN.

FANCY KNITTED STRIPE.

No. 4.—Two or four needles may be used for this design. In working with two needles, *purl* instead of *knitting plain* in the alternate rows. The design is complete in 8 rows or rounds. Cast on any number of stitches divisible by 9 and work as follows :

No. 4.—FANCY KNITTED STRIPE.

First round.—K 3, n, th o, k 4 and repeat.
Second, Fourth, Sixth and Eighth rounds.—Knit plain.
Third round.—K 2, n, th o, n, th o, k 3 and repeat.
Fifth round.—K 1, n, th o, n, th o, n, th o, k 2 and repeat.
Seventh round.—N, th o, n, th o, n, th o, n, th o, k 1 and repeat.
Knit 8th row as directed and repeat from beginning.

KNITTED DESIGN FOR SHAWLS, STRIPES, SPREADS, AFGHANS, ETC.

No. 5.—Cast on any number of stitches divisible by 6 and knit across plain.
Next row.—* K 1, th o 3 times and repeat across the row.
Next row.—Slip 1, drop the put-overs and repeat 5 times more until there are 6 stitches on the right-hand needle. Now pass the *first* 3 stitches slipped over the *last* 3, being careful not to twist them in crossing. Then pass them onto the left-hand needle and knit off. Repeat in this way across the work.
Next two rows.—Plain.

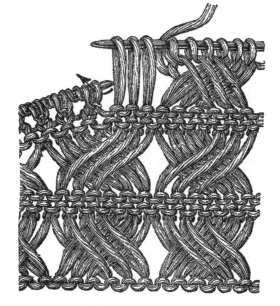

No. 5.—KNITTED DESIGN FOR SHAWLS, STRIPES, SPREADS, AFGHANS, ETC.

Next row.—K 1, th o 3 times and repeat across the row.
Next row.—Slip 1, drop the put-overs and repeat 5 times more, as before. Then pass the 6 stitches onto the left-hand needle, and pass the *last* three over the *first* 3, and then knit as before. Repeat across the row.
Next two rows.—Plain.
Then repeat from * for all the work.

NARROW FANCY STRIPE IN KNITTING.

No. 6.—This design may be made on two needles instead of four if preferred, except that in this case the alternate rows must be purled instead of knitted. Cast on any number of stitches divisible by 4. Four rows or rounds complete the pattern.
First round.—K 1, n, th o, k 1, and repeat.
Second and Fourth rounds.—Plain.
Third round.—N, th o, k 2 and repeat.
Repeat these four rounds to any depth desired.

No. 6.—NARROW FANCY STRIPE IN KNITTING.

FANCY-STRIPE DESIGN.

No. 7.—Use four steel needles. Cast on any number of stitches divisible by 10.
First round.—P 3, k 1, th o, sl and b, k 4, and repeat from beginning of round.
Second round.—P 3, k 2, th o, sl and b, k 3, and repeat from beginning of round.
Third round.—Purl 3, k 3, th o, sl and b, k 2 and repeat.
Fourth round.—Purl 3, k 4, th o, sl and b, k 1 and repeat.
Fifth round.—P 3, k 5, th o, sl and b and repeat. Then repeat from first round for all the work.
This will be found a very pretty pattern for the fronts of stockings or the backs of mittens, and may be continued as far as individual taste may dictate. It is also pretty for the tops of infant's socks.

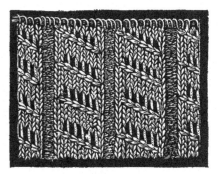

No. 7.—FANCY-STRIPE DESIGN.

FANCY DESIGN IN KNITTING.

No. 8.—Use four needles.

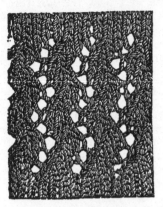

NO. 8.—FANCY DESIGN IN KNITTING.

Cast on any number of stitches divisible by four. Twelve rounds complete the design.

First round.—Knit 2, n, th o and repeat around the work.

Second and every alternate round, including the Twelfth.—Knit plain.

Third round.—K 1, n, th o, k 1 and repeat around the work.

Fifth round.—Narrow, th o, k 2 and repeat.

Seventh round.—K 2, th o, slip and bind and repeat to end of round.

Knit the eighth round as directed, (plain), and then pass the first stitch on each needle to the next needle; this will leave one stitch on the 3rd needle which is considered a part of the 8th round in addition to its other stitches, and is knitted as such before the next round is begun.

Ninth round.—K 2, th o, slip and bind and repeat to end of round.

Eleventh round.—N, th o, k 2 and repeat. In the 12th round knit all but the last stitch; then pass the last stitch on each needle to the next needle. For the next division of the pattern, repeat from the 5th to the 12th rounds inclusive, also making the transfers of the stitches as directed for the first division.

FANCY DESIGN IN KNITTING.

No. 9.—Use four needles. Cast on any number of stitches divisible by 6, and knit 16 rounds for each section of the pattern.

First round.—N, th o and repeat.
Second, Third and Fourth rounds.—Plain.
Fifth round.—K 3, n, th o, k 1 and repeat.
Sixth round.—K 2, n, th o, k 2 and repeat.
Seventh round.—K 1, n, th o, k 3 and repeat.
Eighth round.—N, th o, k 4 and repeat.
Ninth round.—K 2, th o, slip and bind, k 2 and repeat.
Tenth round.—K 3, th o, slip and bind, k 1 and repeat.
Eleventh round.—K 4, th o, slip and bind and repeat.

Twelfth, Thirteenth and Fourteenth rounds.—Plain.
Fifteenth round.—N, th o and repeat.
Sixteenth round.—Plain. Then repeat the 3 plain rounds and all of the directions.

KNOB-STITCH DESIGN.

No. 10.—Cast on any number of stitches divisible by 4, with 2 added for edge stitches.

First row.—K 1, * make 3 stitches out of the next stitch, by purling 1, knitting 1, and purling 1, all out of it. (Do not slip the stitch off until the last purling is made). Then k 3 together and repeat from *, knitting the last stitch.

Second row.—Plain.

Third row.—K 1, * k 3 together. Make 3 out of the next stitch as in first row; and repeat from * across the row knitting the last stitch plain.

Fourth row.—Plain.

These four rows form the design. Repeat until the work is of the required dimensions.

SHELL DESIGN IN KNITTING.

No. 11.—Use four needles. Cast on any number

No. 9.—FANCY DESIGN IN KNITTING.

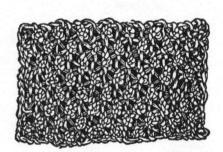

NO. 10.—KNOB-STITCH DESIGN.

of stitches divisible by 8. The design is complete in 7 rounds.

First round.—Slip and bind, k 6, th o and repeat.

Second round.—Slip and bind, k 5, th o, k 1 and repeat.

Third round.—Sl and b, k 4, th o, k 2 and repeat.

Fourth round.—Sl and b, k 3, th o, k 3 and repeat.

Fifth round.—Sl and b, k 2, th o, k 4 and repeat.

NO. 11.—SHELL DESIGN IN KNITTING.

Sixth round.—Sl and b, k 1, th o, k 5 and repeat.
Seventh round.—Sl and b, th o, k 6 and repeat.
Repeat from first round.

FANCY SHELL-STRIPE IN KNITTING.

No. 12.—Use four needles. Cast on any number of stitches divisible by 14. The design is complete in 14 rounds.

No. 12.—FANCY SHELL-STRIPE IN KNITTING.

First round.— K 7, th o, k 5, n, and repeat.

Second and Ninth rounds.—Plain.

Third round.— Sl and b, k 5, th o, k 1, th o, k 4, n, and repeat.

Fourth round.—Sl and b, k 4, th o, k 3, th o, k 3, n, and repeat.

Fifth round.—Sl and b, k 3, th o, k 5, th o, k 2, n, and repeat.

Sixth round.—Sl and b, k 2, th o, k 7, th o, k 1, n, and repeat.

Seventh round.—Sl and b, k 1, th o, k 9, th o, n, and repeat.

Eighth round.—Sl and b, k 5, th o, k 7 and repeat.

Tenth round.—Sl and b, k 4, th o, k 1, th o, k 5, n, and repeat.

Eleventh round.—Sl and b, k 3, th o, k 3, th o, k 4, n, and repeat.

Twelfth round.—Sl and b, k 2, th o, k 5, th o, k 3, n, and repeat.

Thirteenth round.—Sl and b, k 1, th o, k 7, th o, k 2, n and repeat.

Fourteenth round.—Sl and b, th o, k 9, th o, k 1, n, and repeat.

Repeat from first round for remainder of pattern.

HERRING-BONE DESIGN.

No. 13.—Cast on any number of stitches divisible by 3.

First row.—K 1, k 2 together, th o, and repeat across the row, ending with k 2.

Second row.—P 1, p 2 together, th o, and repeat, ending the row with p 2.

Repeat these two rows for all the work.

HERRING-BONE DESIGN (No. 2).
(No Illustration.)

Cast on an uneven number of stitches.

First row.—K 1, * th o, k 2 together, and repeat from * across the row.

Second row.—Same as first.

This makes a very open effect, such as is seen in knitted laces.

FANCY DESIGN IN KNITTING.

No. 14.—Four needles are necessary in knitting this design, which is complete in 14 rounds.

Cast on any number of stitches divisible· by 6.

First round.—Narrow, th o and repeat around the work.

Second, Third and Fourth rounds.—Plain.

Fifth round.—K 4, n, th o and repeat.

Sixth round.—K 3, n, th o, k 1 and repeat.

Seventh round.—K 2, n, th o, k 2 and repeat.

Eighth round.—K 1, n, th o, k 3 and repeat.

Ninth round.—N, th o, k 4 and repeat.

Tenth, Eleventh and Twelfth rounds.—Plain.

Thirteenth round.—N, th o and repeat.

Fourteenth round.—Plain; repeat from the 3rd round for rest of work.

SHELL DESIGN IN KNITTING.

No. 15.—Use four needles and cast on any number of stitches divisible by 9. The design is complete in 12 rounds.

First round.—Slip and bind, k 5, th o, k 1, th o, k 1 and repeat.

Second, Fourth, Sixth, Eighth, Tenth and Twelfth

No. 13.—HERRING-BONE DESIGN.

No. 14.—FANCY DESIGN IN KNITTING.

rounds.—Slip and bind, k 8 and repeat. In each of these rounds there will be 10 stitches on each needle instead of 9.

Third round.— Slip and bind, k 4, th o, k 1, th o, k 2 and repeat.

Fifth round.— Slip and bind, k 3, th o, k 1, th o, k 3 and repeat.

Seventh round.— Slip and bind, k 2, th o, k 1, th o, k 4 and repeat.

Ninth round.— Slip and bind, k 1, th o, k 1, th o, k 5 and repeat across the row.

Eleventh round.—Slip and bind, th o, k 1. th o, k 6 and repeat.

No. 15.—SHELL DESIGN IN KNITTING.

Knit 12th round as directed and repeat from beginning of these details for all of the pattern, making it as deep as desired.

KNOT-STITCH DESIGN.

No. 16.—This stitch looks best in heavy wool and is suitable for afghans, spreads, cushion-covers, etc., etc. Use two steel needles. Cast on any number of stitches required.

NO. 16.—KNOT-STITCH DESIGN.

First row.—Throw the wool over the needle twice, k 1, and repeat across the row.

Second row.—K the first stitch; then out of the two throw-overs, purl one, k the other; then pass the 1st and 2nd stitches on the right-hand needle over the 3rd; repeat from beginning across the row.

Repeat these two rows for all of the work.

FANCY PATTERN IN KNITTING.

No. 17.—To be knitted with four needles. Cast on any number of stitches divisible by 6. The design is complete in 8 rounds.

First round.—Knit 1, n, th o, k 3 and repeat.
Second, Fourth, Sixth and Eighth rounds.—Knit plain.
Third round.—N, th o, k 1, th o, slip and bind, k 1 and repeat.

After knitting the fourth round pass the first stitch on each needle onto the next needle; this will leave 1 stitch on the 3rd needle which is considered as a part of the 4th round and is knit as such before the fifth round is begun.

Fifth round.—Th o, k 3, th o, slip 1, n, pass slipped stitch over and repeat.
Seventh round.—Th o, k 4, n, and repeat.
Eighth round.—Plain, as directed, and repeat from 1st round for rest of work.

DESIGN FOR FANCY KNITTING.

No. 18.—Cast on any number of stitches divisible by 6. The design is complete in 20 rows or rounds which are knit as follows:
First round.—K 1, n, th o, k 3 and repeat.
Second and every alternate round including the Twentieth.—Plain.
Third round.—N, th o, k 1, th o, slip and bind, k 1 and repeat.
Fifth round.—K 1, n, th o, k 3 and repeat.

Seventh round.—N, th o, k 1, th o, slip and bind, k 1 and repeat.

Knit the eighth round plain (as directed) then pass the first stitch on each needle to the next needle. This will leave 1 stitch on the 3rd needle which is considered a part of the 8th round and is knitted as such before beginning the 9th round.

Ninth round.—Th o, k 3, th o, sl 1, n, pass slipped stitch over and repeat.
Eleventh round.—Th o, slip and bind, k 1, n, th o, k 1 and repeat.
Thirteenth round.—K 1, th o, sl 1, n, pass slipped stitch over, th o, k 2 and repeat.
Fifteenth round.—K 1, n, th o, k 3 and repeat.
Seventeenth round.—N, th o, k 1, th o, sl and bind, k 1 and repeat.
Nineteenth round.—K 1, n, th o, k 3 and repeat.

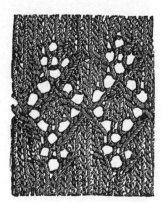

NO. 18.—DESIGN FOR FANCY KNITTING.

In repeating the pattern, knit 2 plain rounds, then begin with the first round for the next row of holes.

DESIGN FOR KNITTED BORDER.

No. 19.—To make this border in Shetland wool requires one thick wooden knitting-needle and two fine steel ones. With the latter, three rows are knitted backward and forward, and then one row with the wooden needle. By drawing up the

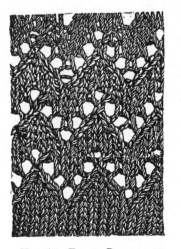

NO. 17.—FANCY PATTERN IN KNITTING.

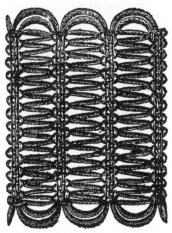

NO. 19.—DESIGN FOR KNITTED BORDER.

side stitches, the edge scollops are made, in which, if desired, a few open scollop rows can be crocheted or netted. In this example of the design, which may be widened at pleasure, sixteen stitches are to be cast on.

OPEN-WORK DESIGN.

No. 20.—Two or four needles may be used for this design. If made on two needles *knit* the second and every alternate following row.

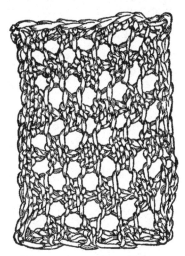

NO. 20.—OPEN-WORK DESIGN.

Cast on any number of stitches divisible by 4, using four needles.

First round.—* Make 1, k 1, make 1, k 3 and repeat from * across the work.

Second round.—Purl.

Third round.—* K 3, make 1, sl 1, k 2 together, pass slipped stitch over, make 1 and repeat from * across the work. At the end of this row, (when using two needles) in making the stitch, pick it up from the preceding row, after the method explained for making stitches, on page 9.

Fifth round.—* Make 1, sl 1, k 2 together, pass slipped stitch over, make 1, k 3 and repeat from * for the whole round.

Seventh round.—Like third round.

Ninth round.—Like fifth round.

Tenth round.—Purl, as directed, and then repeat from third round.

DIAMOND STRIPE.

No. 21.—Cast on any number of stitches divisible by 14.

First row.—K 1, th o, k 2 together at the back, th o, k 2 together at the back, k 5, k 2 together, th o, k 2 together, th o and repeat from beginning, ending with make 1 instead of th o.

Second and every alternate row.—Purl.

Third row.—* K 2, th o, k 2 together at the back, th o, k 2 together at the back, k 3, k 2 together, th o, k 2 together, th o, k 1 and repeat from *.

Fifth row.—* K 3, th o, k 2 together at the back, th o, k 2 together at the back, k 1, k 2 together, th o, k 2 together, th o, k 2, and repeat from *.

Seventh row.—K 4, th o, k 2 together at the back, th o, k 3 together, th o, k 2 together, th o, k 3 and repeat as before.

Ninth row.—K 3, k 2 together, th o, k 2 together, th o, k 1, th o, k 2 together at the back, th o, k 2 together at the back, k 2 and repeat.

Eleventh row.—K 2, k 2 together, th o, k 2 to-

gether, th o, k 3, th o, k 2 together at the back, th o, k 2 together at the back, k 1 and repeat.

Thirteenth row.—K 1, k 2 together, th o, k 2 together, th o, k 5, th o, k 2 together at the back, th o, k 2 together at the back and repeat.

Fifteenth row.—K 2 together, * th o, k 2 together, th o, k 7, th o, k 2 together at the back, th o, k 3 together and repeat from *. At the end of the last repetition in this row there will be only 1 stitch to knit instead of 3 together.

Purl the sixteenth row. Then repeat from the first row, but at the end of this row, there will be an extra stitch which you knit instead of making 1.

PEACOCK'S TAIL PATTERN.

No. 22.—Cast on any number of stitches divisible by 9, with 4 added for the edge stitches. The

NO. 22.—PEACOCK'S TAIL PATTERN.

edges, which are in plain knitting on the right side of the work, are not mentioned after the first row. In knitting these stitches, knit them on the right side of the work and purl them on the wrong side.

First row.—K 2 (for edge) k 2, * th o, k 1; repeat 4 times more from *; th o, k 2. Repeat from beginning, ending with knit 2.

Second row.—* P 2, k 11, p 2 and repeat from * across the row.

Third row.—* N, k 11, n, and repeat from * across the row.

Fourth row.—P 2 together, p 9, p 2 together and repeat.

Fifth row.—N, k 7, n, and repeat.

Sixth row.—Purl.

NO. 21.—DIAMOND STRIPE.

NO. 23.—FANCY STRIPE IN KNITTING.

Now repeat from 1st row for all the sections of the work.

FANCY STRIPE IN KNITTING.

No. 23.—This may be knitted on two needles as well as four; but in using two needles, in the alternate rows you knit 2, and purl 12, instead of knitting 12 and purling 2. Cast on any number of stitches divisible by 14. Twelve rows or rounds complete the design.

First round. (Four needles).—K 2, th o, k 1,

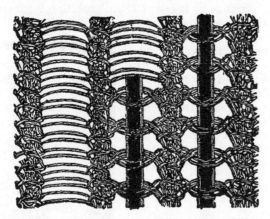

No. 24.—KNITTED STRIPE FOR SHAWLS, JACKETS, ETC., ETC.

th o, k 1, slip and bind, k 3, n, k 1, p 2 and repeat.

Second and every alternate round including the Twelfth.—K 12, p 2 and repeat.

Third round.—K 2, th o, k 3, th o, k 1, slip and bind, k 1, n, k 1. p 2 and repeat.

Fifth round.—K 2, th o, k 5, th o, k 1, slip 1, n, pass slippd stitch over, k 1, p 2 and repeat.

Seventh round.—Slip and bind, k 3, n, k 1, th o, k 1, th o, k 3, p 2 and repeat.

Ninth round.—Slip and bind, k 1, n, k 1, th o, k 3, th o, k 3, p 2 and repeat.

Eleventh round.—Slip 1, .n, pass slipped stitch over, k 1, th o, k 5, th o, k 3, p 2 and repeat.

Knit the 12th round as directed and repeat from beginning.

KNITTED STRIPE FOR SHAWLS, JACKETS, ETC., ETC.

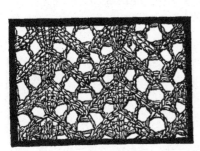

No. 25.—VANDYKE DESIGN.

No. 24.— This stripe may be made of Shetland or Berlin wool, and run through with narrow ribbon, after which it is sewed to the garment it is to decorate. The stripe is complete in two rows. Cast on any number of stitches divisible by 4, casting on as many as will be necessary to make the stripe as wide as required.

First row.—Slip 1, th o, k 3 and repeat across the row.

Second row.—Slip 1, draw the slipped stitch over the first 3 stitches, and then knit 4 plain. Draw the second slip stitch over the next 3 stitches. Knit 4, and so on across the row at the end of which

there will be only 3 to knit. Repeat these rows until the stripe is as long as required. When the stripe is long enough (ending with the second row) every 4th plain stitch is dropped and pulled down to make the running places for the ribbon, which may be satin, velvet or grosgrain.

VANDYKE DESIGN.

No. 25.—Use two needles and cast on any number of stitches divisible by 9.

First row.—K 3, * th o, n at the back of the work, k 4 and repeat from *.

Second row.—Purl.

Third row.—* K 1, n, th o, k 1, th o, n at the back, and repeat from *.

Fourth row.—Purl.

Fifth row.—N, * th o, k 3, th o, sl 1, n, pass slipped stitch over, and repeat from *.

Sixth row.— Purl.

Repeat all the details from the first row until the work is as deep as required.

CABLE PATTERN.

No. 26.—CABLE PATTERN.

No. 26.—Cast on any number of stitches, arranging them so that six stitches will be used for every cable, and six stitches will also occur between the cables.

The following directions are for one cable or stripe with six stitches at each side.

Cast on 18 stitches.

First, Third and Fifth rows.—P 6, k 6, p 6.

Second and Fourth rows.—K 6, p 6, k 6.

Sixth row.—K 6; take a third needle and purl 3, leaving them on the needle at the back. Now with the first right-hand needle purl the next 3 stitches and knit 6.

Seventh row.—P 6, k the 3 stitches on the needle at the back of the work; k 3 stitches on the left-hand needle and purl the remaining 6

Eighth row.—Like the second.

Then repeat from the first row for all of the work.

DESIGN FOR TOPS OF MITTENS, ETC., ETC.

No. 27.—Use four needles and cast on any num

No. 27.—DESIGN FOR TOPS OF MITTENS, ETC., ETC.

ber of stitches divisible by 7. The design is complete in 11 rounds.

First round.—Slip and bind, k 5, th o, and repeat.

Second round.—Slip and bind, k 4, th o, k 1 and repeat.

Third round.—Slip and bind, k 3, th o, k 2 and repeat.

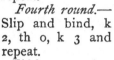

NO. 28.—FANCY DESIGN IN KNITTING.

Fourth round.—Slip and bind, k 2, th o, k 3 and repeat.

Fifth round.—Slip and bind, k 1, th o, k 4, and repeat.

Sixth round.—Slip and bind, th o, k 5, and repeat. Now pass the first stitch on each needle to the next needle. This will leave one stitch on the third needle which is considered a part of the sixth round and is knitted before beginning the next round.

Seventh round.—Knit 1, th o, k 4, n, and repeat.

Eighth round.—K 2, th o, k 3, n, and repeat.

Ninth round.—K 3, th o, k 2, n, and repeat.

Tenth round.—K 4, th o, k 1, n, and repeat.

Eleventh round.—K 5, th o, n, and repeat.

Pass the last stitch on each needle to the next needle, and repeat from the second round.

FANCY DESIGN IN KNITTING.

No. 28.—Cast on any number of stitches divisible by 6. The design is complete in 12 rounds.

First round.—K 2, n, th o, k 2 and repeat.

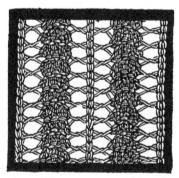

NO. 29.—FANCY-STRIPE DESIGN.

Second and every alternate round including the Twelfth.—Plain.

Third round.—K 1, n, th o, k 3 and repeat.

Fifth round.—N, th o, k 4 and repeat.

After knitting all of the 6th round except the last stitch, pass the last stitch on each needle onto the next needle.

Seventh round.—N, th o, k 1, th o, sl and b, k 1 and repeat.

Ninth round.—K 4, th o, sl and b and repeat.

After knitting the 10th round, pass the first stitch on each needle onto the next needle; this will leave 1 stitch on the 3rd needle which is considered a part of the 10th round and is knitted as such before the next round is begun.

Eleventh round.—K 1, n, th o, k 1, th o, sl and b, and repeat.

Knit the 12th round and then repeat from the 5th round to the 12th, inclusive, for all of the work.

FANCY-STRIPE DESIGN.

No. 29.—This design may be used as an insertion, or as a heading to knitted lace.

Cast on any number of stitches divisible by 6, with 1 added.

First row.—K 1, th o, k 1, k 3 together, k 1, th o and repeat from beginning ending with k 1.

Second and every alternate row.—Purl the 1st stitch and the single stitch between every 2 made stitches, and knit the rest.

Repeat these 2 rows for all the work.

CABLE AND HERRING-BONE PATTERN.

No. 30.—Cast on any number of stitches divisible by 9 with 3 added. Knit 4 rows plain.

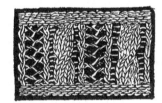

NO. 30.—CABLE AND HERRING-BONE PATTERN.

Fifth row.—Sl 1, th o, n, * take the next 3 stitches off on a 3rd needle, and keep this needle in front; k the next 3 stitches; then knit the 3 taken off onto the extra needle; k 1, th o, n, and repeat from *.

Sixth row.—Sl 1, th o, p 2 together, * p 7, th o, p 2 together, and repeat from * until the last repetition, when you purl 6, th o, p 2 together.

Seventh row.—Sl 1, th o, k 2 together, * k 7, th o, k 2 together and repeat from *.

Eighth row.—Like second.

Repeat from 5th row for each section of the work. The four plain rows may be knitted after every two sections if desired, or the pattern may form one continuous stripe by omitting the plain rows and repeating only from the 5th to the 8th rows, inclusive.

LOOP KNITTING.

No. 31.—Cast on any number of stitches required by

NO. 31.—LOOP KNITTING.

the dimensions of the work to be done. Always knit the first stitch.

First row.—Plain.

Second row.—Throw the yarn around the needle as if for knitting, but do not knit it; then carry the yarn down around the left forefinger and up across the needle; then again around the finger and across the needle; then knit the wind-overs off as one stitch. Repeat for every stitch.

Third row.—Knit plain, knitting each group of wind-overs as one stitch.

Repeat the last two rows for all the work.

DESIGN FOR CLOUDS OR SCARFS.

No. 32.—This design may be made of double zephyr and silk or any fine wool. It is made by knitting, alternately, two rows with each variety of yarn or thread, with coarse needles. Do not break the ma-

NO. 32.—DESIGN FOR CLOUDS OR SCARFS.

terial at the ends of the rows; simply carry it along from one row to the other. Two colors or one may be used in knitting articles by this pattern. This would form a handsome design for a square shawl of white zephyr and white knitting silk, if a border of hair-pin work in silk and wool were added. A number of borders of this description are illustrated in our book upon "The Art of Crocheting."

In combining colors use wool for the white stripe with some pale tint of pink, blue, lavender, yellow, etc., etc. Ice wool would look pretty with zephyr or Germantown yarn.

DESIGNS FOR FANCY STRIPES, TOPS TO MITTENS AND SOCKS, BORDERS, SCARFS, SHAWLS, ETC., ETC.

CORAL STRIPE.

No. 1.—Cast on any number of stitches divisible by 21.

First row.—K 2 together, k 3, k 2 together, k 1, th o, k 1, th o, k 1, k 2 together, k 3, k 2 together, k 1, th o, k 1, th o, k 2.

Second, Fourth, Sixth, Eighth, Tenth and Twelfth rows.—Purl.

Third row.—K 2 together, k 1, k 2 together, k 1, th o, k 3, th o, k 1, k 2 together, k 1, k 2 together, k 1, th o, k 3, th o, k 2.

Fifth row.—Sl 1, k 2 together, pass slipped stitch over, k 1, th o,

NO. 1.—CORAL STRIPE.

k 5, th o, k 1, sl 1, k·2 together, pass slipped stitch over, k 1, th o, k 5, th o, k 2.

Seventh row.—K 2, th o, k 1, th o, k 1, k 2 together, k 3, k 2 together, k 1, th o, k 1, th o, k 1, k 2 together, k 3, k 2 together.

Ninth row.—K 2, th o, k 3, th o, k 1, k 2 together, k 1, k 2 together, k 1, th o, k 3, th o, k 1, k 2 together, k 1, k 2 together.

Eleventh row.—K 2, th o, k 5, th o, k 1, sl 1, k 2 together, pass slipped stitch over, k 1, th o, k 5, th o, k 1, sl 1, k 2 together, pass slipped stitch over.

Twelfth row.—Purl as directed and repeat from first row.

FANCY TOP FOR SOCKS OR MITTENS.

No. 2.—This design is completed with a hem made on the same plan as that described at No. 5 on page 19. The design calls for any number of stitches divisible by 13, and is worked in 10 rounds.

First round.—Slip and bind, k 4, th o, k 1, th o, k 4, n and repeat.

Second, Fourth, Sixth, Eighth and Tenth rounds.—Plain.

Third round.

NO. 2.—FANCY TOP FOR SOCKS OR MITTENS.

—Sl and b, k 3, th o, k 3, th o, k 3, n and repeat.

Fifth round.—Sl and b, k 2, th o, k 5, th o, k 2, n and repeat.

Seventh round.—Sl and b, k 1, th o, k 7, th o, k 1, n and repeat.

Ninth round.—Sl and b, th o, k 9, th o, n and repeat.

Knit tenth round plain as directed, and repeat from first round for all the pattern.

DESIGN FOR THE TOPS OF SOCKS OR MITTENS.

No. 3.—Cast on any number of stitches divisible by 10. The design is formed by two rounds alternately knitted to any depth required. Knit

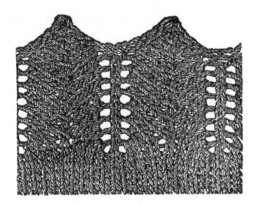

NO. 3.—DESIGN FOR THE TOPS OF SOCKS OR MITTENS.

around once, plain, after casting on.

First round.—K 1, th o, k 3, slip 1, n, pass slipped stitch over, k 3, th o and repeat.

Second round.—Plain. Repeat the rounds as directed.

VINE PATTERN FOR STRIPE.

No. 4.—This stripe is pretty knitted in wool or cotton, or Belding's knitting silk, and may be used as insertion or as a stripe for spreads, afghans, etc., etc.

Cast on 26 stitches.

First row.—Slip 1, k 1, th o, n, th o, n, th o, k 1, th o, k 2, n, k 4, n, k 2, th o, sl and b, th o, sl and b, th o, sl and b, k 1.

Second and every alternate even row. —Purl.

Third row.—Sl 1, k 1, th o, n, th o, n, th o, k 3, th o, k 2, n, k 2, n, k 2, th o, sl and b, th o, sl and b, th o, sl and b, k 1.

Fifth row.—Sl 1, k 1, th o, n, th o, n, th o, k 5, th o, k 2, n, n, k 2, th o, sl and b, th o, sl and b, th o, sl and b, k 1.

Seventh row.—Sl 1, sl and b, th o, sl and b, th o, sl and b, th o, k 2, n, k 4, n, k 2, th o, k 1, th o, n, th o, n, th o, k 2.

Ninth row.—Sl 1, sl and b, th o, sl and b, th o, sl and b, th o, k 2, n, k 2, n, k 2, th o, k 3, th o, n, th o, n, th o, k 2.

Eleventh row.—Sl 1, sl and b, th o, sl and b, th o, sl and b, th o, k 2, n, n, k 2, th o, k 5, th o, n, th o, n, th o, k 2.

Purl the 12th row as directed, and repeat from the 1st row.

A straight edge may be crocheted along either edge of the stripe to convert it into an insertion.

FANCY EDGE FOR MITTENS OR SOCKS.

No. 5.—This design has a hemmed edge made as

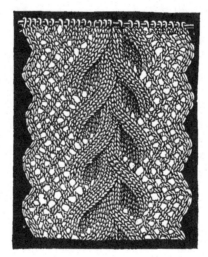

NO. 4.—VINE PATTERN FOR STRIPE.

follows: Cast on loosely (for this design) any number of stitches divisible by 8. Knit six or seven rows plain, then one row of holes, made thus: Narrow, th o and repeat. Then make as many more rows of plain knitting as you made before the holes. The number of stitches now on the needle should be the same as those cast on. Now in the next round turn the edge of the work up inside and pick up and knit with each stitch on the needle, one of the edge or foundation stitches where you commenced the work. This will form a perfect and neatly-made hem, which may be made as wide as desired by increasing the number of plain rows. Now begin the design, which is complete in 7 rounds.

First round.—Th o, k 6, n. and repeat.

Second round.—K 1, th o, k 5, n, and repeat.

Third round.—K 2, th o, k 4, n, and repeat.

Fourth round.—K 3, th o, k 3, n, and repeat.

Fifth round.—K 4, th o, k 2, n, and repeat.

Sixth round.—K 5, th o, k 1, n, and repeat.

Seventh round.—K 6, th o, n, and repeat.

Repeat from the first round.

FANCY HEM-TOP FOR SOCKS, MITTENS, ETC.

No. 6.—Cast on any

NO. 5.—FANCY EDGE FOR MITTENS OR SOCKS.

number of stitches divisible by 13, and work in 5 rounds. Make the hem as directed at No. 69. Then begin the design.

First round.— Sl 1, k 2 together, pass slipped

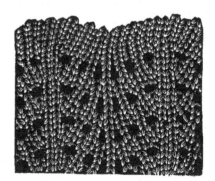

NO. 6.—FANCY HEM-TOP FOR SOCKS, MITTENS, ETC., ETC.

stitch over, th o, n, th o, k 1, th o, k 1, th o, k 1, th o, n, th o, k 3 together and repeat.

Second, Third, Fourth and Fitfh rounds.—Knit plain and repeat from the beginning.

DIAMOND STRIPE.

No. 7.—This stripe develops very handsomely in Saxony yarn, Germantown, Dexter's cotton or any material suitable for making it for spreads, counterpanes, afghans, etc., etc.

The design was taken from a counterpane composed of 10 stripes each 13 diamonds long.

Cast on 63 stitches and knit plain 4 times across; also knit similarly at the end of the stripe.

First row.—K 16, p 11, k 4, th o twice, n, k 3, p 11, k 16. (In knitting back after a row in which there are put-overs, the second half of each double put-over is dropped).

Second row.—K 4, p 8, k 15, p 9, k 15, p 8, k 4.

Third row—K 16, p 11, k 9, p 11, k 16.

Fourth row.—Like second.

Fifth row.—K 30, th o twice, n, th o twice, n, k 29.

Sixth row.—K 4, p 8, k 4, p 31, k 4, p 8, k 4.

Seventh, Fifteenth, Twenty-third, Thirty-first, Thirty-ninth, Forty-seventh, Fifty-fifth, Sixty-third and Seventy-first rows.—Knit plain.

Eighth row.—Like sixth.

Ninth row.—K 16, p 9, k 4, th o twice, n, th o twice, n, th o twice, n, k 3, p 9, k 16.

Tenth row.—K 4, p 8, k 13, p 13, k 13, p 8, k 4.

Eleventh row.—K 16, p 9, k 13, p 9, k 16.

Twelfth row.—K 4, p 8, k 13, p 13, k 13, p 8, k 4.

Thirteenth row.—K 28, th o twice, n, th o twice, n, th o twice, n, th o twice, n, k 27.

Fourteenth and Sixteenth rows.—Like sixth row.

Seventeenth row.—K 4; slip 4 stitches from the left hand needle onto a hair-pin and keep them at the back of the work; k 4 and then replace the slipped stitches on the left hand needle; k 8, p 7, k 4, th o twice, n, th o twice, n, th o twice, n, th o twice n, th o twice, n, k 3, p 7, k 4; slip 4 stitches from the left-hand needle onto a hair-pin; k 4; replace the stitches as before; k 8.

Eighteenth row.—K 4, p 8, k 11, p 17, k 11, p 8, k 4.

Nineteenth row.—K 16, p 7, k 17, p 7, k 16.

Twentieth row.—Like eighteenth row.

Twenty-first row.—K 26, th o twice and narrow, 6 times; k 25.

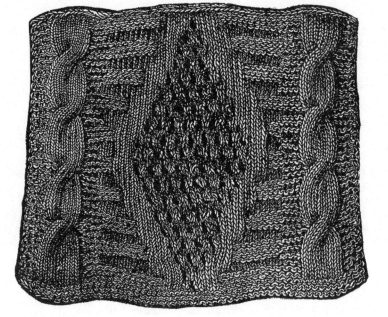

No. 7.—DIAMOND STRIPE.

Twenty-second and Twenty-fourth rows.—Like sixth row.

Twenty-fifth row.—K 16, p 5, k 4; th o and n, 7 times; k 3, p 5, k 16.

Twenty-sixth row.—K 4, p 8, k 9, p 21, k 9, p 8, k 4.

Twenty-seventh row.—K 16, p 5, k 21, p 5, k 16.

Twenty-eighth row.—Like twenty-sixth row.

Twenty-ninth row.—K 24; th o twice and n, 8 times, k 23.

Thirtieth and Thirty-second rows.—Like sixth.

Thirty-third row.—K 4; pass 4 stitches from left-hand needle and slip onto a hair-pin; k 4; replace the 4 slipped stitches; k 8, p 3, k 4; th o twice and n 9 times; k 3, p 3, k 4; slip next 4 stitches onto a hair-pin; k 4; replace the slipped stitches; k 8.

Thirty-fourth row.—K 4, p 8, k 7, p 25, k 7, p 8, k 4.

Thirty-fifth row.—K 16, p 3, k 25, p 3, k 16.

Thirty-sixth row.—Like thirty-fourth row.

Thirty-seventh row.—K 22; th o twice and n, 10 times; k 21.

Thirty-eighth and Fortieth rows.—Like sixth.

Forty-first row.—K 16, p 3, k 4; th o twice and n, 9 times; k 3, p 3, k 16.

Forty-second row.—K 4, p 8, k 7, p 25, k 7, p 8, k 4.

Forty-third row.—K 16, p 3, k 25, p 3, k 16.

Forty-fourth row.—Like forty-second.

Forty-fifth row.—K 24; th o twice and n, 8 times; k 23.

Forty-sixth and Forty-eighth rows.—Like sixth.

Forty-ninth row.—K 4; pass 4 onto a hair-pin; k 4; replace the slipped stitches, k 8, p 5, k 4; th o twice and n, 7 times; k 3, p 5, k 4; slip next 4 onto a hair-pin; k 4; replace the slipped stitches and k 8.

Fiftieth row.—K 4, p 8, k 9, p 21, k 9, p 8, k 4,

Fifty-first row.—K 16, p 5, k 21, p 5, k 16.

Fifty-second row.—Like fiftieth row.

Fifty-third row.—K 26; th o twice and n 6 times; k 25.

Fifty-fourth and Fifty-sixth rows.—Like sixth.

Fifty-seventh row.—K 16, p 7, k 4; th o twice and n, 5 times; k 3, p 7, k 16.

Fifty-eighth row.—K 4, p 8, k 11, p 17, k 11, p 8, k 4.

Fifty-ninth row.—K 16, p 7, k 17, p 7, k 16.

Sixtieth row.—K 4, p 8, k 11, p 17, k 11, p 8, k 4.

Sixty-first row.—K 28; th o twice and n, 4 times; k 27.

Sixty-second and Sixty-fourth rows.—Like sixth.

Sixty-fifth row.—K 4; slip 4 onto the hair-pin; k 4; replace slipped stitches; k 8, p 9, k 4; th o twice and n, 3 times; k 3, p 9, k 4; slip 4 onto the hair-pin; k 4; replace slipped stitches and k 8.

Sixty-sixth row.—K 4, p 8, k 13, p 13, k 13, p 8, k 4.

Sixty-seventh row.—K 16, p 9, k 13, p 9, k 16.

Sixty-eighth row.—Like sixty-sixth row.

Sixty-ninth row.—K 30; th o twice, n, th o twice, n, k 29.

Seventieth and Seventy-second rows.—Like sixth row.

Repeat from the first row for the next and following diamonds. Twist the cable at the third row of holes in the second diamond.

STRIPE FOR AN AFGHAN OR COUNTERPANE.

No. 8.—The stripe may be made of Germantown or Spanish knitting yarn, or of Dexter cotton, according to the purpose for which it is intended. Cast on 50 stitches.

First row.—Purl.

Second row.—Slip 1, purl 2, knit 2, thread over, knit 2 together, purl 3, knit 11, knit 2 together, thread over, knit 1; wrap the thread once around the needle, purl 2, thread over, knit 1, thread over, slip 1, knit 1, pass slipped stitch over, knit 11, purl 3, knit 2, thread over, knit 2 together, purl 3.

Third row.—Sl 1, k 2, p 2, wrap thread once around the needle, purl 2 together, k 3, p 10, p 2 together crossed (to "cross," insert the needle from left to right at the back through both stitches at once and purl them off together); purl 3, k 2, p 3, p 2 together, p 10, k 3, p 2, wrap thread around the needle, p 2 together, k 3.

Fourth row.—Sl 1, p 2, k 2, th o, k 2 together, p 3, k 9, k 2 together, k 1, th o, k 1, th o, k 1, p 2, k 1, th o, k 1, th o, k 1, sl 1, k 1, pass slipped stitch over, k 9, p 3, k 2, th o, k 2 together, p 3.

Fifth row.—Sl 1, k 2, p 2, wrap the thread

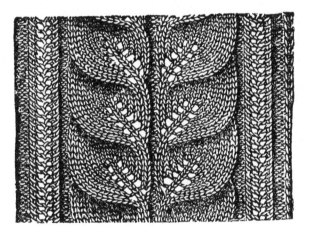

No. 8.—STRIPE FOR AN AFGHAN OR COUNTERPANE.

around the needle, p 2 together, k 3, p 8, p 2 together crossed, p 5, k 2, p 5, p 2 together, p 8, k 3, p 2, wrap the thread around the needle, p 2 together, k 3.

Sixth row.—Sl 1, p 2, k 2, th o, k 2 together, p 3, k 7, k 2 together, k 2, th o, k 1, th o, k 2, p 2, k 2, th o, k 1, th o, k 2, sl 1, k 1, pass slipped stitch over, k 7, p 3, k 2, th o, k 2 together, p 3.

Seventh row.—Sl 1, k 2, p 2, wrap thread around the needle once, p 2 together, k 3, p 6, p 2 together crossed, p 7, k 2, p 7, p 2 together, p 6, k 3, p 2, wrap thread around the needle, p 2 together, k 3.

Eighth row.—Sl 1, p 2, k 2, th o, k 2 together, p 3, k 5, k 2 together, k 3, th o, k 1, th o, k 3, p 2, k 3, th o, k 1, th o, k 3, sl 1, k 1, pass slipped stitch over, k 5, p 3, k 2, th o, k 2 together, purl 3.

Ninth row.—Sl 1, k 2, p 2, wrap thread around the needle, p 2 together, k 3, p 4, p 2 together crossed, p 9, k 2, p 9, p 2 together, p 4, k 3, p 2, wrap thread around the needle, purl 2 together, k 3.

Tenth row.—Sl 1, p 2, k 2, th o, k 2 together, p 3, k 3, k 2 together, k 4, th o, k 1, th o, k 4, p 2, k 4, th o, k 1, th o, k 4, sl 1, k 1, pass slipped stitch over, k 3, p 3, k 2, th o, k 2 together, p 3.

Eleventh row.—Sl 1, k 2, p 2, wrap thread around the needle, p 2 together, k 3, p 2, p 2 together crossed, p 11, k 2, p 11, p 2 together, p 2, k 3, p 2, wrap thread around the needle, p 2 together, k 3.

Twelfth row.—Sl 1, p 2, k 2, th o, k 2 together, p 3, k 1, k 2 together, k 5, th o, k 1, th o, k 5, p 2, k 5, th o, k 1, th o, k 5, sl 1, k 1, pass slipped stitch over, k 1, p 3, k 2, th o, k 2 together, p 3.

Thirteenth row.—Sl 1, k 2, p 2, wrap thread around the needle, p 2 together, k 3, p 2 together crossed, p 13, k 2, p 13, p 2 together, k 5, wrap thread around the needle, p 2, together, k 3.

Fourteenth row.—Sl 1, p 2, k 2, th o, k 2 together, p 3, k 14, p 2, k 14, p 3, k 2, th o, k 2 together, p 3.

Begin again at the first row and repeat all the details just given for the next section of the pattern, and work in this manner until the stripe is about a yard and a-half long. Each of the other stripes are of the same length.

KNITTED DESIGN FOR THE BOTTOM OF AN UNDER-SHIRT OR A PETTICOAT.

No. 9.—This is a very pretty border for the bottom of either of the garments named, or for infants' sacks, cloaks and dresses. It may also be used for an edging. Unlike most edgings, however, it is knitted back and forth the long way of the work, and for a long strip of edging to be sewed to a garment would have to be knitted in sections. Cast on enough stitches to make the garment as wide as necessary (if an under-vest) using a number divisible by 6 with 1 over.

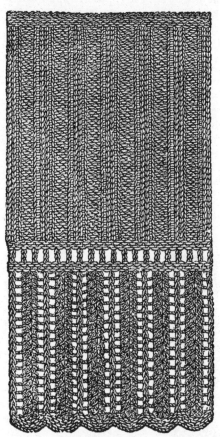

No. 9.—DESIGN FOR THE BOTTOM OF AN UNDER-SHIRT OR PETTICOAT.

First row.—Knit 1, * th o, k 1, slip 1, k 2 together, pass slipped stitch over, k 1, th o, k 1 and repeat from * across the work.

Second row.—Plain.

Repeat these two rows until the edging is 18 holes deep.

Then knit 3 rows, so that they will appear purled on the right side.

To make the next row of holes: Knit 1, th o, n and repeat across the row, knitting the last stitch. Next make 3 rows like the 3 preceding the row just knit. Then begin the main portion of the garment, which is knitted in ribbed style by knitting 2 and purling 2 alternately. Make this portion according to instructions for ribbed under-shirts, which will be found elsewhere in the book.

In knitting a petticoat with this border, it may be knitted in strips or breadths which can be joined by over-and-over stitches or single crochet. Personal judgment must be exercised in deciding how wide or how long to make these strips or breadths, since their dimensions will depend upon the size the garment is desired to be, and also somewhat upon the material from which it is made.

FANCY-EDGE DESIGN WITH A HEM.

No. 10.—Two or four needles may be used in knitting this design. If two are used, *purl* the alternate rows instead of *knitting* them. Cast on any number of stitches divisible by 9, and complete the design in 6 rounds. Make the hem as directed at No. 69. Then begin the design.

First round.—Sl and b, k 2, th o, k 1, th o, k 2, n and repeat.

Second Fourth and Sixth rounds.—Plain.

Third round.—Sl and b, k 1, th o, k 3, th o, k 1, n, and repeat.

Fifth round.—Sl and b, th o, k 5, th o, n, and repeat.

Knit 6th round as directed and repeat from beginning of design.

No. 10—FANCY-EDGE DESIGN WITH A HEM.

LEAF AND TRELLIS PATTERN.

No. 11.—Cast on any number of stitches divisible by 20, as 20 stitches are needed for each pattern.

To knit the stripe as illustrated cast on 40 stitches, using Belding's silk, or crochet cotton.

First and every alternate row.—Purl.

Second row.—K 6; * th o and n 3 times; th o, k 2, n, k 10, and repeat from *. At the end of the last repetition 4 stitches only instead of 10 will remain to be knitted.

Fourth row.—K 2, * n, k 2, th o, k 1; th o and n 5 times; k 5, and repeat from *.

Sixth row.—K 1, * n, k 2, th o, k 3, th o and n

No. 11.—LEAF AND TRELLIS PATTERN.

3 times; th o, k 2, n, k 3, and repeat from *.

Eighth row.—N, k 2, th o, k 5, th o and n 3 times, th o, k 2, n, k 1 and repeat from beginning of row.

Tenth row.—K 3, * th o, k 7; th o and n 3 times; th o, k 2, sl 1, n, pass slipped stitch over, k 2 and repeat from *. In the last repetition there will be but 1 stitch to pass the slipped stitch over, before the edge stitches.

Twelfth row.—N, k 5; * n and th o 5 times; k 1, th o, k 2, n, k 5 and repeat from *.

Fourteenth row.—K 5, * n, k 2; th o and n 3

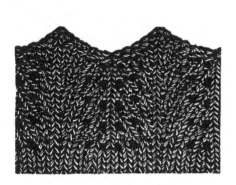

NO. 13.—DESIGN FOR TOPS OF SOCKS OR MITTENS.

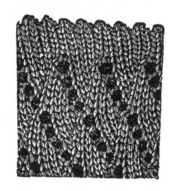

NO. 14.—DESIGN FOR TOPS OF SOCKS OR MITTENS, WITH A HEM.

times; th o, k 3, th o, k 2, n, k 3 and repeat from *.

Sixteenth row.—Knit 4, * n, k 2; th o and n 3 times; th o, k 5, th o, k 2, n, k 1, and repeat from *.

Eighteenth row.—K 3, n, k 2; * th o and n 3 times; th o, k 7, th o, k 2, sl 1, n, pass the slipped stitch over, k 2 and repeat from *.

Repeat from 3rd row for all the work.

DESIGN FOR TOPS OF SOCKS OR MITTENS.

NO. 13.—Use four needles. Cast on any number of stitches divisible by 11 and knit once around plain. The design is complete in 4 rounds.

First round.—N, n, th o, k 1, th o, k 1, th o, k 1, th o, n, n, and repeat.

Second, Third and Fourth rounds.—Plain.

Repeat these directions in the order given until the work is as deep as you desire it to be.

DESIGN FOR TOPS OF SOCKS OR MITTENS, WITH A HEM.

NO. 14.—Begin with a hem made as directed at No. 69, casting on (for the design) any number of stitches divisible by 5. The design is complete in 8 rounds.

First round. (After fastening the hem).—Th o, k 3, n, and repeat.

Second Fourth Sixth and Eighth rounds.—Plain.

Third round.—K 1, th o, k 2, n, and repeat.

Fifth round.—K 2, th o, k 1, n, and repeat.

Seventh round.—K 3 th o, n, and repeat.

Knit 8th round as directed and repeat from 1st round for all the work.

DESIGN FOR SCARF SHAWLS.

NO. 15.—This design is very pretty for scarf-shawls made of Saxony yarn or Shetland wool, and is knitted on medium-size steel needles.

Cast on any number of stitches divisible by 5. Knit back and forth 5 times so that all the stitches will appear to be plain knitting on the right side.

Sixth row.—* K 1, th o twice, k 2 together; repeat from * across the work.

Seventh row.—* Knit 1; k 1 and purl 1 out of the put-over, and repeat from * across the work.

Eighth to Twelfth rows (inclusive).—Purl 2, k 1 alternately across the row. In coming back knit the purled stitches and purl the knitted ones of the preceding row.

Thirteenth row.—Th o, k 2 together; repeat across the row.

Fourteenth row.—Purl.

Fifteenth and Sixteenth rows.—Knit.

Seventeenth row.—Purl.

Eighteenth row.—* Purl 3, k 2 together, th o and repeat from * across the row, making an extra stitch at the end.

Nineteenth to the Twenty-first row (inclusive).—Knit 3, purl 2, but in the 20th row (working back), purl the knitted stitches and knit the purled ones.

Twenty-second row.—* Purl 3, th o, k 2 together; repeat from * across the work.

Twenty-third to the Twenty-fifth row.—K 3, purl 2; in working back in the 24th row, knit the purled stitches and purl the knitted ones.

Now repeat all the details from the 18th row,

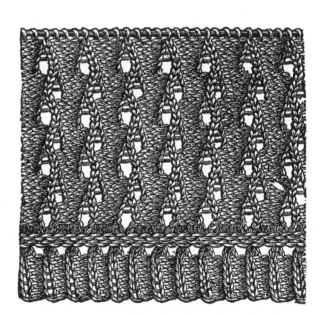

NO. 15.—DESIGN FOR SCARF SHAWLS.

until the shawl is as long as required. Then knit the border to correspond with the one first knitted. Turn the plain knitting at the lower edge of each border up underneath the first row of holes and fasten it in hem fashion.

KNITTED EDGINGS AND INSERTIONS.

KNITTED POINTED EDGING AND INSERTION.

NOS. 1 AND 3.—*For the Edging.*—Cast on 32 stitches and knit across plain.

First row.—Knit 4, * th o, n; th o, n, k 3, and repeat twice more from *. * Th o, n, and repeat twice more from last *; th o, k 1.

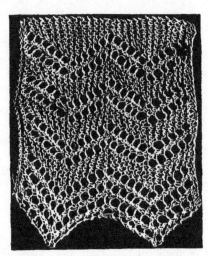

NO. 1.—KNITTED POINTED EDGING.

Second row.—Knit plain.

Third row.—Knit 5, th o, n, th o, n, k 3, and repeat first row from first* for balance of 3rd row.

Fourth row.— Plain.

Fifth row.—K 6, then like first row from first *

Sixth row.—Plain.

Knit in this manner, increasing by one stitch at the beginning of each row, until there are 11 rows with 9 stitches at the beginning of the 11th row, and 6 holes.

Twelfth and Thirteenth rows.—Plain.

Fourteenth row.—K 2 together, * th o, n, and repeat 3 times more from *. * K 3, th o, n, th o, n, and repeat twice more from last *. Knit remainder of row plain.

Fifteenth row.—Plain.

Sixteenth row.—Same as 14th. Continue to knit like this for the last half of the point until there are 24 rows, with 32 stitches on the needle in the last row.

Twenty-fifth and Twenty-sixth rows. — Plain.

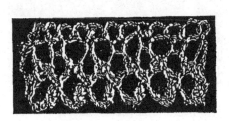

NO. 2.—KNITTED PASSEMENTERIE EDGING.

Repeat from 1st row for all the points. At each point and angle, be sure to make 2 rows of plain knitting, otherwise the angles will not come out as distinctly as they should to be effective.

FOR THE INSERTION.

Cast on 29 stitches and knit across plain.

First row.—K 4, * th o, n, th o, n, k 3, and repeat twice more from * Knit the rest plain.

Second row.—Knit plain. Continue in the same order as in the edging, omitting the holes for the point and knitting plain at each side of the holes made at the middle. In the 6th row of holes, there will be 9 plain stitches *before* narrowing, and 2 at the end of the row. Then knit across twice, plain; and at the beginning of the *next* row, knit 4 plain before beginning to narrow. Then follow the preceding directions for the rest of the point.

KNITTED PASSEMENTERIE EDGING.

No. 2.—This lace is very pretty to use as passementerie in edging velvet bands, or collars, sleeves, etc., etc. In making it, use crochet silk and No. 19 steel needles.

Cast on 5 stitches, and knit as follows:

First row.—Thread over twice, purl 2 together, thread over, purl 2 together, thread over, purl 1.

NO. 3.—KNITTED POINTED INSERTION.

Second row.—Knit 1, (knit 1, purl 1 in loop), knit 1, (knit 1, purl 1 in loop), thread over, purl 2 together.

Third row.—Thread over twice, purl 2 together, knit the rest plain.

Fourth row.—Bind off 3, knit 2, put thread over, purl 2 together. Repeat from first row.

VANDYKE EDGING.
(See next Page.)

No. 4.—Cast on 11 stitches and knit across plain.

First row.—Sl 1, k 2, th o, k 2 together, k 1, th o twice, k 2 together, th o twice, k 2 together, k 1.

Second row.—Sl 1, k 2, p 1, k 2, p 1, k 3, th o, k 2 together, k 1.

Third row.—Sl 1, k 2, th o, k 2 together, k 3, th o twice, k 2 together, th o twice, k 2 together, k 1

Fourth row.—Sl 1, k 2, p 1, k 2, p 1, k 5, th o, k 2 together, k 1.

Fifth row.—Sl 1, k 2, th o, k 2 together, k 5, th o twice, k 2 together, th o twice, k 2 together k 1.

Sixth row.—Sl 1, k 2, p 1, k 2, p 1, k 7, th o, k 2 together, k 1.

Seventh row.—Sl 1, k 2, th o, k 2 together, k 7,

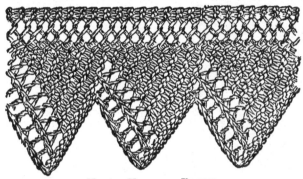

NO. 4.—VANDYKE EDGING.

(For Directions see Page 24.)

th o twice, k 2 together, th o twice, k 2 together, k 1.

Eighth row.—Sl 1, k 2, p 1, k 2, p 1, k 9, th o, k 2 together, k 1.

Ninth row.—Sl 1, k 2, th o, k 2 together, k 9, th o twice, k 2 together, th o twice, k 2 together, k 1.

Tenth row.—Sl 1, k 2, p 1, k 2, p 1, k 11, th o, k 2 together, k 1.

Eleventh row,—Sl 1, k 2, th o, k 2 together, k 11, th o twice, k 2 together, th o twice, k 2 together, k 1.

Twelfth row.—Sl 1, k 2, p 1, k 2, p 1, k 13, th o, k 2 together, k 1.

Thirteenth row.—Sl 1, k 2, th o, k 2 together, k 13, th o twice, k 2 together, th o twice, k 2 together, k 1.

Fourteenth row.—Sl 1, k 2, p 1, k 2, p 1, k 15, th o, k 2 together, k 1.

Fifteenth row.—Sl 1, k 2, th o, k 2 together, k 15, th o twice, k 2 together, th o twice, k 2 together, k 1.

Sixteenth row.—Sl 1, k 2, p 1, k 2, p 1, k 17, th o, k 2 together, k 1.

Seventeenth row.—Sl 1, k 2, th o, k 2 together; knit rest plain.

Eighteenth row.—Cast off until there are 10 stitches on the left-hand needle and 1 on the right; knit the rest plain.

Repeat from first row for all the work.

KNITTED POINTED EDGING.

No. 5.—Cast on 22 stitches and knit across plain.

First row.—Knit 3, th o twice, narrow, k 10, th o twice, n, th o twice, n, th o twice, n, k 1.

Second row.—K 3, p 1, k 2, p 1, k 2, p 1, k 12, p 1, k 3.

Third and Fourth rows.—Plain.

Fifth row.—K 3, th o twice, n, th o twice, n, k 12, th o twice, n, th o twice, n, th o twice, n, k 1.

Sixth row.—K 3, p 1, k 2, p 1, k 2, p 1, k 14, p 1, k 2, p 1, k 3.

Seventh row.—Plain.

Eighth row.—K 3, n, * k 1, n, and repeat 7 times more from *; k 2.

Ninth row.—K 3, * th o twice, n, and repeat 8 times more from *; k 1.

Tenth row.—K 3, p 1, * k 2, p 1, and repeat 7 times more from *; k 3.

Eleventh row.—Plain.

Twelfth row.—K 3, n, k 1, and repeat across the row, knitting the last 2 plain.

Thirteenth row.—Knit 3, * th o twice, n, and repeat 8 times more from *; k 1.

Fourteenth row.—K 3, p 1, * k 2, p 1, and repeat 7 times more from *; k 3.

Fifteenth row.—Plain.

Sixteenth row.—Bind off 9 stitches or until there are 21 stitches left on the left-hand needle. Knit these plain and repeat from the first row.

KNITTED EYELET-EDGING.

No. 6.—Cast on 8 stitches and knit across plain.

First row.—Sl 1, knit 1, th o twice, p 2 together, k 2, th o 3 times, k 2.

Second row.—K 2; of the 3 put-overs, knit the 1st, purl the 2nd and knit the 3rd; k 2, th o twice, p 2 together, k 2.

Third row.—Sl 1, k 1, th o twice, p 2 together, k 7.

Fourth row.—K 7, th o twice, p 2 together, k 2.

Fifth row.—Sl 1, k 1, th o twice, p 2 together, k 7.

Sixth row.—Cast off 3, k 3, th o twice, p 2 together, k 2.

Repeat from the first row for all the work.

NO. 5.—KNITTED POINTED EDGING.

NO. 6.—KNITTED EYELET-EDGING.

LATTICE EDGING.

No. 7.—This design is equally suitable for silk or worsted thread or cotton. Cast on 23 stitches, and knit across plain.

First row.—Slip 1, k 2, th o, k 2 together, th o, k 2 together, and repeat across the row.

Second row.—K 17, p 1, k 1, p 1, k 3.

Third row.—Slip 1, k 2, th o, k 2 together, th o, k 2 together, knit plain to end of row.

Fourth row.—Knit plain until 6 stitches are left, then p 1, k 1, p 1, k 3.

Fifth row.—Slip 1, k 2, th o, k 2 together, th o, k 2 together; knit plain to end of row.

Sixth row.—K 1, * thread over the needle 4 times, k 1, th o 4 times, k 1, and repeat from * until 6 are left on the needle; p 1, k 1, p 1, k 3.

Seventh row.—Slip 1, k 2, th o, k 2 together, th o, k 2 together; * slip off the 4-times wound-over thread, letting it fall in front of the needle, and slip the next stitch on the other needle. Repeat from * across the work, thus making 16 long stitches on the needle.

Eighth row.—Slip the 16 long stitches onto the other needle, * then pass 4 of these stitches over 4, and knit the 8 plain; repeat from * across the work.

Ninth row.—Knit plain until there are 6 stitches left on the needle, p 1, k 1, p 1, k 3.

Tenth row.—Slip 1, k 2, th o, k 2 together, th o, k 2 together; knit remainder plain.

Eleventh row.—Knit plain until 6 are left; then p 1, k 1, p 1, k 3. Repeat from the first row for all the work. The needles used should be of a size adapted to the thread.

NARROW POINTED EDGING.

No. 8.—This edging may be made of Belding's silk or of fine cotton.

Cast on 5 stitches and knit across plain.

First row.—Sl 1, th o, n, th o, k 2.

Second and every alternate row.—Sl 1, k rest plain.

Third row.—Sl 1, th o, n, th o, n, th o, k 1.

Fifth row.—Sl 1, th o, n, th o, n, th o, k 2.

Seventh row.—Sl 1, th o, n, th o, n, th o, n, th o, k 1.

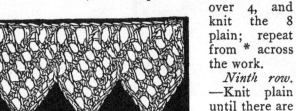

NO. 7.—LATTICE EDGING.

NO. 8.—NARROW POINTED EDGING.

Ninth row.—Sl 1, th o, n, th o, n, th o, n, th o, n, k 2.

Eleventh row.—Sl 1, th o, n, th o, n, th o, n, th o, n, th o, k 1.

Thirteenth row.—Sl 1, th o, n, th o, n, th o, n, th o, n, th o, k 2.

Fifteenth row.—Cast off 8, th o, n, th o, k 1.

Sixteenth row.—Plain. Repeat from first row for all the points.

KNITTED LEAF EDGING.

No. 9.—Cast on 19 stitches and knit across plain.

First row.—Sl 1, k 1, th o, n, th o, n, p 2, k 1, th o, k 1, th o, k 1, p 2, k 2, th o, twice, n, th o twice, k 2.

Second row.—K 3, p 1, k 2, p 1, k 4, p 5, k 2, p 5, k 1.

Third row.—Sl 1, k 1, th o, n, th o, n, p 2, k 2, th o, k 1, th o, k 2, p 2, k 9.

Fourth row.—K 11, p 7, k 2, p 5, k 1.

Fifth row.—Sl 1, k 1, th o, n, th o, n, p 2, k 3, th o, k 1, th o, k 3, p 2, k 2, th o twice, n, th o twice, n, th o twice, n, k 1.

Sixth row.—K 3, p 1, k 2, p 1, k 2, p 1, k 4, p 9, k 2, p 5, k 1.

Seventh row.—Sl 1, k 1, th o, n, th o, n, p 2, k 4, th o, k 1, th o, k 4, p 2, k 12.

Eighth row.—K 14, p 11, k 2, p 5, k 1.

Ninth row.—Sl 1, k 1, th o, n, th o, n, p 2, k 11, p 2, k 12.

Tenth row.—Cast off 5, k 8, p 11, k 2, p 5, k 1.

Eleventh row.—Sl 1, k 1, th o, n, th o, n, p 2, sl and b, k 7, n, p 2, k 2, th o twice, n, th o twice, n, k 1.

Twelfth row.—K 3, p 1, k 2, p 1, k 4, p 9, k 2, p 5, k 1.

Thirteenth row.—Sl 1, k 1, th o, n, th o, n, p 2, sl and b, k 5, n, p 2, k 9.

Fourteenth row.—K 11, p 7, k 2, p 5, k 1.

Fifteenth row.—Sl 1, k 1, th o, n, th o, n, p 2, sl and b, k 3, n, p 2, k 2, th o twice, n, th o twice, n, k 1.

Sixteenth row.—K 3, p 1, k 2, p 1, k 2, p 1, k 4, p 5, k 2, p 5, k 1.

Seventeenth row.—Sl 1, k 1, th o, n, th o, n, p 2, sl and b, k 1, n, p 2, k 12.

Eighteenth row.—K 14, p 3, k 2, p 5, k 1.

NO. 9.—KNITTED LEAF EDGING.

Nineteenth row.—Sl 1, k 1, th o, n, th o, n, p 2, k 3 together, p 2, k 12.

Twentieth row.—Cast off 4, k 12, p 5, k 1. Repeat from the first row for all the work.

INSERTION EDGING.

No. 10.—By omitting the points of this edging, an insertion may be formed which will match the edging. The work may be done with cotton or linen, or with knitting silk.

Cast on 25 stitches and knit across plain.

First row.—Sl 1, k 2, th o, n, k 1, th o, n, k 2, th o, n, k 5, th o, n, k 1, th o twice, n, th o twice, n, k 1.

Second row.—K 3, p 1, k 2, p 1, k 3, th o, n, k 12, th o, n, k 1.

Third row.—Sl 1, k 2, th o, n, k 2, th o, n, k 2, th o, n, k 4, th o, n, k 3, th o, n, th o twice, n, th o twice, n, k 1.

Fourth row.—K 3, p 1, k 2, p 1, k 5, th o, n, k 12, th o, n, k 1.

Fifth row.—Sl 1, k 2, th o, n, k 3, th o, n, k 2, th o, n, k 3, th o, n, k 5, th o twice, n, th o twice, n, k 1.

Sixth row.—K 3, p 1, k 2, p 1, k 7, th o, n, k 12, th o, n, k 1.

Seventh row.— Sl 1, k 2, th o, n, k 4, th o, n, k 2, th o, n, k 2, th o, n, k 12.

Eighth row.—Bind off 6, k 7, th o, n, k 12, th o, n, k 1.

Repeat from first row for all the work.

No. 10.—INSERTION EDGING.

SCOLLOP EDGING.

No. 11.—Cast on 10 stitches and knit across plain.

First row.—Sl 1, k 1, th o, n, th o, n, th o 3 times, n, th o twice, p 2 together.

Second row.—Th o twice, purl 2 together, k 2; then out of the 3 put-overs, p 1, k 1, p 1; k 1, p 1, k 1, p 1, k 2.

Third row—Sl 1, k 1, th o, n, k 1, th o, n, k 4, th o twice, p 2 together.

Fourth row.—Th o twice, p 2 together, k 5, p 1, k 2, p 1, k 2.

Fifth row.—Sl 1, k 1, th o, n, k 2, th o, n, k 3, th o twice, purl 2 together.

Sixth row.—Th o twice, p 2 together, k 4, p 1, k 3, p 1, k 2.

Seventh row.—Sl 1, k 1, th o, n, k 3, th o, n, k 2, th o twice, p 2 together.

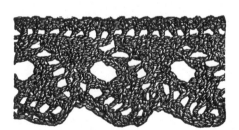

No. 11.—SCOLLOP EDGING.

Eighth row.—Th o twice, p 2 together, k 3, p 1, k 4, p 1, k 2.

Ninth row.—Sl 1, k 1, th o, n, k 4, th o, n, k 1, th o twice, p 2 together.

Tenth row.—Th o twice, p 2 together, k 2, p 1, k 5, p 1, k 2.

Eleventh row.—Sl 1, k 1, th o, n, k 5, th o, n, th o twice, p 2 together.

Twelfth row.—Cast off 3 stitches; place all the stitches on one needle; then, th o twice, p 2 together, k 5, p 1, k 2.

Repeat from the beginning for the next scollop.

POINTED EDGING.

No. 12.—Cast on 22 stitches and knit across plain.

First row.—Sl 1, k 1, th o, k 1, sl 1, n, pass slipped stitch over, k 1, th o, k 2, th o, n, th o, n, th o, k 9.

Second and every alternate row.—Sl 1 and knit the rest plain.

Third row.—Sl 1, k 1, th o, k 1, sl 1, n, pass slipped stitch over, k 1, th o, k 3, th o, n, th o, n, th o, k 9.

Fifth row.—Slip 1, k 1, th o, k 1, sl 1, n, pass slipped stitch over, k 1, th o, k 4, th o, n, th o, n, th o, k 9.

Seventh row.—Sl 1, k 1, th o, k 1, sl 1, n, pass slipped stitch over, k 1, th o, k 5, th o, n, th o, n, th o, k 9.

Ninth row.—Sl 1, k 1, th o, k 1, sl 1, n, pass slipped stitch over, k 1, th o, k 6, th o, n, th o, n, th o, k 9.

No. 12.—POINTED EDGING.

Eleventh row.—Sl 1, k 1, th o, k 1, sl 1, n, pass slipped stitch over, k 1, th o, k 7, th o, n, th o, n, th o, k 9.

Thirteenth row.—Sl 1, k 1, th o, k 1, sl 1, n, pass slipped stitch over, k 1, th o, k 8, th o, n, th o, n, th o, k 9.

Fifteenth row.—Sl 1, k 1, th o, k 1, sl 1, n, pass slipped stitch over, k 1, th o, k 9, th o, n, th o, n, th o, k 9.

Sixteenth row.—Cast off 8, k 21.

Repeat from first row for all the work.

KNITTED LACE.

No. 13.—Cast on 25 stitches.

First row.—K 2, th o twice, purl 2 together, k 6, put 4 stitches over 1 stitch, th o twice, k 2, th o twice, purl 2 together, k 1, th o, n, th o, n, th o, k 2.

Second row.—K 8, th o twice, p 2 together, k 2. Now make 4 stitches out of the long loop of the put-over by knitting one-half stitch and purling one-half stitch alternately, *twice.* K 6, th o twice, p 2 together, k 2.

Third row.—K 2, th o twice, p 2 together, k 12, th o twice, p 2 together, k 2, th o, n, th o, n, th o, k 2.

Fourth row.—K 9, th o twice, p 2 together, k 6. Put 4 stitches over 1 as before. Th o twice, k 2, th o twice, p 2 together, k 2.

Fifth row.—K 2, th o twice, p 2 together, k 2. Now make 4 stitches out of the long loop of the put-over as before. K 6, th o twice, p 2 together, k 3, th o, n, tho, n, th o, k 2.

Sixth row.—K 10, th o twice, p 2 together, k 12, th o twice, p 2 together, k 2.

Seventh row.—K 2, th o twice, p 2 together, k 6. Put 4 stitches over 1. Th o twice, k 2, th o twice, p 2 together, k 4, th o, n, th o, n, th o, k 2.

Eighth row—Bind off 4, which will leave 22 stitches on the left-hand needle; k 6, th o twice, p 2 together, k 2. Make 4 stitches out of the long put-over loop as before. K 6, th o twice, p 2 together, k 2.

Ninth row.—K 2, th o twice, p 2 together, k 12, th o twice, p 2 together, k 1, th o, n, th o, n, th o, k 2.

Tenth row.—K 8, th o twice, p 2 together, k 6. Put 4 stitches over 1. Th o twice, k 2, th o twice, p 2 together, k 2.

Eleventh row.—K 2, th o twice, p 2 together, k 2. Make 4 stitches out of the long put-over. K 6, th o twice, p 2 together, k 2, th o, n, th o, n, th o, k 2.

Twelfth row.—K 9, th o twice, p 2 together, k 12, th o twice, p 2 together, k 2.

Thirteenth row.—K 2, th o twice, p 2 together, k 6. Put 4 stitches over 1. Th o twice, k 2, th o twice, p 2 together, k 3, th o, n, th o, n, th o, k 2.

Fourteenth row.—K 10, th o twice, p 2 together, k 2. Make 4 stitches out of the long put-over. K 6, th o twice, p 2 together, k 2.

Fifteenth row.—K 2, th o twice, p 2 together, k 12, th o twice, p 2 together, k 4, th o, n, th o, n, th o, k 2.

Sixteenth row.—Bind off 4, which will leave 24

stitches on the left-hand needle. K 6, th o twice, p 2 together, k 6. Put 4 stitches over 1. Th o twice, k 2, th o twice, p 2 together, k 2.

Seventeenth row.—K 2, th o twice, p 2 together, k 2. Make 4 stitches out of the long put-over. K 6, th o twice, p 2 together, k 1, th o, n, th o, n, th o, k 2.

Eighteenth row.—K 8, th o twice, p 2 together, k 12, th o twice, p 2 together, k 2.

Nineteenth row.—K 2, th o twice, p 2 together, k 6. Put 4 stitches over 1. Th o twice, k 2, th o twice, p 2 together, k 2, th o, n, th o, n, th o, k 2.

Twentieth row.—K 9, th o twice, p 2 together, k 2. Make 4 stitches out of the long put-over. K 6, th o twice, p 2 together, k 2.

Twenty-first row.—K 2, th o twice, p 2 together, k 12, th o twice, purl 2 together, th o, n, th o, n, th o, k 2.

Twenty-second row.—K 10, th o twice, p 2 together, k 6. Put 4 over 1. Th o twice, k 2, th o twice, p 2 together, k 2.

Twenty-third row.—K 2, th o twice, p 2 together, k 2. Make 4 stitches out of the long put-over. K 6, th o twice, p 2 together, k 4, th o, n, th o, n, th o, k 2.

Twenty-fourth row.—Bind off 4, which will leave 24 stitches on the left-hand needle; k 6, th o twice, p 2 together, k 12, th o twice, p 2 together, k 2.

Repeat from first row for all of the work.

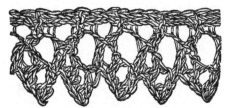

No. 13.—KNITTED LACE.

KNITTED EDGING.

No. 14.—To make this pretty edging, use fine needles and white or unbleached linen, silk, or cotton thread. Cast on 5 stitches.

No. 14.—KNITTED EDGING.

First row.—Slip 1, inserting the needle from the back of the stitch under the working thread; purl 4.

Second row.—Slip 1, k 2, th o 4 times, k 2.

Third row.—Slip 1, k 1; out of the 4 put-overs, k 1 and k 3 crossed (to knit crossed, insert the needle from the back downward); k 3.

Fourth row.—Slip 1, k 8.

Fifth row.—Slip 1, k 1; 3 times by turns, th o and p 2 together; then k 1.

Sixth row.—Slip 1, k 8.

Seventh row.—Cast off 4, inserting needle as before; p 3, k 1.

Repeat from the 2nd to the 7th rows for all the work.

IMPORTED EDGING.

No. 15.—Cast on 26 stitches and knit across plain.

First row.—Slip 1, k 1, n, th o, k 8, p 2 together, th o; (th o here and through the work after purling, means to leave the thread in front of the needle after purling and before knitting the next stitch, in order to increase one stitch) k 1, p 2 together, th o, k 1, p 2 together, th o, k 1, th o, k 2, th o, n, k 1.

Second row.—K 4, th o, n, k 21.

Third row.—Sl 1, k 1, n, th o, k 7, p 2 together, th o, k 1, p 2 together, th o, k 1, p 2 together, th o, k 1, th o, k 1, th o, n, k 1, th o, n, k 1.

Fourth row.—K 4, th o, n, th o, n, k 20.

Fifth row.—Sl 1, k 1, n, th o, k 6, p 2 together, th o, k 1, p 2 together, th o, k 1, p 2 together, th o, k 1, th o, k 1, th o, n, th o, n, k 1, th o, n, k 1.

Sixth row.—K 4; th o and n, 3 times; k 19. (The thread is put over before each narrowing.)

Seventh row.—Sl 1, k 1, n, th o, k 5, p 2 together, th o, k 1, p 2 together, th o, k 1, p 2 together, th o, k 1, th o, k 1; th o and n, 3 times, k 1, th o, n, k 1.

Eighth row.—K 4, th o and n, 4 times; k 18.

Ninth row.—Sl 1, k 1, n, th o, k 4, p 2 together, th o, k 1, p 2 together, th o, k 1, p 2 together, th o, k 1, th o, k 1; th o and n, 4 times; k 1, th o, n, k 1.

Tenth row.—K 4; th o and n, 5 times; k 17.

Eleventh row.—Sl 1, k 1, n, th o, k 3, p 2 together, th o, k 1, p 2 together, th o, k 1, p 2 together, th o, k 1, th o, k 1; th o and n, 5 times; k 1, th o, n, k 1.

Twelfth row.—K 4; th o and n, 6 times; k 16.

Thirteenth row.—Sl 1, k 1, n, th o, k 2, p 2 together, th o, k 1, p 2 together, th o, k 1, p 2 together, th o, k 1, th o, k 1; th o and n, 6 times; k 1, th o, n, k 1.

Fourteenth row.—K 4; th o and n, 7 times; k 15.

Fifteenth row.—Sl 1, k 1, n, th o, k 1, p 2 together, th o, k 1, p 2 together, th o, k 1, p 2 together, th o, k 1, th o, k 1; th o and n, 7 times; k 1, th o, n, k 1.

Sixteenth row.—K 4; th o and n, 8 times; k 14.

Seventeenth row.—Sl 1, k 1, n, th o, k 3, th o, n, k 1, th o, n, k 1, th o, k 3 together, n; th o and n, 6 times; k 1, th o, n, k 1.

Eighteenth row.—K 4; th o and n, 7 times; k 14.

Nineteenth row.—Sl 1, k 1, n, th o, k 4, th o, n, k 1, th o, n, k 1, th o, n, n; th o and n, 5 times; k 1, th o, n, k 1.

Twentieth row.—K 4; th o and n, 6 times; k 15.

Twenty-first row.—Sl 1, k 1, n, th o, k 5, th o, n, k 1, th o, n, k 1, th o, n, n; th o and n, 4 times; k 1, th o, n, k 1.

Twenty-second.—K 4; th o and n, 5 times; k 16.

Twenty-third row.—Sl 1, k 1, n, th o, k 6, th o, n, k 1, th o, n, k 1, th o, n, n; th o and n, 3 times; k 1, th o, n, k 1.

Twenty-fourth row.—K 4; th o and n, 4 times; k 17.

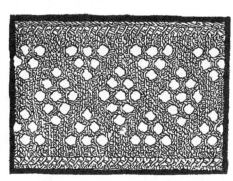

NO. 16.—OPEN-WORK INSERTION.

Twenty-fifth row.—Sl 1, k 1, n, th o, k 7, th o, n, k 1, th o, n, k 1, th o, n, n; th o and n twice; k 1, th o, n, k 1.

Twenty-sixth row.—K 4; th o, and n, 3 times; k 18.

Twenty-seventh row.—Sl 1, k 1, n, th o, k 8, th o, n, k 1, th o, n, k 1, th o, n, n, th o, n, k 1, th o, n, k 1.

Twenty-eighth row.—K 4; th o and n, twice; k 19.

Twenty-ninth row.—Sl 1, k 1, n, th o, k 9, th o, n, k 1, th o, n, k 1, th o, n, n, k 1, th o, n, k 1.

Thirtieth row.—K 4, th o, n, k 20.   Repeat from 1st row.

OPEN-WORK INSERTION.

No. 16.—Cast on 28 stitches.

First row.—Sl 1, th o, k 2 together twice, th o, n, k 5, n, th o, n, k 5, n, th o, n, k 1, th o, n.

Second row.—Sl 1, th o, n, k 1; k 1 and p 1 out of the put-overs; k 7; k 1 and p 1 out of the put-overs; k 7; k 1 and p 1 out of the put-overs; k 2, th o, n.

Third row.—Sl 1, th o, n, k 7, n, th o, k 2 together twice; th o, n, k 8, th o, n.

Fourth row.—Sl 1, th o, n, k 8; k 1 and p 1 out of the put-overs; k 2; k 1 and p 1 out of the put-overs; k 9, th o, n.

Fifth row.—Sl 1, th o, n, k 5, n, th o, k 2 together twice; th o, k 2 together twice, th o, n, k 6, th o, n.

Sixth row.—Sl 1, th o, n, k 6; k 1 and p 1 out of the put-overs; k 2; k 1 and p 1 out of the put-overs; k 2; k 1 and p 1 out of the put-overs; k 7, th o, n.

Seventh row.—Same as third.

Eighth row.—Same as fourth.

Ninth row.—Same as first.

Tenth row.—Same as second.

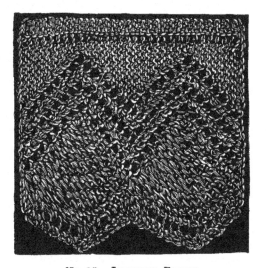

NO. 15.—IMPORTED EDGING.

Eleventh row.—Sl 1, th o, n, k 2; n, th o, n, k 10, n, th o, n, k 3, th o, n.

Twelfth row.—Sl 1, th o, n, k 3; k 1 and p 1 out of the put-overs; k 12; k 1 and p 1 out of the put-overs; k 4, th o, n.

Thirteenth row.—Sl 1, th o, k 2 together twice, th o, k 2 together twice; th o, n, k 6, n, th o, k 2 together twice; th o, n, k 1, th o, n.

Fourteenth row.—Sl 1, th o, n, k 1; k 1 and p 1 out of the put-overs; k 2; k 1 and p 1 out of the put-overs; k 8; k 1 and p 1 out of the put-overs;

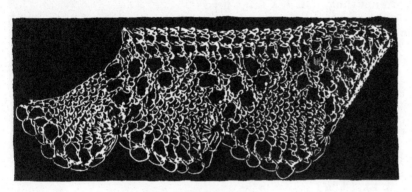

NO. 17.—SHELL LACE.

k 2; k 1 and p 1 out of the put-overs; k 2, th o, n.

Fifteenth row.—Same as eleventh.
Sixteenth row.—Same as twelfth.
Repeat from first row.

SHELL LACE.

No. 17.—This lace may be made of thread or of crochet cotton.

Cast on 18 stitches.

First row.—Slip 1, knit 1, thread over, slip 1, knit 1, pass slipped stitch over last stitch knit, thread over, slip 1, knit 1, pass slipped stitch over, thread over twice, narrow, knit 7, thread over twice, narrow, knit 1.

Second row.—Thread over twice, narrow, knit 1, purl 1, knit 9, purl 1, knit 1, purl 1, k 1, p 1, knit 2.

Third row.—Slip 1, k 1, th o, sl 1, k 1, pass sl st over, th o, sl 1, k 1, pass sl st over, k 11, th o twice, n, k 1, drop 1.

Fourth row.—Th o twice, n, k 1, p 1, k 12, p 1, k 1, p 1, k 2.

Fifth row.—Slip 1, k 1, th o, sl 1, k 1, pass sl st over, th o, sl 1, k 1, pass sl st over, th o twice, n, th o twice, n, k 8, th o twice, n, k 1, drop 1.

Sixth row.—Th o twice, n, k 1, p 1, k 10, p 1, k 2, p 1, k 1, p 1, k 1, p 1, k 2.

Seventh row.—Sl 1, k 1, th o, sl 1, k 1, pass sl st o, th o, sl 1, k 1, pass sl st o, k 15, th o twice, n, k 1, drop 1.

Eighth row.—Th o twice, n, k 1, p 1, k 16, p 1, k 1, p 1, k 2.

Ninth row.—Sl 1, k 1, th o, sl 1, k 1, pass sl st over, th o, sl 1, k 1, pass sl st over, th o twice, n, th o twice, n, th o twice, n, k 10, th o twice, n, k 1, drop 1.

Tenth row.—Th o twice, n, k 1, p 1, k 12, p 1, k 2, p 1, k 2, p 1, k 1, p 1, k 1, p 1, k 2.

Eleventh row.—Slip 1, k 1, th o, sl 1, k 1, pass sl st over, th o, sl 1, k 1, pass sl st over, k 20, th o twice, n, k 1, drop 1.

Twelfth row.—Th o twice, n, k 1, p 1, k 21, p 1, k 1, p 1, k 2.

Thirteenth row.—Sl 1, k 1, th o, sl 1, k 1, pass sl st o, th o, sl 1, k 1, pass sl st over, th o twice, n, th o twice, n, th o twice, n, th o twice, n, k 13, th o twice, n, k 1, drop 1.

Fourteenth row.—Th o twice, n, k 1, p 1, k 15, p 1, k 2, p 1, k 2, p 1, k 2, p 1, k 1, p 1, k 1, p 1, k 2.

Fifteenth row.—Sl 1, k 1, th o, sl 1, k 1, pass sl st o, th o, sl 1, k 1, pass sl st o, k 11, bind over to 1 stitch all the rest on the needle, and knit off binding stitch.

Sixteenth row. K 13, p 1, k 1, p 1, k 2.

Repeat from the first row for all the work.

KNITTED TORCHON LACE.

No. 18.—According to the material used, this lace is suitable for trimming gowns, underwear, counterpanes or knitted or cashmere shawls. It is knitted as follows:

Cast on 34 stitches.

First row.—Slip 1, k 3, make 1, k 2 together at the back, k 3, k 2 together, make 1, p 3, make 1, k 2 together at the back, k 3, make 1, k 2 together at the back, * make 1, k 2 together. Repeat from * 5 times more, k 1.

Second row.—Slip 1, k 23, p 5, k 3; in the next stitch both knit and purl a stitch, knit 1.

Third row.—Slip 1, k 5, make 1, k 2 together at the back, k 1, k 2 together, make 1, p 5, make 1, k 2 together at the back, k 3, * make 1, k 2 together. Repeat from * 5 times more, k 2.

Fourth row.—Slip 1, k 24, p 3, k 5, k 1, and p 1 both in the same stitch, k 1.

Fifth row.—Slip 1, k 7, make 1, k 3 stitches together, make 1, p 7, make 1, k 2 together at the back, k 3, * make 1, k 2 together. Repeat from * 5 times more, k 1.

Sixth row.—Slip 1, k 25, p 1, k 7, k 1 and p 1 both in the same stitch, k 1.

Seventh row.—Slip 1, k 6, k 2 together, make 1, k 3, make 1, k 2 together at the back, p 3, k 2 together, make 1, k 3, k 2 together, make 1, k 1 from the back, * make 1, k 2 together. Repeat from * 4 times more, k 2.

NO. 18.—KNITTED TORCHON LACE.

Eighth row.—Slip 1, k 24, p 3, k 6, knit 2 together, k 1.

Ninth row.—Slip 1, k 4, k 2 together, make 1, k 5, make 1, k 2 together at the back, p 1, k 2 together, make 1, k 3, k 2 together, make 1, k 1 at the back, * make 1, k 2 together. Repeat from * 5 times more, k 1.

Tenth row.—Slip 1, k 23, p 5, k 4, knit 2 together, k 1.

Eleventh row.—Slip 1, k 2, k 2 together, make 1, k 7, make 1, k 3 together, make 1, k 3, k 2 together, make 1, k 1 at the back, * make 1, k 2 together. Repeat from * 5 times more, k 2.

Twelfth row.—Slip 1, k 21, p 7, k 2, k 2 together, k 2. Repeat from first row.

No. 19.—KNITTED EDGING.

KNITTED EDGING.

No: 19.—This edging is pretty whether knitted in silk, cotton or linen, and according to the material selected may be used to trim dresses or under-wear.

Cast on 13 stitches and knit across plain.

First row.—Sl 1, k 1, th o twice, p 2 together, k 1, n, th o, k 1, th o, n, k 1, th o twice, k 2.

Second row.—K 3, p 1, k 2, th o, k 3, th o, k 2, th o twice, p 2 together, k 2.

Third row.—Sl 1, k 1, th o twice, p 2 together, k 2, th o, k 5, th o, n, k 4.

Fourth row.—Cast off 2, k 2, th o, k 3, th o, n, k 2, th o, k 2, th o twice, p 2 together, k 2.

Fifth row.—Sl 1, k 1, th o twice, p 2 together, n, k 1, th o, n, k 3, n, th o, k 1, n, k 1.

Sixth row.—K 4, th o, n, k 1, n, th o, k 1, n, th o twice, p 2 together, k 2.

Seventh row.—Sl 1, k 1, th o twice, p 2 together, n, k 1, th o twice, p 3 together, th o, k 1, n, k 2.

Eighth row.—K 9, th o twice, p 2 together, k 2 and repeat.

Repeat from first row for all the work.

KNITTED LACE.

No. 20.—Cast on 18 stitches.

First row.—Knit 1, * th o, n, k 1, th o, n, k 2, th o, n, k 3, th o, n, k 2, th o, k 1 *.

Second and every alternate even row.—Plain.

Third row.—K 2; then knit like first row between the stars.

Fifth row.—K 3; repeat first row between the stars.

Knit all the alternate *odd* rows in the same manner, except that at the beginning of each row you knit one more stitch than you did in the preceding row. In the 23rd row, 12 stitches will be knitted before beginning the repetition of the first row. There will now, also, be four fancy rows of 12 holes each.

Twenty-fourth row.—In working back k 4; pass the first 3 over the last one knit; then knit 4 more, which with the one already on the right-hand needle will make 5 stitches on this needle. Now pass 4 stitches over the last one knit; knit 5, and pass 5 over the last one knit. This will leave 17 on the left-hand needle and 1 on the right. Knit back plain, and repeat from the 1st row for all the points.

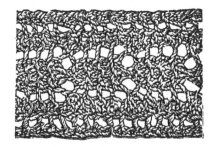

No. 20.—KNITTED LACE

SPIDER INSERTION.

No. 21.—Cast on 15 stitches and knit across plain.

First row.—K 2, th o, n, k 1, th o, n, k 1, sl and b, th o, k 1, n, th o, k 2.

Second, Fourth, Sixth, and Eighth rows.—K 3, p 3, k 3, p 3, k 3.

Third row.—K 2, th o, n, k 1, th o, n, k 1, sl and b, th o, k 1, n, th o, k 2.

Fifth row.—K 2, th o, n, k 2, th o, k 3 together, th o, k 2, n, th o, k 2.

Seventh row.—K 2, th o, n, n, th o, k 3, th o, n, n, th o, k 2.

Ninth row.—K 2, th o, n, k 1, th o, n, k 1, sl and b, th o, k 1, n, th o, k 2.

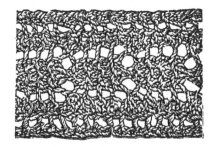

No. 21.—SPIDER INSERTION.

Tenth row.—Same as second and alternate rows. Repeat from first row for all the work.

KNITTED DIAMOND EDGINGS.

NOS. 22 AND 23.—For No. 22 cast on 20 stitches. The *second* and *every following even row* is knitted plain except that out of every thread put over twice, knit 1, purl 1.

First row.—Slip 1, k 1, k 2 together, * th o twice, k 3 together and repeat 3 times more from *; th o twice, k 2 together, k 2.

Third row.—Slip 1, k 2, * th o twice, k 3 together, and repeat 3 times more from *; th o twice, k 2 together, th o twice, k 3.

Fifth row—Slip 1, k 2, k 3 together, * th o twice, k 3 together and repeat twice more from *; th o twice, k 2 together, k 1, k 2 together, th o twice, k 3.

NO. 22.—KNITTED DIAMOND EDGING. (FOUR DIAMONDS).

Seventh row.—Slip 1, k 1, k 2 together, * th o twice, k 3 together, and repeat twice more from *; th o twice, k 2 together, k 3, k 2 together, th o twice, k 3.

Ninth row.—Slip 1, k 2, th o, * k 3 together, th o twice, and repeat twice more from *; k 2 together, k 5, k 2 together, th o twice, k 3.

Eleventh row.—Slip 1, k 2, k 2 together, * th o twice, k 3 together and repeat once more from *; th o twice, k 2 together, th o twice, k 2 together, k 3, k 2 together, th o twice, k 2 together, th o twice, k 3.

Thirteenth row.—Slip 1, k 1, k 2 together, th o twice, k 3 together, th o twice, k 3 together, * th o twice, k 2 together, k 1, k 2 together and repeat twice more from *, th o twice, k 3.

Fifteenth row.—Slip 1, k 2, th o, k 3 together, th o twice, k 3 together, th o twice, k 2 together, k 3, k 2 together, th o twice, k 3 together, th o twice, k 2 together, k 3, k 2 together, th o twice, k 3.

Seventeenth row.—Slip 1, k 2, k 2 together, th o twice, k 3 together, th o twice, k 2 together, k 5, k 2 together, th o twice, k 3 together, k 5, k 2 together, th o twice, k 3.

Nineteenth row.—Slip 1, k 2, th o, k 3 together, th o twice, k 3 together, th o twice, k 2 together, k 3, k 2 together, th o twice, k 2 together, k 3, k 2 together, th o twice, k 2 together, k 1, k 2 together.

Twenty-first row.—Slip 1, k 1, k 2 together, th o twice, k 3 together, th o twice, k 3 together, * th o twice, k 2 together, k 1, k 2 together and repeat 3 times more from *.

Twenty-third row.—Slip 1, k 2, k 2 together, * th o twice, k 3 together and repeat twice more from *; th o twice, k 2 together, k 3, k 2 together, th o twice, k 3 together, th o twice, k 2 together, k 1, k 2 together.

Twenty-fifth row.—Slip 1, k 2, th o, * k 3 together, th o twice and repeat twice more from *; k 3 together, k 5, k 2 together, th o twice, k 3 together, k 1, k 2 together.

Twenty-seventh row.—Slip 1, k 1, k 2 together, * th o twice, k 3 together and repeat twice more from *; th o twice, k 2 together, k 3, k 2 together, th o twice, k 2 together, k 1, k 2 together.

Twenty-ninth row.—Slip 1, k 2, k 2 together, * th o twice, k 3 together and repeat twice more from *; th o twice, k 2 together, k 1, k 2 together, th o twice, k 2 together, k 1, k 2 together.

Thirty-first row.—Slip 1, k 2, th o, k 3 together, * th o twice, k 3 together and repeat 3 times more from *; th o twice, k 2 together, k 1, k 2 together.

Thirty-third row.—Slip 1, k 1, k 2 together, * th o twice, k 3 together and repeat 4 times more from *; k 1, k 2 together.

Repeat from 3rd row for all the work.

For No. 23 cast on 32 stitches. Knit the same as No. 22, except that the extra stitches are used in making an extra row of diamonds (see picture) which are knitted on the same plan as the first row. Any one accustomed to knitting can make this edging after knitting the one seen at No. 22.

KNITTED DIAMOND INSERTION.
(For Illustration see next Page.)

No. 24.—Cast on 21 stitches.

The second and every following row is made plain except at the beginning of each, where you slip 1, k 2, th o, k 2 together for the heading; at the end knit the last 3 stitches as follows: Th o, k 2 together, k 1.

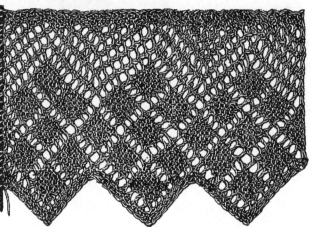

NO. 23.—KNITTED DIAMOND EDGING. (NINE DIAMONDS).

First row.—Slip 1, k 2, th o, k 2 together, k 4, th o, k 3 together, th o, k 6, th o, k 2 together, k 1.

Third row.—Slip 1, k 2, th o, k 2 together, k 2, k 2 together, th o, k 3, th o, k 2 together, k 4, th o, k 2 together, k 1.

Fifth row.—Slip 1, k 2, th o, k 2 together, k 1, k 2 together, th o, k 5, th o, k 2 together, k 3, th o, k 2 together, k 1.

Seventh row.—Slip 1, k 2, th o, k 2 together twice, th o, k 7, th o, k 2 together, k 2, th o, k 2 together, k 1.

Ninth row.—Slip 1, k 2, th o, k 3 together, th o, k 9, th o, k 2 together, k 1, th o, k 2 together, k 1.

Eleventh row.—Slip 1, k 2, th o, k 2 together, k 1, th o, k 2 together, k 5, k 2 together, th o, k 3, th o, k 2 together, k 1.

NO. 24.—KNITTED DIAMOND INSERTION.
(For Directions see this and preceding Page.)

Thirteenth row.— Slip 1, k 2, th o, k 2 together, k 2, th o, k 2 together, k 3, k 2 together, th o, k 4, th o, k 2 together, k 1.

Fifteenth row.— Slip 1, k 2, th o, k 2 together, k 3, th o, k 2 together, k 1, k 2 together, th o, k 5, th o, k 2 together, k 1.

Repeat from the first row for all the work.

FANCY KNITTED EDGING.

NO. 25.—Cast on 19 stitches and knit across plain.

First row.—Sl 1, k 1, th o twice, p 2 together, th o, p 2 together, th o, p 2 together, k 2, th o twice, p 2 together, k 3, th o twice, p 2 together, th o, p 2 together.

Second row.—Th o, p 2 together, th o, p 2 together, k 5, p 1, k 2, th o twice, p 2 together, th o, p 2 together, th o, p 2 together, k 2.

Third row.—Sl 1, k 1, th o twice, p 2 together, th o, p 2 together, th o, p 2 together, k 8, th o twice, p 2 together, th o, p 2 together.

Fourth row.—Th o, p 2 together, th o, p 2 together, k 8, th o twice, p 2 together, th o, p 2 together, th o, p 2 together, k 2.

Fifth row.—Sl 1, k 1, th o twice, p 2 together, th o, p 2 together, th o, p 2 together, k 2, th o twice, p 2 together, th o, p 2 together, k 2, th o twice, p 2 together, th o, p 2 together.

Sixth row.—Th o, p 2 together, th o, p 2 together, k 4, p 1, k 2, p 1, k 2, th o twice, p 2 together, th o, p 2 together, th o, p 2 together, k 2.

Seventh row.—Sl 1, k 1, th o twice, p 2 together, th o, p 2 together, th o, p 2 together, k 10, th o twice, p 2 together, th o, p 2 together.

Eighth row.—Th o, p 2 together, th o, p 2 to-gether, k 10, th o twice, p 2 together, th o, p 2 together, th o, p 2 together, k 2.

Ninth row.—Sl 1, k 1, th o twice, p 2 together, th o, p 2 together, th o, p 2 together, k 2, th o twice, p 2 together, th o, p 2 together, th o, p 2 together, k 2, th o twice, p 2 together, th o, p 2 together.

Tenth row.—Th o, p 2 together, th o, p 2 to-gether, k 4, p 1, k 2, p 1, k 2, p 1, k 2, th o twice, p 2 together, th o, p 2 together, th o, p 2 together, k 2.

Eleventh row.—Sl 1, k 1, th o twice, p 2 together, th o, p 2 together, th o, p 2 together, k 13, th o twice, p 2 together, th o, p 2 together.

Twelfth row.—Th o, p 2 together, th o, p 2 to-gether, k 13, th o twice, p 2 together, th o, p 2 to-gether, th o, p 2 together, k 2.

Thirteenth row.—Sl 1, k 1, th o twice, p 2 to-gether, th o, p 2 together, th o, p 2 together, k 2, th o twice, p 2 together, th o, p 2 together, th o, p 2 together, th o, p 2 together, k 3, th o twice, p 2 together, th o, p 2 together.

Fourteenth row.—Th o, p 2 together, th o, p 2 together, k 5, p 1, k 2, p 1, k 2, p 1, k 2, p 1, k 2, th o twice, p 2 together, th o, p 2 together, th o, p 2 together, k 2.

Fifteenth row.—Sl 1, k 1, th o twice, p 2 to-gether, th o, p 2 together, th o, p 2 together, k 17, th o twice, p 2 together, th o, p 2 together.

Sixteenth row.—Th o, p 2 together, th o, p 2 to-gether, k 17, th o twice, p 2 together, th o, p 2 to-gether, th o, p 2 together, k 2.

Seventeenth row.—Sl 1, k 1, th o twice, p 2 together, th o, p 2 together, th o, p 2 together, k 17, th o twice, p 2 together, th o, p 2 together.

Eighteenth row.—Th o, p 2 together, th o, p 2 together, k 7; pass all the other stitches and loops on the right hand needle over last stitch knit, leaving but 1 on the right hand needle then k 10,

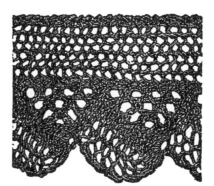

NO. 25.—FANCY KNITTED EDGING.

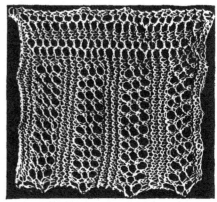

NO. 26.—KNITTED STRAIGHT-EDGE LACE.

th o twice, p 2 together, th o, p 2 together, th o, p 2 together, k 2.

Repeat from first row for all the work.

KNITTED STRAIGHT-EDGE LACE.

NO. 26.—Cast on 32 stitches to begin the work.
First row.—Knit plain.

Second row.—Knit 2, thread over twice, purl two together; repeat once more. K 2, th o, narrow, * th o, n, and repeat from * across the row.

Third row.—K 24 plain, * th o twice, purl 2 together, k 2 and repeat once more from *.

Repeat the last 2 rows twice more, which will make 3 upright rows of holes. Knit across plain 6 times except the heading, which knit the same as in 2nd and 3rd rows.

Now repeat 2nd and 3rd rows for the holes, then knit across plain 6 times; and so on for all the work.

FLUTED EDGING.

No. 27.—This edging is very pretty whether made of Saxony yarn, silk or thread, or crochet cotton. It presents the appearance of a fluted ruffle when properly knitted, and is suitable trimming for any article of wear.

Cast on 22 stitches.

First row.—Knit across plain.

Second row.—Knit 16 stitches, thread over, narrow, thread over, narrow, thread over, knit 2 plain.

Third row.—K 9, purl 11, leave 3 stitches on the needle, and then turn for the next row.

Fourth row.—K 14, th o, n, th o, n, th o, k 2.

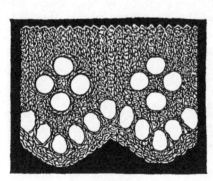

NO. 28.—ANTIQUE EDGING.

Fifth row.—K 10, p 11, k 3.

Sixth row.—K 18, th o, n, th o, n, th o, k 2.

Seventh row.—K 11, p 11, leave 3 on needle and turn for the next row.

Eighth row.—P 11, k 5, th o, n, th o, n, th o, k 2.

Ninth row.—Knit across plain.

Tenth row.—K 3, p 11, k 6, th o, n, th o, n, th o, k 2.

Eleventh row.—K 24, leave 3 stitches on the needle and turn for the next row.

Twelfth row.—P 11, k 7, th o, n, th o, n, th o, k 2.

Thirteenth row.—K 1, bind off 6, thus leaving 21 on the left hand needle. Knit the rest of the row plain.

Repeat from the second row for all the points.

ANTIQUE EDGING.

No. 28.—Cast on 11 stitches.

First row.—K 9, th o twice, k 2.

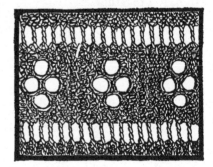

NO. 27.—FLUTED EDGING.

Second row.—K 2; k 1 and p 1 out of the put-overs, k 9.

Third row.—K 9, sl and b, k 2.

Fourth row.—K 2, th o twice, k 10.

Fifth row.—K 6, sl and b, k 2; k 1 and p 1 out of the put-overs, k 2.

Sixth row.—K 2, sl and b, k 3, th o twice, k 6.

Seventh row.—K 6, k 1 and p 1 out of the put-overs; k 4, th o twice, k 2.

Eighth row.—K 2, k 1 and p 1 out of the put-overs; k 4, sl and b, k 6.

Ninth row.—K 4, sl and b, k 1, sl and b, k 2, sl and b, k 2.

Tenth row.—K 2, th o twice, k 3, th o twice, k 3, th o twice, k 4.

Eleventh row.—K 4; k 1 and p 1 out of the put-overs, k 3; k 1 and p 1 out of the put-overs, k 3; k 1 and p 1 out of the put-overs; k 2.

Twelfth row.—K 2, sl and b, k 3, sl and b, k 3, sl and b, k 4.

Thirteenth row.—K 6, sl and b, k 3, n, th o twice, k 2.

Fourteenth row.—K 2; k 1 and p 1 out of the put-overs, n, k 3, th o twice, k 6.

Fifteenth row.—K 6; k 1 and p 1 out of the put-overs; k 2, n, sl and b, k 2.

Sixteenth row.—K 2, th o twice, k 4, sl and b, k 6.

Seventeenth row.—K 9, n; k 1 and p 1 out of the put-overs; k 2.

Eighteenth row.—K 2, sl and b, k 10.

Nineteenth row.—K 9, n, th o twice, k 2.

Twentieth row.—K 2; k 1 and p 1 out of the put-overs; n, k 8.

Twenty-first row.—K 9, sl and b, k 2.

Twenty-second row.—K 2, sl and b, k 8.

Repeat from first row for every scollop.

ANTIQUE INSERTION.

No. 29.—Cast on 17 stitches.

First row.—k 2, th o twice, n, k 9, n, th o twice, k 2.

Second row.—K 1, n, p 1, k 10, n, p 1, k 2.

NO. 29.—ANTIQUE INSERTION.

Repeat these two rows alternately, twice more.

Seventh row.—K 2, th o twice, n, k 4, sl and b, k 3, n, th o twice, k 2.

Eighth row.—K 1, n, p 1, k 5, th o twice, k 4, n, p 1, k 2.

Ninth row.—K 2, th o twice, n, k 4; k 1 and p 1 out of the put-overs; k 4, n, th o twice, k 2.

Tenth row.—K 1, n, p 1, k 3, * sl and b, and repeat twice more from *; k 2, n, p 1, k 2.

Eleventh row.—K 2, th o twice, n, k 2, th o twice, k 3, th o twice, k 2, n, th o twice, k 2.

Twelfth row.—K 1, n, p 1, * k 3; k 1 and p 1 out of the put-overs and repeat from * once more; k 2, n, p 1, k 2.

Thirteenth row.—K 2, th o twice, n, k 2, sl and b, sl and b, k 1, sl and b, k 2, n, th o twice, k 2.

Fourteenth row.—K 1, n, p 1, k 5, th o twice, k 4, n, p 1, k 2.

Fifteenth row.—K 2, th o twice, n, k 4; k 1 and p 1 out of the put-overs; k 4, n, th o twice, k 2.

Sixteenth row.—K 1, n, p 1, k 5, sl and b, k 4, n, p 1, k 2.

Repeat from first row.

KNITTED ANTIQUE-WHEEL LACE.

No. 30.—Cast on 31 stitches.

First row.—K 2, th o, n, k 1, th o, n, k 4, n, th o twice, n, k 5, th o, n, k 1, th o, n, th o, n, th o, n, th o, k 2.

Second row.—K 11, th o, n, k 4, th o twice, n, n, th o twice, n, knit the rest plain.

Third row.—K 2, th o, n, k 1, th o, n, k 4, seam 1, k 3, seam 1, k 5, th o, n, k 2, th o, n, th o, n, th o, n, th o, k 2.

Fourth row.—K 12, th o, n, k 5, n, th o twice, n, k 11.

Fifth row.—K 2, th o, n, k 1, th o, n, k 6, seam 1, k 7, th o, n, k 3, th o, n, th o, n, th o, n, th o, k 2.

Sixth row.—K 13, th o, n, k 5, th o twice, n, n, th o twice, n, knit the rest plain.

Seventh row.—K 2, th o, n, k 1, th o, n, k 4, seam 1, k 3, seam 1, k 6, th o, n, k 4, th o, n, th o, n, th o, n, th o, k 2.

Eighth row.—K 14, th o, n, k 6, n, th o twice, n; knit the rest plain.

Ninth row.—K 2, th o, n, k 1, th o, n, k 6; drop

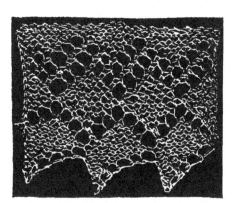

NO. 31.—KNITTED LACE.

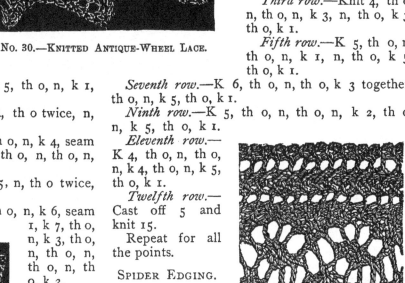

NO. 30.—KNITTED ANTIQUE-WHEEL LACE.

the put-over thread, n, k 6, th o, n, k 5, th o, n, th o, n, th o, n, th o, k 2.

Tenth row.—K 15, th o, n, knit the rest plain.

Eleventh row.—K 2, th o, n, k 1, th o, n, k 13, th o, n, k 14.

Twelfth row.—Slip 1, bind off 5, k 9, th o, n; knit the rest plain.

Repeat these details for all the work.

KNITTED LACE.

No. 31.—This engraving shows a pretty pattern of lace that may be knitted with thread, crochet cotton, Saxony yarn or silk.

Cast on 16 stitches.

First row.—Knit 3, thread over, narrow, thread over, narrow, knit 5, narrow, thread over, knit 1, thread over, knit 1.

Second, Fourth, Sixth, Eighth and Tenth rows.—Knit plain.

Third row.—Knit 4, th o, n, th o, n, k 3, n, th o, k 3, th o, k 1.

Fifth row.—K 5, th o, n, th o, n, k 1, n, th o, k 5, th o, k 1.

Seventh row.—K 6, th o, n, th o, k 3 together, th o, n, k 5, th o, k 1.

Ninth row.—K 5, th o, n, th o, n, k 2, th o, n, k 5, th o, k 1.

Eleventh row.—K 4, th o, n, th o, n, k 4, th o, n, k 5, th o, k 1.

Twelfth row.—Cast off 5 and knit 15.

Repeat for all the points.

SPIDER EDGING.

No. 32.—Cast on 15 stitches and knit across plain.

First row.—Knit 2, th o, k 1, sl 1, n, pass slipped stitch over; k 1, th o, k 4, th o twice, n, k 2.

Second row.—Th o, p 2 together, k 2, p 1, k 11.

Third row.—K 2, th o, k 1, sl 1, n, pass slipped stitch over, k 1, th o, k 2, n, th o twice, k 2, th o twice, k 3.

Fourth row.—Th o, p 2 together, k 2, p 1, n, k 1, p 1, k 10.

Fifth row.—K 2, th o, k 1, sl 1, n, pass slipped stitch over, k 1, th o, k 2, n, th o twice, n, k 2, th o twice, k 3.

NO. 32.—SPIDER EDGING.

Sixth row.—Th o, p 2 together, n, p 1, k 2, n, p 1, n, k 8.

Seventh row.—K 2, th o, k 1, sl 1, n, pass slipped stitch over, k 1, th o, k 3, th o twice, n, n, th o twice, k 3.

Eighth row.—Th o, p 2 together, n, p 1, n, k 1, p 1, n, k 8.

Ninth row.—K 2, th o, k 1, sl 1, n, pass slipped stitch over, k 1, th o, k 4, th o twice, n, th o twice, k 3.

Tenth row.—Th o, p 2 together, n, p 1, n, p 1, n, k 9.

Eleventh row.—K 2, th o, k 1, sl 1, n, pass slipped stitch over, k 1, th o, k 5, th o twice, n, k 2.

Twelfth row.—Th o, p 2 together, n, p 1, n, k 10.

Repeat from 1st row.

KNITTED EDGING.

No. 33.—Cast on 30 stitches.

First row.—Slip 1, knit 2, th o, k 2 together, k 3, k 2 together, * th o twice, k 2 together twice and repeat 3 times more from *; th o twice, k 4.

Second, Fourth, Sixth, Eighth, Tenth, Fourteenth, Sixteenth, Twentieth, Twenty-second, Twenty-fourth, Twenty-sixth, Twenty-eighth and Thirtieth rows.—Knit plain, except that you knit 1 and purl 1 out of every 2 put-overs, and at the end or last 3 stitches (working back), th o, k 2 together, k 1.

Third row.—Slip 1, k 2, th o, k 2 together, k 4, k 2 together, * th o twice, k 2 together twice and repeat 3 times more from *; th o twice, knit 4.

Fifth row.—Slip 1, k 2, th o, k 2 together, k 5, k 2 together * th o twice, k 2 together twice; repeat 3 times more from *; th o twice, k 4.

Seventh row.—Slip 1, k 2, th o, k 2 together, k 6, k 2 together, * th o twice, k 2 together twice; repeat 3 times more from *; th o twice, k 4.

Ninth row.—Slip 1, k 2, th o, k 2 together, k 7, k 2 together, * th o twice, k 2 together twice and repeat 3 times more from *; th o twice, k 4.

Eleventh row.—Slip 1, k 2, th o, k 2 together, k 8, k 2 together, * th o twice, k 2 together twice; repeat 3 times more from *; th o twice, k 4.

Twelfth row.—Slip 1, k 3, * k 1, p 1, k 2, and repeat 3 times more from *; k 1, p 1, k 1, k 2 together, th o twice, slip 1, k 2 together, pass slipped stitch over, th o twice, k 2 together, k 3, th o, k 2 together, k 1.

Thirteenth row.—Slip 1, k 2, th o, k 2 together, k 3, p 1, k 2, p 1, k 2, k 2 together; * th o twice,

No. 33.—KNITTED EDGING.

k 2 together twice and repeat 3 times more from *; th o twice, k 4.

Fifteenth row.—Slip 1, k 2, th o, k 2 together, k 1, th o twice, * slip 1, k 2 together, pass slipped stitch over, th o twice; repeat twice more from *; k 2 together, k 1, k 2 together, * th o twice, k 2 together twice and repeat 3 times more from last *; th o twice, k 4.

Seventeenth row.—Slip 1, k 2, th o, k 2 together, k 9, k 2 together, * th o twice, k 2 together twice; repeat 3 times more from *; th o twice, k 2 together, k 4.

Eighteenth row.—Slip 1, cast off 1, k 3, *; k 1, p 1, k 2 and repeat 4 times more from *; k 2 together, th o twice, slip 1, k 2 together, pass slipped stitch over, th o twice, k 2 together, k 3, th o, k 2 together, k 1.

Nineteenth row.—Slip 1, k 2, th o, k 2 together, k 3, p 1, k 2, p 1, k 1, k 2 together, * th o twice, k 2 together twice and repeat 3 times more from *; th o twice, k 2 together, k 4.

Twenty-first row.—Slip 1, k 2, th o, k 2 together, k 7, k 2 together, * th o twice, k 2 together twice and repeat 3 times more from *; th o twice, k 3 together, k 4.

Twenty-third row.—Slip 1, k 2, th o, k 2 together, k 6, k 2 together, * th o twice, k 2 together twice and repeat 3 times more from *; th o twice, k 3 together, k 4.

Twenty-fifth row.—Slip 1, k 2, th o, k 2 together, k 5, k 2 together *, th o twice, k 2 together twice and repeat 3 times more from *; th o twice, k 3 together, k 4.

Twenty-seventh row.—Slip 1, k 2, th o, k 2 together, k 4, k 2 together; * th o twice, k 2 together twice, and repeat 3 times more from *; th o twice, k 3 together, k 4.

Twenty-ninth row.—Slip 1, k 2, th o, k 2 together, k 3, k 2 together, * th o twice, k 2 together twice and repeat 3 times more from *; th o twice, k 3 together, k 4. Knit back as in other rows, except that you knit the 2nd and 3rd stitches together in order to narrow.

Repeat from the 3rd row for all of the work.

KNITTED INSERTION.

(For Illustration see next Page.)

No. 34.—Cast on 35 stitches.

First row.—Slip 1, k 2, th o, k 2 together, k 3, k 2 together, * th o twice, k 2 together twice and repeat once more from *; th o twice, k 2 together, k 1, k 2 together, th o twice, k 3 together, th o twice, k 3 together, th o twice, k 2 together, k 1, th o once, k 2 together, k 1.

Second and every following even row not described.—The first 4 stitches of each of these rows are knit as follows: Slip 1, k 2, th o, k 2 together. The last 3 as follows: Th o, k 2 together, k 1. Knit the rest plain, knitting one-half and purling the other half of each thread put over twice.

Third row.—Slip 1, k 2, th o, k 2 together, k 4, k 2 together, * th o twice, k 2 together twice and repeat once more from *; th o twice, k 2 together, k 11, th o, k 2 together, k 1.

Fourth row.—Slip 1, k 2, th o, k 2 together, k 1, k 2 together, th o twice, k 3 together, th o twice, k 2 together, * k 3, p 1 and repeat twice more from *; k 7, th o, k 2 together, k 1.

Fifth row.—Slip 1, k 2, th o, k 2 together, k 5, k 2 together, * th o twice, k 2 together twice and repeat once more from *; th o twice, k 2 together, k 2, p 1, k 2, p 1; k 4, th o, k 2 together, k 1.

Sixth row.—Like the second.

Seventh row.—Slip 1, k 2, th o, k 2 together, k 6, k 2 together, * th o twice, k 2 together twice and repeat once more from *; th o twice, k 2 together, k 9, th o, k 2 together, k 1.

Eighth row.—Like second.

Ninth row.—Slip 1, k 2, th o, k 2 together, k 7, k 2 together, * th o twice, k 2 together twice and repeat once more from *; th o twice, k 2 together, k 8, th o, k 2 together, k 1.

Tenth row.—Like second.

Eleventh row.—Slip 1, k 2, th o, k 2 together, k 8, k 2 together; * th o twice, k 2 together twice and repeat once more from *; th o twice, k 2 together, k 7, th o, k 2 together, k 1, th o, k 2 together, k 1.

Twelfth row.—Slip 1, k 2, th o, k 2 together, k 6, k 1, p 1, * k 3, p 1 and repeat once more from *; k 1, k 2 together, th o twice, k 3 together, th o twice, k 2 together, k 3, th o, k 2 together, k 1.

Thirteenth row.—Slip 1, k 2, th o, k 2 together, k 3, p 1, k 2, p 1, k 2, k 2 together; * th o twice, k 2 together twice and repeat once more from *; th o twice, k 2 together, k 6, th o, k 2 together, k 1.

Fourteenth row.—Like second row.

Fifteenth row.—Slip 1, k 2, th o, k 3 together, * th o twice, k 3 together and repeat once more from *; th o twice, k 2 together, k 1, k 2 together; * th o, twice, k 2 together twice and repeat once more from

NO. 34.—KNITTED INSERTION.
(For Directions see this and preceding Page.)

last *; th o twice, k 2 together, k 5, th o, k 2 together, k 1.

Sixteenth row.—Like second.

Seventeenth row.—Slip 1, k 2, th o, k 2 together, k 9, k 2 together, * th o twice, k 2 together twice and repeat once more from last *; th o twice, k 2 together, k 6, th o, k 2 together, k 1.

Eighteenth row.—Slip 1, k 2, th o, k 2 together, k 5, k 1, p 1, * k 3, p 1 and repeat from * once more; k 2, k 2 together, th o twice, k 3 together, th o twice, k 2 together, k 3, th o, k 2 together, k 1.

Nineteenth row.—Slip 1, k 2, th o, k 2 together, k 3, p 1, k 2, p 1, k 1, k 2 together, * th o twice, k 2 together twice and repeat once more from last *; th o twice, k 2 together, k 7, th o, k 2 together, k 1.

Twentieth row.—Like second.

Twenty-first row.—Slip 1, k 2, th o, k 2 together, k 7, k 2 together, * th o twice, k 2 together twice and repeat once more from last *; th o twice, k 2 together, k 8, th o, k 2 together, k 1.

Twenty-second row.—Like second.

Twenty-third row.—Slip 1, k 2, th o, k 2 together, k 6, k 2 together, th o twice, k 2 together twice, and repeat once more from *; th o twice, k 2 together, k 9, th o, k 2 together, k 1.

Twenty-fourth row.—Like second.

Twenty-fifth row.—Slip 1, k 2, th o, k 2 together, k 5, k 2 together, * th o twice, k 2 together twice and repeat once more from *; th o twice, k 2 together, k 10, th o, k 2 together, k 1.

Twenty-sixth row.—Slip 1, k 2, th o, k 2 together, k 1, k 2 together, th o twice, k 3 together, th o twice, k 2 together, k 2, p 1, * k 3, p 1 and repeat once more from *; k 8, th o, k 2 together, k 1.

Twenty-seventh row.—Slip 1, k 2, th o, k 2 together, k 4, k 2 together, * th o twice, k 2 together twice and repeat once more from *; th o twice, k 2 together, k 3, p 1, k 2, p 1, k 4, th o, k 2 together, k 1.

Twenty-eighth row.—Like second.

Twenty-ninth row.—Slip 1, k 2, th o, k 2 together, k 3, k 2 together, * th o twice, k 2 together twice and repeat once more from *; th o twice, k 3 together, th o twice, k 3 together; th o twice, k 2 together, k 2, th o, k 2 together, k 1.

Thirtieth row.—Like second.

Repeat from 3rd row for all the rest of the work.

OPEN-WORK DIAMOND EDGING.

No. 35.—Cast on 19 stitches and knit across plain.

First row.—K 2, th o, n, th o, n, k 6, n, th o, k 3, th o, k 2.

Second row.—K 2, th o, k 5, th o, n, k 6, th o, n, th o, n, k 1.

Third row.—K 2, th o, n, th o, n, k 4, n, th o, k 1, n, th o, k 1, th o, n, k 1, th o, k 2.

Fourth row.—K 2, th o, k 1, n, th o, k 3, th o, n, k 1, th o, n, k 4, th o, n, th o, n, k 1.

Fifth row.—K 2, th o, n, th o, n, k 2, n, th o, k 1, n, th o, k 5, th o, n, k 1, th o, k 2.

Sixth row.—K 2, th o, k 1, n, th o, k 3, th o, n, k 2, th o, n, k 1, th o, n, k 2, th o, n, th o, n, k 1.

Seventh row.—K 2, th o, n, th o, n, k 3, th o, n, k 1, th o, n, k 3, n, th o, k 1, n, th o, k 1, n.

Eighth row.—Cast off 1, k 1, th o, n, k 1, th o, n, k 1, n, th o, k 1, n, th o, k 5, th o, n, th o, n, k 1.

Ninth row.—K 2, th o, n, th o, n, k 5, th o, n, k 1, th o, sl 1, n, pass slipped stitch over, th o, k 1, n, k 1, n.

Tenth row.—K 2, th o, n, k 3, n, th o, k 7, th o, n, th o, n, k 1.

Eleventh row.—K 2, th o, n, th o, n, k 7, th o, n, k 1, n, th o, k 3.

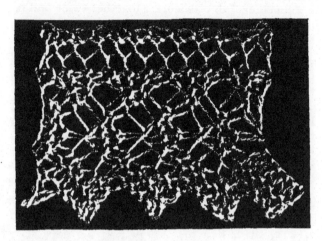

No. 36.—KNITTED TORCHON LACE.

Twelfth row.—Cast off 2, k 1, th o, k 3 together, th o, k 9, th o, n, th o, n, k 1.

Repeat all these details for every scollop.

KNITTED TORCHON LACE.

No. 36.—In this instance this lace is made of Saxony yarn, but cotton, linen or silk may be used for the same pattern.

Cast on 15 stitches.

First row.—Slip 1 k 2, th o, narrow, k 3, th o, k 1. th o, k 6.

Second row.—Slip 1, k 5, th o, k 3, th o, n, k 3, th o, n, k 1.

Third row.—Slip 1, k 2, th o, n, n, th o, k 5, th o, k 6.

Fourth row.—Bind off 4, k 1, th o, n, k 3, n, th o, n, k 1, th o, n, k 1.

Fifth row.—Slip 1, k 2, th o, n, k 1, th o, n, k 1, n, th o, k 3.

Sixth row.—Slip 1, k 2, th o, k 1, th o, slip 2, k 1; pass the two slipped stitches over the knitted one; th o, k 4, th o, n, k 1.

Repeat from first row.

KNITTED NARROW EDGING.

No. 37.—Cast on 12 stitches and knit across plain.

First row.—Knit 2, th o twice, seam 2 together, knit 2, th o twice, n, k 1, th o twice, n, k 1.

Second row.—K 3, seam 1, k 3, seam 1, k 2, th o twice, seam 2 together, k 2.

Third row.—K 2, th o twice, seam 2 together, k 10.

Fourth row.—K 1, bind off 2 (which will leave 11 on the left-hand needle), k 7, th o twice, seam 2 together, k 2. Repeat from first row.

KNITTED LACE.

(No Illustration.)

Cast on 7 stitches and knit across plain.

First row.—Sl 1, k 1, th o, n, k 1, th o twice, k 2.

Second row.—Th o, p 2 together, k 1, p 1, k 2, th o, n, k 1.

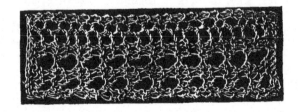

No. 37.—KNITTED NARROW EDGING.

Third row.—Sl 1, k 1, th o, n, k 5.

Fourth row.—Th o, p 2 together, k 4, th o, n, k 1.

Fifth row.—Sl 1, k 1, th o, n, k 5.

Sixth row.—Bind off 3, k 3, th o, n, k 1.

Repeat from first row.

NO. 35.—OPEN-WORK DIAMOND EDGING.

OPEN-POINT EDGING.

No. 38.—This edging may be made of knitting silk or of cotton or linen. Belding's knitting silk in any tint preferred makes a pretty effect.

Cast on 24 stitches and purl across.

First row.—Sl 1, k 2, th o, n, k 11, th o, n, k 1, th o, n, th o twice, n, k 1.

Second row.—K 3, p 1, k 5, th around the needle, p 2 together, p 10, k 1, th o, n, k 1.

Third row.—Sl 1, k 2, th o, n, k 1; th o and n, 4

No. 38.—OPEN-POINT EDGING.

times; k 2, th o, n, k 2, th o, n, th o twice, n, k 1.

Fourth row.—K 3, p 1, k 6, th around the needle, p 2 together, p 10, k 1, th o, n, k 1.

Fifth row.—Sl 1, k 2, th o, n, k 11, th o, n, k 3, th o, n, th o twice, n, k 1.

Sixth row.—K 3, p 1, k 7, th around the needle, p 2 together, p 10, k 1, th o, n, k 1.

Seventh row.—Sl 1, k 2, th o, n, k 1; th o and n, 4 times; k 2, th o, n, k 4, th o, n, th o twice, n, k 1.

Eighth row.—K 3, p 1, k 8, th around the needle, p 2 together, p 10, k 1, th o, n, k 1.

Ninth row.—Sl 1, k 2, th o, n, k 11, th o, n, k 5, th o, n, th o twice, n, k 1.

Tenth row.—K 3, p 1, k 9, th around the needle, p 2 together, p 10, k 1, th o, n, k 1.

Eleventh row.—Sl 1, k 2, th o, n, k 11, th o, n, k 6, th o, n, th o twice, n, k 1.

Twelfth row.—K 3, p 1, k 10, th around the needle, p 2 together, p 10, k 1, th o, n, k 1.

Thirteenth row.—Sl 1, k 2, th o, n, k 11, th o, n, k 12.

Fourteenth row.—Bind off 6, k 7, th around the

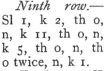

No. 39.—OPEN-WORK EDGING.

needle, p 2 together, p 10, k 1, th o, n, k 1. Repeat from first row for all of the work.

OPEN-WORK EDGING.

No. 39.—Cast on 16 stitches and knit across plain.

First row.—Knit 3, th o, n, k 2, th o, n, k 1, th o twice, n, th o twice, n, th o twice, n.

Second row.—K 2, p 1, k 2, p 1, k 2, p 1, k 2, p 1, k 3, p 1, k 3.

Third row.—K 3, th o, n, k 2, th o, n, k 10.

Fourth row.—Cast off 3, k 7, p 1, k 3, p 1, k 3. Repeat from first row.

KNITTED INSERTION: PEACOCK'S-EYE PATTERN.

No. 40.—Cast on 27 stitches.

First row.—Knit 3, th o, k 2 together, k 18, th o, k 2 together, k 2.

Second row.—K 3, th o, k 2 together, p 1, k 2

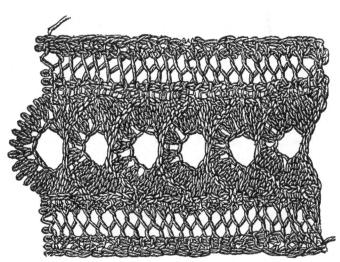

No. 40.—KNITTED INSERTION: PEACOCK'S-EYE PATTERN.

together, k 5, th o 7 times, k 5, k 2 together, p 1, k 2, th o, k 2 together, k 2.

Third row.—K 3, th o, k 2 together. k 1, k 2 together, p 4; knit 7 out of the back; p 4, p 2 together, k 3, th o, k 2 together, k 2.

Fourth row.—K 3, th o, k 2 together, p 1, k 2 together, k 3; * th o, k 1, and repeat 6 times more from *; k 3, k 2 together, p 1, k 2, th o, k 2 together, k 2.

Fifth row.—K 3, th o, k 1, p 2 together, p 18, p 2 together, k 3, th o, k 2 together, k 2.

Sixth row.—K 3, th o, k 2 together, p 1, k 2 together, k 16, k 2 together, p 1, k 2, th o, k 2 together, k 2.

Seventh row.—K 3, th o, k 2 together, p 1, p 2 together, p 14, p 2 together, k 3, th o, k 2 together, k 2.

Eighth row.—K 3, th o, k 2 together, p 1, p 2 together, p 12, p 2 together, p 1, k 2, th o, k 2 together, k 2 and repeat from 1st row.

NARROW TORCHON EDGING.

No. 41.—Cast on 9 stitches and knit across plain.

First row.—K 3, n, th o, n, th o, k 1, th o, k 1.

Second and every alternate row.—Plain.

Third row.—K 2, n, th o, n, th o, k 3, th o, k 1.

Fifth row.—K 1, n, th o, n, th o, k 5, th o, k 1.

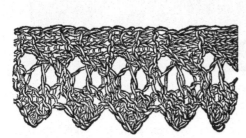

No. 41.—NARROW TORCHON EDGING.

Seventh row.—K 3, th o, n, th o, n, k 1, n, th o, n.

Ninth row.—K 4, th o, n, th o, k 3 together, th o, n.

Eleventh row.—K 5, th o, k 3 together, th o, n.

Twelfth row.—Plain. Repeat from first row for all the details.

KNITTED EDGING.

No. 42.—For this edging use linen thread and fine steel needles. Cast on 7 stitches.

First row.—Slip 1, inserting the needle from the back of the stitch below the working thread; k 6.

Second row.—Slip 1, k 1, th o twice, p 2 together, p 2, k 1.

Third row.—Slip 1, k 3; out of the 2 put-overs k 1 and k 1 crossed (to knit crossed, insert the needle from the back downward); k 2.

Fourth row.—Slip 1, k 2, th o twice, p 2 together, p 2, k 1.

No. 42.—KNITTED EDGING.

Fifth row.—Slip 1, k 3; out of the two put-overs k 1 and k 1 crossed; k 3.

Sixth row.—Slip 1, k 4, th o twice, p 2 together, k 2.

Seventh row.—Slip 1, k 2; out of the put-overs, k 1 and p 1; k 5.

Eighth row.—Cast off 3, inserting the needle as for purling instead of knitting; k 6. Repeat from 1st row for all of the details.

POINTED FLUTED EDGING.

No. 43.—Cast on 21 stitches and knit across plain.

First row.—K 3, th o, n, k 10, th o, n, th o, n, th o twice, n.

Second row.—K 2, p 1, k 4, p 10, k 1, th o, n, k 2.

Third row.—K 3, th o, n, k 1, * th o, n, and repeat 3 times more from *; k 1, th o, n, k 1, th o, n, th o twice, n.

Fourth row.—K 2, p 1, k 5, p 10, k 1, th o, n, k 2.

Fifth row.—K 3, th o, n, k 1, th o, n, k 4, th o, n, k 1, th o, n, k 2, th o, n, th o twice, n.

Sixth row.—K 2, p 1, k 6, p 10, k 1, th o, n, k 2.

Seventh row.—K 3, th o, n, k 1, * th o, n, and repeat 3 times more from *; k 1, th o, n, k 3, th o, n, th o twice, n.

Eighth row.—K 2, p 1, k 7, p 10, k 1, th o twice, n, k 2.

Ninth row.—K 3, th o, n, k 10, th o, n, k 4, th o, n, th o twice, n.

Tenth row.—K 2, p 1, k 19, th o, n, k 2.

Eleventh row.—K 3, th o, n, p 10; leave thread

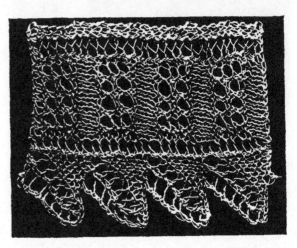

No. 43.—POINTED FLUTED EDGING.

at back of needle to serve as th o; n, k 5, th o, n, th o twice, n.

Twelfth row.—K 2, p 1, k 20, th o, n, k 2.

Thirteenth row.—K 3, th o, n, p 10; leave thread as in 11th row; n, k 6, th o, n, th o twice, n.

Fourteenth row.—Bind off 7, leaving 20 stitches on the left-hand needle; k 16, th o, n, k 2. In binding off, drop the 2nd loop of the two put-over threads.

Repeat from first row for the next and following points.

NARROW EDGING.

No. 44.—Cast on 11 stitches and knit across plain.

First row.—K 3, th o, sl and b, k 1, th o, sl and b, k 1, th o twice, k 1, th o twice, k 1.

Second row.—K 2, p 1, k 2, p 1, k 2, p 1, k 2, p 1, k 3.

No. 44.—NARROW EDGING.

Third row.—K 3, th o, sl and b, k 1, th o, sl and b, k 7.

Fourth row.—Cast off 4, k 3 p, 1, k 2, p 1, k 3. Repeat from first row.

KNITTED INSERTION.

No. 45.—Cast on 13 stitches and knit across plain.
First row.—Sl 1, k 3, n, th o, k 1, th o, n, k 4.
Second and every alternate row. — Plain.

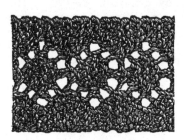

No. 45.—KNITTED INSERTION.

Third row.—Sl 1, k 2, n, th o, k 3, th o, n, k 3.
Fifth row.—Sl 1, k 1, n, th o, k 5, th o, n, k 2.
Seventh row.—Sl 1, k 3, th o, n, k 1, n, th o, k 4.
Ninth row.—Sl 1, k 4, th o, k 3 together, th o, k 5.

Tenth row. — Plain. Repeat from beginning.

NARROW POINTED EDGING.

No. 46.—Cast on 7 stitches.
First row.—Sl 1, k 2 together, th o twice, k 2 together, th o twice, k 2 together.
Second row.—Sl 1; k 1 and p 1 alternately out of each double put-over, knitting the rest plain.
Third row.—Sl 1, k 2 together, th o twice, k 2 together, k 1, th o twice, k 2 together.

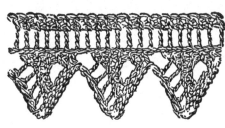

No. 46.—NARROW POINTED EDGING.

Fourth row.—Sl 1, k 1, p 1, k 3, p 1, k 2.
Fifth row.—Sl 1, k 2 together, th o twice, k 2 together, k 2, th o twice, k 2 together.
Sixth row.—Sl 1, k 1, p 1, k 4, p 1. k 2.
Seventh row.—Sl 1, k 2 together, th o twice, k 2 together, k 3, th o twice, k 2 together.
Eighth row.—Sl 1, k 1, p 1, k 5, p 1, k 2.
Ninth row.—Sl 1, k 2 together, th o twice, k 2 together, k 1, th o 3 times, k 2 together, k 1, th o twice, k 2 together.
Tenth row.—Sl 1, k 1, p 1, k 3; p 1 and k 1 out of the rest of the put-overs; k 3, p 1, k 2.
Eleventh row.—Sl 1, k 2 together, th o twice, k 2 together, k 7, th o twice, k 2 together.
Twelfth row.—Cast off 9, leaving 6 on the left-hand needle, k 3, p 1, k 2. Repeat from 1st row.

WIDE POINTED EDGING.

No. 47.—Cast on 30 stitches and knit across plain.
First row.—Knit 2, th o twice, purl 2 together, k 2, th o twice, purl 2 together, k 1, * th o, narrow, and repeat from * to within 1 stitch from the end; then th o, k 1, which will complete 11 holes.
Second row.—Knit plain to within 8 stitches from the end; then th o twice, purl 2 together, k 2, th o twice, purl 2 together, k 2; these last 8

stitches will form the fagoting or heading.
Repeat these two rows, increasing 1 stitch between the fagoting and the holes in every row *worked toward the lower edge*, until there are 17 rows, or 9 stitches, between the fagoting and open work, and 9 holes. This will bring you to the middle of the first point.

In working toward the top (18th row), begin to narrow for the other half of the point in the following manner: Knit 3 stitches together; knit plain to fagoting and knit latter as before.

Begin every row worked toward the top by knit-

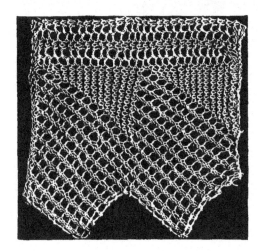

No. 47.—WIDE POINTED EDGING.

ting 3 together as in 18th row; and in every row worked downward increase by 1 plain stitch between the fagoting and holes as before, until there are 15 plain stitches between the fagoting and open work, or 4 holes below them after working back. Then, begin at the top, and repeat from the first row, except that at the end of this row knit the *two stitches* left after putting the thread over, *together*.

KNITTED TORCHON LACE.

No. 48.—Cast on 15 stitches and knit across plain.
First row.—K 3, th o, n, k 3, th o, k 1, th o, k 6.
Second row.—K 6, th o, k 3, th o, n, k 3, th o, n, k 1.
Third row.—K 3, th o, n, n, th o, k 5, th o, k 6.
Fourth row.—Cast off 4, k 1, th o, n, k 3, n, th o, n, k 1, th o, n, k 1.
Fifth row.—K 3, th o, n, k 1, th o, n, k 1, n, th o, k 3.

No. 48.—KNITTED TORCHON LACE.

Sixth row.—K 3, th o, k 1, th o, sl 2, k 1; pass the slipped stitches over the knitted one; th o, k 4, th o, n, k 1.

Repeat from first row for all the work.

LATTICE EDGING.

No. 49.—Cast on 21 stitches and knit across plain.

First row.—K 3, th o, n, th o, n, k 2; k 8 putting thread over 4 times for each instead of once as in ordinary knitting; k 2, th o 4 times, k 2.

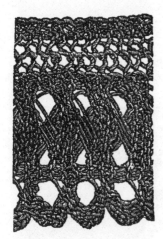

NO. 49.—LATTICE EDGING.

Second row.—K 2, then out of the 4 put-overs, k 1, p 1, k 1, p 1; then k 2; now slip the first 4 put-overs off as 1 stitch; slip each of the following 7 in the same way; this will make 8 long stitches on the right hand needle. With the left hand needle lift or pass the first 4 of these long loops over the second 4, and then keeping them on the left hand needle also slip the second 4 onto this needle. This will cross the loops and leave them on the left hand needle. Now knit them off in the order in which they are now arranged—that is, knitting the second 4 first, and the first 4 last; then k 3, th o, n, th o, n, k 2.

Third row.—K 3, th o, n, th o, n, k 18.
Fourth row.—K 19, th o, n, th o, n, k 2.
Fifth row.—K 3, th o, n, th o, n, k 18.

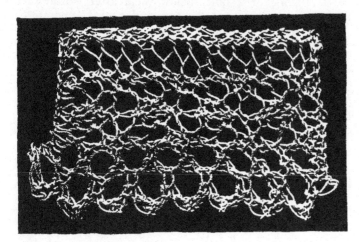

NO. 50.—KNITTED SPIDER-WEB LACE.

Sixth row.—Cast off 4, k 14, th o, n, th o, n, k 2. Repeat from first row for all the work.

KNITTED SPIDER-WEB LACE.

No. 50.—Cast on 15 stitches, and knit across plain.

First row.—Knit 3, thread over and knit 3 together, thread over, knit 3 plain, thread over, narrow, thread over twice, narrow, thread over twice, narrow.

Second row.—Thread over, knit 2, purl 1, knit 2, purl 1, knit 2, thread over, narrow, knit 7.

Third row.—Knit 3, thread over, narrow, thread over, narrow, purl 1, narrow, thread over, knit 8.

Fourth row.—Knit 1, bind off 3, knit 4, purl 6, knit 1, thread over, narrow, knit 1.

Fifth row.—Knit 3, thread over, narrow, knit 1,

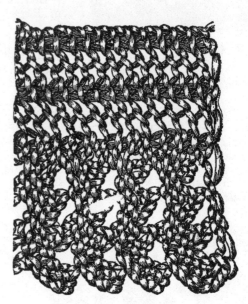

NO. 51.—KNITTED EDGING.

thread over, knit 3 together, thread over, knit 2 plain, thread over twice, narrow, thread over twice, narrow.

Sixth row.—Thread over, knit 2, purl 1, knit 2, purl 1, knit 1, purl 6, knit 1, thread over, narrow, knit 1.

Seventh row.—Knit 3, thread over, narrow, narrow, thread over, knit 1, thread over, narrow, knit 8.

Eighth row.—Same as fourth.
Repeat from first row for all the work.

KNITTED EDGING.

No. 51.—Cast on 15 stitches.
First row.—Knit 3, th o, n, k 1, th o, n, k 1, th o twice, n, th o twice, n, th o twice, n.

Second row.—K 2, p 1, k 2, p 1, k 2, p 1, k 2, th o, n, k 1, th o, n, k 2.

Third row.—K 3, th o, n, k 1, th o, n, k 1; k rest plain.

Fourth row.—K 11, th o, n, k 1, th o, n, k 2,

Fifth row.—K 3, th o, n, k 1, th o, n, k 1; k rest plain.

Sixth row.—Cast off 3, k 7, th o, n, k 1, th o, n, k 2; repeat from the first row for all the points.

LEAF EDGING.

No. 52.—Cast on 19 stitches and knit across plain.

First row.—Sl 1, k 1, th o twice, p 2 together, k 1, th o, k 1, sl 1, n, pass slipped stitch over, k 1, th o, k 1, th o twice, p 2 together, k 1, th o twice, n, th o twice, n, k 1.

No. 52.—LEAF EDGING.

Second row.—K 3, p 1, k 2, p 1, k 1, th o twice, p 2 together, k 7, th o twice, p 2 together, k 2.

Third row.—Sl 1, k 1, th o twice, p 2 together, k 1, th o, k 1, sl 1, n, pass slipped stitch over, k 1, th o, k 1, th o twice, p 2 together, k 3, th o twice, n, th o twice, n, k 1.

Fourth row.—K 3, p 1, k 2, p 1, k 3, th o twice, p 2 together, k 7, th o twice, p 2 together, k 2.

Fifth row.—Sl 1, k 1, th o twice, p 2 together, k 1, th o, k 1, sl 1, n, pass slipped stitch over, k 1, th o, k 1, th o twice, p 2 together, k 5, th o twice, n, th o twice, n, k 1.

Sixth row.—K 3, p 1, k 2, p 1, k 5, th o twice, p 2, together, k 7, th o twice, p 2 together, k 2.

Seventh row.—Sl 1, k 1, th o twice, p 2 together, k 1, th o, k 1, sl 1, n, pass slipped stitch over, k 1, th o, k 1, th o twice, p 2 together, k 7, th o twice, n, th o twice, n, k 1.

Eighth row.—K 3, p 1, k 2, p 1, k 7, th o twice, p 2 together, k 7, th o twice, p 2 together, k 2.

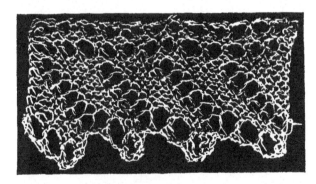

No. 53.—KNITTED LACE.

Ninth row.—Sl 1, k 1, th o twice, p 2 together, k 1, th o, k 1, sl 1, n, pass slipped stitch over, k 1, th o, k 1, th o twice, p 2 together, k 9, th o twice, n, th o twice, n, k 1.

Tenth row.—Cast off 10, k 5, th o twice, p 2 together, k 7, th o twice, p 2 together, k 2 and repeat from first row for all the work.

KNITTED LACE.

No. 53.—Cast on 12 stitches and knit across plain.

First row.—K 1, th o, n, th o, n, th o, n, k 3, th o twice, n.

Second row.—K 2, p 1, and knit rest of row plain.

Third row.—K 6, th o, n, k 5.

Fourth row.—Knit plain.

Fifth row.—K 1, th o, n, th o, n, k 2, th o, n, k 2, th o, twice, n.

Sixth row.—K 2, p 1, knit the rest plain.

Seventh row.—K 8, th o, n, k 4.

Eighth row.—Knit plain.

Ninth row.—K 1, th o, n, th o, n, k 4, th o, n, k 1, th o twice, n.

Tenth row.—K 2, p 1, knit the rest plain.

Eleventh row.—K 10, th o, n, k 3.

Twelfth row.—Bind off 3; this will leave 11 on

No. 54.—DEEP LATTICE EDGING.

the left-hand needle which knit plain, and repeat from first row.

DEEP LATTICE EDGING.

No. 54.—Use Belding's silk or cotton, and fine knitting needles.

Cast on 25 stitches and knit across twice plain.

Third row.—Sl 1, k 3; th o and n, 9 times; th o twice, n, k 1.

Fourth row.—K 3, p 1, k 22.

Fifth row.—Sl 1, k 4; th o and n, 9 times; th o twice, n, k 1.

Sixth row.—K 3, p 1, k 23.

Seventh row.—Sl 1, k 5; th o and n, 9 times; th o twice and n, k 1.

Eighth row.—K 3, p 1, k 24.

Ninth row.—Sl 1, k 27.

Tenth row.—Plain.

Eleventh row.—Slip 1, k 27.

Twelfth row.—Bind off 3, k 24.

Repeat from first row.

DIAGONAL EDGING.

No. 55.—This lace may be made of Belding's knitting silk, or of crochet silk or cotton.

Cast on 22 stitches and purl across.

First row.—Sl 1, n, th o, k 3, th o, n, k 5, th o, k 3 together, k 1, th o, k 1, th o, n, th o, k 2.

Second row.—Th o, n, p 21.

Third row.—Sl 1, k 2, th o, sl 1, n, pass slipped

NO. 55.—DIAGONAL EDGING.

stitch over, th o, k 6, th o, k 3 together, k 1, th o, k 3, th o, n, th o, k 2.

Fourth row.—Th o, n, p 22.

Fifth row.—Sl 1, n, th o, k 3, th o, n, k 3, th o, k 3, together, k 1, th o, k 5, th o, n, th o, k 2.

Sixth row.—Th o, n, p 23.

Seventh row.—Sl 1, k 2, th o, sl 1, n, pass slipped stitch over, th o, k 4, th o, k 3 together, k 1, th o, k 7, th o, n, th o, k 2.

Eighth row.—Th o, n, p 24.

Ninth row.—Sl 1, n, th o, k 3, th o, n, k 1, th o, k 3 together, k 1, th o, k 9, th o, n, th o, k 2.

Tenth row.—Th o, n, p 25.

Eleventh row.—Sl 1, k 2, th o, sl 1, n, pass slipped stitch over, th o, k 12, th o, k 3 together, k 1, th o, n, th o, n, k 1.

Twelfth row.—Th o, n, p 24.

Thirteenth row.—Sl 1, n, th o, k 3, th o, n, k 9, th o, k 3 together, k 1, th o, n, th o, n, k 1.

Fourteenth row.—Th o, n, p 23.

Fifteenth row.—Sl 1, k 2, th o, sl 1, n, pass slipped stitch over, th o, k 10, th o, k 3 together, k 1, th o, n, th o, n, k 1.

Sixteenth row.—Th o, n, p 22.

Seventeenth row.—Sl 1, n, th o, k 3, th o, n, k 7, th o, k 3 together, k 1, th o, n, th o, n, k 1.

Eighteenth row.—Th o, n, p 21.

Nineteenth row.—Sl 1, k 2, th o, sl 1, n, pass slipped stitch over, th o, k 8, th o, k 3 together, k 1, th o, n, th o, n, k 1.

Twentieth row.—Th o, n, p 20.

Repeat from first row for all the work.

KNITTED NORMANDY LACE.

No. 56.—Cast on 22 stitches and knit across plain.

First row.—Knit 3, thread over, n, k 3, thread over, k 3 together, thread over, k 3, thread over, k 3 together, thread over, k 3, thread over, knit 2.

Second row.—Thread over, n, thread over, k 5, thread over, k 1, thread over, k 5, thread over, k 1, thread over, k 6, thread over, n, k 1.

Third row.—K 3, thread over, n, k 7, n, thread over, k 1, thread over, n, k 3, n, thread over, k 1, thread over, n, k 1, th o, k 2.

Fourth row.—Thread over, n, thread over, k 1, n, thread over, k 3, thread over, n, k 1, n, thread over, k 3, thread over, n, k 8, thread over, n, k 1.

Fifth row.—K 3, thread over, n, k 7, thread over, n, k 1, n, thread over, k 3 together, thread over, n, k 1, n, thread over, n, k 1, thread over, k 2.

Sixth row.—Thread over, n, k 1, slip the second stitch on the right-hand needle over the last one, thread over, n, k 1, thread over, k 3 together, thread over, k 3, thread over, k 3 together, thread over, k 10, thread over, n, k 1.

Seventh row.—K 3, thread over, n, k 9, thread over, k 1, thread over, k 5, thread over, k 1, thread over, k 1, n, thread over, k 1, n.

Eighth row.—Thread over, n, k 1, slip the second stitch over the last, thread over, n, k 3, n, thread over, k 1, thread over, n, k 3, n, thread over, k 3 together, thread over, k 6, thread over, n, k 1.

Ninth row.—K 3, thread over, n, k 2, n, thread over, k 3, thread over, n, k 1, n, thread over, k 3, thread over, n, k 1, n, thread over, k 1, n.

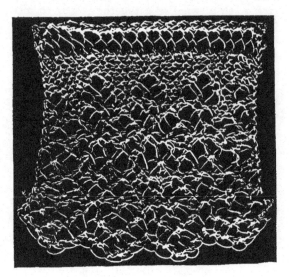

NO. 56.—KNITTED NORMANDY LACE.

Tenth row.—Thread over, n, k 1, slip the second stitch over the last, thread over, k 3 together, thread over, n, k 1, n, thread over, k 3 together, thread over, n, k 1, n, thread over, n, k 3, thread over, n, k 1.

Repeat from first row.

DIAMOND EDGING.

No. 57.—This edging may be made of Belding's knitting silk, or of cotton or linen thread. Cast on 19 stitches and knit across plain.

First row.—Sl 1, k 2, th o, n, k 5, th o, n, th o, n, k 1, p 1, n, k 1.

Second row.—Th o, n, k 13, th o, n, k 1.

No. 57.—DIAMOND EDGING.

Third row.—Sl 1, k 2, th o, n, k 3, n, th o, n, th o, n, k 1, th o, k 1, th o, k 2.

Fourth row.—Th o, n, k 14, th o, n, k 1.

Fifth row.—Sl 1, k 2, th o, n, k 2, n, th o, n, th o, n, k 1, th o, k 3, th o, k 2.

Sixth row.—Th o, n, k 15, th o, n, k 1.

Seventh row.—Sl 1, k 2, th o, n, k 1, n, th o, n, th o, n, k 1, th o, k 5, th o, k 2.

Eighth row.—Th o, n, k 16, th o, n, k 1.

Ninth row.—Sl 1, k 2, th o, n, n, th o, n, th o, n, k 1, th o, k 7, th o, k 2.

Tenth row.—Th o, n, k 17, th o, n, k 1.

Eleventh row.—Sl 1, k 2, th o, n, k 2, th o, n, th o, n, k 1, th o, n, k 3, n, th o, n, k 1.

Twelfth row.—Th o, n, k 16, th o, n, k 1.

Thirteenth row.—Sl 1, k 2, th o, n, k 3, th o, n, th o, n, k 1, th o, n, k 1, n, th o, n, k 1.

Fourteenth row.—Th o, n, k 15, th o, n, k 1.

Fifteenth row.—Sl 1, k 2, th o, n, k 4, th o, n, th o, n, k 1, th o, sl 1, n, pass slipped stitch over, th o, n, k 1.

Sixteenth row.—Th o, n, k 14, th o, n, k 1.

Repeat from first row for all the work.

POMPADOUR EDGING.

No. 58.—Use Belding's knitting silk or crochet cotton. Cast on 24 stitches and knit across plain.

First row.—Sl 1, k 2, th o, n, th o, n, k 12, n, th o, twice, n, k 1.

Second row.—K 3, p 1, k 20.

Third row.—Sl 1, k 3, th o, n, k 11, n, th o twice, n, k 3.

Fourth row.—K 5, p 1, k 18.

Fifth row.—Sl 1, k 2, th o, n, th o, n, k 8, n, th o twice, n, k 3, th o twice, k 2.

Sixth row.—K 3, p 1, k 5, p 1, k 16.

Seventh row.—Sl 1, k 3, th o, n, k 7, n, th o twice, n, k 3, th o, k 1, th o, k 5.

Eighth row.—K 13, p 1, k 14.

Ninth row.—Sl 1, k 2, th o, n, th o, n, k 4, n, th o twice, n, k 3, n, th o, k 3, th o, n, th o twice, n, k 1.

Tenth row.—K 3, p 1, k 12, p 1, k 12.

Eleventh row. -Sl 1, k 3, th o, n, k 3, n, th o twice, n, k 4, n, th o, k 5, th o, k 5.

Twelfth row.—K 19, p 1, k 10.

Thirteenth row.—Sl 1, k 2, th o, n, th o, n, n, th o twice, n, k 5, n, th o, k 1, sl 1, n, pass slipped stitch over, th o 3 times, n, k 1, th o, k 1, n, th o twice, k 2.

Fourteenth row.—K 3, p 1, k 6, p 1, k 12, p 1, k 8. In working off the 3 put-overs, use each one as a stitch.

Fifteenth row.—Sl 1, k 3, th o, n, k 3, n, th o twice, n, k 5, th o, n, k 3, n, th o, k 1, n, k 4.

Sixteenth row.—K 20, p 1, k 10.

Seventeenth row.—Sl 1, k 2, th o, n, th o, n, k 4, n, th o twice, n, k 4, th o, n, k 1, n, th o, k 1, n, th o twice, n, n.

Eighteenth row.—K 3, p 1, k 13, p 1, k 12.

Nineteenth row.—Sl 1, k 3, th o, n, k 7, n, th o twice, n, k 3, th o, sl 1, n, pass slipped stitch over, th o, k 1, n, k 4.

Twentieth row.—K 14, p 1, k 14.

Twenty-first row.—Sl 1, k 2, th o, n, th o, n, k 8, n, th o twice, n 4 times, th o twice, n, n.

Twenty-second row.—K 3, p 1, k 5, p 1, k 16.

Twenty-third row.—Sl 1, k 3, th o, n, k 11, n, th o, sl 1, n, pass slipped stitch over, th o, k 2, n.

Twenty-fourth row.—K 3, p 1, k 20.

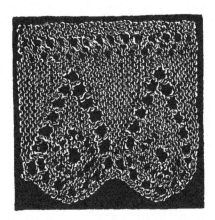

No. 58.—POMPADOUR EDGING.

Twenty-fifth row.—Sl 1, k 2, th o, n, th o, n, k 12, n, th o twice, n, k 1.

Twenty-sixth row.—K 3, p 1, k 20.

Twenty-seventh row.—Sl 1, k 3, th o, n, k 18.

Twenty-eighth row.—Knit plain and repeat from first row for all the work.

FANCY SCOLLOP EDGING.

No. 59.—Cast on 21 stitches and knit across plain.

First row.—K 11, th o, n, th o, n, th o 4 times, n, n, th o, n.

Second row.—K 4; then out of the 4 put-overs,

NO. 59.—FANCY SCOLLOP EDGING.

k 1, p 1. k 1, p 1, slipping off 1 loop or put-over at a time, k 15.

Third row.—K 5, n, th o twice, n, k 3, th o, n, th o, n, k 4, n, th o, k 1.

Fourth row.—K 16, p 1, k 6.

Fifth row.—K 3, n, th o twice, n, n, th o twice, n, k 2, th o, n, th o, n, k 3, n, th o, k 1.

Sixth row.—K 14, p 1, k 3, p 1, k 4.

Seventh row.—K 5, n, th o twice, n, k 5, th o, n, th o, n, k 2, n, th o, k 1.

Eighth row.—K 16, p 1, k 6.

Ninth row.—K 3, n, th o twice, n, n, th o twice, n, k 4, th o, n, th o, n, k 1, n, th o, k 1.

Tenth row.—K 14, p 1, k 3, p 1, k 4.

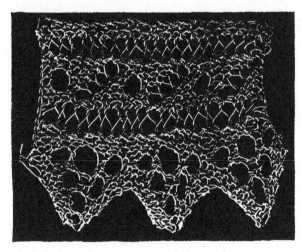

NO. 60.—KNITTED POINTED LACE.

Eleventh row.—K 5, n, th o twice, n, k 7, th o, n, th o, n, n, th o, k 1.

Twelfth row.—K 16, p 1, k 6.

Thirteenth row.—K 17, th o, n, th o, n; slip the stitch just made over onto the left-hand needle, pass the last two stitches on this needle over the

stitch, and then pass the latter back to the right-hand needle.

Fourteenth row.—Knit across plain and repeat from the first row for all the work.

KNITTED POINTED LACE.

No. 60.—This is pretty lace for cotton or linen. It is also especially pretty for trimming flannel garments if knit of Saxony yarn on rather coarse steel needles so that it will be open and lace-like.

Cast on 17 stitches.

First row.—Knit 3, th o, n, th o, n, k 3, th o, n, k 2, th o twice, k 3.

Second row.—K 4, p 1, k 3, th o, n, k 5, th o, n, k 2.

Third row.—K 3, th o, n, k 1, th o, n, k 2, th o, n, k 7.

Fourth row.— K 8, th o, n, k 5, th o, n, k 2.

Fifth row.—K 3, th o, n, k 2, th o, n, k 1, th o, n, n, th o 3 times, n, th o twice, n, k 1.

Sixth row.—K 3, p 1, k 2, p 1, k 3, th o, n, k 5, th o, n, k 2.

Seventh row.— K 3, th o, n, k 3, th o, n, th o, n, k 9.

Eighth row.— K 10, th o, n, k 5, th o, n, k 2.

Ninth row.— K 3, th o, n, k 5, th o, n, k 2, th o twice, n, th o twice, n, th o twice, n, k 1.

NO. 61.—KNITTED EDGING.

Tenth row.—K 3, p 1, k 2, p 1, k 2, p 1, k 3, th o, n, k 5, th o, n, k 2.

Eleventh row.—K 3, th o, n, n, th o twice, n, k 1, th o, n, k 12.

Twelfth row.—K 13, th o, n, k 2, p 1, k 2, th o, n, k 2.

Thirteenth row.—K 3, th o, n, k 5, th o, n, k 12.

Fourteenth row.—Bind off 7; k 5, th o, n, k 5, th o, n, k 2, and repeat from first row.

KNITTED EDGING.

No. 61.—Cast on 22 stitches and knit across plain.

First row.—K 3, th o, n, k 1, th o, n, k 2, th o, k 1, th o, n, k 1, n, th o, k 2, th o twice, n, th o twice, n.

Second row.—K 2, p 1, k 2, p 1, n, k 1, th o, sl 1, n, pass slipped stitch over, th o, k 3, th o, n, n, th o, n, k 1, th o, n, k 1.

Third row.—K 3, th o, n, k 1, th o, n, th o, n, k 1, n, th o, k 1, th o, k 1, n, k 6.

Fourth row.—Cast off 2, k 5, th o, k 3, th o, sl 1, n, pass slipped stitch over, th o, k 3, th o, n, k 1, th o, n, k 1.

Repeat from first row for all the work.

DOUBLE-EYELET EDGING.

No. 62.—Cast on 23 stitches and knit across plain.

First row.—K 2, th o, k 5, th o, n, k 1, n, th o, k 11.

Second row.—K 2, th o, k 1, sl 1, n, pass slipped stitch over, k 1, th o, k 17.

Third row.—K 2, th o, k 1, n, th o twice, sl 1, n, pass slipped stitch over, k 1, th o, sl 1, n, pass slipped stitch over, th o, k 12.

Fourth row.—K 2, th o, k 1, sl 1, n, pass slipped stitch over, k 1, th o, k 10; then k 1, p 1 and k 1 out of the 2 put-overs; k 5.

Fifth row.—K 1, n, th o, n, k 3, n, th o, k 3, th o, n, k 10.

Sixth row.—K 2, th o, k 1, sl 1, n, pass slipped stitch over, k 1, th o, k 17.

Seventh row.—K 1, n, th o, n, k 1, n, th o, k 5, th o, n, k 9.

Eighth row.—K 2, th o, k 1, sl 1, n, pass slipped stitch over, k 1, th o, k 16.

Ninth row.—K 1, n, th o, sl 1, n, pass slipped stitch over, th o, k 1, n, th o twice, sl 1, n, pass slipped stitch over, k 1, th o, n, k 8.

Tenth row.—K 2, th o, k 1, sl 1, n, pass slipped stitch over, k 1, th o, k 5; then k 1, p 1 and k 1 out of the 2 put-overs; k7.

Eleventh row.—K 2, th o, k 3, th o, n, k 3, n, th o, k 10.

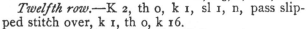

No. 62.—DOUBLE-EYELET EDGING.

Twelfth row.—K 2, th o, k 1, sl 1, n, pass slipped stitch over, k 1, th o, k 16.

Repeat from beginning for all the work.

KNITTED FLUTED EDGE OR BORDER.

No. 63.—According to the material used this design is suitable for a counterpane, a garniture or a child's collar.

Cast on any number of stitches divisible by 6. Then work back and forth for 6 rows, alternately purling 4 stitches and knitting 2; but in the 2nd, 4th and 6th rows you *purl* the *knitted* stitches of the preceding row. and *knit* the *purled* ones, so that there will be a right and wrong side to the pattern.

Seventh row.—* K 2, make 1, k 2, p 2 and repeat from *.

Eighth and every alternate following row.—Alternately purl 5 and k 2, except that in each row the purled stitches will be increased by 2.

Ninth row.—* K 2, m 1, k 1, m 1, k 2, p 2 and repeat from *.

Eleventh row.—* K 2, m 1, k 3, m 1, k 2, p 2, and repeat from *.

Thirteenth row.—* K 2, m 1, k 5, m 1, k 2, p 2 and repeat from *.

Repeat the 13th row, increasing by 2 stitches between each 2 made stitches, until there are 21 rows, and 13 stitches between the made stitches.

Cast off all the stitches. Finish the upper edge with a row of single crochet. Complete the lower edge with 1 double in every other stitch, with 1 chain between; then 1 single in each double, with 1 picot between, the picot being made with 5 chain and 1 slip stitch in 1st stitch of chain.

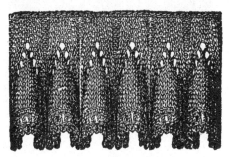

No. 63.—KNITTED FLUTED EDGE OR BORDER.

KNITTED OAK-LEAF EDGING.

No.64.—Cast on 22 stitches and knit across plain.

First row.—* Knit 2, th o twice, p 2 together and repeat 3 times from *. K 1, th o twice, n, th o twice, n, k 1.

Second row.—K 3, p 1, k 2, p 1, k 1, * th o twice, p 2 together, k 2 and repeat 3 times more from *.

Third row.—* K 2, th o twice, p 2 together and repeat 3 times more from *. K 3, th o twice, n, th o twice, n, k 1.

Fourth row.—K 3, p 1, k 2, p 1, k 3, * th o twice, p 2 together, k 2, and repeat 3 times more from *.

Fifth row.—* K 2, th o twice, p 2 together and repeat 3 times more from *. K 5, th o twice, n, th o twice, n, k 1.

Sixth row.—K 3, p 1, k 2, p 1, k 5, * th o twice, p 2 together, k 2 and repeat 3 times more from *.

Seventh row.—* K 2, th o twice, p 2 together and repeat 3 times more from *. K 7, th o twice, n, th o twice, n, k 1.

Eighth row.—K 3, p 1, k 2, p 1, k 7, * th o twice,

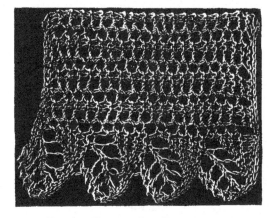

No. 64.—KNITTED OAK-LEAF EDGING.

purl 2 together, k 2 and repeat 3 times more from *.

Ninth row.—* K 2, th o twice, p 2 together; repeat 3 times more from *. K 14.

Tenth row.—Bind off 8, k 5, * th o twice, purl 2 together, k 2 and repeat 3 times more from * Repeat from first row for all the work.

ROSE-LEAF LACE.

No. 65.—Cast on 34 stitches.

First row.—K 2, th o, k 1, slip 1, k 1, pass slipped stitch over, p 1, n, k 1, p 1, k 1, sl 1, k 1, pass slipped stitch over, p 1, n, k 1, th o, k 1, th o, n, th o twice, n, th o twice, n, * th o, n, and repeat three times more from *, th o, k 2.

Second row—K 13, p 1, k 2, p 1, k 1, th o, n, p 3, k 1, p 2, k 1, p 2, k 1, p 3, k 2.

Third row.—K 2, th o, k 1,

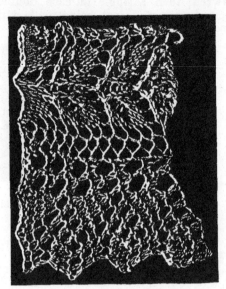

No. 65.—ROSE-LEAF LACE.

th o, sl 1, k 1, pass slipped stitch over, p 1, n, p 1, sl 1, k 1, pass slipped stitch over, p 1, n, th o, k 1, th o, k 1, th o, n, k 7, * th o, n, and repeat three times more from *; th o, k 2.

Fourth row.—K 19, th o, n, p 4, k 1, p 1, k 1, p 1, k 1, p 4, k 2.

Fifth row.—K 2, th o, k 3, th o, sl 1, n, pass slipped stitch over, p 1, sl 1, n, pass slipped stitch over, th o, k 3, th o, k 1, th o, n, th o twice, n, th o twice, n, k 4, * th o, n, and repeat three times more from *; th o, k 2.

Sixth row.—K 17, p 1, k 2, p 1, k 1, th o, n, p 6, k 1, p 6, k 2.

Seventh row.—K 2, th o, k 5, th o, sl 1, n, pass slipped stitch over, th o, k 5, th o, k 1, th o, n, k 13; slip seven of the eight remaining stitches over the first one on the needle, k 1.

Eighth row.—K 15, th o, n, p 15, k 2. Repeat from first row.

VINE EDGING.

No. 66.—Cast on 26 stitches and knit across plain.

First row.—K 2, th o, k 1, sl 1, n, pass slipped stitch over, k 1, th o, k 1, th o, k 1, sl and b, p 1, n, k 1, p 1, k 1, sl and b, p 1, n, k 1, th o, k 1, th o twice, k 1, th o twice, k 1.

Second row.—K 2, p 1, k 2, p 1, k 1, p 3, k 1, p 2, k 1, p 2, k 1, p 3, k 8.

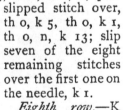

No. 66.—VINE EDGING.

Third row.—K 2, th o, k 1, sl 1, n, pass slipped stitch over, k 1, th o, k 1, th o, k 1, th o, sl and b, p 1, n, p 1, sl and b, p 1, n, th o, k 1, th o, k 7.

Fourth row.—Cast off 4, k 2, p 4, k 1, p 1, k 1, p 1, k 1, p 4, k 8.

Fifth row.—K 2, th o, k 1, sl 1, n, pass slipped stitch over, k 1, th o, k 1, th o, k 3, th o, sl 1, n, pass slipped stitch over, p 1, sl 1, n, pass slipped stitch over, th o, k 3, th o, k 1, th o twice, k 1, th o twice, k 1.

Sixth row.—K 2, p 1, k 2, p 1, k 1, p 6, k 1, p 6, k 8.

Seventh row.—K 2, th o, k 1, sl 1, n, pass slipped stitch over, k 1, th o, k 1, th o, k 5, th o, sl 1, n, pass slipped stitch over, th o, k 5, th o, k 7.

Eighth row.—Cast off 4, k 2, p 15, k 8. Repeat from first row for all the work.

SCROLL-LEAF LACE.

No. 67.—Thread or any preferred make of crochet cotton may be used in knitting this lace.

Cast on 23 stitches.

First row.—Slip 1, knit 1, thread over, slip 1, knit 1, pass slipped stitch over knit stitch, knit 9, thread over, narrow, thread over, narrow, thread over 3 times, narrow, knit 1, thread over, narrow, knit 1.

Second row.—K 6, p 1, k 1, p 1, making 3 stitches of the large loop, k 14, p 1, k 2.

Third row.—Slip 1, k 1, th o, sl 1, k 1, pass slipped stitch over knit stitch, k 3, n, th o twice, n, k 3, th o, n, th o, n, k 4, n, th o, k 2.

Fourth row.—Knit 17, p 1, k 5, p 1, k 2.

Fifth row.—Slip 1, k 1, th o, sl 1, k 1,

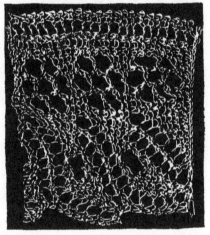

No. 67.—SCROLL-LEAF LACE.

pass slipped stitch over knit stitch, k 1, n, th o twice, n, n, th o twice, n, k 2, th o, n, th o, n, k 3, n, th o, k 2.

Sixth row.—Knit 15, p 1, k 3, p 1, k 3, p 1, k 2.

Seventh row.—Slip 1, k 1, th o, sl 1, k 1, pass slipped stitch over knit stitch, k 3, n, th o twice, n, k 5, th o, n, th o, n, k 2, n, th o, k 2.

Eighth row.—Knit 17, p 1, k 5, p 1, k 2.

Ninth row.—Slip 1, k 1, th o, sl 1, k 1, pass slipped stitch over knit stitch, k 1, n, th o twice, n, n, th o twice, n, k 4, th o, n, th o, n, k 1, n, th o, k 2.

Tenth row.—Knit 15, p 1, k 3, p 1, k 3, p 1, k 2.

Eleventh row.—Slip 1, k 1, th o, sl 1, k 1, pass slipped stitch over knit stitch, k 3, n, th o twice, n, k 7, th o, n, th o, n, n, th o, k 2.

Twelfth row.—Knit 17, p 1, k 5, p 1, k 2.

Thirteenth row.—Slip 1, k 1, th o, sl 1, k 1, pass slipped stitch over knit stitch, k 15, th o, n, th o, n, k 3.

Fourteenth row.—Bind off 3, k 19, p 1, k 2. Repeat from first row for next leaf.

DOTTED LACE.

No. 68.—Cast on 19 stitches.

First row.—K 3, th o, n, k 2, th o, k 1, th o,

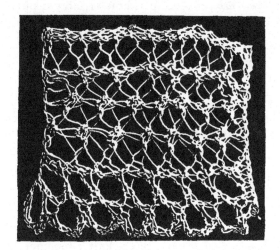

No. 68.—DOTTED LACE.

n, k 1, n, th o, k 2, th o twice, n, th o twice, n.

Second row.—K 2, p 1, k 2, p 1, n, k 1, th o, sl 1, n, pass slipped stitch over, th o, k 3, th o, n, n, th o, n, k 1.

Third row.—K 3, th o, n, th o, n, k 1, n, th o, k 1, th o, k 1, n, k 6.

Fourth row.—Cast off 2 stitches, k 5, th o, k 3, th o, sl 1, n, pass slipped stitch over, th o, k 3, th o, n, k 1.

Repeat from first row for all the work.

INSERTION EDGING.

No. 69.—Cast on 15 stitches.

First row.—Sl 1, k 1, th o twice, p 2 together,

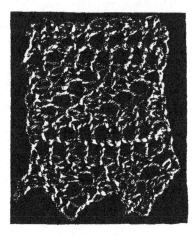

No. 69.—INSERTION EDGING.

k 1, th o, n, k 3, th o twice, p 2 together, k 1, th o, k 2. (The thread over twice before purling only makes 1 extra stitch).

Second row.—K 2, p 1, k 1, th o twice, p 2 together, k 4, p 1, k 1, th o twice, p 2 together, k 2.

Third row.—Sl 1, k 1, th o twice, p 2 together, k 2, th o, n, k 2, th o twice, p 2 together, k 2, th o, k 2.

Fourth row.—K 2, p 1, k 2, th o twice, p 2 together, k 3, p 1, k 2, th o twice, p 2 together, k 2.

Fifth row.—Sl 1, k 1, th o twice, p 2 together, k 3, th o, n, k 1, th o twice, p 2 together, k 3, th o, k 2.

Sixth row.—K 2, p 1, k 3, th o twice, p 2 together, k 2, p 1, k 3, th o twice, p 2 together, k 2.

Seventh row.—Sl 1, k 1, th o twice, p 2 together, k 4, th o, n, th o twice, p 2 together, k 6.

Eighth row.—Cast off 4, k 2, th o twice, p 2

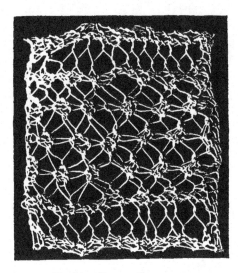

No. 70.—DOTTED INSERTION.

together, k 1, p 1, k 4, th o twice, p 2 together, k 2.

Repeat from first row for all the work.

By omitting the points, an insertion to match may be made.

DOTTED INSERTION.

No. 70.—Cast on 21 stitches and knit across plain.

First row.—K 3, th o, n, k 2, th o, k 1, th o, n, k 1, n, th o, k 1, th o, k 4, th o, n, k 1.

Second row.—K 3, th o, n, n, th o, k 3, th o, sl 1, n, pass slipped stitch over, th o, k 3, th o, n, k 2, th o, n, k 1.

Third row.—K 3, th o, k 3 together, th o, n, k 1, n, th o, k 1, th o, n, k 1, n, th o, n, k 1, th o, n, k 1.

Fourth row.—K 3, th o, n, k 1, th o, sl 1, n, pass slipped stitch over, th o, k 3, th o, sl 1, n, pass slipped stitch over, th o, k 3, th o, n, k 1.

Repeat from first row for all the work.

This insertion matches the edging seen at No. 68, and both may be made of silk or cotton.

KNITTED EDGING.

No. 71.—This pretty design may be used with the insertion seen at No. 34 on page 37.

Cast on 22 stitches.

First row.—Slip 1, knit 2 together, make 1, knit 2 together, knit 8, * make 1, slip 1, knit 1, pass the slipped stitch over, knit 1; repeat from * once more; make 1, knit 3.

No. 71.—KNITTED EDGING.

Second row.—Slip 1, knit 18, knit 1, purl 1 in the made stitch, knit 2.

Third row.—Slip 1, knit 13, * make 1, slip 1, knit 1, pass the slipped stitch over, knit 1, repeat from * once more; make 1, knit 3.

Fourth row.—Slip 1, knit to end of row.

Fifth row.—Slip 1, knit 2 together, make 1, knit 2 together, knit 10, * make 1, slip 1, knit 1, pass slipped stitch over, knit 1, repeat from * once more; end with make 1, knit 3.

Sixth row.—Slip 1, knit 20, knit 1, purl 1 in made stitch, knit 2.

Seventh row.—Slip 1, knit 15, * make 1, slip 1, knit 1, pass slipped stitch over, repeat from * once more; make 1, knit 3.

Eighth row.—Slip 1, knit to end of row.

Ninth row.—Slip 1, knit 2 together, make 1, knit 2 together, knit 12, * make 1, slip 1, knit 1, pass slipped stitch over, knit 1, repeat from * once more, make 1, knit 3.

Tenth row.—Slip 1, knit 22, knit 1, purl 1 in made stitch, knit 2.

Eleventh row.—Slip 1, knit 17, * make 1, slip 1, knit 1, pass slipped stitch over, knit 1, repeat from * once more; make 1, knit 3.

Twelfth row.—Slip 1, knit to end of row.

Thirteenth row.—Slip 1, knit 2 together, make 1, knit 2 together, knit 4, knit 2 together, make 1, knit 3 together, make 1, knit 2 together, knit 3, * make 1, slip 1, knit 1, pass slipped stitch over, knit 1, repeat from * once more; make 1, knit 3.

Fourteenth row.—Slip 1, knit 13, knit 1, purl 1 in the made stitch, knit 1, knit 1, purl 1 in the made stitch, knit 6; knit 1, purl 1 in the made stitch, knit 2.

Fifteenth row.—Slip, 1, knit 7, knit 2 together, make 1, knit 2 together, knit 1, knit 2 together, make 1, knit 2 together, k 1, k 2 together; * make 1, slip 1, knit 1, pass the slipped stitch over, knit 1, repeat from * twice more.

Sixteenth row.—Slip 1, knit 11, knit 1, purl 1 in the made stitch, knit 3, knit 1 and purl 1 in the made stitch; knit to end of row.

Seventeenth row.—Slip 1, knit 2 together, make 1, knit 2 together, knit 4, knit 2 together, make 1, knit 3 together, make 1, knit 2 together, knit 1, knit 2 together, * make 1, slip 1, knit 1, pass the slipped stitch over, knit 1; repeat from * twice more.

Eighteenth row.—Slip 1, knit 11, knit 1, purl 1 in made stitch; knit 1, knit 1, purl 1 in made stitch; knit 6; knit 1 and purl 1 in the made stitch, knit 2.

Nineteenth row.—Slip 1, knit 15, knit 2 together, * make 1, slip 1, knit 1, pass the slipped stitch over, knit 1; repeat from * twice more.

Twentieth row.—Slip 1, knit to end of row.

Twenty-first row.—Slip 1, knit 2 together, * make 1, knit 2 together, knit 10, knit 2 together, make 1, slip 1, knit 1, pass the slipped stitch over, knit 1, repeat from * twice more.

Twenty-second row.—Slip 1, knit 20; knit 1 and purl 1 in the made stitch, knit 2.

Twenty-third row.—Slip 1, knit 13, knit 2 together, * make 1, slip 1, knit 1, pass the slipped stitch over, knit 1, repeat from * twice more.

Twenty-fourth row.—Slip 1, knit to end of row.

Twenty-fifth row.—Slip 1, knit 2 together, make 1, knit 2 together, knit 8, knit 2 together, * make 1, slip 1, knit 1, pass the slipped stitch over, knit 1, repeat from * twice more.

Twenty-sixth row.—Slip 1, knit 18; knit 1 and purl 1 in the made stitch; knit 2.

Twenty-seventh row.—Slip 1, knit 11, knit 2 together, * make 1, slip 1, knit 1, pass the slipped stitch over, knit 1, repeat from * twice more.

Twenty-eighth row.—Slip 2, knit to end of row. Repeat from first row.

KILTED EDGING.

No. 72.—Cast on any number of stitches divisible by 9.

First row.—Purl 8, k 1 and repeat.

Second row.—Purl 2, k 7 and repeat.

Third row.—Purl 6, k 3 and repeat across the row.

No. 72.—KILTED EDGING.

Fourth and Fifth rows.—P 4, k 5 and repeat.

Sixth row.—P 6, k 3 and repeat.

Seventh row.—P 2, k 7 and repeat.

Eighth and Ninth rows.—Like 1st row. Then repeat from 2nd row for all the work.

For the Shell Edge.—Make 1 s. c. into the line between the kilts; skip 3 stitches, make 3 d. c., 3 tr. and 3 d. c. into next stitch; skip 3, make 1 s. c. into next line. Repeat shells for each kilt.

GENERAL RULES FOR KNITTING MITTENS, SOCKS AND STOCKINGS.

For the assistance of knitters who require definite instructions regarding general work, and especially in knitting mittens socks and stockings, we give the following rules. Expert knitters have endorsed them and they will be found correct. But at the same time, they may differ in a few points, from some of the illustrated and other directions found in the following department. This, however, does not signify, since there are many rules and methods for knitting the same kinds of articles, and all work out satisfactorily, according to the selection made by the knitter. We have thought it advisable to mention this fact before proceeding, so that our patrons and students will not be confused by the variety of instructions we offer.

RULE FOR KNITTING MITTENS FROM KNITTING SILK OR FINE YARN.

No. 19 needles, or No. 18, which are one size coarser, are generally selected for knitting mittens when knitting silk or fine yarn is used. The size chosen must depend upon the silk or yarn selected, as the different makes of the latter vary somewhat in texture, some being finer than others.

To make the instructions for knitting mittens found on the following pages more easily understood, we give here some directions of a general character, and two diagrams, Nos. 1 and 2, which will serve to correctly and easily guide the knitter in making mittens of any size, either for children, for ladies, or for gentlemen.

Mittens with fancy knitting at the wrist and back will be chiefly considered; and frequent reference will be made to the diagrams.

[Diagram No. 1 shows the manner of forming the thumb, as referred to in the following directions. The oblong piece, A, B, C, D, shows a section of the wrist. The double lines, a, b, c, d, represent the purled stripes spoken of in the rule, and the dots on the margin of the triangular piece (E) represent the points where the increase is made to form the same. The triangular piece (E) is the lowest portion of the thumb.]

Most mittens are knitted in rounds, forming a tubular web, in one side of which sufficient increase is made during the progress of the work to form a thumb. When the proper length is obtained to cover the wider portion of the hand, the web is decreased at regular intervals until all the stitches are disposed of, thus giving the mittens a round finish like the toe of a stocking.

The knitting of a mitten, therefore, will be best considered in four parts: The wrist, the thumb, the gusset and the remaining portion, which, for convenience, we call the hand.

THE WRIST.

Cast on any number of stitches which is a multiple of the number of stitches required in the fancy design to be used, and knit in rounds according to the rule laid down for the fancy pattern. Repeat the pattern any number of times to suit the length required.

If fancy work is to be extended down the back of the hand, ten or twelve rounds of plain work should be introduced at both sides of the fancy stripe before the increase for the thumb is begun. If fancy work is to be introduced in the wrist only, the pattern should be discontinued ten or twelve rounds before the thumb is commenced, and plain knitting substituted.

In children's mittens from five to eight rounds will be enough, according to the size.

THE POSITION OF THE THUMB.

In all mittens where a fancy design is introduced in the back, great care must be taken to start the thumb at such a point that the fancy stripe will be in the center of the back of mitten *when it is on the hand*. This will not be the case if the stripe be placed in the center of the mitten when the latter is folded as shown in diagram No. 2.

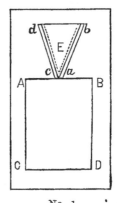 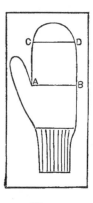

No. 1. No. 2.

The central stitch of the fancy stripe should be about one-third the distance around the hand, measuring from the purled stripe which outlines the thumb. The number of plain stitches, therefore, between the thumb and fancy stripe will vary according to the size of the mitten and the number of stitches employed in the stripe.

It should also be remembered that on a right-hand mitten the thumb must be at the left of the fancy stripe, while on a left-hand mitten it must be placed at the right of the stripe.

Both mittens are made alike where the fancy knitting is only in the wrist.

THE THUMB.

The thumb is formed by taking three stitches as a base, and increasing one stitch on each of the two outside stitches, in every fourth round, until a sufficient number of stitches is obtained for the widest part.

One stitch is to be purled each side of the three base stitches in every round until the point A (No. 2) is reached, thus forming purled stripes which outline the thumb, as shown in diagram No. 1.

The best manner of increasing is to pick up from the back part of work the loop which crosses the base of the stitch on which the increase is made, knit a new stitch in that loop and *afterwards* knit the stitch itself. This method makes two stitches where there was before but one, and leaves the work solid and neat.

The ordinary methods of widening used in knitting are not recommended, as they leave small, round holes in the work, which are not desirable in a mitten. Having obtained, by widening, the requisite number of stitches for the thumb, work three rounds more and place these stitches (not including the purled stitches) upon a piece of strong twine, and tie securely, so that the work may be safe while the hand is being finished. The next step is the formation of a small gusset between the thumb and hand at the point A (No. 2), in order to make a more perfect fit.

THE GUSSET.

This is commenced at the end of the next round, by casting on four extra stitches. In the four rounds which follow, a decrease of one stitch in each round must be made at the point where the extra stitches were cast on, thus disposing of the four extra stitches, and forming one-half of a small diamond-shaped gusset, the other half being formed in the same manner when work on the thumb is resumed.

THE HAND.

We have already described that portion of the hand which includes the gusset, and need only add that, with the exception of the gusset, that section of work comprised between the points A, B, C, D (No. 2) is a simple repetition of rounds of plain or fancy knitting, as best suits the taste.

The number of stitches in the round in this section of the mitten is always three less than were used in commencing the wrist. To knit that portion of the mitten represented above the points C, D (No. 2, observe the following instructions:

Having obtained the proper length for the widest part of the hand, if the number of stitches be not already divisible by 9, narrow in the next round at intervals of 7 stitches until the number is so divisible; then proceed as follows:

First round.—Knit plain.

Second round.—* K 7, n, repeat from * and knit 7 rounds plain.

Tenth round.—K 6, n, repeat from * and knit 6 rounds plain.

Seventeenth round.—* K 5, n, repeat from * and knit 5 rounds plain.

Twenty-third round.—* K 4, n, repeat from * and knit 4 rounds plain. Now narrow once on each needle, in every round, until only 4 stitches are left on a needle; then narrow twice on each needle and cast off. When decreasing once on each needle only, do not narrow at the same point in every round, but at a different place in each successive round.

TO FINISH THE THUMB.

Place the stitches which are on the twine on 3 needles, and pick up 4 loops from the base of the gore formed between the hand and thumb by casting on the 4 extra stitches. Knit once around, and narrow once in each of the next 4 rounds at the point where the gusset is, then knit as many rounds as necessary to give proper length and finish by narrowing once on each needle in every round, until all the stitches are disposed of.

RULE FOR CHILDREN'S MITTENS OF SILK OR FINE YARN.

There are so many sizes required to suit different ages, that we cannot undertake to instruct as to any particular size. The general method of knitting mittens of all sizes has just been given; but to assist our students further, we give the following table as an approximation of the number of stitches which will produce mittens suitable for various ages.

For a child of 1 year, 56 stitches.

For a child of 2 years, 60 stitches.

For a child of 4 years, 64 stitches.

For a child of 6 years, 70 stitches.

The number of stitches used, however, must be a multiple of the number required for the fancy pattern adopted; and for this reason small patterns are more desirable than large.

The pattern used can be repeated to suit the fancy of the knitter. We recommend a narrow hem, as described below for such mittens.

DIRECTIONS FOR KNITTING A HEM.

Very attractive borders for mittens or stockings are easily made by casting on the stitches loosely and knitting several rounds plain, followed by one round of open-work knit thus: N, th o, repeat.

Follow the round of open-work with a number of rounds of plain knitting equal to that which preceded it.

In the next round, turn the edge of work up inside, and pick up and knit with each stitch on the needles one loop from the edge where your work was commenced, thus forming a perfect hem. There will always be exactly the same number of loops on the edge of the work as there are stitches on the needles, if the casting on has been properly done.

These hems may be of any desired width. In our instructions for mittens and also for fancy tops to socks, stockings and mittens we have used some narrow and some wide borders.

The knitted hem is recommended for beginning stockings, either for ladies or children. It forms a neat, strong border, precisely like that seen in expensive, "full-fashioned" French hosiery, and looks much more attractive than the old fashioned method of ribbing.

RULE I. FOR KNITTING MEN'S SILK SOCKS.

No. 19 knitting needles should be used in knitting socks from knitting silk of the ordinary size.

Cast 113 stitches on 3 needles, knit once around plain, then knit in ribs, alternating 4 stitches plain and 2 purl for 70 rounds, which will give about 3½ inches; then knit plain for 6 inches, and commence heel by taking 57 stitches on one needle, * purl across, knit back plain and repeat from * until 57 rows are done, counting each time across as a row.

In knitting the heel, the *first* stitch in each row, whether it be a knitted or a purled row, should be slipped.

Now commence to narrow as follows:

Fifty-eighth row.—K 13, sl and b, k 10, n, k 3, sl and b, k 10, n, k 13.

Fifty-ninth row.—Purl.

Sixtieth row.—K 13, sl and b, k 8, n, k 3, sl and b, k 8, n, k 13.

Sixty-first row.—Purl.

Sixty-second row.—K 13, sl and b, k 6, n, k 3, sl and b, k 6, n, k 13.

Sixty-third row.—Purl.

Sixty-fourth row.—K 13, sl and b, k 4, n, k 3, sl and b, k 4, n, k 13.

Sixty-fifth row.—Purl.

Sixty-sixth row.—K 13, sl and b, k 2, n, k 3, sl and b, k 2, n, k 13.

Sixty-seventh row.—Purl.

Sixty-eighth row.—K 13, sl and b, n, k 3, sl and b, n, k 13.

Sixty-ninth row.—Purl.

Seventieth row.—Commence by knitting 17; ***, then fold the needles together with wrong side of heel out, slip off the first stitch, knit 2 together, taking one from each needle, pass slipped stitch over, and continue knitting 2 together and passing the last made stitch over until all are disposed of but one, which completes the heel, which may now be turned right side out. Pick up and knit 1 stitch in each loop on the side of heel going toward the left, knit across the instep needle; pick up and knit in the loops on the opposite side of the heel, 1 stitch in each as before, which completes the first round in the foot.

In knitting the second round, extra stitches must be made, one in every four on the sides of the heel only (not on instep), and in this round it is necessary also to decrease 2 by narrowing at the right hand corner, and sl and b at the left hand corner next to instep. In the next 2 rounds decrease 2 in the same manner, and afterwards decrease 2 in every alternate round until the whole number of stitches is reduced to 112, then continue knitting until the required length of the foot is obtained. To narrow for the toe, take an equal number of stitches on each needle, commence at the middle of the instep needle, knit all but 3, sl and b, k 1; on the next needle, k 1, n, k until 3 are left, sl and b, k 1; on the next needle, k 1, n, k until 3 are left, sl and b, k 1; at the first corner of instep needle, k 1, n, k to the middle of the needle, which completes first round of decreasing for the toe. Knit plain 3 rounds; then decrease in next round as before. Knit 3 rounds plain and decrease in next round as before. Knit 2 rounds plain and decrease in next round as before; knit 2 rounds plain and decrease in next round as before; knit 2 rounds plain and decrease in every round after, 1 stitch on each needle until 4 stitches are left on each needle; then knit 2 rounds plain and finish off.

When decreasing only 1 stitch on a needle for the toe, care must be taken to narrow at the first corner of the needles in the first round, and sl and b at the last corner in the next round, and so on alternately until done.

This rule will produce socks suitable for a man of full size. The number of stitches should be less for a very small foot or for boys' socks.

This rule for toe is suitable for all sizes of stockings, and a good heel for any size can be made by knitting and purling as many times across as there are stitches on the heel needle, before commencing to decrease.

The rule for decreasing in the heel will need to be slightly changed in different sizes, and any knitter on reading these directions will easily see what changes are required. The general rule for the number of stitches in a heel is to take one-half of the whole number in the ankle, and the number should be odd.

On completion it will improve the appearance of the socks to lay a dry cloth over them and press with a hot iron.

RULE II. FOR KNITTING MEN'S SOCKS.

For plain socks, which may be made by the veriest amateur in knitting, we give the following instructions:

A set of No. 19 needles and knitting silk of the ordinary size will be needed.

Cast 40 stitches loosely on each of 3 needles, and knit around once plain; do not knit too tight. Now knit 2 plain, seam 1; repeat this movement round and round till you have knit a finger in depth; then commence to knit plain, and continue for one finger and a-half, keeping the one seam stitch at the back. Then commence the heel. Put 60 stitches on one needle; knit on these stitches thus: Knit forward plain, and backward seamed, until you have half a finger; now begin to narrow as follows: Knit plain to within 3 stitches of the seam stitch, slip 1, narrow, pass slipped stitch over, knit seam stitch as usual, slip 1, narrow, pass slipped stitch over; finish the row plain.

Repeat this narrowing in every plain row, until you have narrowed 4 times. Knit to the seam stitch, fold together wrong side out, and bind off together; continue until one stitch only is left.

Pick up the stitches on the sides of the heel, and knit around 4 times plain; then at the beginning and end of the heel-needles narrow as follows: Knit 2, slip the 3rd stitch from the first end of the first needle, narrow, pass the slipped stitch over; knit the instep needle plain, slip the first stitch of third needle, narrow, pass the slipped stitch over; knit to the end of the needle plain. Knit 4 plain rounds between the narrowings. Continue to narrow until you have but 120 stitches, the number you had at first; knit a finger and a-half plain; then begin to narrow for the toe; knit two stitches plain at the beginning of the needle, slip 1, narrow, pass the slipped stitch over, knit plain till you have but five stitches left on needle, then slip 1, narrow, pass the slipped stitch over, knit 2 plain; repeat on each needle; knit 4 plain rounds between; repeat these 5 rounds until the toe is narrowed off. Be very careful not to split the silk in knitting; and when finished, spread the sock out in the shape of those you buy, lay over it a wet cloth that has been wrung pretty dry, and press with an iron not too hot. It is impossible to knit silk perfectly smooth, but it will press all right.

Rule III. for Knitting Men's Silk Socks.

In knitting silk socks for men, use 4 needles, No. 18, and 2½ ounces of knitting silk. Decide the length you require the foot of sock to be; 10½ inches is the average size for a man. Take your needles and silk and knit 20 stitches and 20 rows upon them, and fasten them off. Ascertain how many stitches in this piece go to the inch and then multiply that number by the number of inches in the length of foot. This number, when found, will be the right quantity to cast on for the leg of the sock.

The leg of the sock, from the top to the bottom of heel is knitted the length of foot and one-fourth more. The ribbing is half the length of foot. The narrowings are made in one-fourth the length— never as many narrowings as in a stocking; some of the best knitters dispense with them in socks. K 6 rows between each narrowing, and make about 4 narrowings. After that continue to knit until you have the exact length required for the foot.

You now divide for the heel; keep 4 more stitches for the back than for the front, and knit as many rows as you have stitches. When knitted, narrow on each side of the seam stitch once, then knit a plain row. K 3 more narrowed rows, cast off, and knit the last row together, doubling it in the center. For the foot, take the stitches up on the side of the heel. Knit along the front needles. The narrowings in the instep must be made in one-fourth the length of foot, thus:

Ascertain how many rows of your work go to the inch, then how many there will be in the quarter only, then how many stitches have to be reduced to make the back the same as the front of foot, and you thus arrive at the number of rows between each narrowing, remembering that the narrowings are made on each side of the under part of the foot, and thus 2 in a row.

After the instep, knit one-third of the length of the foot plain before commencing the narrowings for the toe. The toe is narrowed on each side of the sock, both the upper and under part, 4 narrowings in the round, and always before and after the first two and after the last two stitches in each half-round. The square toe is the best to wear and to fit. When finished it should be half the width of the foot.

The proportions are given in this manner as they will work out correctly for any-sized sock. It has only to be remembered that the best knitters always leave 2 stitches on each side the seam stitch before and after the narrowings in the leg, and that by making a scale for yourself of your own knitting, using the materials you wish to use, you cannot often get astray in your work.

To Join Wool or Silk in Knitting.

In knitting stockings or other articles in plain knitting join the wool or silk without a knot by beginning the new ball when about half a yard of the old one is left, knitting both together until the first ball is finished.

To Knit Double Heels.

To knit double heels to men's socks, use a second ball of the wool you are knitting with. Take 18 stitches each side of the seam stitch, and knit 4 rows with the double wool; in the next row decrease once near each end of the row. When you have knitted about 2½ inches, decrease once each side of the seam stitch, leaving 1 stitch at each side of the seam stitch between the decreasings; repeat this 3 times, and then take the 7 middle stitches, knit across, and knit the last of the 7 and the next stitch together; turn, and seam back across the 7, seaming the last of the 7 and the next stitch together; repeat till only the 7 are left. This makes a good firm heel, but it is apt to wash hard, and is bad to darn.

The following, though knitted with single wool, doubles the heel quite as effectually as the above, and is much pleasanter to knit. Begin as follows: Divide off 20 stitches each side of the seam.

First row.—Knit 1, slip 1.

Second row.—Seam back along all the stitches. All the rows are the same. Double heels are excellent for children's stockings. Toes may be knitted in the same manner.

KNITTED CLOCKS TO SOCKS.

It is quite easy to knit clocks into socks. After narrowing the sock, calculate how many stitches are to be left for the heel; usually 16 stitches are left at each side the seam stitch. The stitches on each side of these are the loops to use for the clocks. A small ball of silk will be required for each clock, as the silk does not pass round the sock. Begin the clock by knitting 1 stitch with silk; knit round to the other clock, and begin that also by knitting 1 stitch with another ball of silk.

Second row.—Knit 2 stitches with silk, one on each side of the first stitch.

Third row.—Knit 3 stitches, one on each side, and one in the middle.

Fourth row.—Knit 2 stitches as in the second row.

Fifth row.—Knit 1 stitch as at first.

Sixth row.—Knit 2 at each side.

Seventh row.—Knit 1 in the middle; continue this alternate, 2 and 1, down to the heel, but end by a row of 3 like the middle of the heel. You can copy the clocks from any woven stocking; and, if one does not care to use silk, wool of a suitable color will answer just as well.

TO KNIT INITIALS INTO SOCKS OR STOCKINGS.

Take a sampler, or, better still, draw the initials and all the letters required on a piece of checkered paper, making a * for each stitch as if for marking. When knitting, turn this sampler upside down, and purl a stitch to correspond with every * on the sampler.

DIRECTIONS FOR ASCERTAINING THE NUMBER OF STITCHES NEEDED FOR KNITTING STOCKINGS FROM KNITTING SILK.

As the style of work done by different persons varies, some knitting loosely and others very closely, it is not practical to give an exact number of stitches which will answer for any given size of stocking; but the following instructions will enable any one to estimate, in each case, the number of stitches required.

Select the silk and needles you intend using. Cast about 25 stitches onto one needle and knit and purl, say twenty times across, back and forth, in the same manner as for the heel of a stocking.

Now measure the sample piece of knitting so obtained, and count the number of stitches to one inch in width; next select a cotton stocking of good shape and correct size lay, it flat upon a table, and measure across the top just below the hem or, as the case may be, the ribbed part.

This measurement will be one-half the number of inches around the stocking leg in the largest part. Having found the number of stitches to the inch of your work, and the number of inches your stocking measures, multiply one number by the other, and the product will be the whole number of stitches necessary to knit a stocking of the same size as your own cotton pattern.

As an example: If your sample counts 16 stitches to the inch, and your pattern stocking measures 10½ inches around, then it follows that the whole number of stitches needed is 168.

RULE I. FOR KNITTING LADIES' SILK STOCKINGS.

Cast 169 stitches on 3 needles and knit around once plain; then knit in ribs, alternating 4 stitches plain and 2 purl for 10 rounds; then knit plain (purling one stitch in each round in the middle of one needle, which forms the seam), until the leg is 12 inches long; then decrease one stitch each side of the seam in every third round until the whole number of stitches is reduced to 113. The manner of decreasing at each side of the seam is as follows: Commence on the seam needle and knit all but 3 stitches on the right of the seam, then sl and b (to narrow) and k 1; now purl the seam stitch, then k 1 and n again, which completes the operation of decreasing for one round. Then knit 4¼ inches and commence the heel, by taking 28 stitches each side of the seam on one needle, making 57 in all; * purl across, *knit* the seam stitch in this row, and knit back plain, *purl* the seam stitch in this row, then repeat from * until 57 rows are done, counting each time across as a row.

In knitting the heel, the *first* stitch in each row, whether it be a knitted or a purled row, should be slipped.

Now commence to decrease as follows:

Fifty-eighth row.—K 13, sl and b, k 10, n, k 1, p 1, k 1, sl and b, k 10, n, k 13.

Fifty-ninth row.—P 26, k 1, p 26.

Sixtieth row.—K 13, sl and b, k 8, n, k 1, p 1, k 1, sl and b, k 8, n, k 13.

Sixty-first row.—P 24, k 1, p 24.

Sixty-second row.—K 13, sl and b, k 6, n, k 1, p 1, k 1, sl and b, k 6, n, k 13.

Sixty-third row.—P 22, k 1, p 22.

Sixty-fourth row.—K 13, sl and b, k 4, n, k 1, p 1, k 1, sl and b, k 4, n, k 13.

Sixty-fifth row.—P 20, k 1, p 20.

Sixty-sixth row.—K 13, sl and b, k 2, n, k 1, p 1, k 1, sl and b, k 2, n, k 13.

Sixty-seventh row.—P 18, k 1, p 18.

Sixty-eighth row.—K 13, sl and b, n, k 1, p 1, k 1, sl and b, n, k 13.

Sixty-ninth row.—P 16, k 1, p 16.

Seventieth row.—Commence by knitting 17; after this proceed as in Rule I. given for gentlemen's silk socks on page 53, beginning at the point marked ***

EXTRA RULE FOR KNITTING THE TOE OF A STOCKING.

The method of knitting the toe, in the preceding rules, will produce stockings resembling the best French woven goods, but as many prefer a different style, we give the following, which is also very good for finishing off a mitten in the hand:

Commence at corner of the instep needle. The manner of decreasing each side of seam—referred to before—is as follows: Commence on the seam needle and knit all but 3 stitches on the right of the seam, then sl and b to narrow, and k 1; now purl the seam stitch, then k 1 and n again, which completes the operation of decreasing for one round.

First round.—K 7, n, repeat until the number of stitches on all the needles is reduced so as to be divisible by 9, and knit balance of round plain. In case the number of stitches on the needles is already divisible by 9, then the 1st and 2nd rounds should be omitted, commencing at once with the 3rd round instead of the first.

Second round.—Knit plain.

Third round.—K 7, n, and repeat; knit 7 rounds plain.

Eleventh round.—K 6, n, repeat, and knit 6 rounds plain.

Eighteenth round.—K 5, n, repeat, and knit 5 rounds plain.

Twenty-fourth round.—K 4, n, repeat, and knit 4 rounds plain.

Now narrow once on each needle in every round until only 4 stitches are left; then narrow twice on each needle, and cast off. When decreasing once only on each needle, do not narrow at the same point in every round, but at a different place in each successive round.

RULE FOR KNITTING HEELS.

Decreasing in the heel is made at four points in every row where plain knitting is done, no decrease being made in the purled rows.

The number of stitches in a heel should always be odd, the central or seam stitch dividing the whole number into two sections, each containing an even number of stitches.

The decreasing should be done at two points in each section, once next the seam, and again at a point about one-half way between this decrease and the edge of the heel on either side the seam, thus disposing of 4 stitches in each decreased row. The first stitch on either side of the seam should be knit plain in every decreased row.

The manner of decreasing is shown in Rule I, and to further illustrate the principle which should govern the work in hand, the details are given below for completing the heel of a child's stocking with 5-inch foot. (See table, page 58.)

The number of stitches in this heel is 39. After completing 39 rows, decrease as follows:

Fortieth row.—K 8, sl and b, k 6, n, k 1, p 1, k 1, sl and b, k 6, n, k 8.

Forty-first row.—P 17, k 1, p 17.

Forty-second row.—K 8, sl and b, k 4, n, k 1, p 1, k 1, sl and b, k 4, n, k 8.

Forty-third row.—P 15, k 1, p 15.

Forty-fourth row.—K 8, sl and b, k 2, n, k 1, p 1, k 1, sl and b, k 2, n, k 8.

Forty-fifth row.—P 13, k 1, p 13.

Forty-sixth row.—K 8, sl and b, n, k 1, p 1, k 1, sl and b, n, k 8.

Forty-seventh row.—P 11, k 1, p 11.

Forty-eighth row.—Commence by knitting 12; after this proceed as in Rule I. for gentlemen's silk socks, from point marked ***. The number of stitches on the needles will be much less than in this rule, however, and that number will be decreased to shape the instep until only 78 stitches remain.

It will be observed that the number of stitches in the heel *between* the two points of decrease, diminishes by two in each section or four in each decreased row, until none are left, the two points of decrease coming in contact. This forms, when the heel is complete, "gores," which come together on both sides the heel at the bottom like letter V. Thus it will be seen that whenever the point of the V-shaped figure is reached, no further decrease is needed, and the next step is to purl back one row, and commence the following row by knitting one-half the number of stitches and one more; then fold the needles and cast off as described in the rule mentioned.

RULE II. FOR KNITTING LADIES' PLAIN STOCKINGS.

For a medium size cast 152 stitches upon 3 needles, putting 50 on each of 2 needles and 52 on the third. Knit round once plain, catching up the short end left from casting on the stitches, and knitting it in with the regular thread.

Second round.—Knit 2, seam 2 around the work. Repeat the ribbing until you have knitted a section about 2 inches deep, and finish it with a round of seaming. Mark the center stitch (the first one cast on), and knit round and round plain until you have about 12 inches in depth, *always seaming the center stitch.*

For the next round.—Begin to narrow as follows: Seam 1 (the center stitch), knit 2 separately, knit 2 together; then knit plain until 4 stitches of the round remain; knit 2 of these together and 2 plain.

Next five rounds.—Same as those above the last round.

Next round.—Narrow as before. There must be 15 or 16 narrowing rounds, with 5 of the other rounds between every succeeding 2 narrowing rounds. This will bring the work to the ankle, and there should now be about 120 stitches on the needles.

For the Ankle.—Knit plain, seaming the center stitch, until about 3 inches have been worked.

The length of the stocking from the top to the beginning of the heel should measure from 22 to 23 inches, according to the requirements of the figure.

For the Heel.—Divide as follows: Seam 1 (the center stitch), knit 30 plain and leave the rest of the stitches on the needle. Seam the 30 back to beginning of the round, knit 1 for the seam, and seam 30 on the other side of the seam-stitch. The heel is formed of these 61 stitches. Knit as follows:

First row.—Knit 30, seam 1, knit 30.

Second row.—Seam 30, knit 1, seam 30. (Fewer

or more stitches may be divided off for the heel, according to the size of the foot).

Knit these two rows alternately for about an inch, and then begin to narrow as follows, having 30 stitches on one needle and 31 on the other: Knit 26, knit 2 together, knit 2 separately, seam 1, knit 2 separately, knit 2 together, knit 26 plain.

Next three rows.—Seam all except the center stitch, which knit. Knit all except the center stitch, which seam. Seam all except the center stitch, which knit.

Next row.—Narrow as before. Make 5 or 6 narrowing rows, with 3 rows as just given after each narrowing row. The heel should now measure about 2½ inches deep. Close the heel thus: Knit to within 1 stitch of the center; then knit this 1 stitch, the seam-stitch and the next stitch beyond, *together*. Now fold the heel so that the two needles face each other and the stitches on each are exactly opposite each other. Then knit 2 stitches together at once, 1 from each needle, at the same time binding them off. Bind off all the stitches in this way until 1 stitch is left on the needle. Now turn the heel sideways and pick up about 27 stitches along its side, proceeding from right to left. Pick up 3 stitches at the corner of the heel for a gusset. Knit all the stitches left upon the needle until the other corner of the heel

is reached, where you pick up 3 more stitches for a gusset. Next pick up 27 stitches upon the other side of the heel, thus completing 1 round. The needles should now contain about 120 stitches. Knit plain rounds for about 4 inches, and then begin to narrow for the toe as follows: Knit 2 together, knit 8 separately, and repeat to end of round. Knit 8 rounds plain. Knit 2 together, knit 7 separately, and repeat for the round. Knit 7 rounds plain. Knit 2 together, knit 6 separately, and repeat for the round. Knit 6 rounds plain. Knit 2 together, knit 5 separately. Knit 5 rounds plain. Knit 2 together, knit 4 separately, knit 4 rounds plain. After this divide every round into thirds, and narrow once in each third. Continue in this way until each needle contains 2 stitches. Break off the thread, and with a darning-needle draw it through the 6 stitches, drawing them to a point, and fastening the thread on the inside of the stocking.

The heel and toe may be made of white. Clocks may be embroidered at the sides in bright or dull colors. In place of the ribbing at the top a fancy pattern may be knitted; and a similar pattern may be made down the front and over the instep or ankle. The introduction of fancy knitting will in no way interfere with the directions here given for *shaping* the stocking.

HOW TO WASH SILK KNITTED ARTICLES.

Wash in cool, soft water, with pure, white castile soap, ox gall, or fine toilet soap, and use no more of either ingredient than necessary to make a nice suds. Rub as little as possible; press the water out of the articles by placing them in a clean, dry cloth; do not wring, but squeeze them. Wash each one separately. Rinse once in clear cold water, and again in cold water which has been tinctured with some mild acid; cream of tartar, tartaric acid, alum or vinegar will do. Dry quickly. When nearly dry, rub with a piece of soft, dry flannel, always the same way. If you desire to press the article, lay it in or under a heavy book. Do not press with a very hot iron, as it gives the article a starched appearance. Use no acid for black, but add a little liquid ammonia to the washing water. Use no ammonia for colors.

HOW TO WASH WOOL KNITTED ARTICLES.

For the first cleaning of wool knitted articles in white or light colors, a "dry wash" is recommended. This is done with flour, meal or corn starch, the article being dipped into either and rubbed gently with the hands until it looks clean and fresh. Then shake out.

When it becomes necessary to use soap and water, select castile for the former and have the latter luke-warm. Make a suds of the soap and add a little ammonia or borax—preferably the latter—to the suds. Then immerse the article to be washed and allow it to soak for a few minutes. Gently squeeze, but do not rub it, until it looks clean. Then rinse in water of the same temperature and squeeze as dry as possible; do not wring. The article may be straightened out, folded in a towel and pressed firmly with the hands with advantageous results, before hanging it up to dry. The drying should be done as quickly as possible, and it is well to occasionally pull or stretch the article into shape while it is drying.

It is a very good plan to shrink wool that is to be knit into undergarments before using it. Dip the skeins into hot water, squeeze out and hang in the air to dry. Garments made from wool that has been thus treated will shrink comparatively little when washed.

CALCULATION IN KNITTING.

Table showing Number of Stitches required for Stockings of Various Sizes (Ladies', Misses' and Children's) made with No. 19 Knitting Needles, and Knitting Silk of the usual size.

	5 In. Foot.	5½ In. Foot.	6 In. Foot.	6½ In. Foot.	7 In. Foot.	7½ In. Foot.	8 In. Foot.	8½ In. Foot.	9 In. Foot.	9½ In. Foot.
Number of stitches required for top of stocking,	108	112	116	124	132	140	148	156	162	169
Number of rounds before beginning to narrow for ankle, including 20 rounds ribbed,	140	150	160	185	190	200	210	220	230	240
Whole number of rounds before beginning heel,	250	265	295	340	355	370	380	390	400	410
Number of stitches in ankle, after narrowing,	78	82	86	90	94	98	102	106	110	113
Number of stitches in heel, including center or seam stitch,	39	41	43	45	47	49	51	53	55	57
Number of rows in heel, before narrowing, counting each time across,	39	41	43	45	47	49	51	53	55	57
Length of toe, from beginning of narrowing to point,	$1\frac{10}{20}$ in.	$1\frac{11}{20}$ in.	$1\frac{12}{20}$ in.	$1\frac{13}{20}$ in.	$1\frac{14}{20}$ in.	$1\frac{15}{20}$ in.	$1\frac{16}{20}$ in.	$1\frac{17}{20}$ in.	$1\frac{18}{20}$ in.	$1\frac{19}{20}$ in.
Length of foot, before beginning to narrow for toe, including width of heel at widest point,	$3\frac{10}{20}$ in.	$3\frac{19}{20}$ in.	$4\frac{8}{20}$ in.	$4\frac{17}{20}$ in.	$5\frac{6}{20}$ in.	$5\frac{15}{20}$ in.	$6\frac{4}{20}$ in.	$6\frac{13}{20}$ in.	$7\frac{2}{20}$ in.	$7\frac{11}{20}$ in.

The methods of narrowing in the leg, heel and foot have been given in the preceding pages in general and special instructions, and will not need repeating here; and besides, the average knitter will know, without further directions, just where and how to manage this part of the work. The beginner will find the information she seeks in the instructions referred to.

Table showing Number of Stitches required for Stockings of Various Sizes (Ladies', Misses' and Children's) made with No. 22 Needles, and Fine Knitting Silk.

	5 In. Foot.	5½ In. Foot.	6 In. Foot.	6½ In. Foot.	7 In. Foot.	7½ In. Foot.	8 In. Foot.	8½ In. Foot.	9 In. Foot.	9½ In. Foot.
Number of stitches required for top of stocking,	135	140	145	155	165	175	185	195	202	210
Number of rounds before beginning to narrow for ankle, including 24 rounds ribbed,	168	180	192	222	228	240	252	264	276	288
Whole number of rounds before beginning heel,	300	318	354	408	426	444	456	468	480	492
Number of stitches in ankle, after narrowing,	98	102	108	113	118	122	127	132	137	142
Number of stitches in heel, including center or seam stitch,	49	51	55	57	59	61	63	67	69	71
Number of rows in heel, before narrowing, counting each time across,	49	51	55	57	59	61	63	67	69	71
Length of toe, from beginning of narrowing to point,	$1\frac{10}{20}$ in.	$1\frac{11}{20}$ in.	$1\frac{12}{20}$ in.	$1\frac{13}{20}$ in.	$1\frac{14}{20}$ in.	$1\frac{15}{20}$ in.	$1\frac{16}{20}$ in.	$1\frac{17}{20}$ in.	$1\frac{18}{20}$ in.	$1\frac{19}{20}$ in.
Length of foot, before beginning to narrow for toe, including width of heel at widest point,	$3\frac{10}{20}$ in.	$3\frac{19}{20}$ in.	$4\frac{8}{20}$ in.	$4\frac{17}{20}$ in.	$5\frac{6}{20}$ in.	$5\frac{15}{20}$ in.	$6\frac{4}{20}$ in.	$6\frac{13}{20}$ in.	$7\frac{2}{20}$ in.	$7\frac{11}{20}$ in.

It must be remembered that the specifications in the above tables refer to the work of knitters who knit neither too loosely nor too tightly, but with an even and elastic result. Those who knit very tightly may need to increase the number of stitches given, while those who knit loosely may be compelled to undo their work and finish with fewer stitches than those above named.

HOODS, CAPES, SHAWLS, JACKETS, FASCINATORS, PETTI-COATS, LEGGINGS, SLIPPERS, ETC., ETC.

In making the garments and articles illustrated and described in this department, the knitter need not confine herself to the colors and materials named, when, according to her taste and judgment,

No. 1.—LADIES' KNITTED CHENILLE HOOD.

others may be substituted. Owing to the fact that two people rarely knit alike, we have not deemed it advisable to give quantities. These may be ascertained at any store where wool or silk knitting materials are kept, as the people in charge, from the continuous sales of materials for various purposes, can in almost every instance name accurate quantities for different varieties of work.

LADIES' KNITTED CHENILLE HOOD.

Nos. 1 AND 2.—The hood illustrated is made of pale-blue chenille and knitted back and forth, plain (see No. 2), on large ivory or bone needles. Cast on sufficient stitches to make the work wide enough to reach around the head from side to side, back of the face. Knit as directed until the piece is long enough to cover the head and form the frill and cape as seen at figure No. 1. In finishing the upper part of the piece the corners may be rounded by narrowing them off; or, if finished squarely,

they may be turned under when adding the outside to the lining. The latter is made of silk of the same color as the chenille. The chenille portion may be gathered to it at the top and the back of the neck as seen in the picture, and then a lining may be added to the cape-portion. A border of the chenille may be sewed over-and-over about the edges. Finish the hood at the top and the back of the neck with loops of ribbon, and add ties of the same to the lower corners of the front, catching the corners to those of the lining when joining the ties. Cream-white, pale-yellow, rose-color, lavender or any soft tint is pretty for an evening hood knitted in this manner.

If preferred, a lining of the silk may be added as follows: Cut it the size and shape of the knitted portion and fell it in flatly. Then plait the hood over the forehead as seen in the picture. Add a casing or strip of the silk at the back of the neck for the insertion of a rubber strap $4\frac{1}{2}$ inches long by which the hood is drawn into shape. Then add the loops and ties of ribbon as directed.

Eider-down wool, knitted in the same way in any color desired would make a comfortable hood.

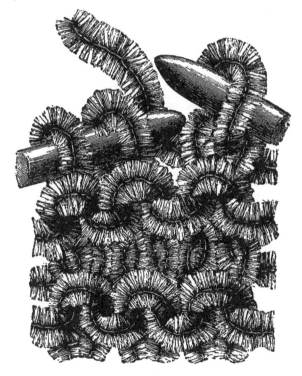

No. 2 —DETAIL FOR KNITTING HOOD.

An edging of Shetland or Ice wool could be added, and the lining either omitted or crocheted with Shetland wool or Saxony yarn.

KNITTED SHOULDER–CAPE.

No. 3.—The cape illustrated is made of Germantown wool, and is knitted as follows: (Use quite coarse needles and work rather loosely).

No. 3.—KNITTED SHOULDER-CAPE.

Cast on 64 stitches, and knit across once, *plain*, and *seam* back. Knit in this order until there are 10 rows. This will form one ridge or rib. Now reverse the order of the knitting and *seam* one row and *knit* one row until there are 6 rows, or a second rib. Repeat these two ribs alternately until there are 63 of them knitted and seamed, altogether.

In the last row of seaming, in the 63rd rib, bind off as follows: Bind off 3 stitches very loosely, and then drop a stitch from off the left-hand needle. * Now pass the stitch on the right-hand needle onto the left-hand needle and knit it off, also loosely. Now bind off 2 more stitches, drop the next stitch and repeat from * until within 9 stitches from the top; then bind these off in the regular way.

Now pull or pick out the dropped stitches entirely across the work, and the ribs will assume the effect of soft open puffs.

To Finish the Neck.—Make single crochets across the top, arranging the crochets so as to draw the cape in to the size of the neck. Then make a treble crochet in the top of every *under* rib, with 2-chains between. Finish with shells made of 6 double crochets in every other space, with a single crochet in each alternate space. Edge the shells with a single crochet in the top of each double, and make a single crochet *over* or *around* every single crochet underneath. Run a ribbon in the spaces and tie it in a bow.

To Make the Fringe.—Begin with a half-double crochet drawn out very long, and then make a chain of 20 stitches and another half-double in the 3rd stitch of the cape.

Repeat chains and half-doubles across the cape, as seen in the picture.

LADIES' KNITTED VEST.

No. 4.—Use Belding's knitting silk and two No. 17 steel needles, 12 inches long.

The front and back of the vest are made alike in 2 pieces, each knitted straight from the lower edge to the neck, when the shaping of the latter and the shoulder straps begins as below directed. The garment is sewed or crocheted together under the arms and on the shoulders, and a gusset, knitted separately, is joined in each under-arm seam at the bottom of the vest, to give breadth at the hips. A very slender figure will not require these gussets.

Cast on loosely, 200 stitches, and knit back plain.

Second row.—Work in rib style as follows: K 3, p 2 alternately across the row. Work back, knitting the purled stitches and purling the knitted ones.

Work in this manner for 24 inches. Then knit off 50 stitches in the usual manner, leaving the remaining 150 on the needle, and put a cork on each end of the needle so that the stitches will not slip off. Now knit to shape the neck edge and shoulder strap as follows:

Work back and forth in rib style as before, on the 50 stitches, narrowing once every time you reach the neck-edge, until there are 20 stitches on the needle. Then rib for 6 inches and bind off.

Next cast off loosely 100 stitches of those left on the first needle, and on the remaining 50 work in rib style to correspond with the other side, being careful to narrow at the neck-edge as before. This completes one half of the vest. Make the other half to correspond and join under the arms as described after making the gussets as follows: Cast on loosely 50 stitches for each, and rib the same as in the body portion for about an inch. Continue to rib, narrowing once at the beginning of every row, until but 1 stitch is left. Insert the gussets in the lower part of the seam with the lower edges of the portions together.

No. 4.—LADIES' KNITTED VEST.

Now fill in the neck of the vest in crochet as follows: Begin at the lower right hand corner and make 1 double crochet, 5 chain, 1 double, and so on across the work making the doubles in the ribs. Break the silk at the end of this and every row.

Second to Ninth row inclusive.—Work same as first row except that the doubles are made under the 5-chains. Increase at the beginning and end of each row by 1 extra 5-chain and 1 double.

Now join each shoulder by making a chain of

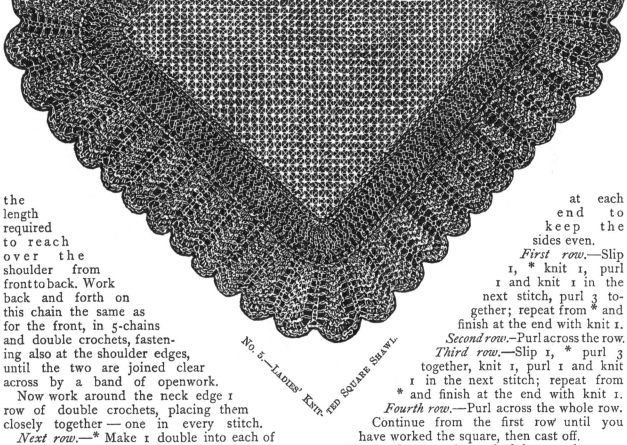

No. 5.—LADIES' KNITTED SQUARE SHAWL.

the length required to reach over the shoulder from front to back. Work back and forth on this chain the same as for the front, in 5-chains and double crochets, fastening also at the shoulder edges, until the two are joined clear across by a band of openwork.

Now work around the neck edge 1 row of double crochets, placing them closely together — one in every stitch.

Next row.—* Make 1 double into each of the 2 doubles underneath, 5 chain, skip 5 doubles and repeat from * entirely across the row.

Next row.—* make 1 double into each of the 2 doubles underneath, 1 chain, 4 doubles, each separated by 1 chain into third of 5-chain, 1 chain and repeat from *.

Next row.—* 1 double into each of the 2 doubles underneath, 1 chain, 4 doubles each separated by 1 chain into the center of the 4 doubles underneath, 1 chain, and repeat from *. Repeat this last row once more, then add a row of scollops as follows: Make about 15 doubles in the center of each group of the 4 doubles underneath, and fasten down to doubles of previous row with single crochets.

Add a similar row of scollops to the edge of each sleeve. Run ribbon into the holes about the neck as seen in the engraving.

Finish the lower edge with several rows of the open-work crochet and a row of scollops.

LADIES' KNITTED SQUARE SHAWL.

No. 5.—This is a light yet warm shawl made of Shetland wool and measuring 18 inches square, without the border. The engraving shows it as it appears when doubled for wearing. The square for the center is in blackberry pattern; the border is worked separately.

For the blackberry pattern cast on about 128 stitches, or any number divisible by 4, and 1 extra at each end to keep the sides even.

First row.—Slip 1, * knit 1, purl 1 and knit 1 in the next stitch, purl 3 together; repeat from * and finish at the end with knit 1.

Second row.—Purl across the row.

Third row.—Slip 1, * purl 3 together, knit 1, purl 1 and knit 1 in the next stitch; repeat from * and finish at the end with knit 1.

Fourth row.—Purl across the whole row. Continue from the first row until you have worked the square, then cast off.

The border must be worked in two pieces, as it is more convenient not to have such a large number of stitches on the needle at once as would be needed to go round the shawl.

Cast on 232 stitches for the border.

First row.—Knit.

Second row.—Knit 1, make 1; (to make 1, put the thread over, and knit it as a stitch in next row) * knit 2, knit 3 together, knit 2, make 1, knit 1, make 1; repeat from * to end of row.

Third row.—Purl.

Fourth row.—Like second row.

Fifth row.—Knit; repeat from second row 6 times more. This will bring you to the 30th row.

Thirtieth row.—Knit.

Thirty-first row.—Purl.

Thirty-second to Thirty-ninth rows.—Make 1, knit 2 together, throughout each row.

Fortieth row.—Knit.

Forty-first row.—Purl.

Forty-second row.—Purl.
Forty-third row.—Knit.
Forty-fourth row.—Like thirty-second.
Forty-fifth row.—Knit, then cast off.
The joining of the two pieces of border should be placed at opposite corners.

DESIGN FOR A SHAWL CENTER.

No. 6.—Cast on 10 stitches for each division of the pattern, using Andalusian or Shetland wool and 2 No. 8 wooden needles.

First row.—K 2 together, th o, k 3, th o, k 3, k 2 together.

Second, Fourth, Sixth, Eighth, Tenth and Twelfth rows.—Purl.

Third row.—K 2 together, k 1, th o, k 4, th o, k 1, k 2 together.

Fifth row.—K 2 together, th o, k 6, th o, k 2 together.

Seventh row.—K 1, th o, k 2, k 2 together twice, k 2, th o, k 1.

Ninth row.—K 2, th o, k 1, k 2 together twice, k 1, th o, k 2.

Eleventh row.—K 3, th o, k 2 together twice, th o, k 3.

After knitting the 12th row, repeat from the 3rd row for all the work.

KNITTED BED ROOM SLIPPERS.

Nos. 7, 8 AND 9.—Use single zephyr or Germantown wool in blue and white, and steel needles, in knitting these slippers.

Commence the slipper at the toe with blue wool. Cast on 10 stitches. Increase 1 stitch by putting the wool over the needle at the beginning of each row. No. 8 shows the outside of work, and No. 9 the inside, with

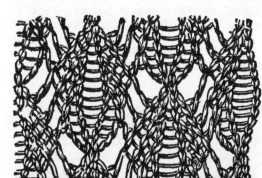

No. 6.—DESIGN FOR A SHAWL CENTER.

No. 7.—KNITTED BED ROOM SLIPPER.

No. 8.—OUTSIDE OF SLIPPER.

Second row.—Make 1, knit 1, * take the double white wool, turn it twice over the needle to form a loop about ¾ inch deep (see design); with the left hand needle pass the last knitted loop over the 4 loops of white, knit 2; repeat from * to the end of the row.

Third row.—Make 1 at the beginning of the row, slip the loops of white wool, knit the blue; in knitting the blue stitch, pass the blue wool with which you are knitting round the double white wool; in knitting the next stitch this will draw up the white wool close to the work, and so carry it to the other side to be ready for working the next row of loops.

Fourth row.—Make 1, knit the blue stitches plain, knit the 4 white loops at the back as 1 stitch.

Fifth row.—Make 1, knit to the end of the row. Repeat from second row, increasing at the beginning of each row until the work is wide enough across the instep.

Now divide the stitches for the sides, casting off 10 in the center; with the third needle continue to work on the side stitches as before, without increase or decrease, until you have the length from the instep to the back of heel; then cast off and work

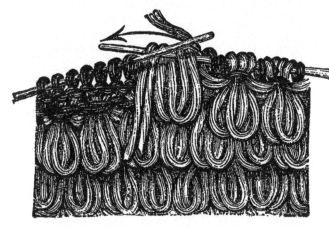

No. 9.—INSIDE OF SLIPPER.

loops of the white wool. When knitting with the white wool take it from two balls so as to have two threads.

First row.—Knit plain.

the other side in the same way; sew the two sides together at the back with a needle and wool.

Now pick up the stitches round the top of slipper on 3 needles and with a 4th needle and blue wool knit 10 rounds and cast off. Turn this plain piece over and hem it down to the top of inside of slipper to form a roll round the edge. Sew the bottom of the slipper neatly and firmly to a strong cork sole lined with wool.

LADIES' FANCY SILK MITTENS.

No. 10.—Four No. 19 knitting needles will be needed in knitting these mittens.

Cast on to each of 2 needles 25 stitches, and on the 3rd needle 30 stitches, making 80 in all. Knit 5 rounds plain for a hem at the top.

Sixth round.—N, o, repeat. Knit 7 rounds plain.

Fourteenth, Fifteenth, Sixteenth and Seventeenth rounds.— Sl and b, k 3, o, repeat.

Eighteenth round.— Knit plain.

Nineteenth round.— K 2, n, o, k 1, repeat.

Twentieth round.— K 1, n, o, k 2, repeat.

Twenty-first round. —N, o, k 2, repeat. Knit 9 rounds plain.

No. 10.—Ladies' Fancy Silk Mitten.

Thirty-first round.—Th o, k 3, n, repeat.

Thirty-second round.—K 1, o, k 2, n, repeat.

Thirty-third round.—K 2, o, k 1, n, repeat.

Thirty-fourth round.—K 3, o, n, repeat. Knit 2 rounds plain.

The last 6 rounds are repeated 7 times to complete the pattern in the wrist. The fancy stripe in the back of hand requires 31 stitches. There are 11 repetitions of the pattern, which are knit in 6 rounds each as follows:

First round.—Sl and b, k 3, o, sl and b, k 3, o, k 2, o, k 2, sl 1, n, pass sl st over, k 2, o, k 2, o, k 3, n, o, k 3, n.

Second round.—Sl and b, k 2, o, k 1, sl and b, k 2, o, k 13, o, k 2, n, k 1, o, k 2, n.

Third round.—Sl and b, k 1, o, k 2, sl and b, k 1, th o, k 4, o, k 2, sl 1, n, pass sl st over, k 2, o, k 4, o, k 1, n, k 2, o, k 1, n.

Fourth round.—Sl and b, o, k 3, sl and b, o, k 17, o, n, k 3, o, n.

Fifth round.—K 12, o, k 2, sl 1, n, pass sl st over, k 2, o, k 12.

Sixth round.—K 31.

The fancy design at end of stripe is knit on the same 31 stitches in rounds as follows:

First round.—K 1, sl and b, k 3, o, sl and b, k 2, o, k 2, o, k 2, sl 1, n, pass sl st over, k 2, o, k 2, o, k 2, n, o, k 3, n, k 1.

Second round.—K 1, sl and b, k 2, o, k 1, sl and b, k 1, o, k 13, o, k 1, n, k 1, o, k 2, n, k 1.

Third round.—K 1, sl and b, k 1, o, k 2, sl and b, o, k 4, o, k 2, sl 1, n, pass sl st over, k 2, o, k 4, o, n, k 2, o, k 1, n, k 1.

Fourth round.—K 1, sl and b, o, k 25, o, n, k 1.

Fifth round.—K 12, o, k 2, sl 1, n, pass sl st over, k 2, o, k 12.

Sixth round.—K 31.

Seventh round.—K 2, sl and b, k 3, o, sl and b, k 1, o, k 2, o, k 2, sl 1, n, pass sl st over, k 2, o, k 2, o, k 1, n, o, k 3, n, k 2.

Eighth round.—K 2, sl and b, k 2, o, k 1, sl and b, o, k 13, o, n, k 1, o, k 2, n, k 2.

Ninth round.—K 2, sl and b, k 1, o, k 7, o, k 2, sl 1, n, pass sl st over, k 2, o, k 7, o, k 1, n, k 2.

Tenth round.—K 2, sl and b, o, k 23, o, n, k 2.

Eleventh round.—K 12, o, k 2, sl 1, n, pass sl st over, k 2, o, k 12.

Twelfth round.—K 31.

Thirteenth round.—K 3, sl and b, k 3, o, sl and b, o, k 2, o, k 2, sl 1, n, pass sl st over, k 2, o, k 2, o, n, o, k 3, n, k 3.

Fourteenth round.—K 3, sl and b, k 2, o, k 17, o, k 2, n, k 3.

Fifteenth round.—K 3, sl and b, k 1, o, k 6, o, k 2, sl 1, n, pass sl st over, k 2, o, k 6, o, k 1, n, k 3.

Sixteenth round.—K 3, sl and b, o, k 21, o, n, k 3.

Seventeenth round.—K 12, o, k 2, sl 1, n, pass sl st over, k 2, o, k 12.

Eighteenth round.—K 31.

Nineteenth round.—K 5, sl and b, k 3, o, k 2, o, k 2, sl 1, n, pass sl st over, k 2, o, k 2, o, k 3, n, k 5.

Twentieth round.—K 5, sl and b, k 2, o, k 13, o, k 2, n, k 5.

Twenty-first round.—K 5, sl and b, k 1, o, k 4, o, k 2, sl 1, n, pass sl st over, k 2, o, k 4, o, k 1, n, k 5.

Twenty-second round.—K 5, sl and b, o, k 17, o, n, k 5.

Twenty-third round.—K 12, o, k 2, sl 1, n, pass sl st over, k 2, o, k 12.

Twenty-fourth round.—K 31.

Twenty-fifth round.—K 31.

Twenty-sixth round.—K 6, sl and b, k 3, o, k 2, o, k 1, sl 1, n, pass sl st over, k 1, o, k 2, o, k 3, n, k 6.

Twenty-seventh round.—K 6, sl and b, k 2, o, k 11, o, k 2, n, k 6.

Twenty-eighth round.—K 6, sl and b, k 1, o, k 13, o, k 1, n, k 6.

Twenty-ninth round.—K 6, sl and b, o, k 6, o, sl 1, n, pass sl st over, o, k 6, o, n, k 6.

Thirtieth round.—K 31,

Thirty-first round.—K 7, sl and b, k 3, o, k 7, o, k 3, n, k 7.

Thirty-second round.—K 7, sl and b, k 2, o, k 9, o, k 2, n, k 7.

Thirty-third round.—K 7, sl and b, k 1, o, k 11, o, k 1, n, k 7.

Thirty-fourth round.—K 7, sl and b, o, k 13, o, n, k 7.

Thirty-fifth round.—K 31.

Thirty-sixth round.—K 10, sl and b, k 3, o, k 1, o, k 3, n, k 10.

Thirty-seventh round.—K 10, sl and b, k 2, o, k 3, o, k 2, n, k 10.

No. 11.—Knitted Fascinator.

Thirty-eighth round.—K 10, sl and b, k 1, o, k 5, o, k 1, n, k 10.

Thirty-ninth round.—K 10, sl and b, o, k 7, o, n, k 10.

Fortieth round.—K 31.

Forty-first round.—K 13, sl and b, o, k 1, o, n, k 13.

Forty-second round.—K 31.

All other portions of this mitten are knit plain (see general instructions page 51). When shaping the tip of hand decrease only in the plain portions of the work. The wrist and fancy back are lined in manner described at No. 23 on page 70.

Eighty stitches at the wrist make a mitten of size No. 6½ to No. 7. More or less stitches must be used to make a larger or smaller mitten care being taken to keep the whole number divisible by 6.

KNITTED FASCINATOR.

No. 11.—This fascinator, as represented, is made of single Germantown yarn used double. If preferred, it may be used single, or single zephyr may be selected instead of Germantown yarn, if the knitter desires.

Cast on 93 stitches. (For a larger or smaller fascinator cast on more or fewer stitches.) Use bone or wooden needles of good size.

To obtain the shape of the fascinator, the better plan is to cut a pattern from paper, making it 46½ inches across the front or longest edge, and 12 inches from the center point to the front edge, sloping the sides regularly from the center point to the ends. Work back and forth in plain knitting for 4 rows (or 2 ribs), without decreasing. Then, continuing to knit plain, narrow once or twice at the end of each row, as the shape of the pattern

necessitates, until you reach the center point. There should now be 50 rows of knitting or 25 ribs.

To make the Fringe.—Crochet *very* loosely, chains of 9 stitches, catching them along the edge with single crochets, at intervals that will cause the fringe to fall as seen in the picture.

By increasing the fascinator in size, it may be used as a shoulder shawl. White or colored yarn may be selected for making it, according to individual taste.

LADIES' KNITTED SHORT DRAWERS.

No. 12.—These drawers are knitted with red and white wool, in patent knitting, with the waistband and lower edge in ribbed pattern. Begin from the upper edge by casting on 188 stitches with the red wool.

First row.—Knit.

Second row.—With white wool knit 1, purl 1 and repeat across the row.

Third to Thirtieth rows.—Like the preceding, except that the last row is knitted with red wool.

Thirty-first row.—Join the white wool. Slip 1, throw wool forward, slip 1, inserting the needle as for purling, knit 1; repeat across the row.

Thirty-second row.—Slip 1; then, alternately, wool forward, slip the stitch knitted in the last row, knit 2 together and repeat.

Thirty-third to Two Hundred and Eighty-eighth row.—Like the preceding, but

No. 12.—Ladies' Knitted Short Drawers.

after the 192nd row, the work is divided in two parts, each of which is continued separately. Then follow 36 rows like those which formed the waistband, the first and last being knitted with red wool.

KNITTED PETTICOAT, WITH DETAIL.

NOS. 13 AND 14.—This pretty petticoat is knitted with coarse steel or medium-sized bone needles, and will generally be made of Germantown wool, in any color preferred, such as cream, scarlet, salmon, turquoise-blue, brown or gray.

The work is done in stripes, which are begun at the top; and after a sufficient number are made, they are crocheted together. Each stripe is finished at the bottom with a fancy border, which is

No. 13.—KNITTED PETTICOAT.

a continuation of the stripe; and after the stripes are all joined, the lower edge of the border is turned up underneath and hemmed down so as to show only the open work at the bottom of the petticoat, as seen in the engravings—No. 13 showing the petticoat fully completed, and No. 14 the lower portion of a stripe with the border turned up as above described.

Begin a stripe by casting on 64 stitches; knit across plain for the 1st row, and purl across for the 2nd row.

Third row.—Slip 1st stitch; * purl 2 together, wool over needle, purl 2 together, purl 5; out of the next stitch purl 2 (1 out of the front of the stitch in the usual manner, and 1 reversed out of the back); purl 3, knit 4 plain, but of these 4 slip the first 2 on a separate needle, which leave at the back; knit the last 2, then slip the first 2 back on the needle and knit them; purl 3, purl 2 out of the next stitch as before, purl 5, purl 2 together, wool over needle, purl 2 together, purl 2; repeat from * once more, ending with purl 1 instead of purl 2 as before.

Fourth row.—Knit back plain.

Fifth row.—Like 3rd row, but knit the group of 4 in *regular order* instead of *crossing* them.

Sixth row.—Slip 1st stitch, purl 10, knit 3, purl 4, knit 3, purl 22, knit 3, purl 4, knit 3, purl 11.

Seventh row.—Slip the 1st; * knit 2 together, wool over, knit 2 together, knit 5; out of the next stitch knit 1 plain and 1 reversed (to reverse, insert the needle from the back downward); purl 3, knit 4, purl 3; out of the next stitch knit 1 plain and 1 reversed; knit 5, knit 2 together, wool over, knit 2

together, knit 2; repeat from * once more, ending with knit 1 instead of knit 2.

Eighth row.—Like the 6th row.

Repeat these rows beginning with the 3rd row, until the stripe is as long as you wish the petticoat to be, and then knit as follows to finish the stripe and make the border: Knit 1 row like the 3rd; next, 1 row plain, and then 2 rows purled. Then, for the border itself, knit 1st row thus: Wool over needle, narrow, and repeat to end of row; 2nd row, purled. Next 4 rows like last 2 by turns; now 4 rows alternate purl and plain, so that the work will be plain on right side, and bind off.

When the stripes are crocheted together and the border is hemmed as described, the petticoat may be sewed to a yoke or a belt, or a crocheted cord may be run in the top; or a row of double or treble crochets may be made along the top and a ribbon inserted for a belt.

KNITTED LACE FOR A FLANNEL PETTICOAT.

(No Illustration.)

Use medium steel needles and knitting silk for this showy lace which is suitable for flannel petticoats. Cast on 22 stitches, and knit across plain.

First row.—K 3, o, n, k 1, o, n, k 2, o, k 1, o, n, k 1, n, o, k 2, o twice, n, o twice, n.

Second row.—K 2, p 1, k 2, p 1, n, k 1, o, sl 1, n, pass sl st over, o, k 3, o, n, n, o, n, k 1, o, n, k 1.

Third row.—K 3, o, n, k 1, o, n, o, n, k 1, n, o, k 1, o, k 1, n, k 6.

Fourth row.—Cast off 3, k 5, o, k 3, o, sl 1, n,

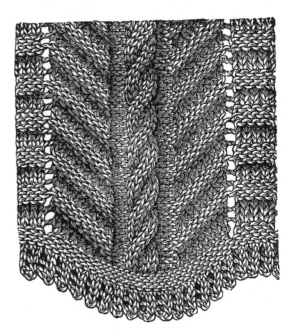

No. 14.—DETAIL FOR KNITTED PETTICOAT.

pass sl st over, o, k 3, o, n, k 1, o, n, k 1. Repeat from 1st row. Knitters will understand that lace is made more or less open according to the size of the needles used.

KNITTED EVENING HOOD. (OR, CHILD'S CAP).

No. 15.—Two colors of single zephyr, German-town wool or any worsted preferred may be used for this natty article, which is appropriate for a young lady or for a child. Worn by a child it is called a cap, and donned by a young lady it becomes an evening hood. An illustration of it as a cap for a child may be seen at No. 1, first page of Children's Department. The decorations may be varied.

Cast on 65 stitches and purl and knit, alternately, 5 rows. Now join the other color, * knit 5 stitches in the usual manner; then knit 5 more, putting the thread over for each, *three times* instead of *once*; then knit 5 in the usual manner, and so on across the row. Now knit back plain, dropping the three put-over threads between the stitches at this part of the row. Repeat *twice* more from *. Then join the other color, knit 1 row plain, purl 1 row, knit 1, purl 1, thus making 4 rows. Alternate the puffed row and the one last made until there are 4 rows of puffs; then beginning to narrow, make 6 more rows of puffs and 7 of the plain stripe, narrowing gradually at each end of the needle until there are about 30 stitches left on it. (If single zephyr is used, the hood or cap should now be about 11 inches across the back, 5 across the top, and 8 inches at each side.) Now take up the stitches around the face, and knit a strip to correspond with that at the beginning of the work. Fold the hood double and sew the top edges together. Finish it with a bow or rosette and ties of ribbon. The work should be done loosely in order to produce the prettiest effect. A very dainty affair of the kind may be made of knitting silk or of any of the fine wools.

No. 15.—KNITTED EVENING HOOD.

KNITTED DESIGN FOR A THREE-CORNERED SHAWL.

No. 16.—This shawl may be made of Saxony and double zephyr wool. Use bone or wooden needles. Cast on with the zephyr, 300 stitches, and knit one row. The shawl is knitted plain throughout and is shaped by knitting 2 together at the end of each row.

Second to Ninth rows.—Use the Saxony yarn.

Tenth row.—Use the zephyr; when knitting the first and second stitches, pick up and knit the corresponding stitches of the last zephyr row with them; k 8, pick up the next 2 stitches, and repeat in this manner across the work.

Eleventh row.—Still using the zephyr, knit plain.

Now repeat from the second row arranging the diamond pattern by picking up the stitches *between* those picked up in the 10th row. (See engraving). Repeat in this manner until the shawl is finished. Finish the upper edge of the shawl with a crocheted shell edge of Saxony, and the other edges with a fringe of the same intermingled with the zephyr knotted in.

This design may be very prettily worked out in white Ice wool with the diamonds of knitting silk in some dainty color, such as pale-blue, rose-color, lavender, Nile-green, etc., etc.; or of dark-blue, black, red or orange.

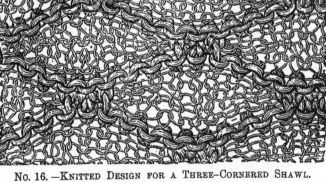

No. 16.—KNITTED DESIGN FOR A THREE-CORNERED SHAWL.

KNITTED EDGING FOR A SHAWL.

(No Illustration.)

A pretty edging for a shawl is knit as follows: Cast on 9 stitches and knit 1 plain row.

First row.—Slip 1, knit 1, th o, slip 1, knit 3, pass the slipped stitch over the three knitted ones, th o, knit 1, th o twice, knit 2.

Second row.—Slip 1, knit 2, purl 1, knit 2, purl 3, knit 3.

Third row.—Slip 1, knit 1, th o, slip 1, knit 3, pass the slipped stitch over, knit 6.

Fourth row.—Cast off 4, knit 2, purl 3, knit 3; repeat from the first row until a length is knitted sufficient to go around the article.

KNITTED SHAWL.

No. 17.—This shawl is made of white double Germantown wool, and is knitted on large bone or wooden needles. A good way in which to make it is as follows: Cut a paper pattern, three-cornered in shape, and measuring from point to point across what will be the top of the shawl, 55 inches; from the top of the shawl down the center to the lower point, 28 inches, and from this point to each end of the shawl, 41 inches. Now cast on 135 stitches and knit back and forth in the ordinary manner, narrowing in each row at the ends as necessary to shape the shawl to the pattern until the shawl is of the size and shape of the pattern.

NO. 17.—KNITTED SHAWL.

To Finish the Top of the Shawl.—Make shells, each formed of 5 double crochets caught down with single crochets.

For the Lower Edges: First row.—Begin at the point with a chain of 4 stitches and make 1 double crochet in about the 3rd stitch; then 1 double crochet back in the first stitch, drawing the stitches and also the last loop on the hook out long. Then skip 1 rib; make a double crochet in the next stitch, and then another double back on the other side of the ridge, drawing the stitches and loop out long as before. Repeat across the work so that the crossed doubles will lie flatly.

Second row.—Make a chain of 3 stitches and then 1 double crochet in the 2nd space, and 1 double back in the first space; 1 double in the 3rd space and 1 back in the 2nd, and work in this order across the shawl.

Third row.—Same as last.

To Make the Fringe.—Very loose chains of 11 stitches each, and catch in the top of every crossed double.

The shawl may be made larger or smaller according to individual taste, and of any color preferred.

KNITTED BEDROOM SLIPPERS.

No. 18.—Use Germantown yarn or single zephyr in two colors. Blue and gray make a pretty combination. The slipper is knitted in a straight strip that is long enough, after it is joined, to go around the sole to be used.

In joining, the *two ends* are not sewed together, but as follows: Turn the corner of one end down so that the end edge will be even with the lower edge. This will make a bias fold which extends along the instep from the toe to the top of the slipper. Then bring the remaining end around and join it to the edge which now crosses the strip from top to bottom, beyond the bias fold, and join the two at this point. This will shape the slipper and make it ready for the sole. In sewing on the latter, the point must be turned under and held a little full to shape it nicely.

The design is in honey-comb pattern, with 2 stitches to a square. For a No. 4 sole 54 squares in length will be needed.

NO. 18.—KNITTED BEDROOM SLIPPER.

Cast on 26 stitches with the blue, and knit across plain. Now to form the squares: Slip off 2 blue stitches, inserting the needle in each as for purling.

Now with the gray yarn, knit 2; slip 2 blue stitches as before, knit 2 with the gray and so on across the needle. In working back, slip 2 blue stitches, and purl 2 gray stitches alternately across the work.

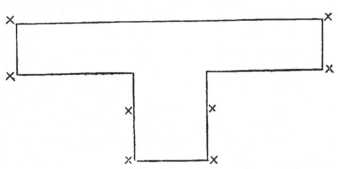

Work back and forth in the same order once more.

Now with the blue, knit back and forth plain 4 times; then repeat the squares with the blue and gray as before. Continue in this manner until the strip is 54 squares in length. Then join the strip as before described to shape the slipper, and sew it to the sole.

Knit a border in loop knitting using both colors, or one, as preferred according to the directions for No. 31 on page 17, making it as wide as desired, and sew it around the top of the slipper. Finish the slipper with a bow of ribbon.

No. 19.—LADIES' KNITTED HUG-
ME-TIGHT, OR ZOUAVE JACKET.

LADIES' KNITTED HUG-ME-TIGHT, OR ZOUAVE JACKET.

No. 19.—This is a very simple garment to make and one exceedingly comfortable to wear either about the house, or on the street under outside wraps. It is made of Germantown wool, and any color preferred may be selected; but black, brown, dark blue, red and gray are the colors generally chosen. It is knitted in a long strip on coarse steel needles, in plain back and forth rows. The one illustrated was knitted on a foundation of 50 stitches and the strip was 204 ribs long when completed. A general rule which will adapt the size of the garment to the figure of the person who is to wear it is as follows: Make the strip as wide as the figure measures from the center of the chest to the arm-socket, and twice as long as the chest measures from one arm-socket to the other. For instance, if the chest measure from arm to arm is 16 inches, make the strip 8 inches wide and 32 inches long.

When the strip is completed, firmly join its two ends by an over-and-over stitch with a coarse needle and the knitting yarn. Now find the center of the strip and fold the latter so that the seam will be even with and over the center. Next, sew the edges at one side of the strip together across

the middle, leaving an unsewed portion at each side large enough for an arm-hole. This seam will extend from shoulder to shoulder when the garment is on, while the seam of the ends will come at the middle of the back *below* this cross-seam. Finish the edges with a shell border in crochet, using the same or a contrasting color as preferred. Put the garment on, draw it together over the bust and sew ties of ribbon at the necessary point to close it. This jacket could be made in fancy ribbed knitting if desired; but as described it adjusts itself very easily and snugly to the figure.

LADIES' ZOUAVE JACKET, OR HUG-ME-TIGHT, KNITTED BY A DIAGRAM.

No. 20.—A garment of the description named and presenting the same appearance as the one illustrated at figure No. 19 except that its seams will be under the arms instead of across the back, may be knitted according to the directions given with this diagram. Plain or fancy knitting as preferred, may be used for the garment.

The narrow sections extend from each side of the back, down the front and under the arm where their ends are joined to the back as indicated by the crosses. To begin properly, cut a pattern of the required size and shaped like the diagram. It will be observed that the long narrow (front) sections are a little more than one-third the width of the other (back) section, and this proportion must be maintained in making any size. Then cast on the stitches for one narrow section of the pattern and knit back and forth until the wide section is reached. Then cast on enough more stitches to reach the full depth of this section and continue knitting until the other narrow section is reached. Bind off the extra stitches cast on, thus reducing the work to the width of the narrow section again; knit until this is long enough, bind off and join the ends to the back as before suggested, as indicated by the crosses. Then crochet a pretty shell-border about the edges, fulling in the edges of the arm-hole in front, if necessary, to make it fit in

No. 20.—DIAGRAM FOR ZOUAVE JACKET, OR HUG-ME-TIGHT.

to the figure. The edge of this jacket, when the latter is adjusted, will roll prettily to the closing, after the manner of a round lapel, such as is seen on cloth jackets closing only over the bust.

KNITTED THREE–CORNERED SHAWL WITH DETAIL.

Nos. 21 AND 22.—This shawl is made of eider-down wool, and is knitted with 3 thick bone or wooden needles. In order to widen it at the point in a neat manner, a chain of 130 loops is crocheted and fastened in at the first row, as will be described later on. In knitting back and forth 2 loops of the chain are taken up in each row.

Begin the shawl as follows: Cast on 2 stitches, and knit back. Now, with the second needle, pick up 2 stitches of the crocheted chain, so that the latter will be next to the point of the needle; then with the first needle, knit them off in regular order. This will leave the chain at the middle of the work.

Next, with the second needle, knit off 2 stitches, and knit 1 loop of the chain; now with a *third* needle, knit another loop of the chain and the two remaining on the first needle. This widens 1 stitch on each of the foundation needles. This widening is done on the same plan throughout the work, and the pattern is made by knitting 2 rows and purling 2 alternately.

At the beginning of each row also widen as fol-

No. 21.—KNITTED THREE–CORNERED SHAWL.

with a crocheted border made as follows:

First row.—Single crochets separated by 7 chains.

Second row.—Two 'double crochets separated by a 5-chain around every 7-chain.

Third row.—One double crochet, 2 trebles, 3 chain, 2 trebles and 1 double around every 5-chain. Any other border preferred may be made, either in knitting or crochet.

KNITTED PETTICOAT.

(No Illustration.)

Germantown wool makes a good warm petticoat for the cold days of winter. Cast on any number of stitches divisible by ten.

First row.—K 9 and p 1.
Second row.—K 2 and p 8.
Third row.—K 7 and p 3.
Fourth row.—K 4 and p 6.
Fifth row.—K 5 and p 5
Sixth row.—K 6 and p 4.
Seventh row.—K 3 and p 7.
Eighth row.—K 8 and p 2.
Ninth row.—K 1 and p 9.
Tenth row.—Knit all plain.

Ten rows complete the pattern; repeat. The skirt should be knitted in stripes and joined; 80 or

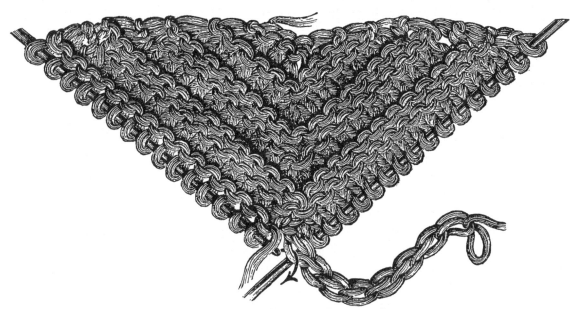

No. 22.—DETAIL FOR THREE–CORNERED SHAWL.

lows: K 1 and p 1 out of the second stitch.

Knit the shawl as large as desired and finish

100 stitches will be found a good number to work upon.

LADIES' MITTENS.

No. 23.—Use No. 19 needles and knitting silk. Cast onto each of 2 needles, 24 stitches, and onto a third, 32 stitches. Knit 5 rounds plain.

Sixth round.—N, th o, and repeat around the work. Knit 7 rounds plain.

Fourteenth round.—K 1, th o, k 2, sl 1, k 2 together, pass slipped stitch over, k 2, th o and repeat.

Fifteenth round.—Plain.

Repeat the last 2 rounds, 3 times more, but after each plain round, pass the first stitch of each needle onto the next needle, knitting the *first* one slipped *only* as the last stitch of the plain round. Now knit 5 rounds plain.

Then, knit 27th to 50th, inclusive, like 14th and 15th, slipping the stitches in the plain rounds, the same as before directed.

Fifty-first round.—Plain.

This completes the wrist portion up to where the fancy stripe for the hand begins. To make this stripe come in the right place, the following plan must be adopted: Knit plain across the first needle containing 24 stitches; knit 19 on the next or second needle, and pass 5 stitches from this needle onto the third needle; then pass 5 from the third needle onto the first, and divide the stitches on the first and second needles so that each will contain 24 stitches. The fancy stripe requires 29 stitches, and is in 12 divisions, each consisting of 8 rounds.

First round.—Sl and b, k 6, th o, k 2, th o, k 3, sl 1, k 2 together, pass slipped stitch over, k 3, th o, k 2, th o, k 6, n. Knit rest plain.

Second round.—Sl and b, k 5, th o, k 15, th o, k 5, n. Knit rest plain.

Third round.—Sl and b, k 4, th o, k 4, th o, k 3, sl 1, k 2 together, pass slipped stitch over, k 3, th o, k 4, th o, k 4, n. Knit rest plain.

Fourth round.—Sl and b, k 3, th o, k 19, th o, k 3, n. Knit rest plain.

Fifth round.—Sl and b, k 2, th o, k 6, th o, k 3, sl 1, k 2 together, pass slipped stitch over, k 3, th o, k 6, th o, k 2, n. Knit rest plain.

Sixth round.—Sl and b, k 1, th o, k 23, th o, k 1, n. Knit rest plain.

No. 23.—LADIES' MITTEN.

Seventh round.—Sl and b, th o, k 8, th o, k 3, sl 1, k 2 together, pass slipped stitch over, k 3, th o, k 8, th o, n.

Eighth round.—Plain. This completes one division. After repeating these 8 rounds 12 times, the fancy tip of the stripe is knit in 6 rounds as follows:

First round.—K 8, n, th o, k 1, th o, k 2, sl 1, k 2 together, pass slipped stitch over, k 2, th o, k 1, th o, sl and b, k 8. Knit rest plain.

Second Fourth and Sixth rounds.—Plain.

Third round.—K 12, th o, k 1, sl 1, k 2 together, pass slipped stitch over, k 1, th o, k 12. Knit rest plain.

Fifth round.—K 13, th o, sl 1, k 2 together, pass slipped stitch over, th o, k 13. Knit rest plain.

The plain portions of the mitten are knit upon the same plan as that given in the general rule for knitting mittens, on page 51. The thumb of this mitten begins in the 76th round.

A lining is knitted for the back and wrist of this mitten as follows:

Pick up on 3 needles the 80 stitches along the top edge and knit plain until you have a piece which is deep enough, together with the first 5 rows of the mitten which are turned down inside for a hem, to reach to the lower edge of the fancy portion of the wrist. Then cast off loosely around the plain portion of the hand, leaving enough stitches to reach across the fancy portion extending down the back. On these knit back and forth until the strip is long enough to extend under the fancy knitting. Fasten so that it will not interfere with the elasticity of the mitten.

KNITTED BED SOCKS.

No. 24.—Use Germantown wool, two colors. Cast on 98 stitches, and knit plain for 13 rows. Then k 46 st, n, k 2, n, and knit the remaining 46 st plain. For the next row, k 45, n, k 2, n, k 45. Now continue to narrow in every row at each side of the center as above directed until there are 60 stitches on the needle, or 28 stitches before the 1st narrowing and also after the 2nd; Then narrow every other time until there are 50 stitches on the needle or 23

No. 24.—KNITTED BED SOCK.

at each side of the narrowings. Now k 2 and p 2 alternately until the length desired is obtained; bind off and crochet a scollop on the edge. Then sew the sock together down the back and along the sole.

LADIES' KNITTED LEGGINGS.

No. 25.—These are warm coverings for the feet and legs, and will be found very useful for ladies who reside in the country and who have to drive some distance to dances or dinner parties, or for daytime drives in cold weather. They may be made of white wool if intended to be worn over white or light silk stockings, or of dark colors or black when for wear over dark stockings. Use Germantown yarn and four No. 10 needles in knitting them.

Begin at the top of the leg, cast 62 stitches on one needle. (This will make a legging of small size, which may be made larger by casting on more stitches when commencing the work).

First to Thirty-fourth rows.—Knit 2 and purl 2 alternately.

Thirty-fifth to Sixtieth rows.—Knit plain.

Sixty-first to One Hundredth rows.—Knit 2 together at the beginning and end of each alternate row, until 22 stitches only remain.

Now cast 23 stitches on a third needle, and work on these 23, and across the 22; cast on 23 more stitches; thus you will have 23 stitches each side the 22 which form the center of the knee. Knit 24 rows on all stitches, then 24 rows of knit 2 and purl 2 alternately; then knit 34 plain rows.

In the next round the decrease for the calf is commenced. Knit 2, knit 2 together, knit 60, knit 2 together, knit 2; knit 5 rows without decrease, then work a row decreasing after the first two and before the last 2 stitches; continue to decrease with 5 plain rows between, until you have decreased 9 times; then work 32 rows plain.

Now divide the stitches on 3 needles, 16 on each side and 18 in the center; knit across the first 16 stitches; knit 1 out of the back and 1 out of the front of the first of 18 stitches; knit 16; knit 1 out of the front and 1 out of the back of the next stitch; knit the 16 on the other needle; turn, and knit back; increase in the same way twice more, with the plain row between.

No. 25—.LADIES KNITTED LEGGING.

Now work only on the 24 stitches on the center needle; work 12 rows on these, then work a row, decreasing by knitting 2 together at the beginning and end of the row; knit 12 rows; then work a row, decreasing by knitting 2 together at the beginning and end of this row; knit 12 rows.

Now pick up 1 stitch at the end of each ridge

No. 26—KNITTED PETTICOAT.

down each side of front; then work 6 rows on all the stitches, and cast off.

Sew the legging together up the back of the leg, and sew the cast-on stitches at the under part of the knee to the edge of the decreased rows; this will form a kind of gusset.

KNITTED PETTICOAT.

No. 26.—In knitting this garment Germantown wool and 2 No. 10 wooden needles are used. The petticoat is made in 2 separate widths each 36 inches long, and 42 wide at the bottom. For each of these widths cast on 273 stitches. Knit back and forth, plain, for 4 rows. Then for the first pattern row, knit as follows: Knit 1, * k 2 together, make 1, k 1, make 1, k 1, k 2 together, k 1. Repeat from * to the end of the row.

Second, Fourth, Sixth, Eighth and Ninth rows.—Purl.

Third, Seventh and Tenth rows.—Plain.

Fifth row.—Same as 1st pattern row. Repeat 3 times more from 1st *. There will then be 40 rows.

Forty-first row.—Knit plain. In this and all following rows, decrease 1 stitch at the beginning to form the slope.

Forty-second row.—Purl.

Forty-third and Forty-fourth rows.—Purl 2, knit 1. Repeat from the 41st row until you have the required length.

Owing to the decrease, the number to be knitted or purled, as the case may be, at the beginning of each row must necessarily be irregular; but care must be taken that the one stitch forming the perpendicular rib is kept in a straight line.

KNITTED CHENILLE HOOD.

NO. 27.—KNITTED CHENILLE HOOD.

Nos. 27 AND 28—This hood is knitted from wired chenille on thick wooden needles and is made in triangular shape. It is 55½ inches long at the longest (front) edge, 12⅝ inches across the middle and 3¾ inches wide at each end.

It is begun at one end on a foundation of 6 stitches and knitted back and forth very loosely. (See No. 28). From the 6th to the 30th rows, increase 1 stitch at the end of every row as you work back, thus increasing by 13 stitches. Knit to the 36th row in which widen 1 stitch. Knit to the 42nd row, and from this row to the 52nd row inclusive, widen by 1 on each row as before. This will make 20 stitches that have been added since the first row.

After 2 rows more without increase, the middle of the hood is reached. Knit the other half to correspond with the first, narrowing instead of widening. The fringe is of chenille in loops 3⅜ inches long. It is crocheted in the manner described for the cape seen on page 74. It may be made as heavy as desired by adding more or less loops to the stitches.

LADIES' KNITTED VEST. (BASKET PATTERN.)
(For Illustration see Page 73.)

No. 29.—This vest is made with Belding's knitting silk and No. 17 steel needles.

Cast on 111 stitches for the lower edge of the front portion to begin the border, and knit back and forth, always slipping the first stitch of every row.

First, Third and Seventh rows.—Knit plain.
Second, Fifth and Eighth rows.—Purl.
Fourth and Sixth rows.—Sl 1, * m 1, k 3, sl 1, k 1, pass slipped stitch over, k 2 together, k 3, m 1, k 1 and repeat from * to end of row.
Ninth row.—Plain.
Repeat from fourth to ninth row inclusive.
Sixteenth row.—K 2 together, k 1, k 2 together, * k 2 together, k 9, and repeat from * till within 7 stitches of the end of the row; k 2 together, k 2,

k 2 together, k 1. This completes the border and leaves 98 stitches on the needle.

Work for the basket pattern as follows:
First and Third rows.—K 5, p 3, * k 7, p 3 and repeat from * to the end of the row.
Second row.—K 3, p 7 and repeat, ending with purl 5.
Fourth row.—Plain.
Fifth and Seventh rows.—P 3, k 7, and repeat ending with purl 5.
Sixth row.—P 5, k 3, * p 7, k 3 and repeat from * to the end.
Eighth row.—Plain.
Repeat these 8 rows until there are 18 blocks or 144 rows of knitting. If desired longer, knit until there are 21 blocks.

For the Shoulders: First row.—K 5, p 3, k 7, p 3, k 7, p 3, k 1, pass the next to the last stitch over the last one, and continue to cast off in this manner until 26 stitches remain on the left-hand needle. Then k 3, p 3, k 7, p 3, k 7, p 3.
Second row.—K 3, p 7, k 3, p 7, k 3, p 2, p 2 together.
Third row.—K 3, p 3, k 7, p 3, k 7, p 3.
Fourth row.—K 24, k 2 together.
Fifth row.—K 7, p 3, k 7, p 3, k 5.
Sixth row.—P 5, k 3, p 7, k 3, p 5, p 2 togther.
Seventh row.—K 6, p 3, k 7, p 3, k 5.
Eighth row.—K 22, k 2 together.
Ninth row.—P 3, k 7, p 3, k 7, p 3.
Tenth row.—K 3, p 7, k 3, p 7, k 1, k 2 together.
Eleventh row.—P 2, k 7, p 3, k 7, p 3.
Twelfth row.—K 20, k 2 together.
Thirteenth row.—K 3, p 3, k 7, p 3, k 5.

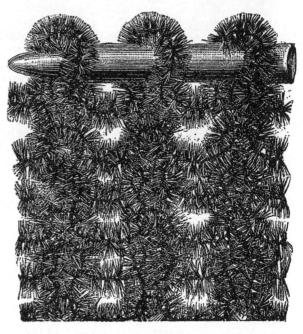

NO. 28.—DETAIL FOR KNITTED CHENILLE HOOD.

Fourteenth row.—P 5, k 3, p 7, k 3, p 1, p 2 together.
Fifteenth row.—K 2, p 3, k 7, p 3, k 5.
Sixteenth row.—K 20.

Seventeenth row.—K 7, p 3, k 7, p 3.
Eighteenth row.—K 3, p 7, k 3, p 7.
Nineteenth row.—K 7, p 3, k 7, p 3.
Twentieth row.—Plain and cast off.

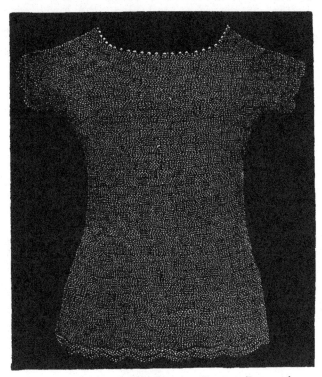

No. 29.—Ladies' Knitted Vest. (Basket Pattern).
(For Directions see Page 72.)

Now work upon the other shoulder beginning at the neck edge. The first row is already knit.
Second row.—K 2 together, p 7, k 3, p 7, k 3, p 5.
Third row.—K 5, p 3, k 7, p 3, k 7, p 1.
Fourth row.—K 2 together, k 24.
Fifth row.—P 3, k 7, p 3, k 7, p 3, k 2.
Sixth row.—P 2 together, k 3, p 7, k 3, p 7, k 3.
Seventh row.—P 3, k 7, p 3, k 7, p 4.
Eighth row.—K 2 together, k 22.
Ninth row.—K 5, p 3, k 7, p 3, k 5.
Tenth row.—K 2 together, p 3, k 3, p 7, k 3, p 5.
Eleventh row.—K 5, p 3, k 7, p 3, k 4.
Twelfth row.—K 2 together, k 20.
Thirteenth row.—P 3, k 7, p 3, k 8.
Fourteenth row.—P 2 together, p 6, k 3, p 7, k 3.
Fifteenth row.—P 3, k 7, p 3, k 7.
Sixteenth row.—K 20.
Seventeenth row.—K 5, p 3, k 7, p 3, k 2.
Eighteenth row.—P 2, k 3, p 7, k 3, p 5.
Nineteenth row.—K 5, p 3, k 7, p 3, k 2.
Twentieth row.—Knit plain and cast off.
Knit the back of vest the same as the front. Join the two at the shoulder edges; also under the arms, leaving a space at the top for the arm-holes.
For the Sleeves.—Cast on 69 stitches for each, and work 15 rows like the border, making 1 additional plain stitch at the beginning and end of each row.
Sixteenth row.—Plain, narrowing once in the row, so as to leave 68 stitches on the needle.

Then knit 8 rows of basket pattern and cast off loosely.

Make a gusset in the sleeve by casting on 16 stitches and knitting 26 plain rows. Cast off. Sew up the sleeve and join it to the body, taking care that the gusset comes under the arm.

Crochet a tiny scollop-edge about the neck, making a row of holes for a ribbon with double crochets.

This vest may be knitted of Saxony yarn, if preferred.

LADIES' KNITTED LEGGINGS.

No. 30.—These leggings are knitted with fine, black, woollen stocking yarn and steel needles. Begin at the top, casting on 104 stitches, and knit in rounds.

First round.—Work in plain knitting throughout.

Second round.—This forms a row of holes through which an elastic braid is run when the article is completed. To make the holes, knit as follows: Th o and knit 2 together, 5 alternately, around the work. In the third round the put-over represents a stitch.

From the 3rd to the 138th rounds, work in ribbed knitting, 2 stitches plain and 2 purled alternately, in each round.

The bend in the knee is worked between the 61st and 91st rounds. In the 61st round knit only 65 stitches, leaving the last 39. In the 62nd round work only 26 stitches which leaves 39 at the other end. After this round, in every successive round including the 90th, add 1 stitch of those left in the 61st and 62nd rounds; at the 91st round add all those which still remain.

No. 30.—Ladies'
Knitted Legging.

From the 139th to the 152nd rounds, the first three rounds are in plain knitting throughout.

Next purl 3 rounds and knit 3 rounds. In the 148th round, knit 1 and purl 3 alternately.

In the 149th to the 151st rounds, purl 1 and knit 3 alternately.

In the 152nd round, knit 1 and purl 3 alternately.

Repeat the last 14 rounds 10 times more; and once more repeat from the 139th to the 147th round; but in the last two repetitions of the 10, at intervals of an equal number of rounds, narrow 4 times in each pattern —making 1 narrowing at the beginning of the round and one at the end.

The next 58 rounds are in the ribbed knitting—2 plain, 2 purled—and these are followed by 10 rounds for the bottom, made as follows:

First round.—* Knit 1, th o, k 1, p 1, th o, p 1, and repeat from * across the row.

Second and Third rounds.—K 3 and p 3 alternately.

Fourth round.—Knit 1, th o, k 1, th o, k 1, p 1, th o, p 1, th o, p 1, and repeat for all the rounds.

Fifth and Sixth rounds.—Knit 5 and purl 5 alternately.

Seventh round.—Knit 2, th o, k 1, tho, k 2, p 2, th o, p 1, th o, p 2, and repeat around the work.

Eight, Ninth and Tenth rounds.— Knit 7 and purl 7 alternately. Bind off and fasten the thread securely.

KNITTED CHENILLE CAPE.

NO. 31.—KNITTED CHENILLE CAPE.

NO. 31.— This cape is made of black feather-chenille and is knitted very loosely on large wooden needles—an inch and a-quarter in circumference. The edge is finished with loops of the chenille crocheted in according to directions given below.

Begin the cape at the lower edge, casting on 64 stitches. It is 40 rows deep.

Knit plain for 26 rows.

Twenty-seventh row.—Knit 15; * th o, k 1 and repeat from * six times more; knit 20, * th o, k 1 and repeat six times more from last *; knit 15.

Twenty-eighth row.—Knit plain, but knit each put-over in the preceding row through the back part of the stitch.

Twenty-ninth row.—K 15, k 2 together 7 times, k 20, k 2 together 7 times, k 15.

Thirtieth row.—Knit 16, k 2 together, k 1, k 2 together, k 22, k 2 together, k 1, k 2 together, k 16.

Thirty-first row.—K 15, k 2 together, k 1, k 2 together, k 20, k 2 together, k 1, k 2 together, k 15.

Thirty-second row.—K 14, k 2 together, k 1, k 2 together, k 18, k 2 together, k 1, k 2 together, k 14.

Thirty-third row.—K 13, k 2 together, k 1, k 2 together, k 16, k 2 together, k 1, k 2 together, k 13.

Thirty-fourth row.—K 12, k 2 together, k 1, k 2 together, k 14, k 2 together, k 1, k 2 together k 12.

Thirty-fifth to Fortieth rows.—Knit plain throughout, but at the beginning of each row cast off 4 stitches. At the end of the 40th row, cast off the remaining stitches.

Finish the neck, first with a row of single crochets and then with a row of picots as follows: * 1 single, a picot made with 3-chain and 1 single in first stitch of chain; skip 1 stitch and repeat from * Draw the thread through at the end of the row and secure it. Then make the fringe down the front as follows:

Bring the thread to the next stitch of the edge, make a loop through it, pull a loop through this loop, drawing it out to a length of 2½ inches.

Secure the first loop by drawing it tight. Remove the hook; take up another loop through the next stitch, draw a long loop as before through it, tighten, and repeat along the entire edge, making several loops through the corner stitches at the bottom of the cape; and along the lower edge make 2 loops in every stitch and draw each out 3 inches long instead of 2½ inches.

KNITTED KNEE CAPS.

NO. 32.—Use Berlin or Germantown wool or single zephyr. Cast 114 stitches onto 4 needles and work with a 5th as follows:

Knit in rib style for 47 rounds. The ribs are formed by purling 2 and knitting 2 alternately.

In the 48th round begin the gore which covers the knee by knitting off the first 26 stiches and knitting them separately back and forth, alternately purling and knitting 2 stitches. After knitting 2 rows in this manner, change the pattern by knitting the stitches that were purled and purling those that were knitted, thus forming small squares.

In knitting this gore, a stitch is taken from the needles at each side of the 26 stitches every time across after the 1st row, (this widens the gore) and the gore is knitted as above described and stitches taken from the needles, until there are only 42 stitches left of the original ribbed portion. This

NO. 32.—KNITTED KNEE CAP.

brings the gore to the points at the side and completes the upper half of it.

Now work the lower half of the gore separately narrowing once at the end of every row until only 26 stitches are left. Now take up 23 stitches at each side of these 26 stitches, along the selvedges of the gore, the same as you pick up the stitches for the heel of a stocking. This will bring you to the side points of the gore. Divide the stitches as evenly as possible on the four needles and then work in rib style, the same as at the top, 47 more rounds, being careful to have the ribs continuous with those of the upper portion of the article.

Finish the edges with a crocheted border worked as follows: 1 single crochet in every rib with 1 chain between. Next row, 4 double crochets under the chains, catching them down so as to lie flatly. Two colors may be used if desired.

KNITTED SKIRT.

No. 33.—Use Berlin wool or three-thread Saxony yarn in two colors, with one pair of bone needles No. 9, and one pair No. 11. The skirt is very quickly and easily made. It is composed of 12 stripes, each knitted separately.

Begin at the lower edge and cast onto one of the No. 9 needles 41 stitches.

First row.—Make 1, knit 19, slip 1, knit 2 together, pass slipped stitch over the two just knitted, knit 19.

Second row.—Make 1; knit to end of row.

Repeat these two rows throughout the work. The 3rd, 4th, 7th, 8th, 11th and 12th rows are knitted with one color and all the rest with the remaining colors.

To decrease the size of the petticoat toward the waist, knit with No. 11 needles after two-thirds of the length has been worked. The length of the petticoat must be regulated according to the size required. When all the stripes are worked, they are joined together on the right side with single stitches worked in crochet.

For the crochet edge, work with blue wool 1 double into the edge of knitting, 4 chain, 1 treble into first of 4 chain, 1 double into petticoat. Repeat all round.

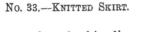

NO. 33.—KNITTED SKIRT.

The top of the petticoat is sewn to a deep yoke of white linen. A knitted lace ruffle may be placed under the lower edge.

LADIES' PLAIN MITTENS WITH FANCY TOPS.

No. 34.—Use 4 No. 19 needles and ordinary knitting silk. Onto each of 2 needles cast 25 stitches, and onto the third, cast 30. Knit 5 rounds plain for a hem at the top.

Sixth round.—N, th o and repeat around the work. Knit 9 rounds plain.

Sixteenth round.—N, th o and repeat. Knit 2 rounds plain.

Nineteenth round.—K 1, th o, k 3, sl 1, n, pass slipped stitch over, k 3, th o, and repeat.

Twentieth round.—Plain.

Now pass the first stitch on the first needle onto the needle back of it, and knit as the last stitch in the plain round.

Twenty-first round.—K 2, th o, k 2, sl 1, n, pass slipped stitch over, k 2, th o, k 1, and repeat.

Twenty-second, Twenty-fourth, Twenty-sixth and Twenty-seventh rounds.—Plain.

Twenty-third round.—Have 27 stitches on the 1st needle, and 24 on the 2nd. Then k 3, th o, k 1, sl 1, n, pass slipped stitch over, k 1, th o, k 2 and repeat.

Twenty-fifth round.—Have 26

NO. 34.—LADIES' PLAIN MITTEN WITH FANCY TOP.

stitches on the first needle, slipping the added stitch from the second needle, not from the third. Then k 4, th o, sl 1, n, pass slipped stitch over, k 3 and repeat.

Twenty-eighth round.—N, th o and repeat. Knit 6 rounds plain.

Thirty-fifth round.—K 1, th o, k 2, sl 1, n, pass slipped stitch over, k 2, th o and repeat.

Thirty-sixth, Thirty-eighth, Fortieth and Forty-first rounds.—Plain. After knitting the 36th round, slip the first stitch on the first needle onto the next one, and knit as the last stitch in the plain round.

Thirty-seventh round.—K 2, th o, k 1, sl 1, n, pass slipped stitch over, k 1, th o, k 1, and repeat.

Thirty-ninth round.—K 3, th o, sl 1, n, pass slipped stitch over, th o, k 2.

Repeat the last 7 rounds 5 times more thus completing the wrist.

Now knit plain for 8 rounds. Then begin the thumb and complete the mitten according to the instructions found in the general rule for knitting mittens, on page 51.

LADIES' KNITTED PETTICOAT.

No. 35.—Brown double zephyr is used for making a petticoat like the one illustrated. It is formed of as many lengthwise stripes as are required to make it as wide as desired, and these are crocheted together. A band of similar knitting is then added to the bottom of the skirt, and a knitted border is added to the lower edge of the band.

No. 35.—LADIES' KNITTED PETTICOAT.

To make each breadth, work as follows:

Cast on 28 stitches and knit plain, back and forth 4 times. This makes the plain stripe. The 7th time across begins the fancy stripe which is made as follows: Slip 1, * th o, slip 1 inserting the needle as in purling, knit the next stitch and repeat from * also knitting the last stitch.

Next row.—Slip 1, *, th o, slip next stitch (which was *knitted* in the last row), inserting the needle as for purling; knit the next stitch (which was slipped in the last row) and the put-over thread together, and repeat from * across the row, knitting the last stitch. Repeat this row 12 times more. Now, to bring the number of stitches down to the original 28: Knit 2, * narrow, k 1, and repeat from * across the row. This really forms the 1st row of the 2nd plain stripe, Knit 3 more plain rows to finish the stripe.

Repeat these two stripes until the breadth is long enough to extend from the belt to the knees, knitting the fancy stripe at the top about 5 inches deep, narrowing it slightly as it approaches the upper edge, making the narrowings 2 stitches in from each edge.

In knitting the breadth to be used as the left-side back-breadth, when within about a-quarter of a yard from the top (see engraving), add 10 more stitches to the work for the foundation for a fly or under-lap and knit them plain each time across. The back-breadths may be made wider than those at each side, by casting on more stitches for each at the beginning of the breadth; 32 may be used.

When all the stripes or breadths are joined by single crochets, add the band, which is knitted exactly like a plain stripe, but on a foundation of 24 stitches and long enough to reach around the petticoat.

Now make the border which is knitted as follows:

Cast on 18 stitches and knit and purl alternate rows until there are 4 rows, knitting the first and purling the last one, and narrowing at the end of the row. This makes one rib of the border.

Now begin the next row, purling a stitch and knitting a stitch out of the first stitch; purl the rest of the row. Then knit, purl and knit the next 3 rows.

This finishes the 2nd rib of the border. Repeat these two ribs until the border is long enough to extend around the skirt; join the ends and sew or crochet it to the lower edge of the band.

Make a band about the waist with single crochets, and close the skirt with button-holes left in the crochet-work, and buttons.

LADIES' JERSEY UNDERVEST.

No. 36.—Use Belding's knitting silk and No. 15 steel needles.

Cast on 108 stitches and knit across plain.

First row.—Sl 1, k 2, * th o, n, and repeat from * 7 times; th o, k remainder plain.

Second row.—Purl to th o in preceding row; k rest plain.

Third row.—Sl 1, k 2, * th o, n, and repeat from * 6 times; th o, k rest plain.

Fourth row.—Plain.

Fifth row.—Sl 1, k 2, * th o, n ; repeat from * 5 times, th o twice; purl remainder.

Sixth row.—Plain.

Seventh row.—Sl 1, k 2, * th o, n, repeat from * 4 times; th o, k rest plain.

Eighth row.—Purl to th o; k rest plain.

Ninth row.—Sl 1, k 2, * th o, n, repeat from * 3 times; th o, k rest plain.

Tenth row.—Plain.

Eleventh row.—K 15 plain; purl remainder.

Twelfth row.—Plain.

Thirteenth row.—Bind off 5, k 2, * th o, n, repeat from * 7 times; th o, k rest plain. Repeat from second row until there are 9 points and 37 ribs; then bind off. This forms one-half of the body. Knit the other half to correspond.

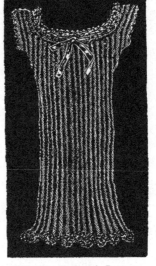

No. 36.—LADIES' JERSEY UNDERVEST.

Cast on 38 stitches, pick up stitches along the top of one side of the body, cast on 38 more, and pick up the stitches across the top of the other side of the body, all on one needle. Knit 3 rows plain.

Fourth row.—Sl 1, k 1, * th o, n, k 2 and repeat from * across the work.

Knit 4 more rows, plain, and bind off. This forms the band and shoulder straps.

For the Sleeve.—Pick up 22 stitches at each side

of the body next to the shoulder strap, and 38 along the shoulder strap. Purl 1st row, narrowing at the beginning and end, and repeat until there are 52 stitches left and 5 ribs formed. (A rib consists of 3 rows). Knit 1 rib without narrowing, and bind off.

Make a similar sleeve at the other side, and then close the sides in under-arm seams.

Finish the band and sleeves with a border of small crocheted scollops.

KNITTED LEGGINGS.

No. 37.—Use Nos. 13 and 14 needles and Germantown yarn in making these gaiters.

Cast 20 stitches on each of two needles and 23 on the third; the odd stitch is for the seam; this is purled at the end of last needle in one round and knitted in the other; as this stitch is worked the same throughout, we shall not mention it in the following directions.

For the ribbed top knit 2 and purl 2, for 2½ inches.

Now purl 2 rounds and knit 1 round; then commence the

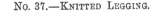
No. 37.—KNITTED LEGGING.

pattern for the leg as follows:
First round.—Knit 1, * purl 4, knit 1, purl 1, knit 1; repeat from * all round and end with knit 1 before the seam stitch.
Second round.—Knit 1, purl 5, * knit 1, purl 6; repeat from * all round and end with knit 1 before the seam.
Third round.—Knit 1, * purl 1, knit 2, purl 1, knit 1, purl 1, knit 1; repeat from * and end with knit 1.
Fourth round.—Knit 1, * purl 1, knit 2, purl 2, knit 1, purl 1; repeat from * all round;knit the last stitch before the seam. Repeat from the first round for 4½ inches.
Now continue the pattern, but decrease for the ankle by knitting the 2nd and 3rd stitches of the first needle together, and the last two stitches but one of the last needle together, that is, decreasing on each side of the seam stitch in every third round, until you have only 50 stitches left, then purl 1 round and knit 1 round; now take the No. 13 needles and knit 1 and purl 1 alternately all round for 2 inches. Now on the 21 stitches at

the back of the leg, that is 10 on each side of the seam, work with 2 needles like the heel of a stocking, knit 1; and purl 1 alternately for 1¾ inch; put the stitches on a piece of cotton, and tie it to prevent their falling off; pick up 12 stitches at the right side of the heel, knit across the front of foot, still preserving the rib; pick up 12 stitches on the other side of heel; continue to work on the side of heel and front stitches backwards and forwards; the side of heel stitches are knitted plain, and the front of foot stitches ribbed; decrease in every 3rd row by knitting the last 2 of side of heel stitches together on the right side of front, and the first 2 on the left side until all the side stitches are taken in, then work on the front stitches for about an inch. Now pick up the stitches down the side of front, take the stitches off the cotton on to a needle and pick up the stitches on the other side of front; purl 4 rounds, then cast off; sew a strap of webbing about 2 inches long to the stitches next the heel.

LADIES' KNITTED MITTENS.

No. 38.—Cast onto each of 2 No. 19 needles, 25 stitches, and onto a 3rd, 30 stitches, making 80 in all. Knit 5 rounds plain.
Sixth round — Narrow, th o and repeat around the work.
Knit 7 rounds plain.
Fourteenth,Fifteenth, Sixteenth and Seventeenth rounds.—Th o, k 3, n, and repeat.
Eighteenth round.—Knit plain.
Nineteenth round.—K 1, th o, sl and b, k 2 and repeat.
Twentieth round.—K 2, th o, sl and b, k 1 and repeat.
Twenty-first round.—K 3, th o, sl and b, and repeat.
Knit 14 rounds plain; then knit 38 rounds in ribbed knitting (k 2, p 2).
The thumb is begun in the 77th round. The first 5 rounds of the mitten are turned in and hemmed. The rest of the directions for knitting the mitten will be found in the

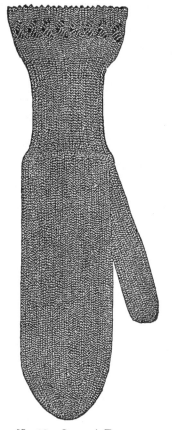
No. 38.—LADIES' KNITTED MITTEN.

general rule for knitting mittens, on page 51.
Plain loose mittens of this style are comfortable articles to wear either over kid gloves on very cold days, or without gloves. Fine wool makes a warmer mitten than silk and is almost as pretty in effect.

LADIES' KNITTED SILK STOCKINGS.

No. 39.—This stocking is knitted with knitting silk of dark color and No. 18 needles. The leg and the top of the foot are in ribbed knitting, and the heel, toe, and sole in plain knitting. Cast 124 stitches equally on 4 needles, and knit 317

rounds for the leg, 2 stitches plain, and 2 stitches purled alternately; begin to narrow for the ankle in the 199th round by knitting 3 stitches together after the first 7 stitches, and before the last 5 on each side of the middle of the back, and in the 200th round narrow in the same manner after the first 6, and before the last 4 stitches; repeat the narrowing in the 222nd and 223rd, 246th and 247th, and 269th, and 270th rounds. After completing the 317th round, put the last 24 and the first 22 stitches together on one

NO. 39.—LADIES' KNITTED SILK STOCKING.

needle for the heel; add a thread of fine silk to the working thread to strengthen it, and knit 38 rows forward and back, 1 plain and 1 purled alternately, so that all will look plain on the right side, and always slipping the first stitch. When there are 18 stitches up each side of the heel leave off with a purled row. In the next row * knit to the 5th stitch pass the middle, slip the 5th, knit the next, and pass the slipped stitch over it; knit the next, turn, slip the first stitch, and purl to the 5th stitch past the middle; slip the 5th, purl the next, and pass the slipped stitch over it; purl the next, turn, and repeat from *, always slipping the first stitch on the other side of the opening formed until all the stitches are knitted off from each side. Take up the 18 stitches on the left side of the heel on a needle, knitting each as it is taken up; knit around to the opposite side, and take up the 18 stitches on the right side in the same manner. In the next 70 rounds the 46 stitches on the top of the foot are worked in ribbed knitting, and the stitches for the gussets and sole in plain knitting; to form the gussets, narrow in the next 2nd and in every following 4th round on the stitches next to the ribbed knitting of the front on each side; narrow 9 times in all on each side. After the 70th about 76 more rounds are required to complete the stocking. In the 23rd of these knit together the first 2 and the last 2 stitches of the instep, and the first 2 and the last 2 stitches of the sole; then in every following 4th round narrow on both sides of each of the first narrowings, 12 times in all. Next, in order to point the stocking, work 2 similar narrowings in a straight line above each of the first narrowings, and then narrow in the manner previously described in every following 2nd round until the narrowings of both

halves meet, whereupon knit 2 stitches together until all the stitches are used up.

KNITTED CUFFS.

No. 40.—Cast on 80 stitches and knit to and fro as follows, for 18 rows: Purl 3 rows, knit 3 rows. The foundation counts as the first row so that it must be purled off in the second row.

Now add or cast on 25 new stitches in the fourth row to begin the first of the loops seen. Knit them in the 5th and 6th rows and cast off in the 7th. At the end of the 10th and 12th rows the last stitches must be knitted together with the end stitches of the loop-part of the work.

Repeat from the 1st to the 18th rows 10 times; and in order to join the separate loops knit together the 5th to the 8th stitches which are cast on for the next loop with the 21st to the 18th cast on for the previous loop, also joining the last loop to the first.

Take up the foundation stitches onto another needle and knit them off together with those of the last row, to close the cuff.

The purled stitches of the loops form the right side when the work is turned back as seen in the picture.

KNITTED SHAWL.
(No Illustration.)

This shawl is not only easy to knit but is very pretty and effective. It may be made of Shetland or any wool of equal fineness. Use long coarse bone needles.

Cast on 225 stitches; knit across 6 times plain. *Seventh row.*—Slip the first stitch, knit 5, knit 3 together, knit last stitch without slipping it from the needle; then bring the wool forward and purl it, still keeping it on the needle; then put the wool back, and knit it this time, slipping it off; this makes 3 stitches out of 1; knit 3 together again, then as before, and so on until but 6 stitches remain; knit these plain. The last stitch before the 6 plain, must always be widened, if you narrow on commencing the row.

Eighth row.—Knit plain.

Ninth row.—Same as 7th, excepting widening the 7th stitch, and so on; that is, always widen the stitch that was narrowed before, and *vice versa.* Knit in this manner 230 times across; then knit 6 times

NO. 40.—KNITTED CUFF.

plain, and bind off loosely to complete the shawl.

TO STRETCH THE SHAWL.

Wring a sheet in clear water, and pin it to the carpet, then stretch the shawl, and pin closely around the edge over the sheet. Pin it at night, and in the morning the sheet will be dry, and the shawl stretched. Deep, crocheted scollops with fluffy edges form a pretty border.

KNITTED SLEEPING SOCKS.

No. 41.—Use Germantown wool and steel needles in two sizes, Nos. 12 and 14; 4 needles of each size will be required.

To begin: Take the No. 12 needles and on each of 2 of them cast 30 stitches, and 34 on a third needle. With the 4th knit.

First row.—Knit 2 and purl 2 alternately. Work in this manner for 1½ inch; then knit a row as follows: Throw the wool forward, and knit 2, alternately.

Work 1½ inch like the first row; then purl 8 rows. Now knit 1, purl 1, alternately for 6 inches.

The decrease is now commenced.

Mark a stitch in the center of a needle by tying a piece of cotton in it, knit 2 together before and after this stitch in every 5th round for 10 inches; in the next round divide the stitches as you would for the toe of a stocking, putting half the stitches on one needle for front of foot; the back half divide on 2 needles and work the stitches off on needles No. 14; decrease by knitting 2 together at the beginning and end of the front needle, at the beginning of the next needle, and the end of the third needle in every other round until 24 stitches only are left; cast off and sew up the toe. The top is turned down on the outside and hemmed leaving the " wool forward and k 2 row" as the edge.

No. 41. – KNITTED SLEEPING SOCK.

KNITTED UNDER CAP FOR ELDERLY LADIES.

No. 42.—This cap is to be worn under a bonnet, for added warmth. Use dark brown Saxony yarn or split zephyr and fine steel needles. Cast on 8 stitches and close into a circle.

First round.—Knit plain.

Second round.—Th o, k 1, and repeat.

Third and every odd round.—Knit plain.

Fourth round.—Th o, k 2 and repeat.

Sixth and every even round to the Twenty-sixth, inclusive.—Like fourth, except that there will be an extra stitch to knit between each put-over, in every round.

Twenty-seventh to the Forty-second round inclusive. —Knit plain.

Now leave 30 stitches for the back of the cap, and knit to and fro on the remaining 82 stitches, 36 rows, all to appear knitted on the right side. This effect is produced by knitting across and purling back.

Next take up the side stitches and knit 6 rounds in rib pattern k 2, p 2, to form the edge. Cast off the stitches and the cap is complete. The cap, knitted in pretty colors may be worn by a child; and in this event it may have a border of looped knitting, crocheted shells or swan's down about its edges.

KNITTED MITTS.

(No Illustration.)

Knitted mitts are necessary luxuries that are easily made of Berlin wool, Saxony yarn, etc., on No. 14 steel needles.

Cast on 39 stitches. Slip the first stitch of every row. K 1 row. For the thumb k 10, turn and k back.

Next row.—K 12, turn, and k back. Continue to k 2 stitches more every 2nd row until there are 28 stitches knitted off.

Next row.—K to the end. K 1 row.

Next row.—K 28, turn, and k back. Continue to leave 2 unknit till there are 10 on the needle.

Next row.—Cast off 10 and k to the end. K 1 row and cast on 10. K 12.

Next row.—K 9, p 1, * k 1, p 1; repeat from * 9 times, k 9. K 7 rows.

Next row.—K 9, p 1, * k 1, p 1; repeat from * 9 times; k 9. Repeat from " k 7 rows."

K 26 rows. Cast off, and on the right side, which is the other side from that on which the pattern rows were knitted, pick up 48 stitches, 1 in each turn along the top. K the 1st stitch of every row. K 36 rows ribbed, 2 plain, 2 purl, alternately, and cast off. Sew up and double over this ribbed piece for a finish at the top of the wrist.

The other mitt is knitted the same, except that the 3 pattern rows on the back of it are knitted on the opposite side.

Mitts of this kind are very useful during shopping expeditions, sleigh-rides, long walks, skating, coasting and various pastimes where an ordinary glove is not warm enough and mittens are considered

No 42.—KNITTED UNDER CAP FOR ELDERLY LADIES.

too clumsy. Mitts leave the finger tips free, thus possessing an advantage over mittens. They may be made of black, blue, brown, drab or dark red; or, two colors may be united in knitting them, one color being used for the wrist-portion and the other for the hand and thumb; or, if two colors are used they may be knitted in stripes.

LADIES' KNITTED EVENING MITTENS.

No. 43.—These mittens, which are worn to protect delicate evening gloves, are knitted with white Saxony wool on rather coarse steel needles, as the work is to be quite loose. Cast 60 stitches on 3 needles, and knit 60 rounds in ribbed knitting, 2 stitches plain and 2 purled. Then follow with 70 rounds of plain knitting for the hand. In the 3rd round of the 70 begin to widen for the thumb gore; widen at both sides of the first 2 stitches to begin, and then 5 times thereafter, with intervals of 2 rounds between, in a line above the previous widenings; for the widenings, having knitted the first 2 stitches mentioned, knit a stitch crossed out of the succeeding horizontal mesh; (for crossed knitting, insert the needle downward at the back instead of upward at the front), and purl

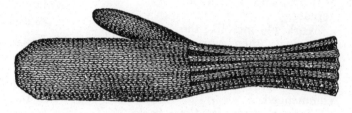

NO. 43.—LADIES' KNITTED EVENING MITTEN.

the following stitch; then having knitted the round, purl the stitch that precedes the 2 named, and knit 1 crossed out of the horizontal mesh succeeding it; at each successive widening round, the number of stitches between the widenings will naturally be increased. After the last widening round (the 18th round) knit two more rounds, then take the stitches of the thumb gore on separate needles and knit 24 rounds for the thumb, in the last four of which point it. Then continue the hand. In the first round, out of the mesh connecting the ends of the thumb stitches, knit two stitches crossed; in the following round knit two stitches together on both sides of these two stitches, and in the succeeding round knit each one of these stitches together with the one beside it, thus forming a small gusset. The hand is narrowed in the last 11 rounds; in the first of these, knit two stitches together at both sides of the first stitch and at both sides of the middle stitch, the narrowing before the stitch to be knit plain and that after crossed. In every following 2nd round narrow in the same manner; then in the last round divide the stitches into halves, and cast off, knitting the stitches of both halves together in pairs.

KNITTED OVER-SHOES.

No. 44.—Germantown wool of any dark rich color preferred may be used in knitting these over-shoes.

Begin at the top part of the back of the heel. Cast on 26 stitches. Work with 2 needles, knitting and purling alternately for 32 rows.

Thirty-third row.—Knit 8. Take a third needle, and knit 10 (leave the 8 stitches on the other needles for the present), purl and knit the 10 stitches alternately for the 10 rows.

After these rows (which must be finished as begun by a knitted row), knit off the 8 stitches

that were left before working the heel.

Forty-fourth row.—Purl 8, pick up the 10 side stitches of the heel, purl 10, pick up the 10 stitches on the other side of the heel, purl 8.

You will now have 46 stitches.

In the next 4 rows decrease 1 in every knitted row by knitting 2 together after the first stitch. Continue for 50 rows without increase or decrease, alternately knitting and purling.

In the 97th row cast on 24 more stitches, knit 6 rounds plain. You will need 4 needles for this.

In the 104th round, * knit 6, slip 1, knit 1, pass the slipped stitch over. Repeat from * all round.

Work 6 rounds without decrease in plain knitting.

One Hundred and Eleventh round.—* Knit 5, slip 1, knit 1, pass the slipped stitch over. Repeat from * all round.

Work 4 rounds plain knitting without decrease.

One Hundred and Sixteenth round.—* Knit 4, slip 1, knit 1, pass the slipped stitch over. Repeat from *.

Work 3 rounds in plain knitting.

One Hundred and Twentieth round.—Knit 3, slip 1, knit 1, pass the slipped stitch over. Repeat from *.

Work 2 rounds in plain knitting.

One Hundred and Twenty-third round.—Knit 2, slip 1, knit 1, pass the slipped stitch over. Repeat.

One Hundred and Twenty-fourth round.—Plain knitting.

One Hundred and Twenty-fifth round.—Knit 1, slip 1, knit 1, pass the slipped stitch over. Repeat.

In the next rounds knit 2 together until reduced to 1 stitch; fasten off on the wrong side.

NO. 44.—KNITTED OVER-SHOE.

With the 4 needles pick up all the stitches on the top of the shoe. Knit as follows:

First round.—Knit 2, purl 2. Repeat all round.

Second, Third, Fourth, Fifth and Sixth rounds.—The same as first.

Seventh and Eighth rounds. — Plain knitting. Cast off.

This shoe is intended to be worn over the boot in cold and frosty weather. It is fastened round the ankle with a bow of ribbon.

DIRECTIONS FOR KNITTING VARIOUS ARTICLES AND GARMENTS FOR WHICH NO ILLUSTRATIONS ARE GIVEN.

TO KNIT A VEST IN ONE PIECE.

This garment is knit all in one piece, beginning at the lower edge of one side, and is sewed up under the arm. Use Saxony or Spanish knitting yarn and quite coarse bone or wooden needles. It is a good plan to shrink the yarn before using or winding it. Dip the skeins in warm water, squeeze and shake them out and hang them in the air to dry.

Cast on 78 stitches, knit backwards and forwards for 22 inches, then increase one at the end of every row until you have 20 more stitches at each end than you had at starting. These 20 stitches form half the gusset under the arm. Now, knit across, and at the end of the row cast on 24 stitches; knit back and cast on 24 at the other end—these are for the sleeve. Knit 15 rows across the whole 166 stitches; then knit 48 stitches and cast off all except 48 stitches at the other end—this is the opening for the head. Knit 54 rows across this last 48 stitches, and then slip them onto a spare needle or a string; knit 54 rows across the first 48, and in the 55th row cast on as many stitches as you cast off (should be 70). Pick up the 48 stitches on the string and knit 15 rows across the lot, then cast off 24 stitches at each end and decrease one at each end till you have 78 stitches; knit 22 inches and cast off. Sew up under each arm, and finish with a crocheted edge around the neck and sleeves. These vests are more comfortable to wear if the body part is ribbed; and the sleeve might have an inch of ribs at the edge instead of crochet, as plain knitting curls up when worn.

Vests of this kind are very easily knitted in ribbed style, by purling 2 and knitting 2 stitches alternately throughout the work. They may be knited without any widenings at all, as they are very elastic and shape themselves to the figure. A sleeveless ribbed Lisle thread or Swiss wool vest is a good pattern to copy after in knitting the neck and shoulders. A crochet border may be added to the neck and arm-hole edges of a knitted vest for the insertion of ribbons; and a wide fancy border may be crocheted about the lower edges, unless a fancy border is knitted while making the garment.

Full or half-length sleeves may be knitted, sewed up and joined to the arm-hole if desired; but the small cap sleeves are not advisable as they roll up about the arm-hole in a very uncomfortable manner.

Some very pretty vests knitted from white Spanish yarn, were made in ribbed style in the low-necked sleeveless shape. The square neck was then filled in in a fancy crochet stitch until high enough to be drawn close about the neck with a ribbon. The top of the crocheted portion was large enough to easily admit the head. (No lengthwise opening had been left, but one could easily be arranged by crocheting the rows back and forth instead of round and round.) A pretty edge was crocheted about the arm-hole, and a border an eighth of a yard deep was crocheted about the lower edge. When the vests were on they fittted very snugly and there were no buttons to come off or imperfectly close them. Ribbon, run into the arm-hole borders held this part of the garment closely to the shoulder.

KNITTED SLEEVES.

Sleeves of this description are very comfortable to slip on under a loose or short cape or wrap. They may be made of Berlin wool, Germantown or Spanish knitting yarn, or any other yarn preferred. Four No. 14 steel needles will be needed in knitting them. Cast on 120 stitches—40 on each of 3 needles —and knit as follows :

For 60 rounds.—Knit 2, purl 2.

61st to 70th rounds.—Plain knitting.

71st to 80th rounds.—Knit 2, purl 2 alternately.

81st to 90th rounds.—Plain knitting.

91st to 100th rounds.—Knit 2, purl 2 alternately.

101st to 226th rounds.—Plain knitting, with the exception of the seam for back of sleeve, which is made in every 3rd round by knitting a stitch at the back instead of the front, as usual, and the decrease, which is made by knitting 2 together—that is, after working 2 stitches from the seam, you knit the 3rd and 4th stitches together, and knit the 3rd and 4th stitches together before the seam at the finish of the round.

The decrease is made in the 107th, 115th, 123rd, 131st, 139th, 147th, 155th, 163rd, and 171st rounds. Eight plain rounds between.

179th round.—After decreasing 2 on each side of the seam, knit 2 together 3 times more at equal distances in the round.

180th to 188th rounds.—Plain knitting.

189th round.—The same as 179th round.

190th to 200th rounds.—Plain knitting.

201st round.—The same as 179th round.

202nd to 209th rounds.—Plain knitting.

210th round.—The same as 179th round.

211th to 219th rounds.—Plain knitting.

220th to 244th rounds.—Knit 2, purl 2. Cast off.

Knit the other sleeve to correspond. If desired, sew a neck strap to the top of the sleeves.

A KNITTED SCARF OR "CLOUD."

A scarf or "cloud" may be easily knitted from Shetland or Ice wool, or from split zephyr as follows: (Use smooth bone or wooden needles.)

Cast on 300 stitches and knit 300 rows back and

forth. The knitting should be very loose, and when completed the "cloud" should be long enough to go twice round the neck and once round the head. Finish the ends with fringe or 2 large tassels made of the same kind of wool.

KNITTED COMBINATION.

Angola wool is used for this garment, which is knitted on No. 16 or 18 needles. Begin at the knee, as follows: Cast on 90 or 100 stitches, and rib a piece 4 inches long; then plain all round, increasing on the inside of the leg each side of the seam (for which 3 stitches should be left), 7 times every 5th row, then 15 times every 4th row, then 13 times every 3rd row. This makes 70 increases. At the seam turn back, purl 2 stitches, and then purl 2 together, then purl to end of row. Knit back plain, knitting twice into the 2nd stitch. Continue purl and plain alternately as though on 2 needles. Purl 2 together in every 4th row 10 times, and increase 1 stitch every 2nd row 20 times at the other end. There will now be 170 or 180 stitches in all. Both legs are done the same so far, except in purling back from the seam in the 2nd leg increase 1st stitch and knit 2 together last, to make the right and left legs. Now take the two ends where 2 stitches have been knitted together, and join them, making plain and purl from one end to the other, and slip the 1st stitch at each end. Continue knitting 2 together every 4th row 14 times in the center as before. Now count 64 stitches each side of the front seam, and then count 4 more stitches for a seam, and knit 2 together each side of the seam. Knit 2 together each side of the 3 seams every 4th row 6 times. There are now 108 stitches inside the two side seams. Take the 72 stitches outside one of the side seams, and knit backwards and forwards on that back piece only. Leave 2 or 3 stitches inside each time to make the outside end longer than the end by the seam. About 30 rows must be done like this, and in the last 10 rows knit 2 together every row at the outside end. Knit round and work the same the other side. Of the 20 stitches that were before increased each side, 10 have been knitted off; the other 10 must now be lapped over each other at the back, where the ends are joined together; and where the 20 stitches lap, each 2 stitches must be knitted as one. Now there are 220 stitches altogether on the needles. Work round all plain on the 4 needles as usual for about 4 inches; then divide in half in front and purl back as on 2 needles. Work thus for 15 or 16 rows, then take 56 stitches by the opening in front, and knit twice into each of the 4 middle stitches; knit to end of row and purl back. Next row knit twice into each of the 8 middle stitches; make 3 rows; then knit twice into each of the 12 middle stitches. There are now 80 stitches. Make 3 inches; then knit the 2 stitches each side of the 24, knit 2 together every 3rd row till the 24 are reduced to 3, as before. Knit 3 inches more; then cast off 12 inches on the inside for the neck, and make 2 inches more to go over the shoulder, and cast off. Make the other front side the same. Take the 108 stitches at the back and work till it is as long as the

front; then cast off 24 stitches in the center. Take the 42 stitches on one side and make 2 inches more, and knit together with the front shoulder-piece and cast off. Make the other shoulder the same.

Now pick up the slip stitches round the arm-hole on 4 needles, and underneath the arm, to make the gusset, leave 2 stitches for the seam, and knit 2 together each side of it every other row, till there are only 70 or 80 stitches left. Knit the sleeve as long as required; rib 2 inches to make it fit closely, and cast off.

With 2 needles pick up the stitches down the opening at the back, and make it as much broader as it is required. Make each side separately. On one side, for the button-hole, cast off 3 stitches, and in their place put on 3 stitches more.

To make a low neck, cast off when the 3 inches are done, after increasing the 24 stitches; the 40 stitches, or the shoulder-piece must also be made longer; cast off at the back as in front.

KNITTED NIGHT OR BED SOCKS.

With No. 12 needles and white Germantown yarn, cast on 70 stitches; this is for the sole of the foot. Knit 18 plain rows, making 1 stitch by knitting 2 in the 2nd stitch at the beginning of each row. Then knit 18 more rows, increasing at the beginning of each alternate row only; this end is for the toe. In the 37th row you ought to have 97 stitches on your needle. Work from the toe to the heel, and knit 60 stitches; turn, knit back; on these 60 stitches knit 22 rows; then at the end of the 60 stitches cast on 37. Now knit 18 rows, decreasing 1 every alternate row at the toe end, then knit 18 rows, decreasing 1 at the beginning of each row, and cast off. Now pick up the 37 stitches for the leg, also pick up 11 stitches along the top of the 22 rows, and then knit the 37 left; on these knit 46 rows of knit 2, purl 2 stitches, then cast off loosely. Sew up the leg and the sole, drawing the toe-tip to form a nice square.

KNITTED EVENING WRAP.

White, double Berlin wool, and blue knitting silk or blue spangled wool, will make a pretty evening wrap. Use thick wooden needles, cast on 80 or 90 stitches with the white, and knit 6 rows; * join on the silk with a neat knot, and knit 4 rows. Break off and join on the white again, and knit 5 rows. Repeat from *, knitting alternate stripes of white and blue, and always being careful to have each fastening of wool on the same edge of the wrap, and there will then be a right and wrong side to the work.

When the silk is nearly used up, make two large tassels about 5 inches deep with the white, interweaving a little of the silk. Having knit with the white last, cast off, draw each end together with a needle, and fasten a tassel at each end. The wrap should be about 2½ yards long. A hood for the head might be formed on one end by omitting the tassel, drawing the ends together in the necessary shape, and finishing with a ribbon bow. Pompadour wool might be used in place of the silk.

KNITTED THREE-CORNERED SHAWL.

The materials required are equal quantities of white and blue single zephyr, or Shetland floss, and one pair of long knitting needles, No. 10.

This shawl is easily made, as it is in plain knitting throughout. It is a half or three-cornered shawl, and the work is begun at the edge of the border; that is, you must cast on the stitches for both sides of the shawl; 700 will be required. Begin with the white yarn.

Work 6 rows, and in each alternate row knit 2 together, at the beginning, middle and end of the row.

Six rows blue, 6 rows white, 24 rows blue, 6 rows white, 6 rows blue. Knit the remainder of the shawl with white.

The fringe is of the blue wool. It is made by knitting the wool four times double upon steel needles—No. 14—as you would knit a garter; knit as tightly as possible. When you have finished the knitting, steam it over boiling water, until quite damp, and while damp, press it with a flat iron until dry. Put a cloth over the wool, and be careful not to scorch it. Pull out the knitting gently, so as not to destroy the crimp. Cut it in lengths of ten inches, keeping the four strands together, and with a large-eyed, wool-needle draw through the outer loops of the border. Bind round four strands of the wool with white silk floss at equal distances. When the fringe is tied in, the shawl is complete. This will be found a very serviceable design for a Summer wrap, as it is comparatively light, yet sufficiently warm.

ROUND SHOULDER CAPE IN LOOP KNITTING.

Round shoulder capes in loop knitting require about 12 ounces of Berlin wool or Germantown, and bone needles No. 9. Cast on 32 stitches. Knit 3 rows plain.

Fourth row.—* Put the needle into the first stitch, wind the wool between the needles and over the two fingers of the left hand 4 times, and again between the needles; draw the stitch through. Knit all the stitches of the row in the same way. Knit 5 rows plain. Repeat from * until there are 8 rows of loops.

Knit 10 more rows of loops with 5 plain rows between, decreasing at the beginning and end of each row of loops by knitting 2 stitches together. Cast off. Knit 7 pieces the same way and sew them together. Knit a strip of loops with the 5 plain rows between for the neck, and sew it to the cape. Line this collar with ribbon, leaving ends to tie.

For a cape of a smaller size, use bone needles No. 8, and cast on 23 stitches. Knit 3 rows plain. Repeat from * to * as for the larger cape, until there are 10 rows of loops, then decrease by knitting 2 together at the end of the 3rd row, and continue to decrease in the same way until there are 10 stitches left. Cast off. Knit 8 of these pieces, and sew them together. For the collar cast on about 8 stitches, and knit rows of loops with 5 plain rows between. Make this of the size required, and sew it on the cape.

KNITTED CLOUD.

This is a simple and showy design for a knitted cloud. For a brunette, contrasting threads of pale lemon Berlin and black Andalusian wool, make a pretty combination. A pretty contrast for a fair person, is delicate blue Berlin and pink Andalusian. For an elderly lady, cream Berlin and pure white Andalusion is extremely effective. The same pattern looks equally well made of Saxony and knitting silk, but whatever threads are used, they must not be of the same size. Two rather large, long rubber needles are needed. With Berlin wool cast on the number of stitches required to make the cloud as wide as you desire it. Eighteen inches wide and two or two and a-half yards in length, make a large cloud or scarf. Knit 2 plain rows, then knit 2 plain rows with Andalusian wool. Repeat the two stripes throughout the entire length of the cloud. It is unnecessary to break the threads at end of each row. Just let the thread you are not working with hang loosely at one side until you knit back again.

BED SOCKS.

Use white Berlin or Germantown wool, and two No. 5 needles. Cast on 40 stitches and for 20 rows knit in rib style—2 plain, 2 purl. At the end of the 21st row cast on 12 more stitches, and knit back plain, casting on 12 more stitches at the end of this (22nd) row. (All the rest of the knitting is plain.) There will now be 64 stitches on the needle. Increase at the end of every row for 10 rows, when you will have 74 stitches on the needle. Next knit 6 rows plain. Then decrease at the end of every row until the number of stitches is again 64, and cast off. Fold the work together and sew it up. The sock will prove to be of excellent shape.

KNITTED BEADED SILK CUFFS.

Thread a whole ball of knitting silk, scantily, with round beads of the same or a contrasting color. The whole ball must be threaded before beginning, because beads cannot be added after the work is begun without breaking the thread.

Use rather fine needles, and cast on 10 stitches; knit back, turn, and knit back again, pushing a bead onto each loop as you knit it. The beads are only on the alternate rows. Continue until you have 45 rows of beads, then cast off, and sew up the cuff. If the cuff is too long, cast on fewer stitches.

KNITTED WRISTERS.

On each of two needles cast 20 stitches, and 30 on 1, and knit around once, plain. Then knit 1, th o, knit 3, slip 1, narrow, pass the slipped stitch over, knit 3, th o, knit 1, th o, knit 3, slip 1, narrow and pass slipped stitch as before, and continue in this way around the work. Make a stitch at the end of each needle. To make a larger wrister, add as many scollops as required, using 10 stitches for each scollop. Bind off loosely.

"SWEATERS," BELTS, SCARFS, TIES, HUNTING CAPS, SUSPENDERS, ETC., FOR GENTLEMEN.

FOOT-BALL SWEATER.

NO. 1.—In making this sweater for a man whose chest measure is 36 inches, a pound and a-half of eight-fold Midnight Germantown wool (white) will be needed; also 3 bone or rubber knitting needles, each measuring half an inch around. Two steel needles, No. 12, will also be necessary in knitting the collar, wrists and border.

The body portion is knitted all in one piece and sewed up under the arms There is no opening except at the neck, which is made large enough to slip the head through.

To make the sweater illustrated, begin by casting 96 stitches onto one of the steel needles for the lower edge. In making a larger or smaller sweater, add or decrease 5 stitches for every inch (chest measure), larger or smaller.

First row.—Knit 2, purl 2, across the row.

Second row.— Work back, *knitting* the *purled* stitches

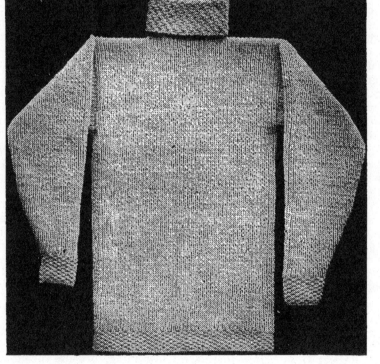

NO. 1.—FOOT-BALL SWEATER.

and *purling* the *knitted* ones to keep the pattern.

Third row.—Reverse the pattern so that the *knitted* stitches will come over the *purled* ones, and the *purled* stitches over the *knitted* ones. This will form the familiar block or basket pattern. Continue these details until the work is 9 blocks or 18 rows deep. This will form a tight, firm border.

Nineteenth row.—Now use the rubber needles and knit in rib style (knit 1, purl 1) for 157 rows.

In the next (158th row) rib 33 stitches for the right shoulder; then bind off 30 for the neck, and on a third needle rib the remaining 33 stitches for the left shoulder. Rib 3 rows on each shoulder; then on the right-hand needle cast 30 stitches to correspond with those bound off for the neck.

Now put all the stitches onto one needle and continue to rib 157 rows for the other side of the sweater.

Then take the steel needles (in the 158th row of this side) and knit 9 blocks for the border to match those first knitted.

Next sew up the sides, over-and-over, for 20 inches, beginning at the lower edges of the sweater.

To make the Sleeves.—For each take up 100 stitches around the arm-hole, using 2 needles and placing 50 stitches on each. The seam of the sleeve must come under the arm. Then rib back and forth for 15 rows.

Sixteenth row.— Put the stitches all onto one needle, and knit as before, narrowing one stitch at each end of the needle in every following fifth row, until you have narrowed 13 times, and the sleeve is 80 rows in length. Then narrow in every other row until the sleeve is 115 rows long.

Now take the steel needles and knit until there are 12 blocks of the border pattern (or 24 rows). Bind off, and sew up the sleeve.

To make and attach the Collar.— The collar is the most important part of the garment, so far as construction is concerned. It must be large enough to slip over the head and yet snugly fit the neck. Use the large needles. Cast on 30 stitches and knit back and forth in the block design until a strip long enough to meet around the head by stretching is made. Then sew the ends together, and try it on again to ascertain if it is large enough to quite easily slip it over the head and at the same time set well around the neck. In the sweater illustrated, the collar has a length of 44 blocks or 88 rows of knitting, and will fit a head of ordinary size. When the collar is made, sew it to the neck of the sweater, holding the latter full or stretching it, as necessary, to make it fit the collar-edge. The collar seam should come a little back of one shoulder. Turn the collar over half-way, as seen in the picture, and the garment is complete.

GENTLEMAN'S KNITTED HUNTING CAP.

No. 2.—This cap may be made with gray zephyr or Germantown yarn on coarse steel knitting needles. It is worked in plain and ribbed knitting, and is begun at the point above the crown in the middle of the front.

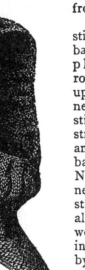

Cast on 20 stitches and knit back and forth, plain, for 55 rows. Now take up on 2 extra needles, the side stitches of the strip just knit, and work 60 rows back and forth. Next, on another needle, cast 24 stitches, and on all of the needles work 24 rounds in ribbed design, by knitting 2 and purling 2. This will form the throat portion.

No. 2.—GENTLEMAN'S KNITTED HUNTING CAP.

Now for the cape portion, divide the stitches onto 2 needles, placing 4 more on the back-portion than on the front, and having the 24 middle stitches of the front portion come directly underneath the 24 cast on above. Work 36 rows for the front portion and 24 for the back, narrowing once at the end of each row. Then cast off the remaining stitches.

Now take up all the stitches around the front edge, using 3 needles, and picking up an even number. Work in rib style, (knit 2, purl 2), for 10 rounds and cast off.

The cap may be made of any dark color such as brown or gray. Bright colors should not be used, as they are too conspicuous in the hunting field.

KNITTED SUSPENDERS.

No. 3.—These suspenders are knitted with Belding's knitting silk and coarse steel needles. To make them sufficiently firm the silk is used doubled.

Begin at the crossed ends, and cast on 14 stitches for each suspender. Knit back and forth plain for 5 rows. Now divide the stitches into two halves to form the button-hole, and knit back and forth on each division or half a sufficient distance to make a button-hole of the size usually seen in suspenders. Then slip the stitches all onto one needle again, and knit back and forth for about an inch and a half. Divide the stitches once more and make a second button-hole like the first one. Now put the stitches again onto one needle and knit back and forth 6 times, increasing one stitch at the end of each row, which will make the number of stitches 20.

Now begin the pattern or widest portion of each suspender as follows:

First row.—* Throw the thread forward, slip 1 as for purling, knit 2 together, and repeat from * across the row.

Knit back in the same manner, and repeat until the suspender is long enough. The length must be decided according to the size of the individual who is to wear the suspenders.

Now knit back and forth plain, decreasing one stitch at the end of each row until there are 16 stitches on the needle. Next divide the stitches evenly on 2 needles—8 on each—to form the straps. Each strap is about 6 inches long when completed. Knit back and forth plain on each division for about an inch and a-half; then divide again to form the button-hole, making it the same as directed before. Next put all the stitches onto one needle, and knit plain until the strap measures about 5 inches long, then make another button-hole, finish as before, knit back and forth two or three times, and bind off.

If preferred, the suspenders may be lined with silk or satin ribbon, and the straps may be of ribbon elastic single or doubled.

KNITTED SUSPENDERS.
(No Illustration.)

Knitted suspenders to be finished the same as the fancy ones seen on page 87 may be made as follows, either Belding's knitting silk or regular crochet silk being used for them: Cast on enough stitches to make the suspenders wide enough, being careful to have the number divisible by 4.

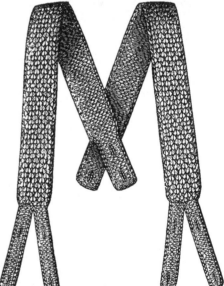

First row.—* K 1, n, th o, k 1 and repeat from * entirely across the row. *Second row.*—Purl. *Third row.*—*Narrow, thread over, knit 2 and repeat from * across the row.

Purl back for the fourth row the same as for the second.

No. 3.—KNITTED SUSPENDERS.

Repeat these four rows until each suspender is long enough, and then proceed to mount them as previously suggested. Pale-blue, Nile-green, old-blue, black, yellow, red and dark-blue are favorite colors for suspenders.

GENTLEMAN'S KNITTED SCARF–TIE.

No. 4.—Use black, blue, deep red or white crochet or knitting silk, and steel needles of a suitable size.

Cast on 32 stitches and knit in ribs as follows:

First row.—Plain.

Second row.—Purl.

Third row.—Plain.

Fourth row.—Purl.

Fifth row.—Plain.

This forms a purled rib.

Sixth row.—Plain.

Seventh row.—Purl.

Eighth row.—Plain.

Ninth row.—Purl.

This forms a plain rib.

Tenth row.—Purl.

Eleventh row.—Plain.

Twelfth row.—Purl.

Thirteenth row.—Plain.

No. 4.—GENTLEMAN'S KNITTED SCARF–TIE.

Fourteenth row.—Purl.

This forms the second purled rib.

Fifteenth row.—Purl.

Sixteenth row.—Plain.

Seventeenth row.—Purl.

Eighteenth row.—Plain.

Repeat from the first row for all the work.

The first purled rib comes on the outside of the work.

The scarf may be knitted in the four-in-hand or Ascot style as preferred. Either of the scarfs named may be used as a guide by which to shape the knitted tie; and the latter may be lined with satin ribbon or worn unlined, as preferred. Get the ribbon as wide as the widest portion and fell it in place, cutting and turning it under along the edges of the neck-band portion. The work should be narrowed down to 12 stitches for the band portion; and then if both ends of the scarf are to be wide, the work must be widened at the other end of the band. Narrow and widen by the usual methods as required to shape the tie to the desired form.

In a four-in-hand, the band portion need not be widened at all but knit to the end on the 12 stitches. A good length for a four-in-hand scarf is 42 inches. The broad portion should be about 18 inches long before the narrowing begins; then narrow quickly down to the 12 stitches and work the remainder of the length on them. See diagram No. 9 on page 88 for shaping a four-in-hand. The dotted lines show how the end may be knitted straight, if the knitter does not wish to widen the end as at the unbroken lines.

KNITTED LAWN TENNIS BELT.

No. 5 —A very handsome tennis belt may be made for either a lady or gentleman by the directions given below. Crochet or knitting silk of any color or colors desired may be used, and the needles selected should be of a size suitable for the silk.

As a rule crochet silk makes firmer work than knitting silk, which is the softer of the two.

Belt clasps of metal may be purchased at many stores, but in case they cannot be found, a cheap belt may be bought and its clasps removed to complete the knitted belt. The colors of a tennis club might be worked into a belt of this style, one color being used for the open-work, while between these sections might appear the other color.

The design illustrated is a strong webbing and showy as well; but any other design preferred may be developed in a belt. A lining of strong silk or satin ribbon, or of belt-webbing may be used, if considered necessary; and the belt may be made as wide or as narrow as desired by using more or fewer stitches for the foundation.

For the belt illustrated, cast on 32 or 34 stitches. Then knit in herring-bone pattern according to

No. 5.—KNITTED LAWN TENNIS BELT.

instructions found at No. 13, on page 13, of this book, making the belt as long as desired. The design used in knitting the scarf-tie illustrated at No. 4 on this page would form a pretty pattern for a belt; or, any of the fancy designs given in the first part of this book that may be deemed appropriate by the knitter, could be utilized in making a tennis belt. The latter may be worn by children as well as by ladies and gentlemen.

Fancy Suspenders.

No. 6.—Knitted suspenders, like knitted or crocheted neck-ties, are very popular gifts from ladies to gentlemen. They are easily made, and may be mounted with the straps and buckles at home, or, they may be taken to a haberdasher's where they will be completed in first-class style. . It is not always an easy matter to obtain the straps and buckles, unless a pair of suspenders is purchased and the attachment removed from them to be applied to the knitted suspenders. This is often done, however. The attachments of the suspenders illustrated were obtained from a manufacturer and the loops and cords were covered with narrow ribbon of the same color as that used for lining (two widths being necessary), the ribbon being neatly over-handed together over the under side of

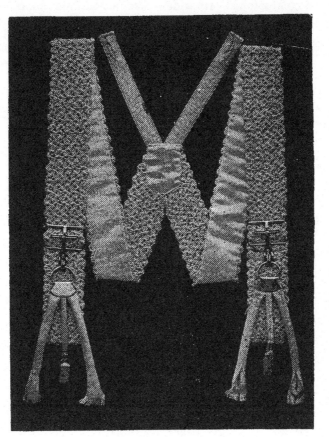

NO. 6.—FANCY SUSPENDERS.

the cords as may be seen by a close inspection of the engraving, which, for this purpose, shows one set of the loops turned wrong side out.

The straps are of ribbon elastic of the same color as the lining, and each has a button-hole made in the end. They are fastened to the suspenders under a machine-stitched shield of the satin ribbon used for the lining. These straps may be made double if desired; and they may be covered with satin ribbon put on very full in order to permit them to stretch as much as required.

The suspender portions may be knitted in knob-stitch, herring-bone, or any of the fancy patterns seen in the front part of this book or that may be otherwise known to the knitter.

Knitted Narrow Tie.

No. 7.—The knob-stitch design, found on page 12 of this book, will be a pretty pattern for a narrow tie.

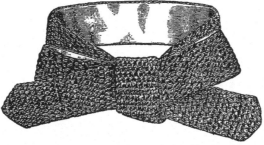

NO. 7.—KNITTED NARROW TIE.

Cast on enough stitches to make the tie about an inch wide, or a trifle wider if desired, and knit until the strip is long enough to extend around the neck and tie in the knot seen in the engraving. It may be lined or not, as preferred.

Knitted Jersey or Tennis Sash.
(No Illustration.)

A knitted silk sash for lawn tennis is a handsome present for a gentleman; or, it can be worn by small children under the name of a Jersey sash. Two ounces of smooth knitting-silk and two large steel needles are required in making it. It should be about two and one-half yards long when finished, or stretched, and may be knit by either of the following designs or patterns:

The first pattern is in *brioche* knitting, 3 stitches to a pattern, and is as follows: Cast on 54 stitches. (Knit loosely, and when completed also cast off loosely.) Make 1, slip 1, knit 2 together; repeat to the end, making all the rows alike.

The second design is like a web, every row the same, with 3 stitches to a pattern. It is knitted as follows: Cast on 54 stitches. Make 1, knit 2 together, knit 1; repeat to the end.

If the *brioche* design is used, you will need 360 lengths of fringe, each 14 inches long. The web design requires 340 lengths. Cut these lengths off first and knit all of the remaining silk into the sash.

Fringe each end by knotting 10 lengths of the silk into each of the *brioche* patterns or ribs, or into each of the holes formed by the web design. Knot half of each tassel together with half of the next one at about 1 inch from the top. The whole of each outside tassel must be knotted in with the next half. Shake out the fringe and cut the edges even. According to individual taste the fringe may be made heavier or lighter than suggested, or it may be knotted in any manner preferred. Blue or red will make a pretty sash.

KNITTED FOUR-IN-HAND TIE. (KNOTTED).

No. 8.—The tie here seen is also knitted in the knob-stitch design and is 42 inches long. Its wide end is about 2¾ inches long, and narrows down to 1⅛ inch for the band portion; and the latter width is kept to the end of the tie, according to the dotted lines in the diagram below, or slightly broadened to the dimensions indicated by the unbroken lines. When so widened, the widened end is about 6 inches long and 2¼ wide. The tie may be lined according to the directions given on this page; or, like the tie seen at No. 10, which is knitted according to the instructions given for

NO. 8.—KNITTED FOUR-IN-HAND TIE. (KNOTTED.)

No. 4, it need have no lining, although the latter renders it firmer. The diagram at No. 9 is simply to show the regular shape of a four-in-hand tie. The usual dimensions have been given in this description, and also in the instructions for No. 4 on page 86.

HOW TO LINE A KNITTED NECK-TIE.

When the neck-tie is knitted, baste under it a strip of silk cut lengthwise of the goods, or a strip of ribbon that is as wide as the widest part of the tie.

The silk strip must be cut wide enough to turn

enough in from the edge of the tie so that it will not show from the outside.

If the tie is lined with ribbon, fell its edges down without turning them in except where the tie narrows; here the ribbon must be cut to follow the outline of the tie and turned under and felled down the same as the silk lining.

No interlining is needed, and the lining should be of the same color as the tie, unless the latter is knitted so closely that the lining will not show through. A handsome cream-white tie was lined with cream-white satin ribbon, and across the ends the lining was confined by fancy stitching done in embroidery silk. The whole effect was both rich and very refined.

GENTLEMAN'S KNITTED NECK-TIE.
(No Illustration.)

A neck-tie may be knitted with silk of any shade desired, though black or white is generally used. Cast on, for the desired width of the tie, any number of stitches that may be divided by four and leave two remainder.

First row.—Knit 2 and purl 2 alternately.

Second row.—Knit 2 for the edge, * knit 2, purl 2, and repeat from *.

Make 6 more rows of the ribbed work and then begin on the pattern as follows:

First row.—* Knit 2, purl 2 together, th o, and repeat from *, knitting 1 at the end.

Second row.—Knit 4, * purl 2, knit 2 and repeat from *.

Third row.—Knit 2, * th o, purl 2 together, knit 2 and repeat from *.

Fourth row.—Knit 4, * purl 2, knit 2 and repeat from *

Repeat these two designs until the tie is as long as you desire; then finish the end with ribbed work to correspond with the other end.

NO. 10.—FOUR-IN-HAND TIE, UNLINED AND UNKNOTTED. (For Description, see Description No. 8.)

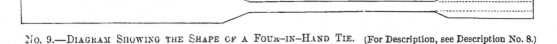

NO. 9.—DIAGRAM SHOWING THE SHAPE OF A FOUR-IN-HAND TIE. (For Description, see Description No. 8.)

in about one-fourth of an inch at each edge, and shaped to follow the outer edges of the tie. Fell it neatly along the edge and at the ends, just far

Made of Saxony or single zephyr this would form a pretty scarf for a child, and could be finished at the end with fringe.

GENTLEMAN'S STORM OR HUNTING CAP.

NOS. 11 AND 12.—In making this cap, use two shades of brown or drab Germantown yarn, and

No. 11.—GENTLEMAN'S STORM OR HUNTING CAP.

steel needles of two sizes. The cap may be worn with the shield or flap turned up, or let down as illustrated.

Begin at the crown, casting on one of the two finer needles, 210 stitches with the light wool. Work in rib stitch as follows:

First row.—K 1, m 1, sl 1 and repeat across the work.

Second row.—Knit plain except that every made stitch and every adjoining slipped one are knitted off *together*.

Repeat these two rows until there are 132 rows in all, or until the work measures 6½ inches in depth; its width should be 45¾ inches. The first 4 rows are light, the next 4 dark, the next 120 light and the next 4 dark.

Now cast off 48 stitches at the middle of the knitting for the face, leaving 81 stitches at each side. Continue to knit on each of the side divisions for 4 rows. Then cast the 48 stitches on again, and divide all of the stitches as evenly as possible on 4 needles, closing the circle when beginning the first row of the edge. Begin with the light wool and knit 1 row and * purl 3 rows. Then join the dark wool and knit 5 rows plain. In each row, after every 6th stitch, slip 2, with the wool at the back of the work. In the 6th row, knit all the stitches off with the light wool, which has been joined for the purpose. Repeat from *, but the stitches slipped in this division of the pattern come between those slipped in the first division (see No. 12) and in this way the pattern is reversed.

Ninety-three rows, knitted as directed, should make the edge or shield deep enough; but this point must be allowed for by tight or loose knitting.

Sew the seam of the head portion, rounding off the corners during the joining.

A "CABMAN'S COMFORTER."
(No Illustration.)

A "cabman's comforter" of Germantown wool is warm and useful for any person exposed to the cold, as it protects the back, chest and throat. The front and back are knitted first in separate pieces, then joined by knitting with 4 needles all around the neck. It is put on over the head, worn under the coat, and comes up to the ears, without covering them so as to muffle sounds. The directions are for one of a medium size, but they can easily be made larger or smaller.

About 5 ounces of wool are necessary and 4 No. 9 bone neeedles, 2 to be used in knitting the front and back, and all 4 for the neck. Cast on 10 stitches, and knit 1 row plain. * Knit the 1st stitch, throw wool forward to make 1; knit plain to last stitch; with the wool forward, slip the last stitch as if to purl. Repeat from * until there are 46 stitches on the needle. Knit plain 52 rows; knit the 1st stitch of every row, and with the wool forward, slip the last stitch as if to purl.

Knit another piece exactly like this, then commence the neck, using 4 needles. Join the two

No. 12.—DETAIL FOR BORDER TO HUNTING CAP.

pieces by knitting 2 together twice at each joining; knit 2, purl 2. There will now be 88 stitches. Knit this ribbed piece for the neck for about 6 inches, then cast off loosely.

GENTLEMAN'S KNITTED MITTS.
(For Illustration see next Page.)

No. 13—These useful mitts are worked with wool of two good contrasting colors, say black and white, ruby and grey, blue and fawn, or other colors according to taste, the first-named colors being for the wrist and edging of the mittens, the latter for the hand part. With black wool, cast 64 stitches on a No. 10 steel needle, and knit in ribbing, 2 stitches plain and 2 stitches purled for 40 rows. Take the white wool and for the hand part, knit as follows:

First row.—Plain.

Second row.—1 purl, 1 plain, and repeat.

Third row.—1 plain, 1 purl, and repeat.

Fourth row.—1 purl, 1 plain, and repeat. Repeat the last two rows 4 times.

Thirteenth row.—Beginning at the side where the tag end of wool hangs, slip 1, increase 1 by picking up the thread that lies directly under the next stitch and knitting it, purl 1, * knit 1, purl 1, and repeat from * to the end of the row.

Fourteenth row.—Purl 1, knit 1 and repeat.

Fifteenth row.—Slip 1, increase 1, knit 1, purl 1, * knit 4, purl 1 and repeat from * to the end.

Sixteenth row.—Purl 1, knit 1, and repeat. Continue thus, always knitting the stitch that was purled, and purling the stitch that was knitted in the last row, and increasing at the beginning of every row that commences on the tag-end side of the work, till you get 88 stitches on the needle, and 60 rows are knitted.

Sixty-first row.—Without any increase, work 24 stitches in ribbing (knit 1, purl 1) for the thumb; turn the work, and continue backwards and forwards on these 24 stitches till 10 rows are done; then take the black wool and with it knit 1 plain row and 4 rows of ribbing, and cast off. Recommence with white wool where you divide for the thumb, and knit 16 rows in pattern on the 64 stitches; then take the black wool and knit 1 plain row and 4 rows of ribbing, and cast off. This is the mitt for the left hand. The right-hand mitt is worked in the same manner, only you commence the increasing for the thumb at the end of the 13th row instead of at the beginning and consequently when you get to the 61st row you have the 64 hand-stitches to begin upon; so you complete the hand part first, and finish off the thumb afterwards. Sew the mitts up neatly.

KNITTED GLOVES.

No. 14.—With Andalusian wool and four No. 16 needles, this instruction will work out a large-sized glove for a lady, or one of small size for gentlemen. To make the glove larger or smaller, increase or diminish the number of stitches cast on, also using more or fewer for the fingers and thumb.

Cast on 65 stitches—that is, 23 on one needle, 22 on another, and 20 on the third; knit 3 and purl 2 for four inches.

For the hand, work 10 plain rounds.

Eleventh round.—Begin the increase for the thumb by knitting 1 and purling 1 in the first stitch. Finish the round plain.

Twelfth round.—Knit the first stitch; knit 1 and purl 1 in the next stitch; knit the rest plain.

Thirteenth round.—Plain.

Repeat the last three rounds until you have increased 26 stitches, making 91 stitches on the needles. Thread a Berlin needle with coarse cotton, and pass it through the 27 stitches knitted for the thumb; tie the cotton. Continue to work in the round for 21 rounds with the four needles.

We are now giving directions for working the right-hand glove, the palm of which is next the knitter and the thumb at the right side.

Now Commence Knitting the First Finger.—Knit 6; take a needle and cotton and pass it through all the stitches of the hand except the 13 last stitches; tie the cotton so as to secure the stitches. On a third needle cast on 4 stitches; this is for the inside of the finger; divide the stitches for the finger equally on 3 needles, and continue to knit plain in the round for 30 rounds; then decrease by knitting 2 of the inside stitches together; knit 8 rounds plain, and decrease by knitting 2 together as before. Knit 6 rounds plain, knit 2 together, and knit 3 all round until you have 8 stitches remaining on the needle; draw the wool through the 8 stitches, draw together, and fasten off the wool firmly on the wrong side.

For the Second Finger.—Put the 7 next stitches from the inside of hand on a needle; cast 4 stitches onto another needle and take the last 8 stitches off the cotton onto a needle; now pick up the 4 cast-on stitches of first finger and work as before, making the finger 6 rows longer previous to beginning the decrease.

For the Third Finger.—Take seven stitches from inside of hand, cast on 4, take the last 7 stitches off the cotton, pick the 4 stitches from the inside of the second finger; knit as directed for the first finger, working 3 rows more before beginning the decrease.

Fourth Finger.—Take all the stitches remaining on the cotton and pick up the 4 stitches from the inside of third finger, knit 36 rounds, decrease as before described, and finish the same way.

Now finish the thumb by taking the stitches off the cotton onto 3 needles. Work 30 rounds plain; finish as directed for the fingers. For the left-hand

No. 14.—KNITTED GLOVE.

glove work as directed for the right-hand until you have put your stitches for the thumb onto the cotton.

The thumb must now be at the right-hand side, and the back of the glove toward the knitter. With this way of holding your work each finger must be begun.

No. 13.—GENTLEMAN'S KNITTED MITT.

(For Description see this and preceding Page.)

GENTLEMAN'S KNITTED DRIVING OR SHOOTING GLOVES.

No. 15.—This glove is knitted with brown-mixed camel's-hair wool, and is faced with leather on its inner surface. Begin the work at the wrist, casting on 60 stitches, and knit 30 rounds in ribbed knitting, 2 stitches plain and 2 purled. Next work 46 rounds in plain knitting, but in the 22nd round of these, after knitting the first 16 stitches, set the rest aside for the present, and cast on 16 new stitches added to the other 16, making 32 stitches for the thumb; knit 42 rounds on these; in the 8th round narrow 1 stitch at both ends of the 16 stitches cast on, and narrow the same 3 times thereafter at intervals of 3 rounds; in the last 8 of the 42 rounds point the thumb by decreasing gradually. Take up 16 stitches out of the 16 cast on for the thumb; these now forming the first stitches of the round, add them to the stitches set aside, and complete the remainder of the 46 rounds for the hand. For the forefinger take on

No. 15.—GENTLEMAN'S KNITTED DRIVING OR SHOOTING GLOVE.

separate needles the first 9 stitches, cast on 3 new stitches, and take the last 9 stitches of the round; knit 34 rounds on these, in the last 8 of which point the finger. For the middle finger take the next 8 stitches of the back and palm, cast on 3 stitches between, and take 3 stitches out of the 3 cast on for the forefinger, and on these 22 stitches knit 42 rounds, in the last 8 of which point the finger. For the third finger take 7 of the remaining stitches of both back and palm, cast on 3 between, and take up 3 out of the 3 cast on for the middle finger; knit it to the same length as the forefinger. For the little finger take the remaining stitches of the hand, and take up 3 from those cast on for the third finger; knit 29 rounds, pointing the finger in the last 6. These directions are for the right glove, and must be reversed for the left; they are for gloves of average size; the fingers can be lengthened or shortened as needed.

KNITTED SUSPENDERS.

No. 16.—These suspenders may be made of coarse crochet cotton in two colors, or one; or they may be made of silk, in which case they may be lined with ribbon or silk of the same or a contrasting color. The wide portion must be made as long as required, according to the size of the individual who is going to wear the suspenders.

Begin a button-hole end as follows: Cast on 8 stitches. Then, from the 1st to the 22nd row, slip 1; * then purl 1 and slip 1 alternately, inserting the needle for the second slipped stitch as for purling; repeat from * across each row, after slipping the first stitch. In working back the slipped stitches are purled and the purled knitted; and from the 2nd to the 18th rows, increase by one stitch at the beginning of each row.

To make the button-hole, divide the stitches equally, and on each half of the work knit 28 rows as above; then knit 6 rows more along all the stitches.

Now cast on 4 stitches at each side of the work and begin the wide part as follows:

First to Eleventh row.—Same as preceding rows.

Twelfth row.—Four times, alternately, slip 1, purl 1, same as in beginning of work; then knit 16 plain, (in working back purl these 16 plain stitches); then 4 times alternately, slip 1, purl 1 as before.

Repeat this pattern as often as necessary to make the suspenders long enough. Then knit 11 plain rows like the 11 at the other end of the pattern. Next cast off 4 stitches at each side, and knit a button-hole end to correspond with the one at the beginning of the work, except, of course, that you narrow instead of widen at the sloping edges.

To complete the edge, take colored cotton and crochet as follows: * 1 double, 2 chain and 3 trebles into the same stitch; skip 2 and repeat from * all around the wide part of the work and across its ends as seen in the picture.

With the colored cotton darn across the center pattern of the suspenders as seen in the engraving.

If preferred,

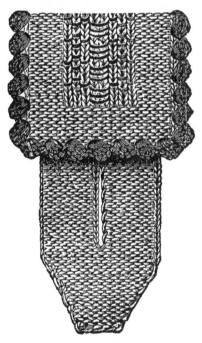

No. 16.—KNITTED SUSPENDER.

a design in cross-stitch might be made down the center of the suspender instead of the darning illustrated. Or, a design in any color preferred could be knitted in after the manner of knitting in initials or clocks, as described on page 55.

COUNTERPANES, SPREADS, BORDERS, DOILIES, MATS, ETC.

SQUARE FOR A COUNTERPANE.

No. 1.—This square may be used for other purposes than that named, and made of cotton, linen or silk, according to the purpose intended by the knitter. It is worked in rounds and requires 5 needles.

Cast 2 stitches on each of 4 needles.

First round.—Plain.

Second round.—* K 1, th o, k 1, and repeat 3 times more from *.

Third and every alternate round.—Plain.

Fourth round.—* K 1, th o, k 1, th o, k 1, and repeat 3 times more from *.

Sixth round.—* K 1, th o, k 3, th o, k 1 and repeat 3 times more from *.

Eighth round.—* K 1, th o, k 5, th o, k 1, and repeat 3 times more from *.

From this last round to the 18th inclusive, knit in the same manner, only in every pattern-round the number of stitches between the made stitches

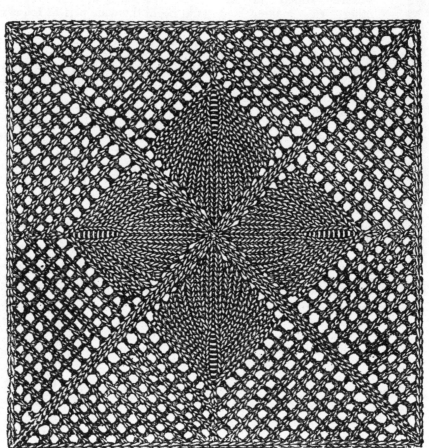

NO. 1.—SQUARE FOR A COUNTERPANE.

increases by 2, so that in the 18th round 15 stitches are knitted between the made stitches.

Twentieth round.—* K 1, th o, k 1, th o, k 5, sl 1, k 1, pass slipped stitch over, k 1, k 2 together, k 5, th o, k 1, th o, k 1; repeat 3 times more from *.

Twenty-second round.—* K 1, th o, k 1, th o, sl 1, k 1, pass slipped stitch over, th o, k 4, sl 1, k 1, pass slipped stitch over, k 1, k 2 together, k 4, th o, k 2 together, th o, k 1, th o, k 1; repeat 3 times more from *.

Twenty-fourth round.—* K 1, th o, k 1, th o, sl 1, k 1, pass slipped stitch over, th o, sl 1, k 1, pass slipped stitch over, th o, k 3, sl 1, k 1, pass slipped stitch over, k 1, k 2 together, k 3, th o, k 2 together, th o, k 2 together, th o, k 1, th o, k 1; repeat 3 times more from *.

Twenty-sixth round.—* K 1, th o, k 1; 3 times alternately th o, sl 1, k 1, pass slipped stitch over; th o, k 2, sl 1, k 1, pass slipped stitch over, k 1, k 2 together, k 2; 3 times alternately th o, k 2 together; th o, k 1, th o, k 1; repeat 3 times more from *.

Twenty-eighth round.—* K 1, th o, k 1: 4 times alternately th o, sl 1, k 1, pass slipped stitch over; th o, k 1, sl 1, k 1, pass slipped stitch over; k 1, k 2 together, k 1; 4 times alternately th o, k 2 together; th o, k 1, th o, k 1 and repeat 3 times more from *.

Thirtieth round.—* K 1, th o, k 1; 6 times alternately, th o, sl 1, k 1, pass slipped stitch over; k 1; 6 times alternately, k 2 together, th o; k 1, th o, k 1, and repeat 3 times more from *.

Thirty-second round.—* K 1, th o, k 1; 6 times alternately, th o, sl 1, k 1, pass slipped stitch over; th o, k 3 together; 6 times alternately th o, k 2 together; th o, k 1, th o, k 1, and repeat 3 times more from *

Thirty-fourth round.—* K 1, th o, k 1; 7 times alternately, th o, sl 1, k 1, pass slipped stitch over; k 1; 7 times alternately, k 2 together, th o; k 1, th o, k 1, and repeat 3 times more from *.

Thirty-sixth round.—* K 1, th o, k 1; 7 times alternately th o, sl 1, k 1, pass slipped stitch over; th o, k 3 together; 7 times alternately th o, k 2 together; th o, k 1, th o, k 1; repeat 3 times more from *.

Thirty-eighth round.—* K 1, th o, k 1; 8 times alternately, th o, sl 1, k 1, pass slipped stitch over;

k 1; 8 times alternately, k 2 together, th o; k. 1, th o, k 1; repeat 3 times more from *.

Fortieth round.—* K 1, th o, k 1; 8 times alternately, th o, sl 1, k 1, pass slipped stitch over; th o, k 3 together; 8 times alternately, th o, k 2 together, th o, k 1, th o, k 1; repeat 3 times more from *.

There should now be 41 stitches on each needle. Knit 1 round plain and cast off.

DESIGN FOR A COUNTERPANE SQUARE.

No. 2.—Use fine knitting cotton and five steel needles. Make in blocks like that seen at No. 2, join them and add the border seen at No. 3 on page 95.

To begin a Block.—Cast 2 stitches each on 4 needles.
First round.—Plain.
Second round.—Four times alternately, th o, k 2.
Third round.—Four times alternately, purl 1 and knit 2.
Fourth round.—* Th o, p 1, th o, k 2, and repeat 3 times more from *.
Fifth round.—Alternately purl 3 and knit 2.
Sixth round.—* Th o, p 3, th o, k 2, and repeat 3 times more from *.
Seventh round.—Four times alternately, p 5, k 2.
Eighth round.—* Th o, p 2, th o, p 1, th o, p 2, th o, k 2; repeat 3 times more from *.
Ninth round.—Four times alternately, p 9, k 2.
Tenth round.—* Th o, p 3; 3 times alternately, th o, p 1; th o, p 3, th o, k 2 and repeat 3 times more from *.
Eleventh round.—Four times alternately p 15, k 2.
Twelfth round.—* Th o, p 2; twice alternately th o, p 1; th o, p 7; twice alternately th o, p 1; th o, p 2, th o, k 2, and repeat 3 times more from *.
Thirteenth round.—Four times alternately, p 23, k 2.
Fourteenth round.—* Th o, p 3; 4 times alternately, th o, p 1; then cast off 8 stitches as follows:

Purl 3 together, purl 3 together, ** p 1, take the last 2 stitches of the right-hand needle upon the left-hand needle, and draw the last stitch over the one before; take this stitch again upon the right-hand needle, and repeat twice more from **; after the last movement of the last repetition, slip the stitch before the last one put back on the needle over the last one, to draw the little puff closely together. Now, 4 times alternately, p 1, th o; p 3, th o, k 2, and repeat 3 times more from the * at the beginning of the round.

Fifteenth round.—Four times alternately, p 25, k 2.
Sixteenth round.—* Th o, p 2; twice alternately, th o, p 1; th o, p 7; 3 times alternately, th o, p 1; th o, p 7; twice alternately, th o, p 1; th o, p 2, th o, k 1 and repeat 3 times more from *.
Seventeenth round.—Four times alternately p 37, k 2.
Eighteenth round.—* Th o, p 3. ** 4 times alternately th o, p 1, cast off 8 as directed in the 14th round; p 1, and repeat once more from **; 3 times alternately, th o, p 1, th o, p 3, th o, k 2 and repeat 3 times more from *.
Nineteenth round.—Four times alternately, p 35, k 2.
Twentieth round.—* Th o, p 4, **, th o, p 7; 3 times alternately th o, p 1, and repeat once more from **; th o, p 7, th o, p 4, th o, k 2 and repeat 3 times more from *.
Twenty-first round.—Four times alternately p 47, k 2.
Twenty-second round.—* Th o, p 5; ** cast off 8 as before directed, p 1; 4 times alternately th o, p 1, and repeat once more from **. Cast off 8 as before, p 5, th o, k 2 and repeat 3 times more from *.
Twenty-third round.—Four times alternately, p 33, k 2.
Twenty-fourth round.—* Th o, p 8, th o, p 7; 3 times alternately, th o, p 1, th o, p 7, th o, p 8, th o, k 2.

NO. 2.—DESIGN FOR A COUNTERPANE SQUARE.

Twenty-fifth round.—Four times alternately, p 41, k 2.

Twenty-sixth round.—* Th o, p 9; cast off 8 as before, p 1; 4 times alternately, th o, p 1, cast off 8, p 9, th o, k 2 and repeat 3 times more from *.

Twenty-seventh round.—Four times alternately p 31, k 2.

Twenty-eighth round.—* Th o, p 12, th o, p 7, th o, p 12, th o, k 2; repeat 3 times more from *.

Twenty-ninth round.—Four times alternately p 35, k 2.

Thirtieth round.—* Th o, p 13, th o, cast off 8 as before, p 13, th o, k 2, and repeat 3 times more from *

Thirty-first round.—* P 13, p 2 together, p 14, k 1 and repeat 3 times more from *.

Thirty-second round.—Th o, k 28, th o, k 2.

Thirty-third round.—Plain.

Thirty-fourth round.—* Th o, k 30, th o, k 2 and repeat 3 times more from *.

Thirty-fifth round.—* K 1, k 2 together; 14 times alternately, th o, k 2 together; k 3.

Thirty-sixth round.—* Th o, k 31, th o, k 2; repeat from * 3 times more.

Thirty-seventh round.—Plain.

Thirty-eighth round.—* Th o, k 33, th o, k 2 and repeat 3 times more from *.

Thirty-ninth round.—Four times alternately, p 35, k 2.

Fortieth round.—* Th o, p 35, th o, k 2 and repeat 3 times more from *.

Forty-first round.—Four times alternately, p 37, k 2.

Forty-second round.—* Th o, k 37, th o, k 2 and repeat 3 times more from *

Forty-third round.—Plain.

Forty-fourth round.—* Th o, k 39, th o, k 2 and repeat 3 times more from *.

Forty-fifth round.—* K 2; 19 times alternately th o, k 2 together; k 3 and repeat 3 times more from *.

Forty-sixth round.—* Th o, k 41, th o, k 2 and repeat 3 times more from *

Forty-seventh round.—Plain.

Forty-eighth round.—* Th o, k 43, th o, k 2 and repeat 3 times more from *

Now knit back and forth on the next needle as follows:

Forty-ninth row.—Narrow 1 as follows: Sl 1, k or p next stitch, as required by the design; then pass the slipped stitch over. P 9, th o, k 1, th o, * p 7, th o, k 1, th o and repeat twice more from *; p 11.

Fiftieth row.—Narrow 1 as at beginning of last row; k 9, 3 times alternately p 3, k 7; p 3, k 10.

Fifty-first row.—Narrow 1 as before; p 8, th o, k 3, th o, * p 7, th o, k 3, th o, repeat twice more from *; p 10.

Fifty-second row.—Narrow 1 as before; k 8; 3 times alternately, p 5, k 7; p 5, k 9.

Fifty-third row.—Narrow 1 as before; * p 7, th o, k 5, th o and repeat 3 times more from *; p 9.

Fifty-fourth row.—Narrow 1 as before; 4 times alternately k 7, p 7, k 8.

Fifty-fifth row.—Narrow 1 as before; p 6, * th o, k 7, th o, p 7; repeat twice more from *; th o, k 7, th o, p 8.

Fifty-sixth row.—Narrow 1 as before; k 6; 4 times alternately p 9, k 7.

Fifty-seventh row.—Narrow 1 as before; p 5, * th o, k 9, th o, p 7, and repeat 3 times more from *

Fifty-eighth row.—Narrow 1 as before; k 5, p 11; 3 times alternately, k 7, p 11; k 6.

Fifty-ninth row.—Narrow 1 as before; p 4, k 4; narrow 2 stitches as follows: sl 1, k 2 together, pass slipped stitch over; k 4, * p 3, th o, k 1, th o, p 3, k 4, n 2 as before, k 4, and repeat twice more from *; p 6.

Sixtieth row.—Narrow 1 as before, k 4, p 9, * k 3, p 3, k 3, p 9, and repeat twice more from *; k 5.

Sixty-first row.—Narrow 1 as before; p 3, k 3, narrow 2 as before; k 3, * p 3, th o, k 3, th o, p 3, k 3, n 2 as before, k 3 and repeat twice more from *; p 5.

Sixty-second row.—Narrow 1 as before. K 3, p 7, * k 3, p 5, k 3, p 7, and repeat twice more from *; k 4.

Sixty-third row.—Narrow 1 as before; p 2, k 2, n 2 as before, k 2, * p 3, th o, k 5, th o, p 3, k 2, n 2 as before, k 2, and repeat twice more from *; p 4.

Sixty-fourth row.—Narrow 1 as before; k 2, p 5, * k 3, p 7, k 3, p 5, and repeat twice more from *; k 3.

Sixty-fifth row.—Narrow 1 as before, p 1, k 1, n 2 as before, k 1, * p 3, th o, k 7, th o, p 3, k 1, n 2 as before, k 1, and repeat twice more from *; p 3.

Sixty-sixth row.—Narrow 1 as before, k 1, p 3, * k 3, p 9, k 3, p 3, and repeat twice more from *; k 2.

Sixty-seventh row.—Narrow 1 as before; * n 2 as before, p 3, th o, k 9, th o, p 3, and repeat twice more from *; n 2 as before, p 2.

Sixty-eighth row.—Narrow 1 as before; * p 1, k 3, p 11, k 3, and repeat twice more from *; p 2.

Sixty-ninth row.—Narrow 1 as before; p 3, k 4, n 2 as before, k 4, * p 3, th o, k 1, th o, p 3, k 4, n 2 as before, k 4, and repeat once more from *; p 5.

Seventieth row.—Narrow 1 as before; k 3, p 9, * k 3, p 3, k 3, p 9, repeat once more from *; k 4.

Seventy-first row.—Narrow 1 as before; p 2, k 3, n 2 as before, k 3, * p 3, th o, k 3, th o, p 3, k 3, n 2 as before, k 3, repeat once more from *; p 4.

Seventy-second row.—Narrow 1 as before, k 2, p 7, k 3, * p 5, k 3, p 7, k 3, and repeat once more from *.

Seventy-third row.—Narrow 1 as before; p 1, * k 2, n 2 as before, k 2, p 3, th o, k 5, th o, p 3 and repeat once more from *; k 2, n 2 as before; k 2, p 3.

Seventy-fourth row.—Narrow 1 as before, k 1, p 5, * k 3, p 7, k 3, p 5; repeat once more from *, k 2.

Seventy-fifth row.—N 1 as before, k 1, n 2 as before, k 1, * p 3, th o, k 7, th o, p 3, k 1, n 2 as before, k 1, and repeat once more from * ; p 2.

Seventy-sixth row.—N 1 as before, p 3, * k 3, p 9, k 3, p 3, and repeat once more from * ; k 1.

Seventy-seventh row.—Sl 2, k 2 together, pass slipped stitches over, * p 3, th o, k 9, th o, p 3, n 2 as before, and repeat once more from * ; p 1.

Seventy-eighth row.—N 1 as before, k 3, p 11, k 3, p 1, k 3, p 11, k 3, p 1.

Seventy-ninth row.—N 1 as before, p 2, k 4, n 2 as before, k 4, p 3, th o, k 1, th o, p 3, k 4, n 2 as before, k 4, p 3, k 1.

Eightieth row.—N 1 as before, k 2, p 9, k 3, p 3, k 3, p 9, k 3.

Eighty-first row.—N 1 as before, p 1, k 3, n 2 as before, k 3, p 3, th o, k 3, th o, p 3, th o, k 3, n 2 as before, k 3, p 3.

Eighty-second row.—N 1 as before, k 1, p 7, k 3, p 5, k 3, p 7, k 2.

Eighty-third row.—N 1 as before, k 2 ; n 2 as before, k 2, p 3, th o, k 5, th o, p 3, k 2, n 2 as before, k 2, p 2.

Eighty-fourth row.—N 1 as before, p 5, k 3, p 7, k 3, p 5, k 1.

Eighty-fifth row.—N 1 as before, n 2 as before, k 1, p 3, th o, k 7, th o, p 3, k 1, n 2 as before, k 1, p 1.

Eighty-sixth row.—N 1 as before, p 2, k 3, p 9, k 3, p 3.

Eighty-seventh row.—Sl 2, k 2 together, pass slipped stitches over, p 2, th o, k 9, th o, p 3, n 2 as before.

Eighty-eighth row.—N 1 as before, k 2, p 11, k 3.

Eighty-ninth row.—N 1 as before, p 1, k 4, n 2 as before, k 4, p 3.

Ninetieth row.—N 1 as before, k 1, p 9, k 2.

Ninety-first row.—N 1 as before, k 3, n 2 as before, k 3, p 2.

Ninety-second row.—N 1 as before, p 7, k 1.

Ninety-third row.—N 1 as before, k 1, n 2 as before, k 2, p 1.

Ninety-fourth row.—N 1 as before, p 3, k 1.

Ninety-fifth row.—N 1 as before, k 3.

Ninety-sixth row.—Cast off the stitches.

This completes one corner of the block. Repeat the details from the 48th row, on each needle, for the remaining corners.

BORDER FOR COUNTERPANE.

No. 3.—Cast on 25 stitches.

First row.—Sl 1, k 2, th o, k 2 together (these first 5 stitches are worked off the same in every

following uneven row, therefore they will not be again *given* in these rows ; but the knitter must not forget that they are to be knitted as just directed). K 3, th o, k 1, th o, k 5, th o, k 2 together crossed, k 1 ; then th o, k 2 together crossed 3 times in succession ; k 2 together.

Second row.—Th o, k 10, th o, k 2 together, k 3, p 3, k 5, th o, k 2 together, k 1.

Third row.—Twice alternately, k 3, th o ; k 5, th o, k 2 together crossed, k 2 ; 3 times alternately th o, k 2 together crossed ; k 1. (The last 7 stitches of each uneven row, up to the 29th row are knit in the same way, and will not be mentioned again in these rows ; but the knitter must be careful to knit them as just directed.)

Fourth row.—Th o, k 11, th o, k 2 together, k 3, p 5, k 5, th o, k 2 together, k 1.

Fifth row.—K 3 ; twice alternately th o, k 5 ; th o, k 2 together crossed, k 3.

Sixth row.—Th o, k 12, th o, k 2 together, k 3, p 7, k 5, th o, k 2 together, k 1.

Seventh row.—K 3, th o, k 7, th o, k 5, th o, k 2 together crossed, k 4.

Eighth row.—Th o, k 13, th o, k 2 together, k 3, p 9, k 5, th o, k 2 together, k 1.

Ninth row.—K 3, th o, k 9, th o, k 5, th o, k 2 together crossed ; k 5.

Tenth row.—Th o, k 14, th o, k 2 together, k 3, p 11, k 5, th o, k 2 together, k 1.

Eleventh row.—K 7, n, k 9, th o, k 2 together crossed, k 6.

Twelfth row.—Th o, k 15, th o, k 2 together, k 3, p 9, k 5, th o, k 2 together, k 1.

Thirteenth row.—K 6, n, k 8, th o, k 2 together crossed, k 7.

Fourteenth row.—Th o, k 16, th o, k 2 together, k 3, p 7, k 5, th o, k 2 together, k 1.

Fifteenth row.—K 5, n, k 7, th o, k 2 together crossed, k 8.

Sixteenth row.—Th o, k 17, th o, k 2 together, k 3, p 5, k 5, th o, k 2 together, k 1.

Seventeenth row.—K 4, n, k 6, th o, k 2 together crossed, k 9.

Eighteenth row.—Th o, k 18, th o, k 2 together, k 3, p 3, k 5, th o, k 2 together, k 1.

Nineteenth row.—K 3, n, k 5, th o, k 2 together crossed, k 6, th o, p 1, th o, k 3.

Twentieth row.—Th o, k 21, th o, k 2 together, k 3, p 1, k 5, th o, k 2 together, k 1.

Twenty-first row.—(For the stripe at the upper edge of the lace, repeat the stitches from the first to the twentieth row. A description of the point

NO. 3.—BORDER FOR COUNTERPANE (SEE DESIGN AT NO. 2).

now follows.)—K 6 ; 3 times alternately, th o, p 1, th o, k 4.

Twenty-second row.—Th o, k 26.

Twenty-third row.—K 4, th o, p 1, th o, k 1, th o, p 7, th o, k 1, th o, p 1, th o, k 3.

Twenty-fourth row.—Th o, k 33.

Twenty-fifth row.—K 4; 3 times alternately, th o, p 1 ; th o, k 1 ; cast off 8 as directed for the puffs in the square ; k 1, 3 times alternately, th o, p 1, th o, k 4.

Twenty-sixth row.—Th o, k 34.

Twenty-seventh row.—K 2, * th o, p 1, th o, k 1, th o, p 7, th o, k 1 and repeat once more from *; th o, p 1, th o, k 3.

Twenty-eighth row.—Th o, k 45.

Twenty-ninth row.—K 2, * 3 times alternately th o, p 1 ; th o, k 1, cast off 8 as before, k 1, and repeat once more from * ; 3 times alternately th o, p 1 ; th o, k 4.

Thirtieth row.—K 42.

Thirty-first row.—K 2, * th o, p 7, th o, k 1, th o, k 1. Repeat once more from * ; th o, p 7, th o, k 1, th o, k 1, th o, k 2 ; 3 times alternately, k 2 together, th o ; k 2 together twice. (The last 10 stitches of every uneven row up to the 57th row are knitted the same as the last 10 stitches just given. They will not be mentioned again in these rows ; but the knitter must be careful to knit them according to the instructions just given.)

Thirty-second row.—Th o, k 51.

Thirty-third row.—K 2, * cast off 8 as before ; k 1 ; 3 times alternately th o, p 1 ; th o, k 1, and repeat once more from * ; cast off 8 as before, k 1.

Thirty-fourth row.—Th o, k 34.

Thirty-fifth row.—K 4, th o, p 7, th o, k 1, th o, p 1, th o, k 1, th o, p 7, th o, k 2.

Thirty-sixth row.—Th o, k 39.

Thirty-seventh row.—K 4 ; cast off 8 as before, k 1 ; 3 times alternately th o, p 1 ; th o, k 1 ; cast off 8 as before, k 1.

Thirty-eighth row.—Th o, k 26.

Thirty-ninth row.—K 6, th o, p 7, th o, k 2.

Fortieth row.—Th o, k 27.

Forty-first row.—K 6 ; cast off 8 as before, k 1.

Forty-second row.—Th o, k 18.

Forty-third row.—K 7.

Forty-fourth row.—Th o, k 17.

Forty-fifth row.—K 6.

Forty-sixth row.—Th o, k 16.

Forty-seventh row.—K 5.

Forty-eighth row.—Th o, k 15.

Forty-ninth row.—K 4.

Fiftieth row.—Th o, k 14.

Fifty-first row.—K 3.

Fifty-second row.—Th o, k 13.

Fifty-third row.—K 2.

Fifty-fourth row.—Th o, k 12.

Fifty-fifth row.—K 1.

Fifty-sixth row.—Th o, k 11.

Fifty-seventh row.—In the last 10 stitches k 2 together ; then 3 times alternately, th o, k 2 together crossed ; k 2 together.

Fifty-eighth row.—Th o, k 10.

Fifty-ninth row.—K 1 ; 3 times alternately th o,

k 2 together ; k 2 together crossed.

Sixtieth row.—Th o, k 10.

Repeat from the first row for all the work.

KNITTED DOILY.
(For Illustration see next Page.)

No. 4.—This doily may be made of thread or fine crochet cotton. Use 4 needles of a size suitable for the thread. On 3 of them cast 1 stitch each.

First round.—Knit plain, increasing 1 on each needle, by knitting a second stitch out of the back of each stitch.

Second round.—Knit and increase in the same manner, thus making 4 stitches on each needle.

Third round.—K 1, m 1, k 2, m 1, k 1 and repeat for each of the other needles.

Fourth and every following alternate round.—Plain.

Fifth round.—K 1, m 1, k 3, m 1, k 2 and repeat.

Seventh round.—K 1, m 1, k 4, m 1, k 3 and repeat.

Ninth round.—K 1, m 1, k 5, m 1, k 4 and repeat.

Eleventh round.—K 1, m 1, k 1, m 1, k 2 together, k 3, m 1, k 1, m 1, k 2 together, k 2 and repeat.

Thirteenth round.—K 1, m 1, k 3, m 1, k 2 together, k 2, m 1, k 3, m 1, k 2 together, k 1 and repeat.

Fifteenth round.—K 1, m 1, k 5, m 1, k 2 together, k 1, m 1, k 5, m 1, k 2 together and repeat.

Sixteenth round.—Plain, as before directed.

(After knitting this round, all except the last stitch, pass this stitch onto the next needle, and also pass the last stitch of each of the other two needles onto the ones next it, before beginning the seventeenth round.)

Seventeenth round.—N, m 1, k 7, m 1, k 2 together, m 1, k 7, m 1 and repeat. Be careful to make 1 at the end of the 3rd needle. In knitting around plain, knit the made stitch on the needle with 19 stitches, thus making 20 stitches on each needle, and replacing the stitch that was moved in the 16th row on its original needle.

Nineteenth round.—K 1, m 1, k 1, m 1, k 2 together, k 7, m 1, k 1, m 1, k 2 together, k 6 and repeat.

Twenty-first round.—K 1, m 1, k 3, m 1, k 2 together, k 6, m 1, k 3, m 1, k 2 together, k 5 and repeat.

Twenty-third round.—K 1, m 1, k 2 together, k 1, m 1, k 2, m 1, k 2 together, k 5, m 1, k 2 together, k 1, m 1, k 2, m 1, k 2 together, k 4 and repeat.

Twenty-fifth round.—K 1, m 1, k 2, m 1, k 2 together, m 1, k 2 together, k 1, m 1, k 2 together, k 4, m 1, k 2, m 1, k 2 together, m 1, k 2 together, k 1, m 1, k 2 together, k 3 and repeat.

Twenty-seventh round.—K 1, m 1, k 4, m 1, k 2 together, k 3, m 1, k 2 together, k 3, m 1, k 4, m 1, k 2 together, k 3, m 1, k 2 together, k 2 and repeat.

Twenty-ninth round.—K 1, m 1, k 3, m 1, k 2 together, k 3, m 1, k 2 together, k 1, m 1, k 2 together, k 2, m 1, k 3, m 1, k 2 together, k 3, m 1, k 2 together, k 1, m 1, k 2 together, k 1 and repeat.

Thirty-first round.—K 1, m 1, k 3, m 1, k 2 together, m 1, k 2 together, k 1, m 1, k 2 together, m 1, k 2 together, k 1, m 1, k 2 together, k 1, m 1, k 3, m 1, k 2 together, m 1, k 2 together, k 1, m 1, k 2 together, m 1, k 2 together, k 1, m 1, k 2 together and repeat.

Thirty-third round.—K 1, m 1, k 5, m 1, k 2 together, k 3, m 1, k 2 together, k 3, m 1, k 2 together, m 1, k 5, m 1, k 2 together, k 3, m 1, k 2 together, k 3, m 1, k 1 and repeat.

Thirty-fifth round.—Pass the first stitch on each needle off onto the needle behind. * M 1, k 16, m 1, k 2 together, m 1, k 17, m 1, k 2 together and repeat from *. Knit the 36th round plain, as directed, and cast off.

ROUND MAT IN BRIOCHE.

(No Illustration.)

Use a pair of bone needles No. 9 or 10, and blue and white double Berlin wool.

Cast on with white wool 26 stitches.

First row.—Knit 8, * th o, slip 1, knit 1 (slip the stitch as if for purling), repeat from * to the end of the row.

Second row.—Th o, slip 1 as for purling, knit 2 together to form a rib; repeat from * 8 times more. Take the next stitch on the needle to knit it, but before doing so, pass the wool over the right-hand needle only, and over the first two fingers of the left hand; do this three times, then take off the stitch as if you were knitting it. Now put the point of the left needle into the stitch made by the loops, and knit the stitch again. Repeat this on the next 7 stitches.

Third row.—Slip 1, knit 7 plain, then th o, slip 1, knit 2 together 8 times; leave the last 3 on the needle; turn.

Fourth row.—Knit 8 ribs, then repeat the loops in the second row.

Fifth row.—Eight plain, knit 7 ribs; turn.

Sixth row.—Knit 7 ribs, knit 8 loops of wool.

Seventh row.—Knit 8, knit 7 ribs; turn.

Eighth row.—Knit 6 ribs, knit 8 loops.

Ninth row.—Knit 8, knit 5 ribs; turn.

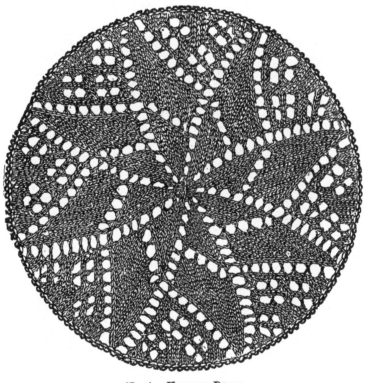

No. 4.—KNITTED DOILY.
(For Directions see this and preceding Page.)

Tenth row.—Knit 5 ribs, knit 8 loops.

Eleventh row.—Knit 8, knit 4 ribs; turn.

Twelfth row.—Knit 4 ribs, knit 8 loops.

Thirteenth row.—Knit 8 plain, knit 3 ribs; turn.

Fourteenth row.—Knit 3 ribs, knit 8 loops.

Fifteenth row.—Knit 8, knit 2 ribs; turn.

Sixteenth row.—Knit 2 ribs, knit 8 loops.

Seventeenth row.—Knit 8, knit 1 rib, turn, knit 1 rib, knit 8 loops.

Eighteenth row.—Knit 8, then knit each of the ribs on the left needle successively, until all nine are knitted; join the colored wool without severing the white, and repeat from the 2nd row. The piece knitted forms one-sixteenth of the whole. You will require 8 white and 8 colored sections. Join the sides of the sections and gently draw the center together.

SQUARE FOR A COUNTERPANE.

(For Illustration see next Page.)

NO. 5.—Begin with the raised pattern. Cast on 3 stitches, using Dexter's cotton, and steel needles of suitable size for the cotton chosen.

First row.—Knit plain.

Second row.—Slip 1, make 1 by knitting the horizontal thread which lies under the next loop; (all of the widenings at the beginning and end of each alternate row are made in this manner); k 1, make 1, k 1.

Third row.—Sl 1, and knit plain to end of row.

Fourth row.—Sl 1, m 1, k 1; th o, k 1, th o (this begins the raised pattern), k 1, m 1, k 1.

Fifth row.—Sl 1, k 2, p 3, k 3.

Sixth row.—Sl 1, m 1, k 2, th o, k 3, th o, k 2, m 1, k 1.

Seventh row.—Sl 1, k 3, p 5, k 4.

Eighth row.—Sl 1, m 1, k 3, th o, k 5, th o, k 3, m 1, k 1.

Ninth row.—Sl 1, k 4, p 7, k 5.

Tenth row.—Sl 1, m 1, k 15, m 1, k 1.

Eleventh row.—Sl 1, k 5, p 7, k 6.

Twelfth row.—Sl 1, m 1, k 5, k 2 together at the back, k 3, k 2 together, k 5, m 1, k 1.

Thirteenth row.—Sl 1, k 6, p 5, k 7.

Fourteenth row.—Sl 1, m 1, k 6, k 2 together at the back, k 1, k 2 together, k 6, m 1, k 1.

Fifteenth row.—Sl 1, k 7, p 3, k 8.

Sixteenth row.—Sl 1, m 1, k 7, k 3 together, k 7, m 1, k 1.

Seventeenth row.—Sl 1, knit to end of row.

Eighteenth row.—Sl 1, m 1, k 3, th o, k 1, th o, k 9, th o, k 1, th o, k 3, m 1, k 1.

Nineteenth row.—Sl 1, k 4, p 3, k 9, p 3, k 5.

Twentieth row.—Sl 1, m 1, k 4, th o, k 3, th o, k 9, th o, k 3, th o, k 4, m 1, k 1.

Twenty-first row.—Sl 1, k 5, p 5, k 9, p 5, k 6.

Twenty-second row.—Sl 1, m 1, k 5, th o, k 5, th o, k 9, th o, k 5, th o, k 5, m 1, k 1.

Twenty-third row.—Sl 1, k 6, p 7, k 9, p 7, k 7.

Twenty-fourth row.—Sl 1, m 1, k 35, m 1, k 1.

Twenty-fifth row.—Sl 1, k 7, p 7, k 9, p 7, k 7.

Twenty-sixth row.—Sl 1, m 1, k 7, k 2 together at the back, k 3, k 2 together, k 9, k 2 together at the back, k 3, k 2 together, k 7, m 1, k 1.

Twenty-seventh row.—Sl 1, k 8, p 5, k 9, p 5, k 9.

Twenty-eighth row.—Sl 1, m 1, k 8, k 2 together, k 1, k 2 together, k 9, k 2 together, k 1, k 2 together, k 8, m 1, k 1.

Twenty-ninth row.—Sl 1, k 9, p 3, k 9, p 3, k 10.

Thirtieth row.—Sl 1, m 1, k 9, k 3 together, k 9, k 3 together, k 9, m 1, k 1.

Thirty-first row.—Sl 1, m 1, k 5, th o, k 1, th o, k 9, th o, k 1, th o, k 9, th o, k 1, th o, k 5, m 1, k 1.

Thirty-second row.—Sl 1, k 6, p 3, k 9, p 3, k 9, p 3, k 7.

Thirty-third row.—Sl 1, m 1, k 6, th o, k 3, th o, k 9, th o, k 3, th o, k 9, th o, k 3, th o, k 6, m 1, k 1.

No. 5.—Square for a Counterpane.
(For Directions see this and preceding Page.)

Thirty-fourth row.—Sl 1, k 7, p 5, k 9, p 5, k 9, p 5, k 8.

Thirty-fifth row.—Sl 1, m 1, k 7, th o, k 5, th o, k 9, th o, k 5, th o, k 9, th o, k 5, th o, k 7, m 1, k 1.

Thirty-sixth row.—Sl 1, k 8, p 7, k 9, p 7, k 9, p 7, k 9.

Thirty-seventh row.—Sl 1, m 1, k 55, m 1, k 1.

Thirty-eighth row.—Sl 1, k 9, then knit like 11th row, knitting 9 between the puffs, and 10 at the end.

Thirty-ninth row.—Sl 1, m 1, k 9; then knit like 12th row and so on for the other half of the puff. Work 4th row of puffs to correspond.

Now begin the other half of the square, having finished the puffs, by slipping the first stitch and narrowing once at the beginning of each row.

First row.—Knit.

Second row.—Purl.

Third row.—Knit.

Now make the holes as follows:

Fourth row.—Sl 1, p 2 together, *th o, p 2 together, and repeat from *, purling 3 together at the end.

Fifth row.—Purl.

Sixth row.—Knit.

Seventh row.—Purl.

Eighth row.—Knit.

Ninth row.—Purl.

Tenth row.—Purl.

Now repeat from the first row until the square is complete. In knitting the last stitch of each row, pass the needle from front to back instead of in the usual way.

BORDER FOR A COUNTERPANE OR SPREAD.
(For Illustration see next Page.)

No. 6.—Cotton No. 8 and rather large steel needles are generally selected in making this border for the purposes above named, but Saxony yarn will also be found very effective for the design. The puff-edge and the heading are crocheted on.

Cast on 12 stitches.

First row.—Sl 1, k 1, th o twice, k 3 together, th o twice, narrow at back of work, k 3, th o, n.

Second row.—Sl 1, k 6, p 1, k 2, p 1, k 2.

Third row.—Sl 1, k 1, th o twice, n, k 1, narrow at the back, th o twice, narrow at the back, k 2, th o, n.

Fourth row.—Sl 1, k 5, p 1, k 4, p 1, n at the back.

Fifth row.—Sl 1, k 1, th o twice, n, k 1, th o, k 1, n at the back, th o twice, n at the back, k 1, th o, n.

Sixth row.—Sl 1, k 4, p 1, k 6, p 1, k 2.

Seventh row.—Sl 1, k 1, th o twice, n, k 5, n, th o twice, narrow at the back, th o, n.

Eighth row.—Sl 1, k 3, p 1, k 8, p 1, k 2.

Ninth row.—Sl 1, k 4, n, th o.

To make the puff in the center of each diamond, work as follows: Draw 1 loop of the cotton through the hole in the middle of the 5th row, with the right needle; pass it onto the left needle and knit it off. Repeat this 4 times more; k 1, and then slip the 5 loops over the last stitch knit; then th o, n, k 4, th o, n.

Tenth row.—Sl 1, k 3, n at the back, k 10.

Eleventh row.—Sl 1, n, th o twice, n, k 1, n at the back, th o, k 2, n at the back, th o twice, k 1, th o, n.

Twelfth row.—Sl 1, k 3, p 1, k 8, p 1, n at the back.

Thirteenth row.—Sl 1, n, th o twice, n, k 3, n at the back, th o twice, n, k 1, th o, n.

Fourteenth row.—Sl 1, k 4, p 1, k 6, p 1, n at the back.

Fifteenth row.—Sl 1, n, th o twice, n at the back, k 1, n, th o twice, n, k 2, th o, n.

Sixteenth row.—Sl 1, k 5, p 1, k 1, n at the back, k 1, p 1, n at the back.

Seventeenth row.—Sl 1, n, th o twice, n, th o twice, n, k 3, th o, n.

Eighteenth row.—Sl 1, k 6, p 1, k 2, p 1, n at the back.

Nineteenth row.—Sl 1, k 9, th o, n.

Twentieth row.—Sl 1, k 11.

Repeat from first row for all the diamonds.

For the Puff-Edging: First row.—Each puff is crocheted as follows: * Th o, pick up a loop at the point seen in the picture; repeat from * 3 times more, then th o, draw through all the loops, th o, draw through the last stitch. Make chains of 5 stitches between all the puffs except the 2 at the angles. Here no chain at all is made.

Complete the edge as seen in the picture with 5-chains and single crochets.

For the Heading: First and Third rows.—Double crochets with 2-chains between.

Second row.—Cross trebles, with 2-chains between.

To make a cross treble work as follows: Fasten the thread and make a chain of 4. * Throw the yarn throw it over again and take up the third chain stitch beyond the one first taken up. Five stitches will now be on the hook. Put the yarn over and

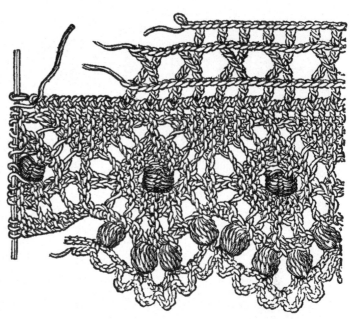

No. 6.—Border for a Counterpane or Spread.
(For Description see this and preceding Page.)

draw through 2 of them, over again and through 2 more, over again and through 2 more, over again and through the last 2. Now make one chain, and a double crochet in the junction of the cross. Make 2-chain, skip 2, and repeat from *.

DESIGN FOR COUNTERPANES, AFGHANS, ETC.

No. 7.—In making a counterpane, afghan, robe, etc., etc., by this design, knit two sections like the engraving and join them along the diagonal edge to form one block. Make as many blocks as desired and unite them in square or oblong shape, as preferred. Finish with a border of fringe or knitted lace. Select needles according to the size of the cotton or wool used. Two or more colors may be united in making a spread or afghan by this design.

Cast on 35 stitches.

First, Third and Fifth rows. — Plain knitting.

Second and Fourth rows.—Purl, purling 2 together at each end of the row.

Sixth, Eighth and Tenth rows.—Plain, knitting 2 together at each end of the row.

Seventh and Ninth rows.— Purl.

Eleventh row.—Plain. Then begin at the second row and repeat until you have only 3 stitches left. Cast off.

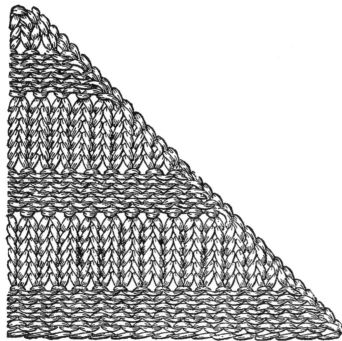

No. 7.—Design for Counterpanes, Afghans, Etc.

over the hook twice, take up the first stitch underneath; there will now be 4 stitches on the hook; throw the yarn over and draw through 2 stitches;

GRANDMOTHER'S TABLE MAT.

No. 8.—This is a neat, serviceable mat which

NO. 8.—GRANDMOTHER'S TABLE MAT.

knitted in squares on a foundation of 134 stitches. It is 11 squares in length and 11 in breadth, and 10 stitches are used for each square which is 14 rows deep; 2 stitches are used in separating the squares across the work, and 2 are also at each side edge; 2 rows of purling are also at the top and bottom of the spread, and separate the squares between these two-edges, so that each square practically has a narrow border of purled stitches.

The designs at the centers of the squares are made by purling stitches, and as the engraving very clearly represents which ones are purled, special directions are not needed. Care must be taken in working back and forth to knit and purl the divisions so that the stitches will assume the effect seen in the picture. This is done by knitting the purled stitches of the preceding row in going forward, and purling the knitted ones.

To begin, purl 2 rows and then divide the work into squares by purling 2 and knitting 10 alternately across. Purl the last 2. When the main portion is completed, work all around its edges as

recommends itself as being easily laundered, and furnishing pleasant employment for the dear aged fingers which are no longer able to handle intricate patterns, yet dislike to be idle.

It is knitted lengthwise of the points in plain back-and-forth knitting, and is sewed together at the first and last points made.

Use Dexter's cotton No. 10. Cast on 44 stitches. Knit 14, turn, knit back to last stitch; cast off this stitch; knit back to 1st turn, and knit 3 more stitches, turn; knit back to last stitch. Cast off as before; knit back to 2nd turn, and knit 3 more stitches, turn, and work in this manner until the last 3 stitches are knitted. This will complete 1 point. Now you have 33 stitches on the needle. Knit back, cast on 11 stitches for the next point, and repeat as for 1st point. Nineteen points form the mat. Sew together as described and press smoothly.

SECTION OF CARRIAGE SPREAD IN KNITTING, WITH CROCHETED BORDER.

No. 9.—This spread, a section of which is here illustrated, is made of red and white cotton, and is

follows: 1 row single crochets; 3 rows double crochets as seen in the picture, the middle row being red; then make the picot edge of the red with 2 single crochets alternating with chains of 5 stitches each. Unbleached, écru or drab cotton may

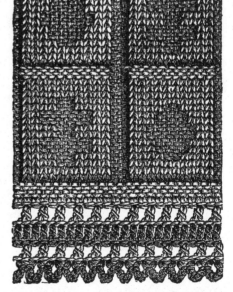

NO. 9.—SECTION OF CARRIAGE SPREAD IN KNITTING, WITH CROCHETED BORDER.

be used for this rug in place of white, with blue instead of red as the intermingling color.

COUNTERPANE DESIGN WITH BORDER.

No. 10.—This design may be worked out in Dexter's or any suitable cotton with two, long, No. 14 knitting needles. It is made in squares that are worked diagonally across.

Cast on 1 stitch.

First row.—Th o, k 1.

Second row.—Th o, k 2.

Third row.—Th o, k 1, th o, k 1, th o, k 1.

Fourth row.—Th o, k 1, p 3, k 2.

Fifth row.—Th o, p 2, th o, k 3, th o, p 2.

Sixth row.—Th o, k 2, p 5, k 3.

Seventh row.—Th o, p 3, th o, k 1, sl 1, k 2 together, pass slipped stitch over, k 1, th o, p 3.

Repeat the 6th and 7th rows, alternately, 5 times more, continuing to increase 1 stitch at the beginning of every row, which will make 1 stitch more to purl before and after the raised pattern in each row.

Eighteenth row.—Th o, k 8, p 5, k 9.

Nineteenth row.—Th o, p 9, k 1, sl 1, k 2 together, pass slipped stitch over, k 1, p 9.

Twentieth row.—Th o, k 9, p 3, k 10.

Twenty-first row.—Th o, p 10, k 3 together, p 10.

No. 10.—COUNTERPANE DESIGN WITH BORDER.

Twenty-second row.—Th o; purl to end of row.

Twenty-third row.—Th o, knit to end of row.

Twenty-fourth row.—Th o; purl to end of row.

Twenty-fifth and Twenty-sixth rows.—Th o; k to end of row.

Twenty-seventh row.—Th o; purl to end of row.

Twenty-eighth and Thirtieth rows.—Th o; k to end of row.

Twenty-ninth row.—Th o; purl to end of row.

Thirty-first row.—Th o, * p 1, sl 1 as if for purling; keep the cotton in front of the needle and repeat from * to the end of the row.

Thirty-second row.—Th o; p to end of row. Repeat the last 2 rows 5 times more.

Forty-third and Forty-sixth rows.—Th o, k to end of row.

Forty-fourth, Forty-fifth, Forty-seventh, Forty-eighth and Fiftieth rows.—Th o; p to end of row.

Forty-ninth row.—Th o; knit to end of row.

Fifty-first row.—Th o, p 2, * th o, k 1, th o, p 5, and repeat from * 7 times more; then p to end of row.

Fifty-second row.—Th o, k 2, * p 3, k 5, and repeat from * 7 times more; then knit 3.

Fifty-third row.—Th o, p 3, * th o, k 3, th o, p 5 and repeat from * 7 times more; purl to end of row.

Fifty-fourth row.—Th o, k 7, * p 5, k 5, and repeat from * 7 times more; k 4.

Fifty-fifth row.—Th o, p 4, * th o, k 1, sl 1, k 2 together, pass slipped stitch over, k 1, th o, p 5, and repeat from * 7 times more; purl to end of row.

Fifty-sixth row.—Th o, k 8, * p 5, k 5; repeat from * 7 times more; k 5.

Repeat last 2 rows, alternately, 5 times more, always increasing by making 1 stitch at the beginning of every row.

Sixty-seventh row.—Th o, p 9, * k 1, sl 1, k 2 together, pass slipped stitch over, k 1, p 5. Repeat from * 7 times more; p to end of row.

Sixty-eighth row.—Th o, k 15, * p 3, k 5, and repeat from * 7 times more; knit to end of row.

Sixty-ninth row.—Th o, p 10, * sl 1, k 2 together pass slipped stitch over, p 5, and repeat from * 7 times more; purl to end of row.

Repeat from the 22nd to the 69th rows inclusive, being very careful to make the regular increase, so as to have 16 raised patterns at the repetition of the 51st row. In the 60th row, begin to decrease for the 2nd half of the square by knitting 2 together. Join the squares by an over-and-over stitch or crochet them together with slip stitches.

DESIGN FOR BORDER OF COUNTERPANE SEEN AT NO. 10.

(For Illustration see next Page.)

No. 11.—Cast on 32 stitches.

First row.—Knit 2, th o, k 2 together, knit to end of row.

Second row.—P 29, th o, k 2 together, k 1.

Third row.—Like 1st row.

Fourth row.—Like 2nd row.

Fifth row.—K 2, th o, k 2 together, p 4, *, th o, k 1, th o, p 5, and repeat 3 times more from *.

Sixth row.—K 5, * p 3, k 5, and repeat from * 3 times more; th o, k 2 together, k 1.

Seventh row.—K 2, th o, k 2 together, p 4, * th o, k 3, th o, p 5, and repeat from * 3 times more.

Eighth row.—K 5, * p 5, k 5, and repeat from * 3 times more; th o, k 2 together, k 1.

Ninth row.—K 2, th o, k 2 together, p 4, * th o, k 1, sl 1, k 2 together, pass slipped stitch over, k 1, th o, p 5, and repeat from * 3 times more.

Tenth row.—K 5, * p 5, k 5, and repeat from * 3 times more; th o, k 2 together, k 1.

Repeat the 9th and 10th rows, alternately, 5 times more.

Twenty-first row. —K 2, th o, k 2 together, p 4, * k 1, sl 1, k 2 together, pass slipped stitch over, k 1, p 5, and repeat from * 3 times more.

Twenty-second row.—K 5, * p 3, k 5, and repeat from * 3 times more; th o, k 2 together, k 1.

Twenty-third row. —K 2, th o, k 2 together, p 4, sl 1, k 2 together, pass slipped stitch over, p 5, and repeat from * 3 times more.

Twenty-fourth row.—K 5, * p 1, k 5, and repeat from * 3 times more; th o, k 2 together, k 1.

Twenty-fifth row.—K 2, th o, k 2 together, k to end of row.

Twenty-sixth row.—P 29, th o, k 2 together, k 1.

Twenty-seventh and Twenty-ninth rows. — K 2 th o, k 2 together, p to end of row.

Twenty-eighth row.—K 29, th o, k 2 together, k 1.

Thirtieth and Thirty-second rows.—Like the 26th.

Thirty-first row.—Like 25th row.

Thirty-third row.—K 2, th o, k 2 together, * p 1, sl 1 as if for purling; keep the cotton in front of the needle, and repeat from * to end of row.

Thirty-fourth row.—Purl 29, th o, k 2 together, k 1.

Thirty-fifth row.—K 2, th o, k 2 together, * sl 1 as for purling, p 1; keep the cotton in front of the needle and repeat from * to end of row.

Thirty-sixth row.—P 29, th o, k 2 together, k 1. Repeat these last 4 rows twice more.

Forty-fifth row.—K 2, th o, k 2 together, k to end of row.

No. 11.—Design for Border of Counterpane Seen at No. 10.
(For Directions see this and preceding Page.)

Forty-sixth row.—P 29, th o, k 2 together, k 1.

Forty-seventh row.—K 2, th o, k 2 together, p 28.

Forty-eighth row.– K 29, th o, k 2 together, k 1.

Forty-ninth row.—Like 47th row.

Fiftieth and Fifty-second rows.—Like 46th.

Fifty-first row.—Like 45th row. Repeat from the 5th row for the required length.

For the Lace on the Border. — Cast on 7 stitches.

First row.—Sl 1, k 4, th o, k 2 together.

Second row.—K 2, th o, k 2 together, th o, k 2 together, k 1.

Third row.—Sl 1, k 1; k 1 and p 1 in the made stitches, k 2, th o, k 2 together.

Fourth row.—K 2, th o, k 2 together, k 4.

Fifth row.—Sl 1, k 5, th o, k 2 together.

Sixth row.—K 2, th o, k 2 together, th o, k 1, th o, k 2 together, k 1.

Seventh row.—Sl 1, k 1; k 1 and p 1 out of the made stitch; k 1; k 1 and p 1 out of the made stitch; k 2, th o, k 2 together.

Eighth row.—K 2, th o, k 2 together, k 7.

Ninth row. — Sl 1, k 8, th o, k 2 together.

Tenth row.—K 2, th o, k 2 together, th o, k 2 together, th o, k 2 together, th o, k 2 together, k 1.

Eleventh row. —Sl 1, k 1; k 1 and p 1 out of the made stitch; k 1; k 1 and p 1 out of the made stitch; k 1; k 1 and purl one out of the made stitch; k 2, th o, k 2 together.

Twelfth row.—K 2, th o, k 2 together, k 10.

Thirteenth row.—Cast off 8, k 4, th o, k 2 together. Repeat all these details for each point.

KNITTED HARLEQUIN QUILT.
(No Illustration.)

A harlequin quilt is made of remnants of colored Germantown wool, with a pound of black to qualify the brilliant effect. Two bone needles, No. 5 or 6, are needed. It is knit in diamonds, in garter stitch, commencing with 1 stitch and widening at the beginning of every row by 1 stitch. Widen until you have 20 stitches on your needle. Then narrow by knitting 2 together at the beginning of every row until you have only 1 left. Then change the color.

Alternate black or dark brown diamonds with the gay-colored ones. Sew the diamonds together with a rug needle, and finish the quilt with a crocheted edge.

KNITTED DOILY.

No. 12.—This doily may be made of crochet cotton, thread or silk.

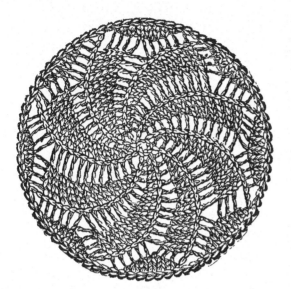

No. 12.—KNITTED DOILY.

Use five needles. Cast 2 stitches on each of 4 needles.

First round.—Knit plain.

Second round.—Make 1, k 1, and repeat to end of round.

Third round.— Make 1, k 2, and repeat to end of round.

Fourth round.—Make 1, k 3, and repeat to end of round.

Fifth round.—Make 1, k 4, and repeat to end of round.

Sixth round.—Make 1, k 5, and repeat to end of round.

Seventh round.—Make 1, k 4, k 2 together and repeat to end of round.

Eighth round.—Make 1, k 6 and repeat.

Ninth round.—Make 1, k 5, k 2 together and repeat.

Tenth round.—Make 1, k 7, and repeat.

Eleventh round.—Make 1, k 6, k 2 together and repeat.

Twelfth round.—Make 1, k 8 and repeat.

Thirteenth round.—Make 1, k 7, k 2 together and repeat.

Fourteenth round.—Make 1, k 9 and repeat.

Fifteenth round.—Make 1, k 1, make 1, k 2 together, k 5, k 2 together and repeat.

Sixteenth round.—Make 1, k 3, make 1, k 2 together, k 5, make 1, k 3, make 1, k 2 together, k 5, and repeat.

Seventeenth round.—Make 1, k 5, make 1, k 2 together, k 2, k 2 together, make 1, k 5, make 1, k 2 together, k 2, k 2 together, and repeat.

Eighteenth round.—Make 1, k 5, make 1, k 2 together, k 2, k 2 together, make 1, k 5, make 1, k 2 together, k 2, k 2 together, and repeat.

Nineteenth round.—Make 1, k 7, make 1, k 2 together, k 2, make 1, k 7, make 1, k 2 together, k 2 and repeat.

Twentieth round.—Make 1, k 9, make 1, k 2 together, make 1, k 2 together, make 1, k 9, make 1, k 2 together, and repeat.

Twenty-first round.—Knit plain and then cast off.

DESIGN FOR A COUNTERPANE.

No. 13.—This design may be made in blocks of any size convenient to the knitter; or if the counterpane is for a child's crib or bed, it might be made in one piece upon very long needles. It may be made of knitting cotton or Saxony yarn, or of any similar materials. In casting on, use any number of stitches divisible by 10, with 9 over. This will bring the beginning of every leaf in every 10th stitch, with 9 stitches at each side edge of the block. After casting on the desired number of stitches knit across plain.

First, Third and Fifth rows.—Knit 9, purl 1, and repeat across the row, ending with knit 9.

Second and Fourth rows.—Plain.

Sixth row.—* Knit to the purled stitch; take up or knit 1 stitch out of the right side of the purled stitch; knit the purled stitch and then take up another stitch out of the left side of the purled stitch which you have just knitted. Repeat from * across the work.

Seventh row.—Knit 9, purl 3 and repeat across the row.

Eighth row.—Knit 8, k 2 together, * take up a

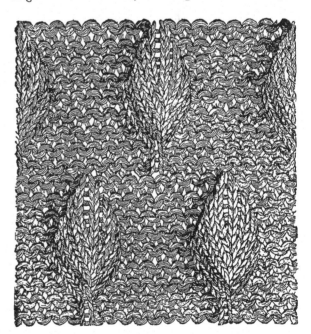

No. 13.—DESIGN FOR A COUNTERPANE.

stitch out of the bar between the last stitch knit and the first one on the left-hand needle; k 1 (center stitch of leaf) take up another stitch as before, k 2 together, k 7, and repeat from * across the row.

Ninth row.—Knit to leaf, * p 5, k 7, and repeat from * across the row.

Tenth row.—K 7, * k 2 together, k 1; make 1

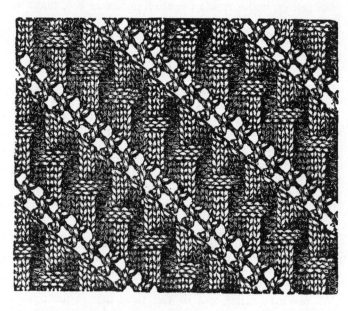

NO. 14.—DESIGN FOR COUNTERPANES, SPREADS, ROBES, ETC.

stitch at each side of the center stitch, knitting the latter as in the eighth row; k 1, k 2 together, k 5, and repeat from * across the row.

Eleventh row.—Knit to leaf, purl 7, and repeat across the row.

Twelfth row.—K 6, k 2 together, k 2, * make 1 at each side of the center stitch, knitting the latter, as before; k to center of next leaf and repeat from * across the row, knitting the last half of the last leaf to correspond with the first half.

Thirteenth row.—K to leaf, p 9 and repeat across the row.

Fourteenth row.—K to leaf; narrow first 2 and last 2 stitches of every leaf, knitting the intervening stitches plain.

Fifteenth row.—K to leaf, purl leaf stitches and k rest plain.

Sixteenth row.—Plain.

Seventeenth row.—Knit to leaf, purl leaf stitches and repeat across the row.

Eighteenth row.—K 6, make 1 by taking up a stitch out of the oblique cross-thread of the stitch just knitted; * k 2 together, k 3, k 2 together, k 1, make 1 as before, k 3, make 1, k 1, and repeat from * across the row, making 1 stitch in knitting between the last leaf and the edge, so as to make 75 stitches.

Nineteenth row.—Knit to leaf, purl leaf and repeat across the row.

Twentieth row.—Same as 18th row except that you knit 7 instead of 6 in beginning, and k 1 between the narrowings instead of 3; and between the leaves k 5 instead of 3.

Twenty-first row.—Like 19th.

Twenty-second row.—K 8, * k 2 together, k 10, and repeat from * across the row, ending with k 9.

Twenty-third row.—Begin the second row of leaves, making them the same as those in the first row, and arranging them as seen in the picture.

DESIGN FOR COUNTERPANES, SPREADS, ROBES, ETC.

NO. 14.—Cast on as many stitches as are necessary, making the number divisible by 18.

First row.—K 4, th o, k 2 together, th o, k 2 together, k 4, p 6, and repeat from beginning of row.

Second and every following alternate row.—Purl all the knitted and made stitches, and knit the purled ones.

Third row.—K 6, th o, k 2 together, th o, k 2 together, k 6, p 2, and repeat from * across the row.

Fifth row.—P 4, * k 4, th o, k 2 together, th o, k 2 together, k 4, p 6, and repeat from *; but in repeating, purl 2 instead of 6, in each repetition.

Seventh row.—K 2, * p 2, k 6, th o, k 2 together, th o, k 2 together, k 6; repeat from *, but at the end of each repetition, k 4 instead of 6.

Ninth row.—K 2, * p 6, k 4, th o, k 2 together, th o, k 2 together, k 4, and repeat from *; but at the end of each repetition, k 2 instead of 4.

Eleventh row.—* K 6, p 2, k 6, th o, k 2 together, th o, k 2 together, and repeat from *.

Thirteenth row.—Th o, k 2 together, * k 4, p 6, k 4, th o, k 2 together, th o, k 2 together and repeat from *.

Fifteenth row. — * Th o, k 2 together, th o,

NO. 15.—DESIGN FOR COUNTERPANE.
(For Description see next Page.)

k 2 together, k 6, p 2, k 6, and repeat from *.

Work in this manner, according to the illustration, until the work is of the desired dimensions.

DESIGN FOR COUNTERPANE.

(For Illustration see preceding Page.)

No. 15.—Use Dexter's cotton, worsted, or any

NO. 16.—DESIGN FOR A COUNTERPANE STRIPE.

thread or yarn suitable for the purpose, and steel needles.

19 stitches are required to work out two blocks (1 open, 1 solid). Cast on as many stitches as will be required to make the work of the desired dimensions, always using a number divisible by 19. Purl back.

First row.—* K 2 together, th o and repeat 3 times more from * ; k 11 and repeat from beginning of the row, across the work.

Second row.—P 11, k 8, and repeat across the work.

Repeat these two rows 10 times more. Then reverse the order of the blocks by knitting as follows:

K 11, * th o, k 2 together and repeat 3 times more from *; then repeat from the beginning of the row.

Next row.—K 8, p 11 and repeat across the work. Make the blocks the same as the previous ones; then reverse again by repeating the first two rows of the work. The stars at the center of the solid square are embroidered by chain stitches.

DESIGN FOR A COUNTERPANE STRIPE.

No. 16.—Cotton or wool may be used for this design as required by the purpose for which it is selected.

Cast on 10 stitches for each section or division of the design, with 2 additional stitches to keep the design even. If a plain edge is desired 5 or 6 stitches must be allowed at each side and knitted plain at the beginning and end of each row.

First row.—K 2, * th o, k 1, th o, k 1, sl 1, k 1,

pass slipped stitch over, k 3, k 2 together, k 1 and repeat from *.

Second, Fourth, Sixth, Eighth, Tenth and Twelfth rows.—Purl.

Third row.—K 2, * th o, k 3, th o, k 1, sl 1, k 1, pass slipped stitch over, k 1, k 2 together, k 1 and repeat from *.

Fifth row.—K 2, * th o, k 5, th o, k 1, sl 1, k 2 together, pass slipped stitch over, k 1 and repeat from *.

Seventh row.—* Sl 1, k 1, pass slipped stitch over, k 3, k 2 together, k 1, th o, k 1, th o, k 1; repeat from * ending with k 2.

Ninth row.—* Sl 1, k 1, pass slipped stitch over, k 1, k 2 together, k 1, th o, k 3, th o, k 1, and repeat from *, ending with k 2.

Eleventh row.—* Sl 1, k 2 together, pass slipped stitch over, k 1, th o, k 5, th o, k 1, and repeat from *, ending with k 2.

Repeat from the first row for next division of the work.

KNITTED COUNTERPANE BORDER.

No. 17.—This border must be made in sections as long as can be conveniently knitted, and then sewed together. Each scollop requires 21 stitches, and the leaf above requires 9; but the scollops and leaves are so arranged that in casting on you must use any number of stitches divisible by 63. Begin at the lower edge.

First row.—* Purl 3, k 3, k 2 together; m 1 (or

NO. 17.—KNITTED COUNTERPANE BORDER.

th o) and k 1, 8 times; k 2 together at the back, k 3 and repeat from *.

Second row.—P 2, p 2 together at the back, p 16, p 2 together, p 2, k 3 and repeat.

Third row.—P 3, k 1, k 2 together, k 16, k 2 together at the back, k 1 and repeat.

Fourth row.—P 2 together at the back, p 16, p 2 together, k 3 and repeat.

Repeat these 4 rows 5 times more. Knit the next 2 rows plain; purl the next and knit the next.

First row of the Leaf Pattern.—M 1, k 1, m 1, p 8 and repeat from the beginning of the row.

Second row.—K 8, p 3, k 8 and repeat.

Third row.—K 1, m 1, k 1, m 1, k 1, p 8 and repeat.

Fourth row.—K 8, p 5 and repeat.

Fifth row.—K 2, m 1, k 1, m 1, k 2, p 8 and repeat.

Sixth row.—K 8, p 7 and repeat.

Seventh row.—K 3, m 1, k 1, m 1, k 3, p 8 and repeat.

Eighth row.—K 8, p 9 and repeat.

Ninth row.—K 2 together at the back, k 5, k 2 together, p 8 and repeat.

Tenth row.—K 8, p 7 and repeat.

Eleventh row.—K 2 together at the back, k 3, k 2 together, p 8 and repeat.

Twelfth row.—K 8, p 5 and repeat.

Thirteenth row.—K 2 together at the back, k 1, k 2 together, p 8 and repeat.

Fourteenth row.—K 8, p 3 and repeat.

Fifteenth row.—Sl 1, k 2 together, pass slipped stitch over, p 8 and repeat.

Sixteenth row.—Plain.

Seventeenth and Eighteenth rows.—Purl.

Nineteenth row.—M 1, k 2 together at the back and repeat throughout the row.

Twentieth row.—Purl.

Twenty-first row.—K 1, * m 1, k 2 together at the back; repeat from *, ending the row with knit 1.

Twenty-second row.—Purl.

Twenty-third row.—Like 19th row.

Twenty-fourth row.—Purl.

Twenty-fifth and Twenty-sixth rows.—Plain.

Twenty-seventh row.—Purl.

Twenty-eighth row.—Knit. Then cast off the stitches.

Finish the lower edge as follows:

First row.—1 single crochet in each stitch.

Second row.—1 single at the point of the scollop, * 4 chain, 1 double into first single, skip 2 stitches, 1 single into next, and repeat from * for each scollop.

KNITTED COVER FOR A PIANO STOOL OR A SMALL TABLE.

No. 18.—This cover may be made of heavy knitting silk or cotton, and requires 5 coarse knitting needles in making.

Cast on each of 4 needles, 1 stitch.

First Round.—4 times alternately, th o, k 1.

Second round and every alternate round to Twenty-first.—Knit plain.

Third round.—* Th o, k 1 and repeat 7 times more from *.

Fifth round.—* Th o, k 2, and repeat from * for the round.

Repeat the last (pattern) round (increasing 1 stitch in each round) and the plain ones alternately, until the twelfth (plain) round is reached, when there will be 7 plain stitches between every 2 putovers in the preceding round.

Thirteenth round.—* Th o, k 2 together, k 4, k 2 together and repeat from *.

Fifteenth round.—Th o, k 1, th o, k 2 together, k 2, k 2 together, and repeat from *

Seventeenth round.—* Th o, k 3, th o, k 2

No. 18.—KNITTED COVER FOR A PIANO STOOL OR A SMALL TABLE.

together, k 2 together and repeat from *.

Nineteenth round.—* Th o, k 5, th o, k 2 together, and repeat from *.

Twenty-first round.—* K 1, th o, k 5, th o, k 2 and repeat from *.

Twenty-second round.—K 2, k 2 together, k 1, k 2 together, k 3 and repeat from *.

Twenty-third round.—* K 2, th o, k 3, th o, k 3, and repeat from *.

Twenty-fourth round.—* K 3, k 2 together, k 5 and repeat from *.

Twenty-fifth round.—* K 3, th o, k 2 together, th o, k 4; repeat from *.

Twenty-sixth round.—Plain.

Twenty-seventh round.—* Th o, k 9, th o, k 1, and repeat from *.

Twenty-eighth, Thirtieth and Thirty-second rounds.—Plain.

Twenty-ninth round.—* K 1, th o, k 9, th o, k 2 and repeat from *

Thirty-first round.—* K 2, th o, k 9, th o, k 3 and repeat from *.

Thirty-third round.—* K 3, th o, k 9, th o, k 4, and repeat from *

Thirty-fourth round.—* K 4, k 2 together, k 5, k 2 together, k 5, and repeat from *.

Thirty-fifth round.—* K 4, th o, k 7, th o, k 5, and repeat from *

Thirty-sixth round.—* K 5, k 2 together, k 3, k 2 together, k 6, and repeat from *.

Thirty-seventh round.—* Th o and k 5 3 times in succession; th o, k 1, and repeat from *.

Thirty-eighth round.—* K 7, k 2 together, k 1, k 2 together, k 8 and repeat from *

Thirty-ninth round.—* K 1, th o, k 6, th o, k 3, th o, k 6, th o, k 2, and repeat from *.

Fortieth round.—* K 9, k 3 together, k 10, and repeat from *.

Forty-first round.—* K 2, th o, k 15, th o, k 3 and repeat from *.

Forty-second round.—* K 3, k 2 together, k 11, k 2 together, k 4, and repeat from *.

Forty-third round.—* K 3, th o, k 13, th o, k 4 and repeat from *.

Forty-fourth round.—* K 4, k 2 together, k 9, k 2 together, k 5 and repeat from *.

Forty-fifth round.—* K 4, th o, k 11, th o, k 5, and repeat from *.

Forty-sixth round.—* K 5, k 2 together, k 7, k 2 together, k 6 and repeat from *.

Forty-seventh round.—* Th o, k 5, th o, k 9, th o, k 5, th o, k 1 and repeat from *.

Forty-eighth round.—* K 7, k 2 together, k 5, k 2 together, k 8, and repeat from *.

Forty-ninth round.—* K 1, th o, k 6, th o, k 7, th o, k 6, th o, k 2 and repeat from *.

Fiftieth round.—* K 2, k 2 together, k 5, k 2 together, k 3, k 2 together, k 5, k 2 together, k 3 and repeat from *.

Fifty-first round.—* K 2, th o, k 6, th o, k 5, th o, k 6, th o, k 3 and repeat from *.

Fifty-second round.—* K 3, k 2 together, k 5, k 2 together, k 1, k 2 together, k 5, k 2 together, k 4 and repeat from *.

Fifty-third round.—* K 3, th o, k 6, th o, k 3, th o, k 6, th o, k 4 and repeat from *.

Fifty-fourth round.—* K 11, k 3 together, k 12 and repeat from *.

Fifty-fifth round.—* K 4, th o, k 15, th o, k 5 and repeat from *.

Fifty-sixth round.—* K 5, k 2 together, k 11, k 2 together, k 6, and repeat from *.

Work in this manner until the cover is as large as desired. Then cut it between the points and turn under to form the latter.

For the Lace Edge.—Cast on 5 stitches.

First row.—Sl 1, th o, k 2 together, th o, k 2.

Second row.—Sl 1, knit the rest.

Repeat 2nd row after every pattern row.

Third row.—Sl 1, th o, k 2 together, th o, k 2 together, th o, k 1.

Fifth row.—Sl 1, th o, k 2 together, th o, k 2 together, th o, k 2.

Seventh row.—Sl 1, th o, k 2 together, th o, k 2 together, th o, k 2 together, th o, k 1.

Ninth row.—Sl 1, th o, k 2 together, th o, k 2 together, th o, k 2 together, th o, k 2.

Eleventh row.—Sl 1, th o, k 2 together, th o, k 2 together, th o, k 2 together, th o, k 1.

Thirteenth row.—Sl 1, th o, k 2 together, th o, k 2 together, th o, k 2 together, th o, k 2 together, th o, k 2.

Fifteenth row.—Cast off 8 stitches, th o, k 2 together, th o, k 1.

Sixteenth row.—Plain. Then begin again at the first row.

KNITTED BATH-BLANKETS FOR INFANTS.

Bath blankets for babies are pretty when made after the following simple plan. Heavy zephyr is used, and somewhat large hard-wood or bone needles. 120 stitches will make a good width for the blanket. Knit it a square and a-quarter in length in plain back and forth knitting. It may be bordered with colors, although nothing except red will bear the washing required to keep the bath-blanket clean.

KNITTED CRADLE-BLANKETS.

Cradle-blankets are knit of single zephyr on smaller needles than are used for bath-blankets. 140 stitches are cast on at the beginning. The blanket may be prettily striped with "baby-blue" and white, with pink and white, or scarlet and white. A wide band of color at the ends and plain white between, looks well. Bind the ends with ribbon or galloon, or edge with knitted worsted lace.

KNITTED AFGHAN FOR BABY-CARRIAGE OR CRIB.

Knit plain or fancy strips, wide or narrow, of harmoniously contrasting zephyr, or Germantown worsted, until each is the whole length required. Then crochet them together with colored worsted to match the principal hue used, or with one that offers a vivid contrast. Crochet a loop-chain at each end, and knot lengths of worsted into the loops as a fringe.

If you prefer, knit squares, instead of strips, and join neatly with crocheted slip stitches.

RUGS.

KNITTED RUG.

NOS. 1, 2, 3 AND 4.—Use the thick heavy yarn that is sold for making rugs and is called Smyrna 1 shows the rug completed, and No. 4 the back of the work, while No. 2 shows the method of knitting in the wool after the latter has been cut in the lengths desired. These lengths must depend on

No. 1.—KNITTED RUG.

wool, for the pattern, and any heavy cotton or linen yarn for the foundation. The design for the rug, with the colors required, is given at No. 3, and each tiny block represents a strand of the wool of the color designated, so that the design may be very easily followed. No.

individual taste, according to the required thickness of the rug.

Cast on enough stitches to make the rug as wide as desired. The wool is knit in with every other stitch of the foundation-work as follows: Knit 1 stitch; lay in a strand of four or five lengths of the

No. 2.—DETAIL FOR KNITTED RUG.

wool, with one-half to the front and the other half to the back ; knit 1, then bring the wool from the back to the front with the ends even, and knit 1 ;

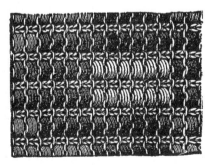

Description of Symbols: ■ Dark Brown ; ⊞ Light Brown ; ❑ Dark Blue; ▨ Light Blue; ▧ Maroon ; ◨ Dark Green ; ◨ Orange.

NO. 3.—DESIGN FOR KNITTED RUG SEEN AT NO. 1.

(For Description see preceding Page.)

lay in another strand and repeat the details given for all the work, being careful to follow the colors of the designs as indicated by the symbols.

The rug may have a lining if preferred, although it is not necessary. Rugs of this description are often made from the ravelings of Brussels carpeting, or from strips of silk or woollen goods cut like ordinary carpet rags but in shorter lengths.

KNITTED RUG.

(For Illustration see next Page.)

NO. 5.—This engraving illustrates a knitted bedroom rug, which is 56 inches long by 34 wide, and is worked with six-thread woolen yarn in three shades of red and one of the beige or natural écru shade. It is composed of 21 strips, set together so that an effect of shaded squares is produced. It is edged with a six-inch-wide border of maroon furniture-plush or of velveteen, which rests in notches on the knitted center. The rug is lined with stout linen crash.

Begin each strip by casting on 20 stitches, and knit to and fro in plain knitting; it will take about 42 rows to make a square, but this will depend on the quality of the work; the knitting must be quite tightly done. The strips are of different lengths, containing a varying number of squares.

For the first strip (see the left-hand upper corner of the illustration) work only a square of the darkest red.

Second strip.—A square of dark red, a square of medium red, a square of dark red. The square composing the 1st strip is joined in the middle square of the 2nd strip; up to the 8th the strips are so joined that they are one block or square longer at each end than the preceding one.

Third strip.—1 square of dark red, 1 of medium red, 1 of light red, 1 of medium red, 1 of dark red.

Fourth strip.—1 dark red, 1 medium red, 1 light red, 1 écru, 1 light red, 1 medium, 1 dark. In all the strips to the 18th inclusive, the first 3 and the last 3 squares are dark, medium and light red; this being understood, in the following directions only the middle squares will be mentioned.

Fifth strip.—3 écru.

Sixth strip.—5 écru.

Seventh strip.—3 écru, 2 light red, 2 ecru.

Eighth strip.—3 écru, 1 light red, 3 medium red, 2 écru.

Ninth strip.—2 écru, 1 light red, 1 medium red, 3 dark red, 2 écru.

Tenth strip.—2 écru, 1 medium red, 1 dark red, 3 medium red, 2 écru.

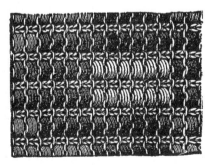

NO. 4.—BACK OF KNITTED RUG.

(For Description see preceding Page.)

Eleventh strip.—2 écru, 1 dark red, 1 medium red, 1 light red, 1 medium, 1 dark, 2 écru.

Twelfth strip.—2 écru, 3 medium red, 1 dark red, 1 medium, 2 écru.

Thirteenth strip.—2 écru, 3 dark red, 1 medium, 1 light, 2 écru.

NO. 5.—KNITTED RUG.

(For Description see this and preceding Page.)

Fourteenth strip.—2 écru, 3 medium red, 1 light, 3 écru.

Fifteenth strip.—2 écru, 2 light red, 3 écru.

The subsequent strips are each a block shorter than the one preceding.

Sixteenth to the Twenty-first strips.—Like the 6th to the 1st.

The strips are over-seamed together from the wrong side.

FELT RUG, WITH KNITTED CENTER.

NO. 6.—For the foundation of the rug use felt of any color desired, and pink or embroider the edges. Use double Germantown wool or any heavy yarn preferred, for the center.

Use two bone or wooden knitting needles and on one cast as many stitches as will be needed to make the center as wide, proportionately, as the one seen in the engraving. Knit across twice, plain.

Now, for the third (or first tufted) row, knit the first stitch; * then wind the wool around the first finger of the left hand (or two fingers if the tufts are desired quite long) from four to six times, according to the desired size of the tufts and the texture of the yarn. Now slip the right-hand needle through the next stitch and the wind-overs, throw the yarn over the needle and draw it through the wind-overs and stitch; keeping the wind-overs still on the fingers, slip the stitch mentioned off from the left-hand needle; knit the next stitch and slip the wind-overs off. Repeat from * across the row, and knit back plain. Repeat these two rows until the center is as long as desired. If the rows of tufts appear too close together, make three rows of plain knitting between the rows.

By the exercise of a little ingenuity this rug may be very economically made. Underneath the center ordinary muslin may be used, and strips of felt may be attached to this foundation in border style, as the tufted center will extend beyond the joining and conceal it. Line the rug with cambric, Silesia or any appropriate fabric, and thus conceal the border joinings on the wrong side. Flannel or remnants of ladies' cloth or broadcloth left over from dresses or other garments of these fabrics may be used in place of the felt strips. If preferred the whole rug may be knitted, and then bordered with fringe or a handsome crocheted edging.

KNITTED RUGS.

Pretty rugs are made by cutting silk, cotton or wool odds-and-ends into fine strips like carpet-rags and sewing them together in the same manner. Then with heavy bone or wooden needles knit back and forth, in strips of different colors, sewing the

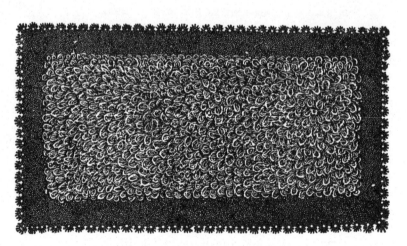

NO. 6.—FELT RUG, WITH KNITTED CENTER.

strips together to form the rugs. A border of black, knit by the plan seen at No. 2 on page 108, will greatly improve the appearance of such a rug.

USEFUL ARTICLES FOR CHILDREN'S WEAR.

CHILD'S CAP.

No. 1.—Full directions for making this cap may be found on page 66, where it is shown and

No. 1.—CHILD'S CAP.

described as an evening hood for a lady. It is therefore unnecessary to repeat the instructions here. For children the cap is usually made of white, or of some bright color such as blue or red. It is a dainty affair in white and may be made of silk and wool.

INFANTS' KNITTED SHIRT.

No. 2.—This little garment is made of Saxony yarn and silk, and is knitted in two sections that are afterward sewed together.

For One-Half of the Shirt.—Cast on 78 stitches for the lower edge.

First row.—K 2, * th o, k 1, th o, k 3; narrow twice, k 2, th o, k 1, th o, k 3, narrow twice, k 2, and repeat from * across the work.

Second row.—Purl across the work.

Third row.—N, k 1, * th o, k 1, th o, k 3, n twice, k 2, and repeat from * across the work.

Fourth row.—Narrow once and knit the rest plain, to reverse the pattern.

Fifth row.—P 2 together, p 1, * th o, p 1, th o, p 3, p 2 together twice (to narrow twice), p 2, and repeat from *.

Sixth row.—Narrow once and knit the rest plain, to reverse the pattern.

Seventh row.—N, k 1, and then repeat first row from first * for rest of row.

Eighth to Twelfth rows.—Same as from 2nd to 6th rows.

Continue the details given until there are thirty-two holes, one directly over the other, and then set the stitches for the ribs, as follows:

K 2, p 2, k 2, p 2 across the needle. Knit in this manner until there are 45 ribbed rows; then knit once across plain, and purl once across.

To make the Holes for the Ribbon.—K 4, * th o, n, k 3, and repeat from * across the row.

Knit back plain, and then knit 6 times across as follows: P 1 row, k 1 row, alternately to the end of the 6 rows, and bind off. This completes one-half of the shirt. Make the other half to correspond.

For the Sleeves.—Cast on 68 stitches, and work the same as for the lower part of the shirt until the strip is 3 holes deep. Then knit across plain and purl back, until there are 5 rows; *but in the third row, after knitting 17 stitches*, make holes the same as in the top of the shirt, for the ribbon. Then bind off and sew the ends of the sleeves together.

Sew the two halves of the shirt together to within an inch and a-half of the top, and then sew in the sleeves. Now crochet a shell-scollop about the neck, making 6 double crochets for each shell, and catching the latter down by a single crochet. Edge these scollops with single crochets of silk.

Finish the sleeves with similar scollops, and, if

No. 2.—INFANTS' KNITTED SHIRT.

desired, edge them with silk to correspond with the neck.

Run No. 1 ribbon in the holes as seen in the engraving, and tie it in a bow at the front.

CHILD'S CHEST PROTECTOR.

No. 3—This comfortable little article may be made of any fine worsted, such as single zephyr or Germantown wool, with Angora wool for the outer

No. 3.—CHILD'S CHEST PROTECTOR.

edge, and of any tint desired, though white is preferable as it may be renovated without losing any of its beauty. The tabs meet at the back of the neck where they may be fastened with a fancy pin.

In knitting this protector, it is advisable to first cut out a stiff paper pattern having the same general outlines as the engraving, but of a size suitable for the child who is to wear the protector.

The protector illustrated is for a child five years of age, and its dimensions are as follows :

Across the lower edge of the front, 5 inches.
From neck to lower edge,-------- 7½ inches.
From neck to point of tab,----- 7 inches.
Width at widest portion, ---13 inches.
From tab to tab at neck edge,--- 2½ inches.

By cutting a pattern by these measurements the proper shape may be obtained, and then a pattern larger or smaller, as required may be cut from it.

To begin the Protector.—Cast on 30 stitches and knit back and forth plain until there are 7 rows. (Once across and back forms one row).

To make the first row of Blocks.—After finishing the first row, turn and knit as follows : Knit 10, purl 5, knit 5, purl 5, knit 5. (In knitting the rows, 5

stitches must be knit plain at each side of every row, in order to form the border seen in the engraving.) Turn.

Knit 10, p 5, k 5, p 5, k 5. Turn.

K 10, p 5, k 5, p 5, k 5. Turn.

Knit back and forth in this order until there are 6 rows, each formed by knitting across and back. This completes the first set of blocks.

To begin the second set of Blocks.—(These blocks must alternate with those of the first set).

Knit 5; then widen by knitting a stitch out of the next stitch, but do not slip it off the needle; then purl out of this same stitch and slip it off; purl 4, k 5, p 5, k 5, now purl 1 out of the next stitch, but do not slip it off the needle, to widen, and then knit 5. Turn.

K 7 but do not slip off the last stitch; p 5, k 5, p 5, k 7 but do not slip the last stitch off the needle; p 1, k 5. Turn.

Complete this set of blocks after this manner, widening as described at each side between the blocks and border. Then make a set of blocks to correspond with the first set, widening as in the second set, and so on until the widest part of the protector is reached.

To make the Tabs.—When the neck edge is reached (in the protector illustrated) pass all the stitches of the border at one side and those of 6 blocks onto another needle; then bind off the stitches of 4 blocks for the neck-edge. Now continue the knitting after the manner before directed, to form the tab at one side, making the plain border at each side of the tab and narrowing at the outer border, instead of widening as before. Complete the other tab to correspond.

For the outer Edge.—Use Angora wool and crochet shells along the border as follows: 1 single crochet and 2 doubles all in the same space, selecting the spaces so that the shells will be perfectly flat. Fasten ties of ribbon at the sides as seen in the engraving, to tie the protector about the waist.

INFANT'S KNITTED LONG MITTENS.

No. 4.—This mitten is particularly easy to make,

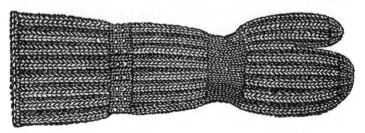

No. 4.—INFANTS' KNITTED LONG MITTEN.

being knitted on two needles, and sewed up after it is knitted. Use four-thread Saxony yarn.

Cast on 48 stitches carefully for the upper edge of the mitten.

Work in patent knitting for 3 inches in depth. (Patent knitting is formed by this method : Throw wool forward, slip 1, knit 2 together.) About 32 rows of this knitting will be required.

Thirty-third row.—Knit.

Thirty-fourth row.—Purl.

Thirty-fifth row.—Knit.

Thirty-sixth row.—Knit 1 and purl 1 alternately across the row.

Thirty-seventh row.—Knit.

Thirty-eighth row.—Purl.

Thirty-ninth row.—Like 36th row.

Fortieth row.—Purl.

Forty-first row.—Knit.

Forty-second to Seventy-second rows.—Patent knitting.

Seventy-third row.—K 1, p 1, repeat to end of row.

Seventy-fourth row.—P 1, k 1, repeat to end of row.

The seventy-third and seventy-fourth rows are repeated alternately 6 times more.

Work in patent knitting for 32 rows.

Take a third needle, and work on 33 stitches from the right-hand side of the mitten (leave 15 on the other needle without working for the present); continue to work in patent knitting for 32 rows on the 33 stitches now on the right side of the work; this is apparent in the engraving by the narrow stripe at the top of the mitten that was knitted next to the first 2 inches of patent knitting; knit a row, knitting 2 stitches together each time.

In the following 3 rows, k 1, p 1, and the one you knit in one row you purl in the next. Now draw the wool through all the stitches on the needle, pull it tight and fasten off.

On the 15 stitches of the thumb, work in patent knitting 28 rows; repeat the last three rows of the hand at the top of thumb; sew up the thumb and the side of the mitten, and it is finished.

Reverse the side on which the thumb is worked for the second mitten; in all other respects the work is the same. If desired two colors may be used for the mittens.

CHILD'S KNITTED HOOD.

No. 5.—This hood is made of four-thread Saxony yarn on medium-sized steel needles. Begin at the front of the hood, under the border. Cast on 115 stitches. Knit back and forth for 23 rows. Purl back in the 24th row.

Twenty-fifth row.—This begins the fancy pattern. K 1, * th o twice, k 2 together, k 1, and repeat from * across the row. Knit back plain, dropping the put-over thread. Then knit back and forth plain 4 times.

Repeat the last 6 rows 4 times more. This will make 5 fancy rows and 5 plain rows for the sides of the hood.

Now knit across once more and purl back. Next cast off 37 stitches; then k 2 together, k 1, * th o twice, k 2 together, k 1, and repeat 10 times more from last *. Then fasten on a thread and cast off the stitches left on the left-hand needle. Then continue knitting the pattern until there are 8 more plain stripes and 8 more fancy stripes; next, after the last plain stripe, knit across once and purl back. Then cast off the stitches. Join the crown-edges to the side-edges by an over-and-over stitch.

To Knit the Border.—Cast on 12 stitches. Knit 1 row plain. In the next and succeeding alternate rows, k 1, wind the yarn twice around the left forefinger, pass the right needle through the next stitch on the left needle and also under the top of the 2 wind-overs; throw the yarn around the needle and draw it under the wind-overs and through the stitch as in ordinary knitting. Repeat across the row, knitting the last stitch plain. Knit the alternate rows plain. Sew the border over the plain portion of the hood.

To Make the Cape.—Make 1 double crochet at one end or lower corner of the hood, 1 chain stitch, skip 1 stitch of the knitting, 1 double in the next; repeat across the work.

Next row.—4 chain, 1 double in each double underneath, with 1-chains between.

Next row.—5 chain, 1 double in the first double underneath, * 2 doubles in the next double with 1 chain between; 1 chain, 1 double in the next double and repeat from * across the row.

Next row.—Same as last except that each of the 2 doubles come in the space made by the 2 doubles underneath.

No. 5.—CHILD'S KNITTED HOOD.

Next two rows.—5 chain, 1 double in the double underneath, * 4 doubles, with 1 chain between the 2nd and 3rd doubles, in the space made by the 2 doubles underneath, 1 chain, 1 double in the next double; repeat from * across the row.

Next row.—Like last row, except that between the 2nd and 3rd doubles make 2 chain and catch with a single crochet in the top of the 2nd double to form a point, and so on across the row.

Run No. 2 ribbon through the fancy stripes as seen in the picture, and also across the neck of the hood, drawing it in a trifle at the back to shape it to the head, and tying it in a bow. Sew on the ties and add a narrow lace ruching; then line the hood with thin silk. Finish the top with a handsome bow of ribbon.

INFANTS' KNITTED SACK.

No. 6.—This little sack is made of pink and white Saxony yarn.

Cast on 281 stitches with the pink wool, and knit back and forth 6 times.

Now begin the pattern at the 7th row as follows:

Knit 1, th o, k 5, * slip 1, k 2 together, pass slipped stitch over last one, k 5, th o, k 1, th o, k 5, and repeat from * across the work, ending with th o, k 1.

Eighth row.—Seam back.

Repeat the 2 rows until there are 5 holes, and then join on the white wool and knit in the same way until there are 5 more holes, or 10 in all.

After the 10th hole is made, knit back and forth 3 times to form a rib, narrowing, *in the last row, once* at each side of every point.

Now knit the pattern again as follows: K 1, th o, k 4, * slip 1, k 2 together, pass slipped stitch over, k 4, th o, k 1, th o, k 4, and repeat from * across the row.

Seam back; and knit in this way until there are 3 rows of holes; and then make another rib *without* narrowing.

Now join on the white and make 4 rows of holes, the same as the last 3 rows of holes.

Join on the pink and knit a 3rd rib, narrowing as in the 1st rib.

Join on the white; k 1, th o, k 3, * slip 1, k 2 together, pass slipped stitch over, k 3, th o, k 1, th o, k 3, and repeat from *.

Make 3 rows of holes in this way; then join on the pink and make a 4th rib without narrowing.

Join on the white, and make 3 more holes the

No. 6.—INFANTS' KNITTED SACK.

same as last 3; join on the pink and make a 5th rib without narrowing.

Now, for each side of the front, take off 5½ points, slipping the stitches onto another needle, and knit 4 divisions and 3 ribs according to the directions for the last division and rib, being careful to keep the work even at the arm-hole edge.

Then make 3 ribs and 2 divisions like the last ones, narrowing *once* each time across, at the shoulder edge.

Then make 1 division of 2 holes, and half a rib; and then a row of holes for the ribbon as follows: K 1, * th o twice, narrow and repeat from * across the work.

Knit back plain, dropping the 2nd half of each of the 2 put-over threads, and bind off.

For the Back.—Knit off 8 whole points and 1 half point at each side, and then knit the divisions and ribs in the same order as those for the front, also narrowing at each shoulder edge and finishing the top with holes, the same as the top of the front.

Next knit the other side of the front the same as the first one, and join the shoulder edges by an over-and-over stitch.

For the Collar.—Cast on 161 stitches with the pink wool, and knit 1 rib. Then k 1, th o, k 3, * slip 1, k 2 together, pass slipped stitch over, k 3, th o, k 1, th o, k 3, and repeat from * across the work, ending with th o, k 1.

Seam back.

Make 3 rows of holes for this division.

Join on the white and make a rib, narrowing once at each side of every point. K 1, th o, k 2, * slip 1, k 2 together, pass slipped stitch over, k 2, th o, k 1, th o, k 2, and repeat from*. This division also has 3 holes.

Join on the pink, make half a rib without narrowing, and finish with a row of holes like those in the top of the sack.

Lay the collar over the sack, and run a ribbon or cord through the 2 rows of holes at the same time.

For each Sleeve.—Cast on 85 stitches with the pink and knit 1 rib. Then knit like the bottom of the sack, 10 holes and 1 rib. Now join on the pink and make a division of 4 holes, and then a rib narrowed once at each side of every point.

Now make 3 divisions of the white and 3 ribs of the pink, knitting 4 stitches at each side of the point instead of 5; and then bind off. Sew up the sleeves and join them to the arm-hole by an over-and-over stitch.

CHILD'S KNITTED PETTICOAT.

No. 7.—Use Saxony yarn of any tint desired, and 4 medium-sized wooden needles.

Begin at the border, casting on any number

NO. 7.—CHILD'S KNITTED PETTICOAT.

of stitches required that may be divided by 19.

First round.—Knit 8, sl 1, k 2 together, pass slipped stitch over, k 8 and repeat.

Second round.—* K 7; k 1 out of the front and 1 out of the back of the next stitch, thus making 1 stitch; sl 1, k 2 together, pass slipped stitch over; make 1 out of the next stitch as before; k 6 and repeat from *

Make 2 more rounds like second.

Fifth round.—* K 4, k 2 together, th o, k 2 together, k 5, th o, k 2 together, th o, k 2 together and repeat from *.

Sixth round.—Plain.

Repeat 5th and 6th rounds until the border is 5 holes deep. There will now be 17 stitches for each scollop.

For the Skirt-Portion, in First round.—K plain, knitting 2 together at the center of each scollop.

Second round.—* K 10 for the *plain* stripe. Then for the *fancy* stripe, p 1 and k 1 out of *each* of the next 6 stitches. Repeat from * to end of round.

Third round.—* K 10, ** sl 1, k 1, pass slipped stitch over, and repeat from ** 5 times more. Repeat from * for all the round. Repeat 2nd and 3rd rounds 27 times, or as many times as will be required by the length desired.

To decrease for the Waist: First round.—K 5, k 3 together and repeat.

Second round.—Plain.

Third round.—K 8, k 2 together and repeat.

For the Bodice.— K 34 rounds plain. Then divide the stitches for the front and back evenly, taking off 3 stitches at the beginning and end of each half and leaving them on a piece of cotton to be used under the arm later.

Now work each half separately for 16 rows, knitting 1 row and purling 1 row alternately, and keeping the end stitches plain in the purled rows.

Then work 8 rows of 1 plain, 1 p, keeping 11 stitches at each end plain. Then knit the 11 stitches at one side, cast off the stitches of the fancy portion, and knit the remaining 11. Then knit back and forth on each 11 stitches, decreasing 1 at the inner edge in every other row until there are but 6 stitches left at each side. Then cast these off.

Work the back in the same manner and join the two on the shoulders by an over-and-over stitch.

To form the Sleeve.—Pick up 39 stitches around each arm-hole, and also the stitches on the cotton under the arm. Knit 6 rounds plain, then 6 rounds as follows: K 1, p 1, and repeat. Then cast off.

Then around the neck and sleeves work with a crochet hook as follows: 1 single crochet, 3 chain, skip 1 stitch, 1 single crochet in the next stitch, and repeat. Insert a tasseled cord or a ribbon in the neck edge and tie at the back.

BOYS' KNITTED VEST, TO WEAR WITH A SAILOR BLOUSE.

No. 8.—This vest is knitted of blue and white Saxony yarn in plain back-and-forth rows. To make it, cut a pattern in paper of the shape illustrated, and of the size desired, or required by the boy who is to wear the vest. Knit back and forth as described above, making each stripe about half an inch wide. Narrow the neck and shoulder edges to fit the pattern, binding off when made necessary by the outlines of the pattern. Join the two sections at one shoulder by an over-and-over seam or by single crochets. Bind the neck with ribbon and fasten the other shoulder edges together with buttons and button-holes. Sew tape loops to the lower corners of the front and tape ties to the corners of the back, and in adjusting the vest pass the tapes through the loops and tie them in front.

If preferred, this vest may be knitted and purled so that the work will have a right and wrong side like a stocking. If desired, the neck edge may have a

NO. 8.—BOYS' KNITTED VEST, TO WEAR WITH A SAILOR BLOUSE.

plain knitted or crocheted edge, and the ribbon may be placed underneath it for a stay. Red may be used in place of white, if desired.

The vest may also be used as a chest protector to be worn under a coat or cloak.

Infant's Knitted, Long Bootees.

No. 9.—This little article for babies' wear is made of pink and white Germantown yarn, and is knitted as follows:

Cast on 52 stitches for the top, with the pink yarn.

First row.—Knit 4, * k 2 together, k 4, and repeat from * across the row.

Second row.—Knit 4, pick up a stitch from the foundation, pass it on to the left-hand needle, * and knit it off; k 5, pick up another stitch and repeat from *

Third row.—Knit 3, k 2 together, * thread over, k 1, th o, k 2 together; then put the right-hand needle through the next stitch, th o, draw through, but do not slip the stitch mentioned off from the left-hand needle; slip the *loop* drawn through onto the left-hand needle by passing the needle through it from the *front* to the *back;* then draw the stitch first mentioned *through* this loop onto the *right-hand* needle, allowing the loop to slip down over it; now k 2 together and repeat from * across the work, ending with knit 2 separately.

Fourth row.—Knit plain.

Join on the white and repeat the last 2 rows alternately until there are 8 holes. Then knit plain, 3 times across, or until there are 2 ribs of white; then 4 times across with the pink, and 5 times across with the white, seaming back the 6th time across. Now knit back and forth 6 times, and then begin the braided knitting as follows:

Knit 10; knit 5 onto another needle; knit 16 with the first needle; knit 5 onto a second extra needle; knit 16 with the first needle. In knitting back, knit 11, and also the 5 on the *last* extra needle; now knit the next 16, and then knit the 5 on the *first* extra needle, and then knit the remaining stitches. Now knit across plain. Then knit 11, seam the 10 in the braid, knit 11, seam the 10 in the braid and knit 10. Now repeat the last two rows, alternately, *twice more.*

Next row.—Like the first row of braided knitting, except that you narrow *once* back (at the outer side) of each braid.

In knitting back: Knit 10, and seam the 5 on the extra needle and also the 5 on the left-hand needle;

No. 9.—Infant's Knitted, Long Bootee.

then knit 11, seam 5 on the second extra needle, seam 5 on the left-hand needle, knit 9. Now complete this section of the braid the same as the first one, by 6 rows more.

Now make 3 more sections of the braided knitting, narrowing the same as in the last one, at the beginning of every section.

Knit the first 15 stitches off onto another needle; then, with another needle knit the next 13, for the top of the foot, and leave the remaining stitches on the left-hand needle. Now, on the 13 stitches, knit back and forth 21 times for the top of the foot, and fasten the yarn. Now with the needle on which are the first 15 stitches, pick up 11 stitches along the right-side edge of the foot, slip the needle through the 13 stitches at the toe and pick up the 11 stitches at the left-side edge of the foot; then join on the yarn and knit off the stitches remaining on the other needle.

Now knit 2 ribs, and seam back; then knit 2 ribs more and join on the pink worsted.

Now use 4 needles, dividing the stitches evenly on 3 of them, so as to close the work at the back. Then knit 9 rounds, and close the foot as follows: Divide the stitches evenly onto 2 of the needles. Knit to within 1 stitch of the center; then knit this 1 stitch, the center stitch and the next stitch beyond, *together.* Now fold the work so that the two needles face each other and the stitches on each are exactly opposite each other. Then knit 2 stitches together at once, 1 from each needle, at the same time binding them off. Bind them all off in this manner and fasten the yarn to the last stitch. If preferred the stitches may be bound off singly and the foot sewed together.

Sew the bootee together at the back. Run a twisted or crocheted cord through the lowest row of holes in the top, tip it with tassels of pink and white and tie in front. Dark colors may be used, if preferred; or, pale tints of gray, blue, pink, yellow or tan-color may be selected.

Plain white bootees are always pretty, especially when the infant is dressed all in white. If preferred, the yarn may be shrunk before it is used, as the little articles may need frequent washings. Spanish knitting yarn is often used for them.

Infant's Napkin Cover.

No. 10.—This convenient article is made of Dexter's cotton No. 8 and may be constructed as follows :

Cast on 25 stitches for the lower edge.

Then knit 16 ridges, widening each time across. (To widen, knit 2 stitches out of 1.)

Now make 12 ridges without widening, and then 8 ridges, narrowing once each time across in the first 4 ridges, and once *every other time* across in the last 4 ridges.

Now knit 4 ridges without widening. Then take off onto another needle at each side, 10 stitches, leaving the remaining ones on a thread or third

style, narrowing each time across until a point is made. Sew tapes to these points and run another tape in the holes at the top. Sew on buttons as seen in the picture, and when adjusting the cover fasten the lower edge in place with safety-pins, and tie the tapes in front.

Girls' Knitted Petticoat.
(For Illustration see next Page.)

No. 11.—Germantown wool or the more expensive camel's-hair wool may be used in knitting this little petticoat. White or colored yarn may be chosen for it, or two colors may be united. It is knitted in two parts which are over-seamed together.

Begin with the border at the bottom of the

No. 10.—Infant's Napkin Cover.

needle. Knit back and forth on each 10 stitches to make 5 ridges, narrowing once at the inner edge for every other rib. Make the button-holes while knitting the last ridge as follows : K 1, th o, n, k 1, th o, n, k 1; knit back plain to complete the 5th ridge, and bind off each side.

Pick up the stitches along the inner or narrowed edges of the sections just knitted, also picking up the stitches that are on the thread. Now work back and forth 4 times, knitting across one way and seaming back. Then make holes for the ribbon after the method described for the button-holes; then knit back plain and bind off.

Now across the ends of the 12 ribs that were not widened, pick up the stitches at each side, as seen in the engraving, and knit back and forth in ridge

skirt, casting on 18 stitches and knitting to and fro as follows:

First row.—Knit 15, th o, k 2 together, th o, k 1.
Second row.—Knit 4, purl 15.
Third row.—K 16, th o, k 2 together, th o, k 1.
Fourth row.—Knit 20.
Fifth row.—Purl 15, k 2, th o, k 2 together, th o, k 1.
Sixth row.—Knit 21.
Seventh row.—Knit 18, th o, k 2 together, th o, k 1.
Eighth row.—Knit 7, purl 15.
Ninth row.—Knit 22.
Tenth row.—Cast off 4 and k 17.
Eleventh row.—Purl 15, th o, k 2 together, th o, k 1.
Twelfth row.—Knit 19.
Thirteenth row.—Same as third.
Fourteenth row.—Knit 5, purl 15.

Fifteenth row.—Knit 17, th o, k 2 together, th o, k 1.

Sixteenth row.—Knit 21.

Seventeenth row.—Purl 15, k 3, th o, k 2 together, th o, k 1.

Eighteenth and Nineteenth rows.—Knit 22.

NO. 11.—GIRLS' KNITTED PETTICOAT.

(For Directions see this and preceding Page.)

Twentieth row.—Cast off 4, k 2, p 15.

Twenty-first row.—Same as first.

Twenty-second row.—Knit 19.

Twenty-third row.—Purl 15, k 1, th o, k 2 together, th o, k 1.

Twenty-fourth row.—Knit 20.

Twenty-fifth row.—Knit 17, th o, k 2 together, th o, k 1.

Twenty-sixth row.—Knit 6, purl 15.

Twenty-seventh row.—Knit 18, th o, k 2 together, th o, k 1.

Twenty-eighth row.—Knit 22.

Twenty-ninth row.—Purl 15, k 7.

Thirtieth row.—Cast off 4 and knit 17.

Repeat these 30 rows (3 scollops) 8 times more; then repeat the first 10 rows once, and cast off.

Now out of the top of this border take up 120 stitches. Begin on the right side and knit 1 row plain.

Second row.—Purl.

Third row.—Knit.

Fourth row.—Purl. This will cause all the stitches to appear purled on the right side.

Fifth row.—Knit plain.

Sixth row.—Knit 1, purl 1 across the row.

Seventh to Twenty-third rows.—Same as last row except that each stitch that appears purled in one row must appear knitted in the next, and *vice versa.*

Twenty-fourth row.—Same as fifth.

Twenty-fifth to Twenty-eighth rows.—Same as 2nd to the 5th rows.

Twenty-ninth row.— (Right side of work.) * Purl 5, k 1, p 1, k 1, and repeat from * across the work.

Thirtieth row.—Knit 1; * purl 1, k 7, and repeat across the work, ending with k 6.

Thirty-first row.—* Purl 1, k 3, p 1, k 1, p 1, k 1, and repeat from * across the work.

Thirty-second row.—K 1, * p 1, k 2, p 3, k 2, and repeat from *, ending with k 1.

Repeat from the 29th to the 32nd row 14 times more. Then repeat once more the 29th and 30th rows.

Now make 1 plain row, and then 38 rows in ribbed knitting, 2 plain and 2 purled stitches forming the ribs. Then make 1 plain row. Then narrow for the belt, by knitting every 2 stitches together, so that all the stitches will appear plain on the right side.

Knit 3 rows like the 2nd to the 4th; then a row of holes as follows: Th o, k 2 together, and repeat across the row. Then make 3 rows like those preceding the last and cast off.

This completes one-half, or the front of the petticoat. Knit the back half in the same manner except that the last 25 rows are divided at the middle and knit separately to form the placket opening. Join the two halves as described at the beginning of these instructions, and insert a tasseled cord or a narrow tie-ribbon in the holes at the top of the skirt.

By increasing the number of stitches for each half and knitting it longer, the skirt could be made for an adult.

INFANTS' KNITTED BOOTS.

NO. 12.—Commence at the top of leg, and cast on 1 needle 36 stitches with blue wool.

First row.—Knit.

Second row.—With white wool, purl.

Third row.—Knit.

Fourth row.—Make 1, k 2 together throughout the row.

Fifth row.—Knit.

Sixth row.—Purl.

Seventh row.—Knit.

Eighth row.—With blue wool, knit.

Ninth row.—With white wool, m 1, k 2 together throughout.

Tenth row.—With blue wool, knit.

Eleventh row.—With white wool, p 1 and k 1 alternately 7 times, k 8, k 1, and p 1 alternately 7 times.

Twelfth row.—Knit the purled and purl the knitted stitches in the last row.

Thirteenth row.—K 1 and p 1 alternately 7 times, k 8, p 1 and k 1 alternately to the end of the row.

Fourteenth row.—P 1 and k 1 alternately 7 times, p 1; take a third needle, p 3; with the first right-hand needle p the 4 next stitches, then k 1 and p 1 alternately to the end of row.

Fifteenth row.—P 1 and k 1 alternately 7 times, k 1, k the 3 stitches on the 3rd

NO. 12.—INFANTS' KNITTED BOOT.

or extra needle then the 4 next stitches on the left-hand needle; k 1 and p 1 alternately to the end of row.

Sixteenth row.—Knit the purled and purl the knitted stitches of last row and repeat from the 13th row 4 times more.

Thirty-third row.—K 1 and p 1 alternately 7 times, k 8; p 1 and k 1, 3 times.

Thirty-fourth row.—P 1 and k 1, 3 times; p 1, take the 3rd needle, p 3; with the right-hand needle p the 4 next stitches, k 1, p 1, k 1, p 1.

Thirty-fifth row.—P 1, k 1 twice; k 1, k the 3 stitches from the extra needle, k 5 from the 1st left-hand needle, p 1 and k 1 twice.

Thirty-sixth row.—P 1 and k 1 twice, p 10, k 1, p 1, k 1.

Thirty-seventh row.—K 1, p 1 twice; k 8, p 1, k 1, p 1, k 1.

Thirty-eighth row.—P 1, k 1 twice; p 1, take the 3rd needle and p 3; with the right-hand needle p 4, k 1, p 1, k 1.

Thirty-ninth row.—K 1, p 1, k 2, k the 3 from the extra needle, k 4 from the left-hand needle, k 1, p 1, k 1

Fortieth row.—P 1, k 1, p 10, k 1.

Forty-first row.—K 1, p 1, k 8, p 1, k 1.

Forty-second row.—P 1, k 1, p 1, p 3 on the extra needle; with the right-hand needle p 4, k 1.

Forty-third row.—K 2, k the 3 stitches from the 3rd needle, k 5 from the left-hand needle.

Forty-fourth row.—P 10; now work on the stitches left for the side of the boot, k 1 and p 1 in each of the 6 next stitches. Knit to end of row.

Forty-fifth row.—K until you have worked across the 10 toe-stitches, then k 1 and p 1 in each of the 6 next stitches; then knit to end of row.

Forty-sixth row.—With blue wool, k 1 and p 1 in the 1st and 10th of the 10 stitches of the toe. Knit the rest.

Forty-seventh row.—With white wool, knit.

Forty-eighth to Fifty-seventh rows.—With blue wool, knit plain; then cast off, sew the boot up on the wrong side with a needle and wool and draw the toe up into a nice shape; run a narrow ribbon through the holes of the ninth row, and tie in a bow in front.

CHILD'S KNITTED LEGGINGS.

NO. 13.—These leggings are made of white Germantown wool, and are for a child of one or two years of age. They are made in two sections, which are joined by a middle seam, as seen in the engraving.

Begin to knit each section as follows: Cast on 80 stitches for the top edge. Knit 2, purl 2, and repeat across the needle. Knit in this way 4 times

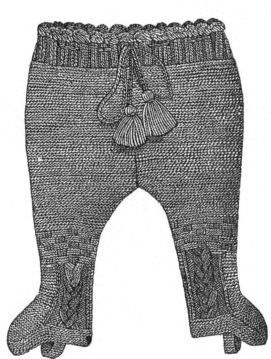

NO. 13.—CHILD'S KNITTED LEGGINGS.

across, being careful to preserve the regular order of the stitches in the ribs.

The Fifth time across.—K 2, p 2, k 1, * th o twice, n, p 1, k 2, p 2, k 1, and repeat from * across the row. In working back, work in the regular order, except that you drop the put-over thread to form the holes for the cord.

Now knit across 8 times more the same as the first 4 times.

Now knit 8 stitches, then knit back on the 8; k 16, and then knit back; k 24, and knit back; k 32, knit back; k 40, knit back; k 48, knit back. This will make 6 ridges at one side of the work before you have knit once entirely across, and they are made to lengthen the back portion of the section. Now knit back and forth entirely across, until there are 43 ridges at the front edge of the section.

Next knit 15 ridges, narrowing once at the beginning of every time across. There should now be 50 stitches on the needle.

To Make the Fancy Portion.—K 3, p 7, and repeat across the needle. In working back, p 7 and k 3, across the needle. Work in this way until there are 3 ridges, and then reverse the design for the next 3 ridges as follows: P 5, k 3, * p 7, k 3, and repeat from * across the needle, except at the end, where you knit 5. In working back, k 5, p 3, k 7, p 3, and repeat across the needle as before.

Repeat this pattern until there are 5 blocks as seen in the picture.

To Make the Braid and Remainder of Section: First row.—K 4, p 3, k 9, p 3, k 12, p 3, k 9, p 3, k 4.

Second row.—K 3, p 1, k 3, p 9, k 3, p 1, k 10, p 1, k 3, p 9, k 3, p 1, k 3.

Repeat first and second rows.

Fifth row.—K 4, p 3; * take another needle and knit 3 very loosely onto it; now knit 3 stitches with the first or right-hand needle; now place the extra needle with its 3 stitches *back of the first needle;* then knit 3 more with the first needle, and with this same needle knit off the 3 stitches on the extra needle to form the twist of the braid.* Now p 3, k 12, p 3, and repeat between the stars; p 3, k 4.

Sixth row.—K 3, p 1, k 3, p 9, k 3, p 1, k 10, p 1, k 3, p 9, k 3, p 1, k 3.

Repeat from the first row of braid until there are 20 ridges at the middle portion of the front.

For the Instep.—Knit 31 stitches; slip the remaining 19 onto another needle; knit back 12 stitches of the 31, and leave the remaining 19 on the first needle. Knit the 12 stitches now on the center needle back and forth until there are 10 ridges; knit 3 more ridges, narrowing once every other time across. Now with the needle left at the right side of the work, pick up the stitches at the adjoining side of the instep-portion and knit across the toe; then with the needle at the left side of the work pick up the stitches along the adjoining edge of the instep, and with the right-hand needle knit them off. Now knit back and forth until there are 6 ridges below the instep-portion, and bind off. Knit a strap 5 stitches wide and 15 ridges long, and sew it to the lower edges of the foot-portion as seen in the picture.

Now sew up each leg-seam, and join the two sections by a middle seam.

Crochet scollops around the top as follows: Make * 4 chain, 2 double crochets drawn up long and caught down flatly by a single crochet; repeat from *.

Run a cord through the holes made for it, and tip it with tassels. A ribbon or an elastic may be used in place of the cord.

CHILD'S KNITTED SHIRT.

NO. 14.—This engraving illustrates a pretty little shirt for a child 3 or 4 years of age. It is made on 4 No. 16 needles, with Shetland wool.

On 3 needles cast 176 stitches, using 11 for each scollop. Divide the stitches as follows: 88 on one needle, and 42 on each of the other two.

First four rounds.—Purl

Fifth round.—K 1, * th o, k 3, k 2 together twice, k 3, th o, k 1, and repeat from * around the work.

Sixth, Seventh and Eighth rounds.—Repeat the 5th round.

Next three rounds.—Purl. Then repeat from the 5th round twice more, being careful to make the holes come over those underneath, and continuing the pattern from where it was left off, to begin the three purled rounds.

Next repeat the 5th round 8 times.

Knit 2 plain rounds.

Then knit 40 rounds of 4 plain stitches and 2 purled ones alternately, in rib style.

Now, on the needle having 88 stitches knit back and forth, preserving the ribbed effect, for 15 rows; then make 16 rows of plain knitting.

Now on the first 14 stitches of the next row, knit back and forth for 20 rows and cast off.

Then cast off the remaining stitches so that there will be 14 stitches left for the other shoulder, which you knit to correspond with the first one.

NO. 14.—CHILD'S KNITTED SHIRT.

Now put all the remaining stitches onto one needle and knit 15 rows of ribbing and 16 plain rows and cast off. Join the ends of the shoulder portions to the top of the edge just finished, and complete the neck edge with crochet as follows:

First row.—Double crochets with 1-chains between in every other stitch of the knitting.

Second row.—Double crochets arranged in clusters, as seen in the picture.

To make the Sleeves.—Cast on either 66 or 88 stitches, according to the size of the arm, and repeat the first 14 rows of the pattern. Then knit and purl alternate rows for 16 rows, cast off and sew to the arm-hole.

KNITTED UNDER-DRESS FOR CHILDREN.

(For Illustrations see next Page.)

NOS. 15, 16 AND 17.—The material used for knitting this little garment is white lambs' wool, but any color preferred may be used. The front and back parts are knitted separately and each is 15¾ inches long. The skirt, when the parts are joined, is 38¾ inches wide or around. Each section is begun at the lower edge, and when completed, all three are seamed together on the wrong side. Begin the front as follows:

Cast on 144 stitches and knit the scolloped portion (see No. 16) as below directed:

First row.—Slip 1 and purl all the rest.

Second row.—Slip 1 and knit all the rest.

Third row.—Slip 1, * k 2 together, k 3, th o, k 1, th o, k 3, k 2 together at the back; repeat from * and at the end of the row k 1.

Fourth row.—Slip 1 and purl the rest.

Fifth, Seventh and Ninth rows.—Like the 3rd.

Sixth row.—Slip 1, knit the rest.

Eighth row.—Slip 1, purl the rest.

Tenth row.—Slip 1, knit the rest.

Eleventh row.—Slip 1, purl the rest.

Twelfth row.—Slip 1, knit the rest.

Repeat from the 3rd row, 5 times more; then repeat the 3rd row once more, except that you *omit* the put-over threads, in order to decrease the 24 stitches. This completes the scolloped portion.

Now begin the basket pattern seen below the holes in illustration No. 17, as follows:

Purl 3, knit 3 across the row; knit back purling the knitted stitches and knitting the purled stitches so as to preserve the effect of the pattern. Knit over and back once more in this order; this will form 1 section of the pattern. Now knit the next section, changing the order of the stitches so that a purled block will come over a knitted one and *vice versa*. Knit in this way for 48 rows, gradually decreasing 1 stitch at a time at each side until 12

NO. 15.—KNITTED UNDER-DRESS FOR CHILDREN.
(For Directions see this and preceding Page.)

stitches are decreased. This brings the skirt portion of the front to the waist-line.

The waist portion is then begun and 28 rows knitted without increase or decrease. This brings you to the left arm-hole.

The first row for the arm-holes is as follows: Cast off 4 stitches at each side and gradually narrow 9 stitches at the sides in the next 12 rows. Then knit 8 rows without decreasing; then cast on gradually, in the next 12 rows, 8 stitches. In the next row cast off from 4 to 6 stitches. Now begin one shoulder on 9 stitches, leaving the remaining stitches unknitted. Knit 12 rows, gradually decreasing the 9 stitches to 1. Knit the other shoulder section to correspond with the first.

For one-half of the Back.—Cast on 108 stitches and work the scolloped pattern as high as that on the front. Then work 48 rows of the basket pattern and then 3 purled rows (see picture No. 17;) but in the *first* purled row knit every 3 stitches on the first 9 blocks together. In this way the skirt is fulled a little at the middle. After knitting these 3 rows, make the holes for the ribbon as follows: Slip 1, * k 1, n, th o twice, k 2 together through the back of the stitches, and repeat from *.

Next row.—Knit plain, purling the second half of each put-over thread. Then make 3 more purled rows. This brings the work to the waist portion. Now make 24 rows of the basket pattern, which brings you to the arm-hole. Then work 4 more rows gradually decreasing 6 stitches at the arm-hole side; now make 16 rows without decreasing. Now knit the shoulder on 9 stitches to correspond with that of the front.

Knit the second half of the back to correspond with the first.

Sew the side seams of the parts as suggested. Slip the stitches of all 3 sections including those of

the shoulders onto 1 needle, and knit the entire upper edge like illustration No. 17, which has been described at the waist line of the back. Finish each arm-hole with a strip knitted like the neck edge and sew on over-and-over.

Finish the edges with single crochets and chains (see No. 17.) Close the seam at the back, leaving an opening as long as desired, and finish its edges with single crochets. Insert narrow ribbons, tying them in bows as seen in the engraving.

DESIGN FOR A CHILD'S KNITTED PETTICOAT.
(No Illustration.)

This is a very pretty design and may be knitted in Germantown wool or Saxony yarn. It is knit in widths that are afterwerd sewed together and finished with any pretty crocheted edge liked. For each width, cast on 135 stitches.

First row.—Knit 2 and purl 1 all the way across.
Second row.—K 2 and p 7 across the row.
Third row.—Knit 6 and purl 3 all the way across.
Fourth row.—K 4 and p 5 all the way across.
Fifth row.—Knit 4 and purl 5 all the way across.
Sixth row.—Knit 6 and purl 3 all the way across.
Seventh row.—K 2 and p 7 all the way across.
Eighth row.—K 8 and p 1 all the way across.

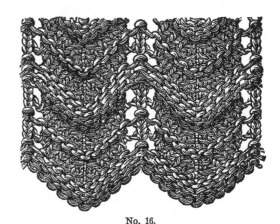

No. 16.

No. 17.

NOS. 16 AND 17.—DETAILS FOR KNITTED UNDER-DRESS.
(For Directions see this and preceding Page.)

The pattern is to be repeated until the skirt is as long as is necessary. The garment is intended either for a girl or boy. If for a boy, it can be used as a kilt skirt, with a waist.

KNITTED COVER FOR A BABY'S FEEDING BOTTLE, WITH DETAIL.

NOS. 18 AND 19.—This cover is useful in keeping the contents of a baby's feeding bottle from becoming cold too quickly, and the cord prevents the child from throwing the bottle to the floor. As illustrated, it is made of red and gray knitting yarn, knitted back and forth in alternate stripes, as

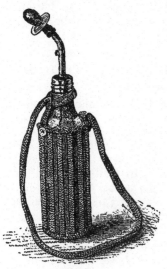

No. 18.

No. 19.

NOS. 18 AND 19.—KNITTED COVER FOR A BABY'S FEEDING BOTTLE, WITH DETAIL.

may be seen by referring to engraving No. 19. To begin it, cast on 50 stitches, and for the flat stripe knit 4 rows, as follows: K 1 row, p 1 row, and repeat once more. This stripe may be of the gray yarn. Then fasten on the red and purl 4 rows. Repeat each stripe 12 times, bind off and close the side edges with a crochet hook and slip stitches.

Crochet a bottom-piece, beginning at the center and working round and round in single crochets. Join it by a row of single crochets.

Finish the top as follows: 1 s c, 1 ch, 2 d c, 1 ch, 1 s c; repeat around the entire edge. The cord is knitted round and round with 4 needles on a foundation of 9 stitches, and is about 26 inches long. A short section of the cord is also added about the neck of the bottle and joined to the long cord as seen in the picture to prevent the cover from slipping off the bottle.

The long cord is fastened on at one end by a button and button-hole, so that the cover may be easily removed when the bottle is to be cleaned.

CHILD'S KNITTED LEGGINGS.

NO. 20.—Use Germantown wool or any yarn of a similar texture and weight. Four needles are necessary.

Cast on 63 stitches, making 20 on each of 2 needles, and 23 on the 3rd; the odd stitch is for the seam, which is purled at the end of the last needle in one round, and knitted in the other; this stitch is knitted in the same way throughout the work.

For the ribbed top, knit 2 and purl 2 alternately for 2½ inches.

For the leg knit 3 rounds and purl 3 rounds alternately, for 1½ inch, then on larger needles knit 2 rounds and purl 2 rounds for 3 inches; now take the smaller needles and continue as before, but decrease for the ankle gradually by knitting or purling, as the case may be, the 2nd and 3rd stitches of the first needle together; and the last 2 stitches but 1 of the last needle together; that is, decreasing on each side of the seam-stitch in every 3rd round until you have only 20 stitches left; knit 1 and purl 1 alternately for 2 inches.

Now on the 21 stitches at the back of the leg, knit 1 and purl 1 alternately in 1 row, and in the next row purl the knitted, and knit the purled stitches; repeat these 2 rows for 1¾ inch, as you would for the heel of a stocking; put the stitches on a piece of cotton and tie it, to prevent their falling off; pick up 12 stitches at side of heel, knit across the front (still preserving the rib); pick up 12 stitches at the other side of the heel, continue to work on the side-stitches and the front of the foot; the side-stitches are knitted plain, and the front is ribbed; decrease in every 3rd row by knitting together the last two stitches of the front side of the heel, and the first 2 on the other side together, until all the side-stitches are taken in; then work on the front stitches for about 2 inches.

Now pick up the stitches at sides of the foot, and those left on the cotton from the heel; purl for 5 rounds, then cast off. Finish the bottom of the foot with a crocheted edging worked as follows: 1 double crochet into a stitch, 3 chain, 1 double into the first; skip 1 stitch, and repeat from the beginning of the row.

Sew on an elastic strap, as seen in the engraving, to keep the legging in place.

Dark brown or blue, or black, is generally selected for making leggings, although a brighter blue, deep red, or gray may be chosen with a pretty effect. The leggings may be made larger or smaller by casting on more or less stitches.

NO. 20.—CHILD'S KNITTED LEGGING.

KNITTED PETTICOAT BODICE, WITH DETAIL.

NOS. 21 AND 22.—This bodice, knitted very easily of white crochet or soft unbleached cotton, will be appreciated by those accustomed to wear

No. 21.

No. 22.

NOS. 21 AND 22.—KNITTED PETTICOAT BODICE, WITH DETAIL.

a woolen bodice in winter, as it gives a most useful one for putting on in Spring and Autumn. The bodice is begun at the lower edge and knitted plain backwards and forwards in two halves on a foundation of from 92 to 101 stitches, the first stitch in each row being slipped; from 200 to 220 rows are required for the length. About 21 stitches are then reckoned for each shoulder and the work is continued as before, while between the shoulders the first and last, and also every third stitch is dropped (see No. 22), so that a transparent foundation is made. The dropped stitches are replaced again in the next row by taking up and knitting the upper bar-like threads, all the stitches in the next row being cast off between the shoulder for the neck-opening. Each shoulder-part is then knitted alone from 14 to 16 rows deep. The number of stitches decreased are now put in again by casting on afresh, and the second half of the bodice knitted in just as many rows as the first. When the worker has reached the lower edge every third stitch, now including the shoulders, is again drop-

ped, only at the side edges 3 stitches are always left. The number of stitches are now completed and cast off as before described. The side edges are crocheted together with a row of singles, leaving arm-holes 6¼ inches long. The neck-opening and edge of the arm-hole are secured and finished off with a picot-row made alternately of double crochets round several of the knitted bars, 5 chain, and 1 double back into the first chain. Narrow ribbon is slipped through these open insertion-rows and tied in bows.

BABY'S KNITTED STOCKINGS.

NO. 23.—This stocking is knitted quite loosely with white Saxony wool. Cast on 48 stitches, and knit back and forth.

First row.—Plain knitting. Always slip the 1st stitch.

Second to Eighteenth rows.—Ribbed knitting, 2 stitches plain and 2 purled.

Nineteenth row.—For a row of holes through which a ribbon is run, by turns knit 2 together and put the wool over. Then follow 58 rows of plain knitting, in the 32nd, 40th, 46th, 52nd and 56th of which, for narrowing, knit together the 3rd and 4th stitches from the beginning and the 4th and 3rd from the end. The succeeding 12 rows are in ribbed knitting, 1 stitch plain and 1 purled. Then knit the heel in 2 separate halves, on the first 11, and on the last 11 stitches of the row, omitting those between; knit 20 rows of plain knitting for each part of the heel, but in the 13th, 15th and 17th of them, at one stitch from the edge, knit 2 together. After completing the 20th row cast off the stitches, take up the 10 edge stitches at the inner edge of the heel, and on all the stitches together knit 44 rows of plain knitting back and forth; but in the 1st row of the 44, for narrowing, knit together the first 2 stitches, the 10th and 11th, then the 11th and 10th from the end, and the last 2 stitches; in the 29th row knit together the 6th and 7th, 13th and 14th, 20th and 21st, and 27th and 28th; in the

No. 23.—BABY'S KNITTED STOCKINGS.

33rd, 37th, 39th, 41st and 43rd rows, narrow in a straight line above the narrowings in the 29th row. Through the stitches left after the last row, draw the wool and fasten off; then sew up the edge-stitches of the stocking from the wrong side.

CHILD'S KNITTED SACK.

NO. 24.—This sack is made of 3-thread Saxony yarn in 2 colors—pale-blue and white.

Cast on 100 stitches for the back and knit as follows: Knit once across plain; then knit 3 and purl or seam 7, and repeat across the row. Knit back as follows: Knit 7, purl 3, and repeat across the row.

Now for the 3rd row, knit 3, purl 7, and repeat across the row.

Fourth row.—Purl.

Fifth row.—Purl 4, knit 3, * purl 7, knit 3 and repeat from * across the row.

Sixth row.—Purl 5, * knit 7, purl 3 and repeat from * across the row.

Seventh row.—Purl 5, knit 3, * purl 7 and knit 3, and repeat from * across the row.

Eighth row.—Purl.

Two sections of the pattern are formed by the details just given. Repeat these two sections, purling every 4th row, until there are 25 sections counting from the bottom.

Now cast on 65 additional stitches for one sleeve; purl back to the other side, and cast on 65 stitches for the other sleeve. Then knit 10 more sections, preserving the order of the design. Purl back.

Now slip onto another needle 98 stitches, and bind off the next 37 stitches for the back of the neck.

Now with the 95 stitches remaining, knit 4 sections of the pattern, being careful to have the design come in the proper order. Now purl back. Then cast on 20 stitches and, working back, purl 5, knit 3, * purl 7, knit 3, and repeat from * in the regular order across the row. Knit 10 more sections and bind off the 65 stitches added for the sleeve and purl the remainder of the row. This completes the sleeve. Then knit 25 more sections to complete one front.

Finish the other sleeve and front to correspond. The purled rows come on the wrong side of the garment. Close the seams of the sleeves and those under the arms by an over and over stitch.

To Make the Edging.—The edging for the front and lower edges of the sack is knitted so as to fit the corners and is made *crosswise* instead of *up and down.* This necessitates casting on at once all of the stitches needed to make a strip long enough to reach along the edges mentioned, and long needles will be required for the work. Cast on 473 stitches and knit across once plain.

First row.—Knit 1, * th o, k 1, slip 1, k 2 together, pass slipped stitch over, k 1, th o, k 1, and repeat from * across the work, ending with th o, k 1.

Second row.—Plain.

NO. 24.—CHILD'S KNITTED SACK.

Repeat these two rows until the edging is 3 holes deep. Then knit back across 18 points in the manner already directed, ending with k 1, th o, k 1. Then knit 4 together, slip 1, knit 3 together, pass slipped stitch over, knit 4 together, slip 1, knit 4 together, pass slipped stitch over, slip 1, knit 4 together, pass slipped stitch over, th o, k 1, th o, k 1; this will draw in the work for the turn at the corner. Now work again according to the directions for the first row across 33 points, ending with k 1, th o, k 1; this will bring you to the other corner which you make the same as the first one, and then finish the row in the regular manner.

Knit back plain to within 1 of the 5 narrowed stitches at the corner; then knit 2 together 3 times in succession, and knit plain to the next corner. Work the same as the first corner and then knit plain to the end of the row.

Now knit back and forth according to the directions for the first 2 rows until the edging is 7 holes deep. Then knit across plain and bind off. Sew the edging on so that the rounding side of the points will be outward.

To Knit the Collar.—Cast on 129 stitches. Knit according to the directions given for the edging, until 3 holes are made. Then work along the first and last 4 points of the collar the same as at the corners in the edging, to turn them. Work back and forth until the collar is 7 holes deep; and in the last row of plain knitting, pick up the stitches at each end, across the edge of the point. Work back as follows, very loosely: Knit 1, * th o 3 times, k 2 together and repeat from * across the row. In knitting back, knit 2 stitches together and drop the remaining 2 put-over threads. Repeat across the work. Then knit across plain twice, and bind off. Then sew the collar to the neck.

For the Sleeve Edging.—Cast on 67 stitches and knit the same as for the lower edge, making 11 points for each sleeve. Join the ends, sew it on and turn it back over the sleeve. Run a ribbon in the holes at the neck and tie as seen in the engraving.

NO. 25.—INFANTS' KNITTED BAND.

INFANTS' KNITTED BAND.

NO. 25.—This band is made of 4-thread Saxony yarn in two sections, and is knitted back and forth in ribbed style—that is, knit 2, purl 2, knit 2, purl 2, etc., etc.

Cast on 76 stitches for each section and knit as directed above until there are 107 rows, or about 8 inches in depth; bind off and sew the sections together by an over-and-over stitch. Finish the edge at the top and bottom with single crochets.

At the center of the front crochet on a little strap, 11 single crochets wide and 5 rows deep.

BABY'S HOOD.

No. 26.—Use Belding's knitting silk and quite coarse steel needles. Cast on 75 stitches. Knit 40 stitches; turn. Knit back 10 stitches. Turn again and knit 20 stitches; turn. Knit back 30 stitches; turn, knit back 40 stitches; turn, knit back 50 stitches. Knit all the stitches the next time. This makes the hood a little deeper at the top than at the sides.

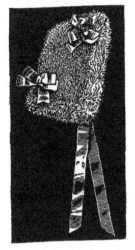

No. 26.—BABY'S HOOD.

Knit 36 rows plain. Bind off 25 stitches; then knit 54 rows plain on the next 25 stitches, for the crown, and bind these stitches off; also bind off the 25 stitches that were left before knitting these.

Sew the sides and crown together. Take up all the stitches at the neck and knit 16 rows for the cape.

Make a row of double crochets all around the hood, working in every stitch. Draw the neck in with a cord, and trim the hood with eider down or any pretty fur, feather or silk trimming. Finish with ribbon ties and bows as seen in the picture.

INFANTS' KNITTED SOCKS.

No. 27.—This sock is made of Saxony yarn in two colors —pink and white—and is a very dainty little affair.

To Make the Foot Portion. —Cast on 35 stitches. Knit back and forth for each row and make 6 rows, widening at the back by 1 stitch, and widening at the front by 2 stitches in every row, so that in the last row there will be 41 stitches. In widening so that no openings will result, two methods may be used. The first is as follows: Put the needle through a stitch in the ordinary manner, throw the thread around it twice and then knit the stitch off in the regular way, but keeping the two thrown-over threads on the needle to make the two new stitches required. In knitting these two new stitches, knit the first in the regular way and the

second through the back. By the other method knit through the front of a stitch in the usual way, but do not slip it off the needle; now knit through the back of the *same* stitch and then slip it off.

The plain knitting first made comes under the sole of the foot.

To Make the Upper Part of the Foot.—After the 6 rows of plain knitting are made, begin the 7th as follows: Knit 2, p 2, k 2, p 2, and repeat across the row until there are 22 tiny blocks, widening by 2 stitches at the front edge or toe of the sock. Turn.

Eighth row.—Purl 4, k 2, * p 2, k 2; repeat from * across the row. These two rows of knitting form one completed row of blocks.

Ninth row.—Begin so as to alternate the order of the blocks, thus:

Purl 2, k 2, p 2, k 2, and repeat across the row, widening as before.

Tenth row.—Knit 4, * p 2, k 2, and repeat from * to end of row. This completes the second row of blocks.

Now make 3 more rows of similar blocks, widening in the same order. Then 4 more rows without widening; 3 more rows, widening by 1 stitch at the front edge.

To Make the Instep and Toe.—Pass 36 stitches (beginning at the back) on another needle. Then make 9 rows of blocks, widening at the toe-edge in every row by 2 stitches, regulating the widening so that the basket effect of the blocks will not be disturbed. This forms one-half of the foot. Knit the other half of the toe and instep (8 rows more) to correspond with the first half, narrowing instead of widening. At the last row cast on 36 stitches, and work the remainder of the foot to correspond

No. 27.—INFANTS' KNITTED SOCK.

with the other side. Double the foot together and join it at the back and along the sole, sewing the toe point into the angle under it. Now pick up all the stitches around the top of the foot portion that are not already on the needle, and then knit back and forth 6 times, thus making 3 rows, and bind off.

For the Top.—Cast on 79 stitches. Purl once across, and knit back plain.

Third row.—Purl 2 separately, then purl 3 together; * purl 3, then purl 3 together, and repeat from * across the row until within 2 of the end, and purl these 2 separately.

Fourth row.—Knit 1, th o, k 3, * th o, k 1, th o, k 3, and repeat from * across the row. Repeat third and fourth rows until the top is 21 holes deep, making the last row like the fourth. Now across four ribs at each side knit plain, and between the plain sections work the same as third row, to preserve the uniformity of the ribs. Now knit plain again at each side, working between the same as in the fourth row.

Fifth row.—Purl 2, th o twice and p 2 together; and repeat to end of plain section. Make open-work between.

Sixth row.—Knit plain at sides, dropping every second put-over thread; make open-work between.

Next two rows.—Knit plain, also knitting plain across the next row of open-work and the next rib at each side. This will leave 4 rows of open-work and ribs at the center of the needle.

NO. 28.—BABY'S KNITTED BOOTEES.

Now bind off 30 stitches, then knit across in open-work style until there are 30 stitches left on the needle; bind off the 30, leaving the open-work on the needle. Join the yarn and knit the remainder of the instep in open-work, so that there will be 32 holes from the top of the sock to the lower edge of the instep. Then bind off.

Now sew the top of the sock together at the back, and join its lower edge to the foot portion on the inside, where the plain knitting around the top begins.

Run a cord through the holes in the plain portion back of the instep, tip it with balls or tassels, and tie it in front of the ankle.

BABY'S KNITTED BOOTEES.

NO. 28.—These bootees are knitted with white Saxony wool on coarse steel needles; they are done in a ribbed pattern and finished with a knitted edging turned over the top. The scollop of the edging and the toe of the bootee are ornamented in light blue floss-silk.

Cast on 60 stitches to begin, and knit to and fro. Knit the first 4 rows all to appear plain on the right side (as the work is done to and fro, and consequently turned at the end of each row, one row will be knitted plain and the next purled); then knit 4 rows to appear purled on the right side, then 4 more plain rows followed by 4 more purled rows, making 16 rows. Knit 40 more rows (5 ribs) to carry the work to the top; but in the 18th row begin the instep. For this take the middle 10 stitches on a separate needle, leaving the rest aside, and knit 17 rows of the pattern on them,

and at the end of each row narrow by knitting the last of the middle stitches together with the first of the stitches set aside, the narrowed stitch to be plain on the right side; slip the first stitch of every row. After completing the 17 rows take up all the stitches again, but narrow 7 more times, in each succeeding 2nd row, in a straight line above the previous narrowings; in the 34th row and 3 times thereafter in each succeeding 2nd row, widen after the first stitch from the beginning and before the last stitch from the end of the row; (to widen, knit 2 stitches out of 1, 1 plain and 1 purled). At the end of the 56th row cast off the stitches. Fold the foundation stitches through the middle and over-seam them together on the wrong side; then over-seam the end stitches of the 56 rows.

For the edging cast on 58 stitches and knit to and fro, as follows :

First row.—Slip the 1st, k 1, th o, * k 2, n 2 (to narrow 2, slip 1, knit the next 2 together, and cast off the slipped stitch over the knitted stitch), k 2, th o, k 1, th o ; repeat 6 times more from *. Omit the last th o at the end.

Second row.—Purl throughout.

Repeat the 1st and 2nd rows 3 times more.

Next knit a plain row, in which narrow 18 stitches at intervals ; then 4 rows to appear purled on the right side, and 3 rows plain on the right side, after which cast off, join the ends, and over-seam the lace to the bootee. Trim the front with silk cord and tassels as illustrated.

KNITTED TOQUE OR TOBOGGAN CAP.

NO. 29.—Use Germantown yarn and work as follows :

For the Crown.—Cast on 42 stitches. Knit plain for 120 rows and bind off loosely. Join the two ends by an over-and-over seam.

NO. 29.—KNITTED TOQUE OR TOBOGGAN CAP.

For the Border.—Cast on 16 stitches and knit until you have a piece long enough to sew on the crown portion. Join its ends, sew it to the lower edge of the crown, placing the seams together, with the border *inside* the crown; then turn the border up on the outside to conceal the seam.

Fold the toque so that the seam will come at the middle. Now lay a box-plait in the top, turn the latter down for about a finger and fasten it under a satin bow at the top of the border.

This toque may be worn by adults as well as children, and may be made of any color prefered, or of a combination of two colors. It may be made to match a toboggan suit in colors, and pompons may be substituted for the bow.

KNITTED ALPINE OR STORM HOOD.

No. 30.—The hood here illustrated may be made of Germantown wool or four-thread Saxony yarn, and is for a child 8 or 10 years of age. In a larger size, which may easily be made by increasing

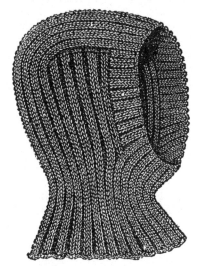

NO. 30.—KNITTED ALPINE OR STORM HOOD.

the number of stitches given, the hood is much used by gentlemen compelled to travel out of doors in severe weather, and is also worn by them for night travelling in winter.

Children wear this hood under their hats when out in frosty weather during play hours, or when they are taking long rides or going to school, as it covers the throat and ears and protects the head generally from the cold.

The hood may be made in any color preferred, and is begun at the neck and knitted as follows: Cast on 120 stitches, making 40 on each of 3 needles. Work round and round, purling 2 and knitting 2 alternately for 5 inches.

For the back of the head work as you would for the heel of a stocking, using 70 stitches; the stitches that are purled in one row must be knitted in the next, and *vice versa*, to preserve the rib. Continue to work backward and forward in ribs for 6½ inches.

For the Top of Crown.—Cast off 18 stitches at each end of the 70 you have been working upon; on the stitches which remain continue to work in ribbed knitting, picking up a stitch from the cast-off stitches, and knitting it together with the last stitch of each row; in this way you take up a stitch from the right side in one row, and one from the left in the next. Continue to work as described until all the side stitches are taken up. Then pick up the stitches down each side of the 6½ inches of ribbed knitting, and then work round and round, including the 50 stitches left for the under-part of chin, knitting 2 and purling 2 alternately for 2½ inches; then bind off.

The hood is slipped on over the head and fits closely about the neck and face.

BABY'S KNITTED DRAWERS.

No. 31.—These drawers are knitted with Germantown wool on coarse steel needles. Begin at the top, casting on 96 stitches, and work to and fro.

First to Third rows.—Knit so that all stitches will appear purled on the right side.

Fourth row.—To make a row of holes through which to run a ribbon, knit as follows: * Knit 2 stitches together, put the wool over twice, knit 2 together crossed; repeat from *.

Fifth row.—By turns knit 2 and purl 2.

Sixth to Sixteenth rows.—Knit all stitches so that on the same side they will appear the same as in the last row. Next make 94 rows of plain knitting; then knit up to the middle 24 stitches, and separating them from the rest, knit 126 rows of plain knitting on them, but beginning in the 36th row of the 126 knit each end-stitch together with the next nearest edge stitch of the 94 rows worked previously; and when doing this in the 37th row, and every second row thereafter to the 59th inclusive, increase 1 stitch on both sides; then in the 80th row, and every second row after, narrow 1 stitch at the same place, so that all the stitches will be used up. Then take up the edge stitches at the lower edge, and on these, together with those left aside before, knit 14 rows of ribbed knitting like the 5th to the 16th rows, after which cast off, and join the edge stitches of the first 16 rows from the wrong side.

TO KNIT A DOUBLE KNEE TO A STOCKING.
(No Illustration.)

A double knee is very useful in children's stockings on account of added durability. It is very simply done, as follows: Knit as much of the stocking as you wish above the knee in the ordinary manner. Then add another thread of yarn

NO. 31.—BABY'S KNITTED DRAWERS.

and knit with the two taken together until the knee is as deep as you desire. Then break off the second thread and finish the stocking with one thread. The heels and toes may be made double, using the same yarn or one half as coarse.

Baby's Knitted Bootees.

No. 32.—Pink and white Berlin wool and four steel needles, No. 14, are used in making these little bootees.

With white wool cast 19 stitches on the first

No. 32.—Baby's Knitted Bootee.

needle, 19 on the second, and 18 on the third.

Knit 2, purl 2, for 28 rounds.

Twenty-ninth round.—M 1, sl 1, k 1, pass the slipped stitch over the knit one. Repeat.

Thirtieth round.—The same as the 1st round.

Continue for 7 more rounds the same, then join on the pink wool. Knit and purl each alternate round for 8 rounds. Divide 26 stitches for the front, leaving the other stitches on the two other needles for the sole. On the needle with the 26 stitches, knit backward and forward in stripes of 3 rows, in pink and white wool. In the beginning of the fourth white stripe the decrease is begun and made by slipping the second stitch, and passing it over the knitted one; (at the beginning of each row the first stitch is to be purled to make a ridge in picking up the stitches for the sole) ; continue the decrease until you have 6 stitches on the needle ; then pick up the side stitches to meet those on the other needles ; knit and purl alternately 6 rounds, then decrease at the back of heel by knitting 2 together twice, and at the toe by slipping the second stitch over the first at the beginning of each knitted round. Continue this for 9 more rounds, divide the stitches onto 2 needles, then cast off the stitches on both together. A chain is run through the holes of the boot, and finished with a small tassel.

For the top, cast on 75 stitches with the pink wool. M 1, sl 1 (as if to purl), k 2 together. Repeat.

The next row is the same; then join on the white wool, and work, alternately, 2 rows, pink and white, for 13 rows. Cast off, and sew on neatly to the top.

A Patch, Knitted into a Stocking.

No. 33.—This plan of mending will be found superior to darning, as it is strong and quite imperceptible. Decide what sized patch will be required. Cut the stocking carefully across the

top and bottom of the patch, taking care to cut along one row of the knitting. As the stocking is knit from the top it will be necessary, if ribbed, to begin at the top of the patch. Rip a row or two till all the stitches are clear of broken threads. Do not break off the threads at each side, but cut them in the center. Pick up all the stitches along the top of the patch. Now clear the stitches at the bottom of the patch. You will have to cut the thread sometimes to get it free of the stitches if the stocking is ribbed, but always leave threads at each side at least an inch long. Now cut out the patch, keeping it about one-half an inch narrower on each side than the piece you intend to knit in. Ravel this out one-half an inch on each side, leaving the ends as they are. Be sure to stop raveling so that the sides of the patch will be quite even. Now knit backwards and forwards as many rows as you have taken away. Turn the stocking wrong side out and lay the stitches you have just knit beside the stitches you picked up at the bottom of the patch and knit them together, as in the heel of a stocking. Sew up each side of the patch, keeping

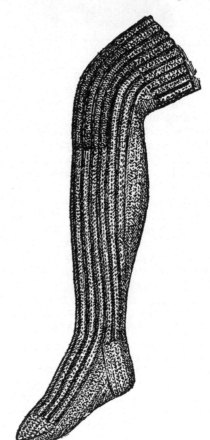

No. 33.—A Patch, Knitted into a Stocking.

the rows perfectly even, and keeping all the loose threads on the wrong side. Take a darning needle and run each thread to the right or left of the patch. If the stocking is knit plain, you can begin at the bottom of the patch and knit up, which is, of course, neater, as the join is out of sight, being near the top of the stocking.

KNITTED CHEST PROTECTOR.

No. 34.—This chest protector is knitted with white zephyr wool and steel needles, and finished with an edging in crochet. Begin the work at the lower edge of the front, casting on 22 stitches.

No. 34.—KNITTED CHEST PROTECTOR.

Knit 6 rows in plain knitting, slipping the first stitch at the beginning of each row, and increasing by 1 stitch at the end of each, to do which knit 1 stitch and purl 1 out of the last stitch. Beginning at the 7th row, work the first 6 and the last 6 stitches in each row in plain knitting, while on the rest of the stitches alternately knit 2 and purl 2 to form the block pattern shown in the illustration; the blocks are 2 rows deep, and in every 3rd row the pattern is changed, bringing plain blocks over the purled ones below and purled ones over the plain blocks. Work from the 7th to the 144th row in this manner, always increasing at the end of the row as described above until the 41st row is completed, after which neither increase nor decrease to the close of the 144th. Having completed the 144th row, finish the front in three parts; on the middle 16 stitches knit 4 rows in the usual pattern, narrowing 1 stitch at the end of each row, then cast off; cast off the stitches between the middle 16 and the outer 20 on each side, and on the latter knit 16 rows as in the part below, narrowing 1 stitch at the inner edge in each of the first 14 rows, so that in the last 2 rows only the 6 plain stitches remain; cast these off on the right side, but on the left, to form a tab with 2 button-holes, knit 4 rows on the first 3 stitches, then 4 rows on the last 3 stitches, after that 6 rows on all 6 stitches, but in every second row knit the middle 2 stitches together, so that, in the last row all will be used up. Knit the back in the same manner, but 17 rows shorter than the front; omit the 4 rows on the middle 16 stitches at the top, casting off these stitches, and work both shoulders like the right shoulder of the front; join the right shoulder to that of the front, and provide the left with a button. For the crocheted edging work as follows: 1 single crochet in the next stitch, skip 2, and make a picot formed of 5 chain stitches and a single crochet in the first one, in the next stitch. Repeat.

INFANTS' KNITTED LOW-NECKED SHIRT.

No. 35.—This little shirt is made of Saxony yarn and is formed of two sections, which are sewed together under the arms.

To Knit the Back.—Cast on 85 stitches and knit back and forth for 61 rows or a space of 5½ inches, working as follows: Knit 1, purl 1, knit 1, purl 1, and so on across each row. In working back, be careful to *knit* the stitches you *purled*, and *purl* those you *knitted* in the last row. This will preserve the order of the ribs.

Now take the finer needles and knit 40 rows (or 3¼ inches).

Then take the coarser needles and knit 36 rows (or 3¼ inches).

In the 33rd row knit and purl 9 stitches, then thread over twice, knit 2 together; then knit and purl 4 stitches, thread over twice, and knit 2 together; work in this way until there are 9 stitches left, and work them off in the previous order. In working back knit 1 put-over thread and drop the other, in each group. This will form holes for the ribbon.

To Make the Front.—Make the front exactly like the back, except that after working 11 rows on the coarse needles for the upper part of the front, you divide the work equally on two needles, and knit separately on each needle in order to make the front opening.

Now sew up the seams under the arms to within an inch and a-half of the top.

To Make the Sleeve or Shoulder-Portion.—Join

No. 35.—INFANTS' KNITTED LOW-NECKED SHIRT.

the wool at the outer edge of the front, and crochet a chain of 3 stitches; 1 double crochet in every stitch of the knitted portion (9 in all); turn, 2 chain, then 1 half-double crochet *around* each double crochet underneath; turn, 3 chain, 1 double crochet in each half-double crochet underneath. Work in this order until there are 4 rows of each kind, and sew the last row to the top of the shirt at the back. Make the other sleeve to correspond.

For the Border.—Finish the top, bottom, arm-hole and left side of the front opening with scallops formed of 5 double crochets caught down with singles so that the scallops will lie flatly.

Run ribbon in the holes at the top of the shirt, and tie it in front.

CHILD'S JERSEY CAP.

No. 36.—This cap is very simply and easily made, and is knitted from Berlin wool or Saxony yarn on No. 9 bone or wooden needles.

Cast on 108 stitches. Then knit a row and purl

NO. 36.—CHILD'S JERSEY CAP.

a row until your work measures about 5 inches; then double it and knit the stitches that were first cast on with the stitches now on the needle, so as to form the hem. Still keep knitting a row and purling a row until you have made 10 inches in all; then cast off, and sew up the top and back very neatly, gathering the top in a little. Crochet a cord, leaving two ends on which two balls are tied. Work a small flower in the front. To make wool balls see illustrations on page 54.

INFANTS' KNITTED SOCKS.

No. 37.—*For the Foot-Portion of the Sock.*— Cast on 36 stitches, and knit across 6 times to make 3 ridges, widening every other time across at the *back only.* In the next 6 ridges narrow at the front edge in every row or every other time across.

In the next 3 ridges widen at the front edge. The last time across (in the last of the 3 ridges) working from the back, knit 27 stitches; then take another needle and knit off the rest of the stitches to begin the instep. Now knit across 7 times, widening every other time at the front or toe-edge. (There will now be 14 stitches on the needle.) Now knit back and forth 13 times, or until there are 10 ridges across the open space; now narrow every other time across until there are 13 ridges for the instep. Then cast on 27 stitches and finish the remaining half of the foot to correspond with the first half, binding off the stitches of the last row.

Now with the needle on which there are still 27 stitches, pick up the stitches across the instep and the other side of the foot, knit across twice and bind off.

For the Upper Portion.—Pick up 14 stitches across the instep, picking them up on the wrong side of the work under the edge-finish, and purl 1 row.

For the Fancy Stripe and the Basket Stripe.—Knit 5 for the fancy stripe. Knit 2 and purl 2 for the basket stripe; knit 5 for the fancy stripe. This forms the first row of the instep.

Second row.—Purl 1, * thread over, purl 1, and repeat 3 times more from * for the fancy stripe. Knit 2, purl 2 for the basket stripe. Repeat for fancy stripe.

Third row.—Knit 2 together, knit 5 plain, knit 2 together for the fancy stripe. Purl 2, knit 2 for the basket stripe; and repeat fancy stripe.

Fourth row.—Purl 2 together, purl 3 separately, purl 2 together for fancy stripe. Purl 2, k 2 for the basket stripe and repeat fancy stripe.

Now repeat from first row until there are 3 holes, one over the other, or 12 rows of knitting; fasten the yarn and break it off. Begin at the back edge of the foot fastening on the white yarn, and, holding the right side toward you, pick up 20 stitches along the inside of one side-edge, slipping the needle downward through the crosswise threads of the stitches, and pulling the white yarn up through each, much after the manner of crochet. Now knit across the instep as follows: Purl 2 together, purl 3 separately, purl 2 together for the fancy stripe. Purl 2, knit 2 for the basket stripe, and repeat the fancy stripe once more. Now pick up the remaining 20 stitches the same as at the other side (there will now be 54 stitches on the needle), and *purl* back and forth 3 times. Now *knit* back and forth 3 times, and then knit as follows to make the holes for the cord and balls: Purl 1, thread over twice, purl 2 together, * thread over twice, purl 2 together, and repeat from * to end of row.

NO. 37.—INFANTS' KNITTED SOCK.

In working back, knit 2, purl 1, knit 2, purl 1, and continue thus across the work.

Now, knit back and forth plain, once; then purl 3 times across. This brings the work to the ankle. There are six fancy and six basket stripes in the leg portion of the sock, and they are knitted by the same directions as those given for the similar stripes over the instep. A basket stripe comes at the back of the leg, one half of it being knitted at each end of the needle; and in knitting this stripe, be careful to knit so that the blocks will alternate as in a whole stripe. Knit until the leg has 9 holes one

NO. 38.—BABIES KNITTED SACK.

over the other in the fancy stripes; then knit back and forth 4 times and bind off. Now sew the sock together down the back, along the sole and across the toe. Run a cord into the holes made for it at the ankle, and finish it with balls or tassels.

Blue and white Saxony yarn were used for this sock, but any other combination of colors preferred may be used, or any color alone may be selected.

BABIES' KNITTED SACK.

NO. 38.—This little sack is made of 4-thread Saxony yarn in white and pale-blue, and is formed in one section and joined under the arms and along the sleeves.

Cast on 70 stitches with the white wool for the lower edge of the back, and knit back and forth until there are 33 ridges. (Two rows of knitting make a ridge.) Now at each side of this center-piece cast on 35 stitches and knit until there are 19 more ridges. Then knit back 55 stitches at one side; take another needle and bind off 29 stitches; knit off the remaining stitches on the needle. Knit at each side, 6 ridges; then cast on 18 stitches and knit 19 ridges; then bind off 35 stitches for each sleeve, knit 33 ridges for each front, and bind off across the bottom. Sew up the garment under the arms and along the sleeves. Now, with the blue yarn, pick up the stitches across the bottom, and knit across once.

Now knit 2, th o twice, n; then knit plain until within 3 stitches from the end; th o twice, n, k 1. In knitting back, k 3, p 1 and knit plain until within 3 stitches of the end; then p 1, k 1.

Knit in this way until there are 9 ridges, then pick up the stitches along each front, beginning at the bottom, and knit back plain.

Now knit 1, th o, n, and knit plain to the top of the sack. Knit back plain to within 2 of the end; then p 1, k 1.

Knit in this manner until there are 9 ridges, and overhand the slanting corners of the border together.

Now pick up the stitches across the neck and border, and knit 5 ridges. Then knit 6 stitches, th o twice, n; * k 7, th o twice, n, and repeat from * across the work. In working back drop the last half of every put-over thread.

Now knit 10 more plain ridges, and bind off. Run ribbon in the holes to tie the garment about the neck.

INFANT'S MITTENS.

NO. 39.—Cast on 36 stitches with colored wool, dividing the stitches onto 3 needles; then work thus, knitting 2 and purling 2 for 20 rounds; then purl 1 round; next round knit 2, make 2, knit 2 together, next round purl, taking care to purl the made stitch as 1, and not as 2. Next with white wool knit 1 plain round; then knit 10 rounds, purling and knitting alternately, taking care that the stitch that was plain in one round is purled in the next, thus making a pretty spotted pattern; then work backwards and forwards 14 rows; this leaves a space open between 2 of the needles where the thumb is to be sewn in; then work 10 rounds as before by drawing the two end needles together.

Eleventh round.—Purl or knit plain 2 stitches together, so as not to disturb the pattern, and work till you come to the middle 4 stitches on the center needle, then purl or knit 2 together twice, and work to the end of the next needle, and decrease again; then work 3 rounds more and decrease again in the same way; work 2 rounds more and decrease again; work 1 round and decrease again. There will now be 20

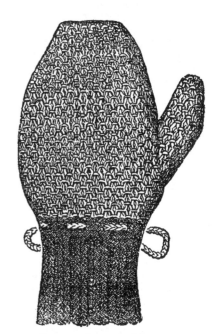

NO. 39.—INFANT'S MITTEN.

stitches in all; divide onto 2 needles, 10 on each and cast off; then turn the mitten and sew together, this being much easier done than turning the mitten with the needle in it to cast off.

For the thumb, begin with 1 stitch, and increase 1 stitch at the end of every row till you have 14 stitches on the needle, taking care to keep the pattern by knitting and purling alternately.

Fifteenth row.—Knit 10, turn the needles round, slip 1 and knit 5; turn the needles round again, slip 1, and work to the end; then work 1 row, knitting and purling; next row, decrease by knitting or purling 2 together twice in the center of the row; work 3 rows and decrease again; work 2 rows and decrease again; work 1 row and cast off. Next sew the thumb neatly together and into the mitten. The point of the thumb began with 1 stitch coming to the bottom of the hole for the thumb; this of course must be done on the inside of the mitten; next crochet a chain about 14 inches long to run through the holes round the wrist; fasten a tassel to each end, and the mitten is finished.

BABY'S KNITTED SOCKS.

No. 40.—This pretty little sock is made of pink and white Saxony yarn.

Cast on 62 stitches with the pink yarn, by method No. 1, and knit across plain.

First row.—Knit 1, th o, k 2, * n, n, k 2, th o, k 1, th o, k 2, and repeat from * across the work. Purl back. Repeat these 2 rows until the scollop is 4 holes deep.

For the 5th row of holes: K 1, th o, * narrow 4 times in succession, th o, k 1, th o, and repeat from * across the row.

Next, knit 1 row and purl 1 row, and join on the white wool.

Next row.—K 1, * th o, n, and repeat from *

NO. 40.—BABY'S KNITTED SOCK.

across the work, ending with k 1. This makes a new row of holes.

Next row.—K 1, p 1, and repeat across the row. Now make 7 more rows like this row, making the *knitted* stitches in each row come over the *purled* ones of the preceding row, and the *purled* stitches over the knitted ones. Next make another row of holes like the last ones, and repeat the holes and solid portions until there are 5 rows of holes and 4 solid rows.

After making the last row of holes, purl back and break off the yarn, leaving it quite long. Now slip the 1st 16 stitches onto a piece of thread or yarn; join the yarn again, then knit and purl alternately the next 15 stitches, and slip the remaining stitches onto another thread. Knit back and forth

across the center, the same as in the solid rows above, 29 times more; then knit once across plain.

Now pick up the stitches on the 1st thread, and 17 stitches along the side of the instep; slip the toe-stitches onto the same needle, pick up 17 along the other side of the instep and finally slip those on the remaining thread onto the needle. Join the white wool to the end that was broken off and knit across plain, once. Then join on the pink wool and knit plain 11 times across, or until there are 5½ ribs. In the next row, at each end and at the center of the toe, narrow once. This completes the 6th rib.

Next row.—Knit plain.

Next row.—Narrow at each end and twice at the middle of the toe.

Next row.—Knit plain.

Next row.—Narrow at each end and once at the middle of toe.

Next row.—Knit plain.

Next row.—Narrow at each end and once at the middle.

Next row.—Knit plain.

Next row—Knit plain, narrowing at each end, and then bind off.

Sew up the sock and insert a narrow ribbon at the top, as seen in the picture.

KNITTED VEIL FOR AN INFANT.

(No Illustration.)

Cream-white Shetland wool and a pair of bone needles of medium size will be needed in making this veil.

Cast on 203 stitches. Knit across and seam back, and then begin the design.

First row.—K 2 plain, * n, 3 plain, m 1, 1 plain, m 1, 3 plain, n *; repeat from star to star till end of row, except last 2 stitches, which are knit plain.

Second row.—Purl.

Third row.—Like the 1st.

Fourth row.—Like the 2nd.

Repeat these 4 rows till the border is 5 inches deep. The upper part of the veil is knitted as follows:

First row.—All plain.

Second row.—All seam.

Third row.—1 plain, narrow till only 1 stitch is left; knit that plain.

Fourth row.—Knit plain, picking up the loop where the 2 were knit together, and the stitches before each 2. Be sure to have 203 stitches before beginning the next row.

Repeat the last 4 rows till the veil is long enough.

INFANTS' KNITTED JACKET.

No. 41.—This jacket is a most useful little garment for infants to wear under cloaks, or even under robes in very cold weather.

Commence at the bottom; cast 94 stitches on one needle.

First row.—Knit.

Second row.—Knit 2, purl 2 throughout the row.

No. 41.—INFANTS' KNITTED JACKET.

These 2 rows are repeated 9 times more.

Twenty-first row.—Knit 1, * th o, knit 2 together; repeat from * to end of row, knitting the last stitch.

Twenty-second row.—Knit.

Twenty-third row.—Knit 14; knit 1 and purl 1 in the next stitch; knit 24; knit 1 and purl one in the next stitch; repeat from the beginning of the row once more; end with knit 14.

Twenty-fourth row.—Knit.

Twenty-fifth row.—Like 23d row, with the exception that you knit 15 instead of 14, as mentioned in 23d row.

Twenty-sixth row. — Knit; continue to increase with a plain row between until you have increased 9 times in all; then increase only in the back, until you have increased at the back in all 13 times; now work 4 rows on all the stitches.

Now for the Right front.—Work on 35 stitches.

First to Tenth rows.—Knit.

Eleventh row.—Leave 8 stitches on another needle, and for the shoulder on the remainder of the stitches, knit 2 together, knit to end of row in each alternate row for 5 times; (the intermediate rows are plain); knit 10 rows without decrease, then cast off.

Work the other shoulder in the same way as described for this. Take 13 stitches from each side of back stitches; work on the remaining 42 stitches 10 rows, then decrease at the beginning and end of each alternate row for 18 rows more, sew up the shoulders, pick up 1 stitch at the end of each ridge of both fronts, and knit across in a row with the 24 stitches of the back to form the neck.

First row.—Knit.

Second row. — Wool forward, knit 2 together throughout; repeat the 1st row 3 times more, then cast off.

For the Sleeve.—Commence at the wrist; cast on 27 stitches.

First row.—Knit.

Second to Twentieth rows.—Knit 2, purl 2 throughout.

Twenty-first row.—Knit 1 and purl 1 in the first stitch; knit 25, knit 1 and purl 1 in the last stitch.

Twenty-second to Twenty-sixth rows.—Knit; repeat from the 21st row 5 times more; work 8 more rows without increase, then cast off; sew up the sleeves and sew into the armholes. Run ribbon into the holes at the neck and waist and tie.

INFANTS' KNITTED BOOTS.

No. 42.—This little boot is made of Saxony yarn on two knitting needles. It is very simply and quickly made, being sewed up the front from the toe to the top of the ribbed knitting, and is also slightly gathered at the heel and toe to shape it and draw the sole to the right length.

Begin at the sole, casting on 144 stitches. Work in patent knitting thus : * Th o, sl 1, k 2 together and repeat from * across the work, knitting one at the end. Work back and forth in this manner for an inch and a-quarter.

Now begin the decrease as follows :

First row.—* Th o, sl 1, k 2 together and repeat from * 3 times more. Th o, sl 1, k 2 together, pass slipped stitch over, k 3 together and continue in patent knitting to the end of the row. Repeat this row until you have worked 3 inches, measuring from the bottom of the boot.

To make the ankle, which is worked in ribbed knitting :

First row.—K 1, p 2 together, and repeat across the row.

Next row.—K 1, p 1, and repeat across the row, and repeat this row until you have 2 inches more, being careful to preserve the ribbed effect by reversing the order of the stitches in knitting back.

For the Top of the Leg.—To increase the number of stitches sufficiently: Th o, k 1, and repeat across the row. Then work in patent knitting

No. 42.—INFANTS' KNITTED BOOT.

for an inch and a-half and cast off. Turn this portion down, as seen in the engraving.

For the Edge of the Turned-Down Portion — Crochet * 1 d c into a stitch of the knitting, skip 1; 2 trebles, 2 chain, 2 trebles in next stitch; skip 1 and repeat from * around the work. Sew a ribbon bow to the top of the ankle, as seen in the picture.

INFANTS' KNITTED BOOTS.

No. 43.—Use Saxony yarn and four steel needles of suitable size. Commence at the top of leg, cast loosely 40 stitches on 3 needles, that is 14 on each of 2, and 12 on the 3rd.

First and Second rounds.—Knit plain.

Third round.—Bring the wool forward, knit 1 in the front, 1 at the back, and again 1 in the front of next stitch, making 3 stitches in 1; put the 3 stitches back on the left-hand needle, knit them, put them a second time back, and knit them; bring the wool forward, knit 3; repeat from the beginning of the round.

Fourth round.—Knit.

Fifth round.—Cast off 4, knit 3; you will now have 4 stitches on the right-hand needle; repeat from the beginning of the round.

Sixth round.—Knit plain.

Seventh round.—Knit 2 before beginning the raised pattern as described in the third round; this makes the patterns lie between those of the third round; end the round with wool forward, knit 1. Continue to work as described, until you have 9 raised patterns in a diagonal line.

For the next round, knit 5, make 1 by bringing the wool forward; repeat; this increases the number of stitches to 47 in the round.

For the ankle, knit 22 rounds plain.

For the heel:

First row.—Knit 28, turn.

Second row.—Knit 1, purl 26, knit 1.

Repeat these 2 rows until you have worked 18 rows.

Nineteenth to Twenty-second row.—Knit; this forms 2 purl ridges.

Twenty-third row.—Knit 19 and then turn the work.

Twenty-fourth row.—Knit 10, this leaves 9 stitches each side of heel. Turn and knit back.

Twenty-fifth row.—Knit 9, knit the next stitch, and 1 of the side stitches together; turn and repeat this last row until all the side stitches are worked in, leaving 10 stitches only on the heel needle.

Now pick up 13 stitches down each side of heel, turn and work back on the heel, (with the right side of the work towards you) and so on around for 24 rounds.

Twenty-fifth round.—Knit the stitches for top of foot, knit 5, knit 2 together, knit 22, knit 2 together, knit 5; knit 3 rounds without decrease.

In the next round decrease again at the same places, but there will be only 20 stitches between the 2 decreases this time; continue to decrease 4 times more with 3 plain rounds between each decreas-

No. 43.—INFANTS' KNITTED BOOT.

ing round; then at the top knit 1, purl 1 across (for the remainder of the boot) reversing the stitches in each alternate round, but continuing the decreasings at sole for another 4 times, making in all 10 decreasings on each side. Turn the boot inside out, put 2 stitches from each side of sole stitches to the top stitches; knit together, 1 stitch from the top, and 1 stitch from the sole, then 2 from the top and 1 from the sole (casting off each time) across the whole stitches, until there are left but 1 at top and 1 at bottom; knit these 2 together, and cast them off.

For the crocheted trimming round the top, work with wool as follows:

First round.—One double into a stitch, 1 chain, pass over 1 stitch, 3 trebles each separated by 1 chain into next stitch, 1 chain, pass over 1 stitch and repeat all round.

Second round.—With silk: 1 double into each stitch.

For the line below the scollops, with silk, work 1 double into each stitch.

For the rosette, with silk, make a chain of 14 stitches, turn, work 1 double, 3 trebles, and 1 double into each of 3 stitches, 1 double, 4 trebles, and 1 double into each of 4 stitches, 1 double, 5 trebles, and 1 double into each of 5 stitches. Roll the work round, with the smallest scollops in the center, sew securely at the back of work, and sew to the toe of boot. The ribbon round the ankle is sewn to the boot at the back, and is tied in front.

BABY'S KNITTED SHIRT.

(For Illustration see next Page.)

No. 44.—This shirt is made of Saxony yarn and is in one piece which is sewed together under the arms.

To Knit the Back.—Cast on 73 stitches for the lower edge, and work back and forth 58 times or until you have a piece 4¼ inches deep. Work as follows: Knit 1, seam 1, knit 1, seam 1, each time across, being careful in coming back to *knit* the stitches you *seamed* and *seam* those you *knitted* in working the last row. This will preserve the ribs in regular order.

Now knit the work onto finer needles and make 35 rows (or 2½ inches.) Then knit the work back onto the original needles and make 34 rows (or about 3 inches); but in the 31st row of this last section, and beginning at the 21st stitch, put the thread over twice and knit 2 together; knit 4 stitches, th o twice, and knit 2 together; repeat this until there are 20 stitches left on the needle and then finish the row plain. In working back, drop the put-over threads, This will form holes for the ribbon. Begin the 35th row and knit and purl

23 stitches; then cast off the center stitches for the neck until there are 23 left on the needle.

Now on the last 23 stitches knit 14 rows, making the holes for the ribbon along the neck edge, in every 3rd row, 3 stitches from the end, to correspond with those across the back. Now cast on, or add to the 20 you are working on, 15 more stitches, and knit 3 rows. Then make the ribbon-holes as across the back, and work until there are 22 rows counting from the added stitches. This will form the shoulder and front.

No. 44.—BABY'S KNITTED SHIRT.
(For Description see this and preceding Page.)

Now begin at the 20 stitches left on the needle at the other side of the work, and knit the shoulder and upper part of the front exactly the same as the side just completed.

Now slip all the stitches onto one needle. Then take the fine needles and knit 35 rows (or 2¼ inches), and complete the lower part of the front to correspond with that of the back. Sew the section together under the arms, from the lower edge to the top of the fine knitting, leaving the rest for the arm-holes.

To Knit the Sleeves.—Cast on 61 stitches for each, and with the coarse needles knit 53 rows or 4½ inches, and with the finer ones 24 rows or 1¼ inch. Sew up the sleeves and sew them in.

For the Border.—Edge the neck, bottom, wrists and the right-side edge of the opening in the front with crocheted scollops made as follows: 6 double crochets, caught down with single crochets so that they will lie flatly. Finish the other edge of the opening with single crochets. Run ribbon in the holes at the top and tie it to draw it in to the neck.

A shirt of this kind may be knitted in any size required for an infant, child or adult, by simply casting on fewer or more stitches to begin the work and making the number of rows or inches less or greater according to the size desired. Plain shirts of this kind are often completed with a deep border at the bottom, of fancy knitting or of crochet.

KNITTED STOCKINGS FOR A GIRL FROM 6 TO 8 YEARS OLD.

No. 45.—This stocking is knitted with black or dark colored silk, partly in plain, partly in ribbed and fancy knitting.

Cast on 104 stitches, and work the first eight rounds, in plain knitting; in the 9th round, alternately, th o and k 2 together, then knit eight more plain rounds. For the 18th round take up the stitches originally cast on on another set of needles, and knit off the stitches in pairs, forming the double notched edge at the top of the stocking. Work the 19th to the 96th rounds plain throughout. In the next round set off the middle 40 stitches on which to knit the fancy pattern on the middle of the front and instep, the rest of the stitches being in ribbed knitting. Work as follows:

Ninety-seventh round.—On the 32 stitches before the middle 40, alternately knit 2 and purl 2 eight times; then th o, k 2 together; twice p 2 together; then * 4 times alternately th o and k 1; then 4 times p 2 together; repeat from * twice, but in the last repetition, only p 2 together twice instead of 4 times, then th o, k 2 together; then for the ribbed knitting on the next 32 stitches, p 2 and k 2 eight times.

Ninety-eighth and Ninety-ninth rounds.—Eight times alternately p 2 and k 2; k the next 40, then eight times p 2 and k 2.

One Hundredth to One Hundred and Third rounds.—Work as in the preceding round, but in the 100th knit together the first 2 and the last 2 stitches, previously putting the thread around the needle.

Repeat the 97th to 103rd rounds until the leg is long enough (33 repetitions in the model), but in the last two rounds of the 11th, 15th, 19th, and 24th repetitions knit together the first 2 and last 2 stitches as in the 100th round, so that the number of stitches will be decreased by 4 in each of these patterns without breaking in on the ribbed knitting. Take the 22 stitches on each side of the middle of the back for the heel, and work 36 rows forward and back, one plain and one purled alternately, seaming the middle and the end stitches on each side. Slip the first stitch in every row, and knit until there are 18 loops at each side; leave off with a purled row. In the next row * k to the 5th stitch past the seam (which is now discontinued), slip the 5th, k the next and pass the slipped stitch over it, k the next, turn, slip the first stitch and p to the 5th past the seam, slip that, p the next stitch and pass the slipped stitch over it, p the next stitch and turn again; repeat from *, always slipping the first stitch on the other side of the opening formed, until all the stitches are knitted off from each side. Pick up the 18 loops on the left side of the heel, knitting each as picked up; knit around the stocking to the 18 loops on the other side, and pick up these also, knitting

No. 45.—KNITTED STOCKING FOR A GIRL FROM 6 TO 8 YEARS OLD.

them for the gussets; narrow by 1 stitch at the side of the 18 stitches picked up, in every 3rd round, until there are 8 narrowings on each side. Knit the stitches on the instep in the fancy pattern, and the rest plain, narrowing down to the toe.

BABIES' KNITTED BOOTEES.

No. 46.—This dainty little affair is made of white split zephyr and salmon-colored silk.

For the Foot.—Cast on 25 stitches and knit back and forth, widening alternately in the rows at the front and back until there are 5 ridges; then knit 12 more ridges, widening at the front only.

In working back from the last row, narrow 1

No. 46.—BABIES' KNITTED BOOTEE.

stitch at the front, and knit across. Now bind off 27 stitches. Then knit 2 ridges, widening at the toe-edge in each ridge. Now make 3 ridges, narrowing in each at the toe-edge. Next make 4 ridges, widening in each at the toe-edge; and then 5 ridges, widening in *each row*. Then make 5 ridges, narrowing in *each row* at the toe; and 4 more, narrowing in *each ridge*. Knit 3 ridges, widening in each at the toe. Now cast on 27 stitches, and knit the remainder to correspond with the first side. Bind off the stitches, and sew up the foot along the sole and toe.

To Knit the Top.—Cast on 25 stitches and knit 4 ridges, and then at each side cast on 28 stitches and knit 9 ridges. Now to make the holes, knit 3 stitches, th o, n, *k 4, th o, n, and repeat from * across the row. Knit back, and make 18 more ridges.

For the Fancy Portion.—P 1, *k 2 together, k 2 plain, th o, k 1, th o, k 2, k 2 together, p 1, and repeat from * across the row.

Next row.—K 1, p 9, k 1, p 9, and repeat across the row.

Repeat these two rows until there are 8 holes. Sew the section up at the back.

For the Border.—With the silk make 1 single crochet at one side of a scollop, then 12 doubles and another single; then 1 long double down between the scollops, as seen in the picture.

Sew the top and foot together by an over-and-over stitch, and then conceal the joining by short and long button-hole stitches of the silk. Run ribbon in the holes and tie it in front. Fasten a tiny bow of the same over the toe of the bootee, and turn the top down as seen in the picture.

CHILD'S KNITTED UNDER-DRAWERS.

No. 47.—These drawers are for a child from 2 to 4 years of age and are made from Saxony yarn with No. 10 needles, in one design throughout.

Begin at the bottom of the leg. Cast on 64 stitches.

First row.—Knit.

Second row.—Purl.

Third, Fourth and Fifth rows.—Knit.

This forms a rib across the work, of 3 rows on one side and one on the other side.

Now repeat from the 2nd row 12 times more, which will make 52 rows in all. In the 6th and 7th rows, increase 1 stitch at the beginning of each row.

Next knit 4 rows without increasing; then 2 rows, increasing 1 at the beginning of each. Repeat the 4 plain rows and the 2 increased rows alternately until 36 rows are worked. Then increase at the beginning of every following row until the 52nd row is completed. This forms one leg.

Knit another section like the first, and when completed turn or hold the work so that the thread will be at the right-hand side; then slip the stitches of the other section onto the same needle, at the left-hand side. Now knit across, knitting the two adjoining stitches of the sections together.

In the *second* (next) row, knit without any decrease; in the *third* row, knit 2 together at each side of the center stitch. Repeat these 2 rows 3 times more. After this knit plain in the middle and decrease at the beginning of every 3rd and 4th row. Work in this way until there are 50 rows above the joining, binding off the last row. Sew

No. 47.—CHILD'S KNITTED UNDER-DRAWERS.

up the legs. Now take a crochet hook and work across the top as follows:

First row.—Treble crochets with single chains between.

Second and Third rows.—1 double crochet in every stitch.

Fourth row.—1 double, * 3 ch., skip 2 doubles, 1 double in the next and repeat from *.

Edge for the Legs.—Make to correspond with the top. Run a ribbon in the top and tie it at the back.

SILK SOCKS FOR A CHILD TWO YEARS OLD.
(No Illustration.)

To knit these socks use 4 No. 16 needles, and 2-fold knitting silk.

Cast 33 stitches onto each of 2 needles and 30 onto 1, and knit in rib pattern thus: 2 purl, 2 plain. Knit to a depth of 6½ inches, and then divide for the heel as follows: Take half the number of stitches and 8 more (or 56 stitches). Knit back and forth, for a depth of 1¾ inches in ribs. (In working back reverse the details in order to preserve the rib-effect.) Now knit plain and narrow at each side of the center stitch for 1 row. Then purl a row. Make 2 more rows narrowed at the center with an extra row between, and cast off. Double the heel together and sew it along the cast-off stitches. This forms the "manufacturers' heel."

Next take up 52 stitches on the side of the heel for the under part of the foot and knit this plain; rib the top part. Narrow the underpart on each side in the 4th, 7th, 10th, 13th and 16th rows; then knit until your work measures from the heel where you have taken up the stitches, 2¼ inches. Then begin the narrowings for the toe—one on each side of the front and back part, always in the 2nd and 3rd stitches. Knit 3 plain rounds between the first 2 narrowed rounds, 2 plain rounds between the next 2 narrowed rounds, and 1 plain round between the remaining narrowed rounds. When the stitches are reduced to about 58 in number, cast off and sew the edges together.

TO STRENGTHEN THE KNEE OF A CHILD'S STOCKING WHILE KNITTING IT.

An excellent plan for strengthening the knee of a child's stocking is to have a second ball and knit every second row double across the front of the knee, breaking off the wool at the end of each double row. If you leave about an inch of wool at the beginning and end of each double row, it will not require to be fastened, and will never appear on the right side. A diamond-shaped double-piece is all that is necessary, and does not make the stocking clumsy under the knee. It is formed thus: When you have knit to the knee, knit almost half round the stocking, counting from the seam stitch. Now knit a few stitches double. Break off the wool and finish the row. Next row plain. In the next row, knit about six more double stitches, taking care to keep them exactly in the centre of the stocking. Proceed in this way till about half the width is double. Knit a few rows without increasing the number of double stitches, then decrease their number gradually till only a few remain, and cease the double-knitting altogether. A patch knitted into a stocking may easily be made double, but need not be shaped.

KNITTED CROSS-OVER FOR A CHILD.
(No Illustration.)

A cross-over for a child of 6 years is easily knitted of single Berlin or Germantown wool on bone needles. First take the length of the little girl's back, from her neck to her waist, then cast on 10 stitches and knit a piece the length of her back, increasing at the beginning of every row thus: Wool over the needle, knit (not slip) the next stitch; (this forms a sort of open edge, which, when the crossover is quite completed, is secured by 2 rows of double crochets the whole way round, working 3 doubles in one at all the corners); knit plain to the end.

Every row is the same until you have knitted the depth of the child's back; then divide your stitches into 3 parts, and knit off the first part plain. Take your third needle and cast off the middle set of stitches. This is for the back of the neck. Leave the first set of stitches on the first needle, now knit the remaining set of stitches for 20 rows, and then knit every row plain, decreasing 1 stitch at the beginning of each row, always at the neck end, by knitting the first 2 together, until only 2 stitches remain, and you have knitted, in fact, to a point.

Do precisely the same on the other side to form the other front, and sew a ribbon on each point. After you have made 2 rows of double crochets the whole way round, knot in a pretty fringe by taking two strands of the wool about 8 inches in length, and doubling them for each knotting. Slip the doubled part through the space for it and pass the cut ends through the doubled end, drawing the loop tightly.

BABY'S KNITTED PETTICOAT, WITH BODICE.
(No Illustration.)

This little garment may be made from Germantown wool with No. 8 needles. Two colors may be used, according to the directions given below.

It is begun at the bottom and has an open work pointed edge, with imitation tucks in color. It is made in 2 pieces as follows:

For one section of the garment, cast on, in color, 112 stitches, and then work 1 row plain, 1 row purl, 1 row plain. Then with white wool * k 1, k 2 together, k 3, wool forward, k 1, wool forward, k 3, sl 1, k 1, pass the slip stitch over; repeat from * across the row and purl back. Repeat these 2 rows 4 times. Then, in color, knit 2 plain rows, 1 purl, 1 plain. Continue the fancy pattern in white, and the pink tucks till there are 5 of the latter. Then knit in white, in the fancy stitch, till there are 10 of the open-work rows, decreasing by putting 2 plain stitches in the fancy pattern where the 3 were; then decrease here and there till the stitches are reduced to 56. This completes the skirt part. Then rib the 56 stitches. Now work 4 plain, 4 purl, for 56 rows, for the body, and cast off. Make another piece of knitting just the same, only adding a strap for the shoulders at the beginning and end of the 56 stitches, making it 12 stitches wide and 20 rows long. Cast off the middle stitches, sew up the sides, and join the ends of the straps on to the top of the other piece. Finish with a crochet edging for the neck and arms and run in a string.

DOLLS, REINS, BALLS, ETC., FOR CHILDREN.

KNITTED HARLEQUIN.

No. 1.—Berlin wool in green and black, flesh-color, scarlet, olive-green, white and yellow will be needed in knitting this harlequin.

These illustrations represent a comical knitted harlequin which would make a charming present for a little boy or girl. It is 32¼ inches tall, and will not be difficult to make for those who are very good knitters, after the stitches are given; but a detailed description, with the exact number of stitches required for the use of inexperienced knitters, could not be given for the want of space. The worker must begin the harlequin at the grey pointed cap, for which (without the brim), 60 stitches must be cast on and divided evenly on 4 needles. After a few plain rounds, the stitches are gradually decreased at the end of each needle until all are used. The point is reached at the 70th round. The brim, 18 rounds deep and 15 inches round, with the outer edge supported by a piece of wire, is knitted separately and afterwards sewn on. The 60 foundation stitches of the cap are again taken up on 4 needles, and the knitting is continued for the head, working separately on two with black wool and two with flesh-colored; 3¾ inches is the length of the black back part of the head; in knitting this towards the neck, the stitches must be decreased so that at last only 10 are left on each needle. With the flesh-colored wool about 1⅛ inch is now knitted plain, and the worker must then take up the stitches necessary for the length of the nose, between the two needles to about 20, closing the small gusset shape again when the nose is knitted. After a few rows more, in which a decrease is made here and there on

NO. 1.—KNITTED HARLEQUIN.

the outer side of the needles, 6 stitches are increased again in the middle of the needle for the chin, then decreased again so much, that when the work is as long as the back part of the head made before, 10 stitches may remain on each needle. The neck is next knitted in 14 rounds with flesh-colored wool, the side edges of the head part and face are sewn together, and the head and face are stuffed with cotton-wool before knitting further. This must be done with great care and taste so that the features may be well moulded. The red wool is now to be put on for the body and the width of the shoulder reached in 20 rounds, by folding the knitting over to the half and taking up 1 stitch on both sides at the beginning and end of each needle (therefore 4 stitches in every row) and knitting 2 rows over; the worker must also take up a few stitches here and there in the knitted part, until the width of the chest and back consists of 48 stitches. Now the armholes are formed, and therefore 20 rows are knitted backwards and forwards for the back as well as the chest, in purl and plain. The arms are knitted separately with 36 stitches divided on 4 needles and first knitted 3⅜ inches long plain; then 6 stitches are to be increased and again decreased, and the arm finished with a length of 3¾ inches, narrowing during the knitting so that at last only 5 stitches are left on each needle. The flesh colored wool is now to be put on and the hand knitted plain for 25 rounds long, 4 stitches being narrowed off, after 10 rounds for the thumb. It is then completed separately in 8 or 10 rounds with the help of 3 stitches cast on afresh. After the hand and arm have been stuffed and the figures each marked by close stitching, the arms are to be sewn into the armholes. The upper part of the body is then knitted for 3¾ inches long down to the waist, narrowing so much under the arms and at the beginning and end of each needle that 12 stitches are left on each of the 4; 6 plain rounds finish the waist. For 5¼ inches long (lower part of the body), the worker must gradually increase all round, so

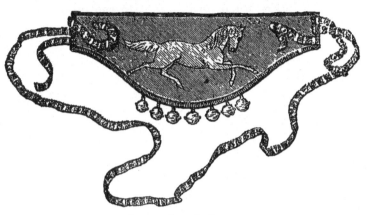

No. 2.—Child's Reins.

that when the middle of this is reached, 25 stitches are on every needle and must again be decreased at the end so that 20 stitches remain. The legs are now begun with green wool, and require each 40 stitches of those now in use and 5 cast on afresh. Before knitting the above, it is necessary to stuff the body, and the stitches taken up for each leg must also be sewn very close together. The legs are each 4⅜ inches long as far as the knee, for which 12 stitches are again to be narrowed in 12 rows; at the same time a few stitches are to be narrowed at the bend of the knee. From the knee to the ankle the leg is 3¾ inches long; at the calf of the leg the stitches are again increased and decreased, so that in beginning the boots 8 stitches are on every needle. When the leg has been stuffed, the black is fastened on for shoes and 10 rows knitted round, then the heel and foot are formed as in making a stocking. Before the last stitches are sewn together at the point of the toe, the boot is to be stuffed. Black buttons and a yellow cord of crocheted chain with tassels at the ends, imitate the closing of a shoe. For the vandyke points with small bells trimming the neck, sleeves and shoulders, the worker has to cast on 12, 6 and 3 stitches and to increase to 23, 12 and 6 stitches; then decrease again. The vandykes ornamenting the hips have a small yellow scollop edge; the upper part is also fastened by a narrow band crocheted on. The hair is knitted like a garter with black wool, wetted and ironed, cut in half lengthwise and then raveled out as long as required. Eyebrows are imitated by black dashes; the eyes themselves are made with beads; red stitches form the mouth and a few threads of black wool the

beard. A little rouge on the cheeks gives the whole face a more natural appearance.

CHILD'S REINS.

No. 2.—Cut a piece of wiggan for the front piece 16 inches long by 9 inches wide; then cut two pieces of flannel or felt, and on one of them embroider or fasten on a transfer-pattern of a horse. Lay a piece of goods each side of the wiggan and bind the three pieces together; then at each end make a band or strap large enough to fasten round the child's waist. For the reins use single zephyr in bright colors and No. 12 needles. Cast on 14 stitches and in plain knitting, make a length of 3 yards and fasten the reins just above the band that goes round the waist. Knit 4 strips each about three-eighths of a yard long and sew them to the corners to tie the piece on with (see engraving). Sew tiny bells to the lower edge of the piece. The flannel used may be gray, blue, red, yellow or black, as preferred.

KNITTED REINS AND WHIP FOR CHILDREN.

No. 3.—Little folk may make the reins for themselves from remnants of bright colored wools, when mamma has begun the work for them as follows:

Cast on 12 stitches and knit back and forth in one color for 4 inches. Then join another color and knit another 4 inches and so on until a strip as long as desired is made. Then sew the strip together over a stout cord, and make a loop of the covered cord at each end of the strip, using 9¾ inches for each loop. These loops are for the arms to pass through.

The whip-handle may be covered with a strip

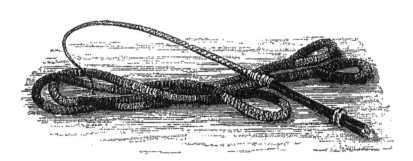

No. 3.—Knitted Reins and Whip for Children.

similarly knitted. The reins may be shaped like either of the other sets illustrated. The whip-handle may be made at home from a smooth pliable bit of wood or a tapering branch of willow or any other flexible shrub. A handsome set of reins and whip-cover may be made from crochet or knitting silk.

KNITTED "SAMBO."

No. 4.—This "Sambo" is made of zephyr in the following colors:

For the Face and Hands: Écru. (Black or white may be used if preferred.)

For the Hat and Body: Blue.

For the Legs: Red and white.

For the Garters, Belt and Trimmings: Black.

The figure must be stuffed with cotton as you knit it.

Begin at the Foot.—Cast on each of 3 needles, 15 stitches. Knit 3 rounds plain. Then for the center of the front, narrow as follows: K 2 together at the end of the needle, and 2 together at the beginning of the next. Narrow in this way until there are but 5 stitches on these 2 needles, and the original 15 on the other needle.

Now divide the stitches so that there will be 8 stitches each on the needle at each side of the center of the front, and 9 on the other. K 3 rounds plain, and knit to the center of the back. * Join the white and make a seam stitch by knitting 1 at the front and 1 at the back of the middle stitch. Knit 2 rounds of the white. Join the red; knit 5 rounds widening at each side of the seam in the first round. Repeat 4 times more from *.

Join the black and knit 5 rounds for the garter. Knit 5 rounds of red.

To begin the Trousers.—Knit in rib style; (k 2 seam 2 ; * k 4 rounds. In next round widen twice on the inside of the leg. Repeat from * 5 times more. In widening be careful to preserve the order of the ribs. This completes one leg. Make the other like it.

Join the legs by placing the two needles together at the inner side of the legs and knitting 6 stitches from them at the same time—that is, you slip the needle through 1 stitch on each needle, draw through both with one thread and slip them off as if they were but one stitch. Then cast off these 6 stitches.

Divide the remaining stitches onto four needles, and knit twenty-five rounds. In the next round narrow once at the end of each needle. Next, join the black and knit 6 rounds for the belt.

Now join the blue for the waist, and knit 46

No. 4.—Knitted "Sambo."

rounds or about 3 inches. Then divide your stitches so that the needles will cross at the center of the front and back and on each shoulder. Now knit, narrowing in every other round, at each side of each shoulder as follows: Knit the last 2 of the first needle you knit from, together; slip the first stitch of the next needle, knit the next and pass the slipped stitch over. Knit to the other shoulder and narrow in the same way. Knit and narrow in this manner until there are 34 stitches, and knit the next round plain.

Now join the color for the face. Knit 6 rounds; then widen 16 stitches in the next 4 rounds (once on each needle). Knit plain for 1 inch; then widen 1 on each needle. Then knit plain for ½ inch; next narrow 2 on each needle; knit 3 rounds; then narrow 2 on each needle; knit 3 rounds; narrow 2 on each needle; knit 2 rounds; narrow 2 on each needle; knit 1 round; narrow 1 on each needle; knit 1 round and bind off.

For the Arm.—Cast 6 stitches on each of 3 needles; k 2 rounds. In the next 3 rounds widen to 27 stitches. Knit plain until the section is an inch deep from the edge. Then, in the next round narrow one on each needle. Then knit plain until the section is 2½ inches long. In the next round, narrow 1 on each needle; knit 3 rounds; then narrow 1 on each needle. There should now be 18 stitches. Knit 7 rounds; then narrow 1 on each needle. K 12 rounds; then narrow 1 on each needle; k 1 round; join the écru, knit 10 rounds; then narrow 1 on each needle; k 1 round; then narrow all the stitches off by knitting 2 together each time.

To make the Wool or Hair.—Cast on 10 stitches and knit in garter style until you have a strip about 12 inches long. Dampen and press with a hot iron, cut lengthwise through the center and ravel.

For the Cap.—Cast 25 stitches onto each of three needles. Knit 6 rounds plain; then * narrow at the beginning and end of each needle. Knit 3 rounds plain, and repeat from * until there are 13 stitches on each needle. Knit 3 rounds, narrow as usual, and also knit the middle 2 stitches on each needle together. Knit 2 rounds plain; narrow the same as in last narrowed round. Knit 1 round plain; narrow at the beginning and end of each needle, and knit the 3 center stitches together. Knit 1 round plain. Then thread a needle with the yarn you are using and draw through the 3 stitches on each needle. Draw closely and fasten.

Finish the neck and wrists with chain-stitching.

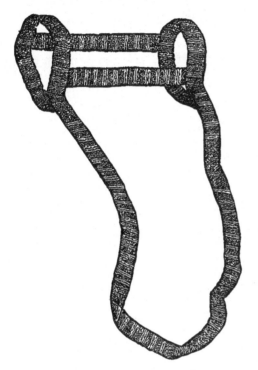

No. 5.—Knitted Reins for a Child.

Simulate buttons with tiny knots of the wool, and a lacing with the same wool in cross stitch.

Any colors preferred to those named may be used.

Knitted Reins for a Child.

No. 5.—There is no amusement that little children are so fond of as that of "playing horse," and for this purpose they are always asking mothers, sisters, etc., to buy or make reins for them.

We give, above, a design for some reins in plain knitting. They are knitted with coarse yarn or Germantown wool. No. 12 needles are required.

Cast on 14 stitches, and in plain knitting knit a length of 3 yards for the reins, and 4 pieces of half a-yard each for the arms and cross pieces. Work the name of the child, or of a favorite horse, on the front, in cross-stitch, with white wool, and add little bells, front and back, to complete it. Or, if preferred, make the reins plain as seen in the engraving.

No. 6.—Knitted Ball.

Knitted Ball

No. 6.—The materials required are twelve different colors of Berlin wool, and two bone knitting needles, No. 10. The ball is composed of twelve sections, each one of a different color. To commence, cast on 24 stitches. Work throughout in patent knitting; that is, m 1, sl 1, k 2 together.

First row.—Work as above described.

Second row.—Work on all but the last 3 stitches; leave them on the needle, and turn.

Third, Fourth, Fifth and Sixth rows.—Work on all but the first and last 3 stitches.

Seventh row.—Work on all but the first 3 and last 6.

Eighth row.—Work on all but the first 6 and last 6 stitches.

Ninth and Tenth rows.—Work to the end of the needle; then take another color, and repeat from the second row. When you have worked the 12 sections, cast off the stitches, and sew together on the wrong side. The ball must be drawn together at one end, and then filled with odds and ends of wool or wadding, then neatly drawn together at the other end. Work a chain loop about two inches in length, and fasten to the top of the ball. A soft ball of this kind will be found very appropriate for the nursery, as it will not injure anything it may come in contact with.

Doll's Knitted Leggings.

No. 7.—These leggings are knitted with blue and white split zephyr wool and fine steel needles.

Cast on 40 stitches and knit 18 rounds in ribbed knitting, 2 stitches plain and 2 purled alternately.

Next knit 36 rounds in plain knitting, alternating 4 rounds with white and 4 rounds with blue wool; in the 15th, 23rd, 31st and 36th rounds, narrow by knitting the first 2 stitches together. After the 36 plain rounds knit 26 in ribbed knitting with white wool; in the last 6 of these, to form the gusset at the side, widen by knitting 2 stitches out of one on both sides of the middle 18 stitches; work the stitches gained

No. 7.—Doll's Knitted Legging.

by widening in plain knitting. At the end of the 26th round cast off all but the middle 18 stitches between the gusset and on these work 17 rows in ribbed knitting for the foot, narrowing at both edges in every 4th row, after which cast off the remaining stitches and work a round in single crochet around the bottom of the legging. Set buttons along the side, and sew a ribbon strap to pass under the sole at the bottom. If preferred, but one color need be used.

Knitted Soldier Doll.

(For Illustrations see next Page.)

No. 8.—This doll is made of zephyr in white, black, dark green, red and blue, the latter color being used for the shoes, the crown of the cap and the decorations on the waist; the white for the face and hands, and the black for the back of the

No. 8.—KNITTED SOLDIER DOLL.
(For Directions see this and preceding Page.)

head and the green for the top. It is knitted, with the exception of the feet, in proportions similar to but smaller than those of the doll seen at No. 4, but is all in plain knitting. The directions, for the knitted "Sambo" will, however, be a sufficient guide for shaping this doll.

Narrow knitted red bands, made with four needles and trimmed with over-and-over stitches of blue are about the waist, neck and arm-holes. The wrists are finished with an over-and-over stitch, and 3 red stitchings are down the back of each hand, in imitation of glove-stitchings. Buttons and bars of blue are embroidered on the front of the waist. Knitted pockets are added to the trousers and a handkerchief of white lawn, over-handed with blue, is in one pocket. Red lacings are worked on the shoes and tied in front of the ankle.

A crocheted chain of red is sewed about the face where its white and the black and green of

the head meet, and the cap is crocheted as follows: Begin with a chain of 3 and work round and round in single crochets, widening now and then until the cap is large enough around for the head, and is 1½ inches deep. Then add 2 rows of red, then 2 rows of blue, then 2 rows of red to complete the edge. Tack the top of the cap down and complete it with a tassel.

To knit the Doll.—Begin at the bottom of the waist and knit upward, seaming a stitch at the center of the front, and narrowing on the shoulders the same as in making the doll referred to. Knit the face and the back of the head separately, widening each, and purling back after every knitted row, so as to keep the work the same on the outside. Sew up at the sides, and finish the top of the head with 4 needles, narrowing it down to nothing. The knitter must use personal judgment in shaping the face and the top of the head, and must stuff the lower part of the doll as she knits.

Now, pick up the stitches around the waist, and knit round and round for 2¼ inches, seaming a stitch at the center of the front. Then divide the stitches evenly and use half of them for each leg, knitting the legs separately and narrowing them gradually to the ankle. Then join the blue and have one needle at the back of the leg for the heel. Knit back and forth, like a heel, until the strip is long enough to form a heel as seen in the picture. Cast off these stitches and sew the heel together along the lower edge and for two or three stitches up the sides. Now pick up the stitches on each side of the heel, as in a stocking, and with the stitches on the other needles finish each foot the same as a stocking, narrowing down to 1 stitch. Fasten firmly and then with a needle arrange the stuffing so as to nicely shape the foot.

Knit and sew on the arms on the same plan as those on the doll at No. 4.

The doll may be made as large or small as desired by casting on more or less stitches. This point must be made a matter of personal judgment.

KNITTED BALL.

No. 9.—Get a small India-rubber ball or a cork and wind it over with coarse wool until it is of the size required. Then knit the cover, which is 7½ inches around, as follows:

Cast on 24 stitches and knit back and forth in 2

No. 9.—KNITTED BALL.

colors—6 rows of each, until there are 14 stripes of the 2 colors. Then join the two sides of the stripes, slip the cover over the ball and draw its ends down tight by a row of gathering-stitches so that the stripes will form points. Any bright colors preferred may be used in working a ball like this. The rainbow colors, two stripes of each, are pretty for it.

MISCELLANY.

KNITTED TWINE-BALL CASE.

No. 1.—This ball is made of Nile-green knitting or crochet silk. String 450 beads upon the silk before beginning to knit. Cast on 50 stitches. Knit back and forth as follows:

Knit 1 row, purl back for 9 rows. This maks a plain, flat section. Now, the last row being knit; to reverse the knitting to produce a purled section and introduce the beads, knit back 9, slip a bead forward, knit 8, slip another bead forward, and repeat in this manner until there are 5 beads in the row; then knit 9. Now purl back for the next row.

Third row.—Knit 8, slip a bead, k 2, slip another bead; * knit to within 1 stitch of the next bead in the preceding row; slip a bead, k 2, slip another bead and repeat from * to end of row. Purl back.

Fifth row.—Same as 3rd row between the stars. Purl back.

Seventh row.—Like 3rd. Purl back.

Ninth row.—Like 1st. Knit back to reverse the pattern.

Repeat plain and beaded sections until there are 10 of each, and sew it together at the sides. Gather it closely at one end, slip in the ball of twine, and gather the other end, leaving an end of the twine extending through the tiny opening left by the

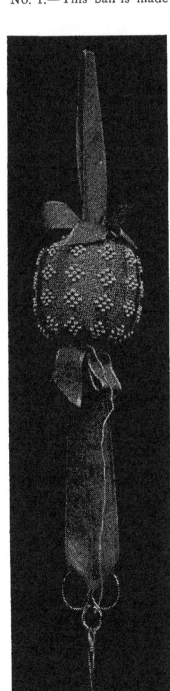

No. 1.—KNITTED TWINE-BALL CASE.

gathering. Sew a ribbon loop at the top to hang it up by (see engraving); and suspend a pair of scissors as seen in the picture, from the lower part of the case. Fasten both long loops on with shorter fancy loops and ends.

KNITTED PURSE.

No. 2.—Use Belding's knitting silk and 4 No. 17 needles.

Cast on 40 stitches, putting 14 on the first needle, 12 on the second and 14 on the third. Knit once around plain.

First, Second, Fifth, Sixth, Ninth and Tenth rounds.—P 10, k 2 crossed, p 2, k 2 crossed, p 2, k 2 crossed, and repeat for the round.

Third, Fourth, Seventh, Eighth, Eleventh and Twelfth rounds.—K 10, k 2 crossed, p 2, k 2 crossed, p 2, k 2 crossed and repeat.

Thirteenth, Fourteenth, Seventeenth, Eighteenth, Twenty-first and Twenty-second rounds.—K 2 crossed, p 2, k 2 crossed, p 2, k 2 crossed, p 10 and repeat.

Fifteenth, Sixteenth, Nineteenth, Twentieth, Twenty-third and Twenty-fourth rounds.—K 2 crossed, p 2, k 2 crossed, p 2, k 2 crossed, k 10, and repeat.

Repeat these twenty-four rounds twice more, making 72 rounds in all. Then knit once around plain.

Seventy-fourth round.—K 2; then alternately th o, k 2 together, to within 2 of the end; knit these plain.

No. 2.—KNITTED PURSE.

Seventy-fifth round.—Purl back instead of working around to form an opening at the middle of the purse. Purl *back* and *forth* in this way until you have a strip 2½ inches long. Then knit once *around* plain.

Now resume the pattern and knit it 3 times. Then bind off; draw one end together and finish with an ornamental tassel; sew the other end together straight, and finish with bead fringe or as illustrated.

A purse of this shape may be made of plain knitting, casting on 50 to 60 stitches as a foundation. Or, doubling the stitches, use 2 needles and knit back and forth until a strip 9 inches long is made. Bind off and sew up, leaving a slit at the middle. One color or different colors in stripes may be used.

KNITTED PURSE.

NO. 3.—Four No. 18 knitting needles and knitting silk of any color preferred are to be used in making this purse. To begin, use 2 needles only, and leave an end of the silk about 10 inches long with which to sew up the purse when made.

Cast on 20 stitches, and knit in garter fashion for 5 rows.

Sixth row.—Knit 3, th o, k 14, th o, k 3.

Seventh row.—Knit 22. In every uneven row up to the 21st row, knit plain like last row, knitting 2 more stitches in each row. In the 21st row there will be 36 stitches.

Eighth row.—K 3, th o, k 16, th o, k 3.

Tenth row.—K 3, th o, k 18, th o, k 3.

Twelfth row.—K 3, th o, k 20, th o, k 3.

Fourteenth row.—K 3, th o, k 22, th o, k 3.

Sixteenth row.—K 3, th o, k 24, th o, k 3.

Eighteenth row.—K 3, th o, k 26, th o, k 3.

Twentieth row.—K 3, th o, k 28, th o, k 3. After the 21st row, cut the silk, leaving an end about 10 inches long. Do not cast off. This completes the first portion of the 2 parts which form the mouth of the purse.

Make another section like the first, but do not break the silk.

Now transfer 12 stitches from each needle to a third needle, and begin knitting in rounds as follows: Knit 6 rounds plain.

Seventh round.—N, th o, and repeat. Knit 5 rounds plain.

Thirteenth round.—K 3, th o, sl 1, n, pass slipped stitch over, th o, k 2, and repeat.

Fourteeenth, Sixteenth and Eighteenth rounds.—Plain.

Fifteenth round.—K 1, n, th o, k 3, th o, sl and b and repeat.

Seventeenth round.—Like 13th. Knit 2 rounds plain. Transfer the first 4 stitches on each needle to the next needle; this will leave 4 stitches on the 3rd needle which are to be knitted as a portion of the 20th round.

Twenty-first and Twenty-fifth rounds.—Like 13th.

Twenty-second, Twenty-fourth and Twenty-sixth rounds.—Plain.

Twenty-third round.—Like 15th.

Twenty-seventh round.—Plain.

Twenty-eighth round.—Plain to last 4. Transfer the last 4 stitches on each needle to the next

NO. 3.—KNITTED PURSE.

needle and consider the 28th round completed.

Twenty-ninth and Thirty-third rounds. — Like 13th.

Thirtieth, Thirty-second and Thirty-fourth rounds.—Plain.

Thirty-first round.—Like 15th. Knit 2 rounds plain; transfer the first 4 stitches on each needle, to the next needle, which will leave 4 stitches on the 3rd needle, and these are to be knitted as a part of the 36th round in addition to those already knit.

Thirty-seventh and Forty-first rounds.—Like 13th.

Thirty-eighth, Fortieth and Forty-second rounds.—Plain.

Thirty-ninth round.—Like 15th. Knit 5 rounds plain.

Forty-eighth round.—N, th o and repeat. K 6 rounds plain.

Fifty-fifth round.—K 4, n, and repeat. K 2 rounds plain.

Fifty-eighth round.—K 3, n and repeat. K 2 rounds plain.

Sixty-first round.—K 2; n and repeat. K 2 rounds plain.

Sixty-fourth round.—K 1, n, and repeat. Knit 1 round plain, and narrow twice in every round after that until all the stitches are disposed of but 6. Then cast off, leaving enough silk to secure the stitches and sew on the metallic ornament.

Now turn the bag wrong side out, as the purled side is shown in the engraving. The knitted side, however, may be used for the outside of the purse if desired.

With the ends of silk left hanging where the stitches were cast on, and a coarse needle, secure one of the metal bars to each edge, passing the threaded needle over the bar, and through each and every loop at the top of the purse.

KNITTED WASH RAG.
(No Illustration.)

Use No. 12 white knitting cotton and two steel needles of the largest size.

Cast on 54 stitches. Knit plain 12 rows (rather loosely.)

Thirteenth Row.—K 12, * o, n, o, n, repeat from (*) 14 times; k 12, repeat the 13 rows for the length required; then k plain 12 rows. Edge it all around with narrow lace, knitted with white cotton in any design preferred.

KNITTED HOLDER.

No. 4.—This pretty holder is knit in imitation of an ear of corn. It is made of yellow Germantown yarn and green silk. Use quite coarse steel needles.

Cast on 45 stitches and then work with 2 threads as follows:

First row.—Knit 5 with 1 thread; take the other thread and draw it tightly across the back of the knitted stitches to produce a curved effect, like a kernel of corn. Knit the next 5 with the second thread and draw them up with the first thread. Use these 2 threads alternately, in this way, across the row.

Second row.— Knit back, taking first the thread which was used in making the next to the last kernel. Knit as in preceding row, except that you must keep the threads on the *wrong* side of the work which, in this row is next to you. The secret of success in knitting this holder is the drawing of the threads to form the kernels. They must be drawn tightly and not allowed to slip.

Knit back and forth in this manner until the holder is 25 kernels deep. Then, instead of casting off, take a yarn needle and draw the knitting threads through the stitches tying them tightly. Draw the other end together to correspond in shape. Add a tassel of green silk at one end, and a crocheted ornament of the same silk at the other end. To make this ornament crochet as follows: Pick up a loop through the end-kernel, make 3 chain; 1 double, very loose, in each of the remaining 8 kernels; 3 chain, 2 doubles between

No. 4.—KNITTED HOLDER.

every double underneath and fasten to the 3-chain.

KNITTED PURSE.

No. 5.—Use Belding's silk and No. 18 needles. Cast onto 1 needle 59 stitches and knit across plain.

Second row.—P 2 together, th o and repeat until one stitch remains. Knit this. Repeat this row up to the 65th row inclusive. Now make 83 rows of plain knitting; then 65 rows of the fancy knitting. Knit 1 row plain and cast off.

You will now have a long, flat piece, a little narrower at the center than at the ends. Sew up the edges, leaving an opening 2½ inches long at the middle. Join one end flatly and draw the other together as seen in the picture, and finish with steel trimmings.

KNITTED HAMMOCK.
(No Illustration.)

A hammock may be knitted by the following instructions, and will be found comfortable as well as pretty. A small hammock in the nursery is a convenience to a mother and a delight to her baby; and a hammock slung from the window-sill across the corner of a room and fastened to the wall, will, when completed with cushions, form a delightful lounging place for reading.

Use strong cord, macramé or any variety that is well covered or twisted, and with one or two colors, knit with two large wooden needles, as follows:

Cast on 25 stitches and knit in a plain or fancy stitch a strip about 5 feet long. Make 4 such strips and join them with the same cord by an over-and-over stitch. Then fasten the ends of the hammock to wooden bows, such as may be either purchased or

No. 5.—KNITTED PURSE.

made at home. A fringe of the cord may be knotted on the edges and across the bows of the hammock with a pretty effect, and it may be of one color, or both colors if two are used. Colored twine may be selected as the material from which to make such a hammock. For an infant's hammock cast on about 15 stitches and make the strips about a yard long.

KNITTED PENCE JUG.

No. 6.—For making this useful jug for holding odd pennies, a small quantity each of heavy, black and scarlet Germantown yarn will be required, and 5 No. 16 needles.

Take the red yarn and on one needle cast 12 stitches for the spout of the jug; and 10 on each of three other needles.

First, Second, Third and Fourth rounds.—Plain.

Fifth round.—Knit 2, purl 2 alternately all round until the stitches for the spout are reached; then knit 2 together, knit 8 plain, knit 2 together.

No. 6.—KNITTED PENCE JUG.

Repeat the 5th round 3 times more.

Ninth round.—Purl 2, knit 2 alternately until you reach the spout; then knit 2 together, knit 8 plain.

Tenth round.—Purl 2, knit 2 alternately. For the spout, knit 7 plain, knit 2 together.

Repeat the 9th and 10th rounds 3 times more. This will complete the spout. Cast off by knitting the 2 remaining stitches together. There will now be 30 stitches on the remaining needles. Then knit as follows:

* Purl 2 rounds, knit 2 rounds and repeat from * 4 times more. Join on the black and begin the bowl as follows:

First round.—Make 2 in 1, purl the rest plain.

Second round.—Purl.

Then knit 4 rounds in scarlet, and 1 round in black, increasing every 4th stitch; purl 2 rounds.

Knit 4 rounds in scarlet, and 1 round in black, increasing every 6th stitch; purl 2 rounds.

Knit 6 rounds in scarlet; knit 1 round in black; purl 2 rounds in black; knit 4 rounds in scarlet; knit 1 round in black, decreasing by knitting the 7th and 8th stitches together.

Purl two rounds in black, knit 4 in scarlet, knit 1 in black, decreasing by knitting the 12th and 13th stitches together.

Purl 2 rounds in black. There should now be 72 stitches. Divide these by 6, marking the divisions. Knit 11 rounds in scarlet, decreasing 6 stitches in each round by knitting 2 together at the commencement of each division. This will leave 6 stitches.

Draw these together with a needle and the wool, and sew them securely.

For the Handle.—Cast on 6 stitches and knit and purl alternately until you have made a strip 3 inches long. Then bind off and sew the handle to the jug.

KNITTED BATH MITTEN. (ESPECIALLY ADAPTED FOR BATHING INFANTS.)

No. 7.—This useful article is made of Dexter's cotton No. 8, and is knitted on two needles and sewed together at the side.

Cast on 36 stitches, and knit in rib style for about two inches as follows: Knit 3, seam 3 and repeat across the row. In knitting back, seam the knitted stitches and knit the seamed ones.

Next knit 2 plain ridges across the work.

Then knit 17 stitches, th o, k 2, th o, k 17. This begins the widening for the thumb portion. Knit back plain.

Next row.—K 17, th o, k 4, th o, k 17. Knit back plain.

Make 8 ridges by this plan, knitting 17 both before and after widening each time. Then knit 2 ridges without widening.

Next slip off the 17 stitches at each side of the thumb onto a thread, and knit back and forth across the thumb portion until there are 6 ridges; then knit 3 more ridges, narrowing once each time across; there will then be 10 stitches left on the needle. Draw the yarn through these 10 stitches, drawing them into as small a space as possible; fasten them and sew up the thumb with the same piece of yarn.

Take up the slipped stitches on a needle and knit 18 ridges without narrowing. In the next 6 ridges narrow once at each side and once in the middle of the needle to shape the mitten. There will then be 19 stitches the last time across. Draw the yarn through them and fasten them, and sew up the mitten the same as the thumb.

No. 7.—KNITTED BATH MITTEN.

To make the Loop.—Fasten on a piece of yarn to make a loop as long as desired, and then work over it in button-hole stitch or in tatting style. If preferred, the loop may be crocheted.

KNITTED HOLDER.

No. 8.—Lavender and white zephyr and fine needles were used in knitting this holder. Cast on 64 stitches. Knit across plain with the lavender yarn. Knit back 12 stitches plain; then add the white yarn and knit: 8 white, 8 lavender, 8 white, 8 lavender, and 8 white, following the same plan as in knitting the corn-design at No. 4; then 12 lavender plain. Knit back and forth in this way 8 times. This forms one division of the design. In the next row knit with the lavender so as to reverse the order of the blocks, making the second block of white instead of lavender. Knit 8 rows also for this division. Knit in this order until the holder is 8 blocks wide and cast off.

NO 8.—KNITTED HOLDER.

Gather the block portion at each end under a tiny bow.

Holders of this style are very handsome made of knitting silk, and the ends may be arranged in a variety of ways.

KNITTED HOLDER.

No. 9.—The holder illustrated by this picture is made of ordinary yarn in two colors, although it may also be made of odds and ends of wool left over from fancy work. It is knitted on steel needles in alternate squares of plain and purled (or seam) stitches. When finished there must be seven rows of one color all round the holder between the sqares and the border. The holder here pictured is made of red and gray yarn.

Cast on 64 stitches, and knit 7 rows of one color plain; then of the same color knit 7 stitches plain; join the other color, and purl 10; carry the first yarn along the back, and knit 10 plain; then with the second color purl 10; then with the first color knit 10; with the other color purl 10; and then with the first color knit 7.

Turn, knit 17 plain, joining the second color at the 8th stitch; purl 10, knit 10, purl 10, knit 17, joining the second color to correspond with the other side.

Knit 10 rows for each row of squares, and reverse the order of the colors for the alternate rows, as seen in the engraving.

When six rows of squares are completed, knit 7 rows plain; and then knit the border as follows, and sew it on:

Cast on 7 stitches.

First row.—Slip 1, knit 2, put the thread over, and knit 2 together, knit 2.

Second row.—Slip 1, knit 1, put thread over; knit 2, put thread over, knit 2 together; knit 1.

Third row.—Slip 1, knit 2, put thread over, knit 2 out of the next stitch, putting the thread over before making each stitch; knit 1, purl 1, knit 2.

Fourth row.—Slip 1, knit 7, put thread over, knit 2 together, knit 1.

Fifth row.—Slip 1, knit 2, put thread over, knit 2 together, make 1 dot; for this dot take the next 2 stitches on another needle, wind the yarn four times around these two stitches from the wrong side toward the right, and then knit them off; then knit 1, make a dot as before, and knit 1.

Sixth row.—Cast off 4 stitches, knit 3, put thread over, knit 2 together, knit 1.

This edging is very quaint-looking and pretty, and can be made of thread or silk for any purpose.

DOUBLE KNITTING (ON FOUR NEEDLES).
(No Illustration.)

Cast on any even number of stitches, * bring the thread forward, slip a stitch, put the thread back to cross last stitch knit; knit 1 plain, putting the thread twice round the needle; repeat from *. In knitting with two needles every row back and front is the same, but you must take care, however, to knit the stitch that was slipped in the last row, and slip the one that was knitted; but, of course, it is

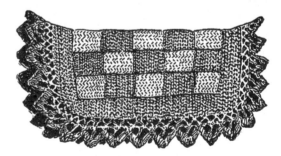

NO. 9.—KNITTED HOLDER.

not so with four needles. Then you cast on twice the number of stitches that you wish to have on the right side, and knit the first row by the above directions. It is well to put in a bit of colored wool or cotton to mark the beginning of the rounds, otherwise it may be a little difficult to distinguish it, and, of course, it is there that the pattern changes.

Second row.—The first stitch you come to is the

one slipped in the last round, and that is to be purled with the thread twice around the needle. The next is the one that was knitted in the last round, which you will always easily recognize by the thread being twice round the needle; this is to

NO. 10.—KNITTED NIGHT-DRESS CASE.

be slipped, bringing the thread forward first, and replacing it when the stitch is taken off. Both put-overs of the thread are to be slipped as one stitch; purl the next, putting the thread twice round; bring the thread forward, slip the next, put the thread back, and continue these two stitches alternately throughout the round.

Third row.—Like the first.

Fourth row.—Like the 2nd; and so on.

If rightly done, both sides of the work will look exactly alike, and will be quite detached from each other. If finer work is desired, we have no doubt it could be knitted as well with the thread once round, in the ordinary way; the purled stitch for the back must also be knitted to correspond.

KNITTED NIGHT-DRESS CASE, WITH DETAILS.
(For Illustrations see this and next Page.)

NOS. 10, 11, 12 AND 13.—This case is a very pretty addition to the dainty adjuncts of my lady's wardrobe. It is made of crochet cotton and may be lined with white or tinted silk or cotton fabric.

To Knit the Middle or Fancy Stripe (See No. 12).—Cast on 47 stitches and purl or seam across once.

First row.—* Knit 2 together, th o, and repeat twice more from *; knit 5, * th o twice, k 2 together twice and repeat from last * 5 times more; th o twice, knit 5, * th o, slip 1, knit 1, pass slipped stitch over and repeat twice more from last *; knit 1.

Second row.—Purl. Also purl every alternate or even following row, being careful to *knit* the *last* half of each thread that is put over *twice*; and also in purling back, *knit* the stitches in the small diamonds, that were *purled* in the preceding row.

Third row.—Knit 2, * th o, slip 1, knit, 1, pass slipped stitch over and repeat twice more from *; knit 2, * k 2 together twice, th o twice, and repeat 5 times more from last *. K 2 together twice, k 2; * k 2 together, th o, and repeat twice more from last *; k 3.

Fifth row.—K 3, * th o, slip 1, k 1, pass slipped stitch over, and repeat twice more from *. K 2, * th o twice, k 2 together twice, and repeat twice more from last *. Th o, * k 2 together twice, th o twice, and repeat twice more from last * K 2, * k 2 together, th o, and repeat twice more from last *. K 4.

Seventh row.—K 4, * th o, slip 1, k 1, pass slipped stitch over and repeat twice more from *. * K 2 together twice, th o twice and repeat once more from last * K 2 together twice, k 1, wrap thread around the needle once, purl 1, th o, k 1, * k 2 together twice, th o twice and repeat once more from last *. Knit 2 together three times, th o, * k 2 together, th o, repeat once more from last *. K 5.

Ninth row.—K 2, * k 2 together, th o, and repeat twice more from *. K 3, * th o twice, k 2 together twice and repeat once more from last *. Th o twice, k 2 together, wrap the thread once around the needle, purl 3, th o, k 2 together, * th o twice, k 2 together twice and repeat once more from last *. Th o twice, k 3, * th o, slip 1, k 1, pass slipped stitch over and repeat twice more from last *. K 3.

Eleventh row.—K 1, * k 2 together, th o, and repeat twice more from *. K 3, * k 2 together twice, th o twice and repeat once more from last *. K 2 together twice, wrap the thread around the needle once, purl 2, k 1, purl 2; * k 2 together twice, th o twice, and repeat once more from last *; k 2 together twice, k 3, * th o, slip 1, k 1, pass slipped stitch over and repeat twice more from last *. K 2.

Thirteenth row.—* Knit 2 together, th o, and repeat twice more from *. K 5, * th o twice, k 2 together twice and repeat once more from last *. K 1, wrap the thread around the needle once, purl 2,

NO. 11.—DETAIL FOR BORDER TO CASE.
(For Description see page 150.)

k 3, purl 2, th o, k 1. * K 2 together twice, th o twice and repeat once more from last *. K 5, * th o, slip 1, k 1, pass slipped stitch over and repeat twice more from last *. K 1.

Fifteenth row.—K 2, * th o, slip 1, k 1, pass

slipped stitch over, and repeat twice more from *. K 2, * k 2 together twice, th o twice and repeat once more from last *. Purl 2 together, wrap thread once around the needle, purl 3, k 3, purl 3, th o, k 2 together, * th o twice, k 2 together twice and repeat

NO. 12.—FANCY STRIPE FOR CASE.

(For Description see this and preceding Page.)

once more from last *. K 2, * k 2 together, th o and repeat twice more from last *. K 3.

Seventeenth row.—K 3, * th o, slip 1, k 1, pass slipped stitch over and repeat twice more from *. K 2, * th o twice, k 2 together twice and repeat once more from last *. Wrap thread once around the needle, purl 1, th o, purl 2 together, purl 2, k 1, purl 2, purl 2 together, wrap thread once around the needle, purl 1, th o, * k 2 together twice, th o twice, and repeat once more from last *. K 2, * k 2 together, th o, and repeat twice more from last *. K 4.

Nineteenth row.—K 4, * th o, slip 1, k 1, pass slipped stitch over and repeat twice more from * K 2 together twice, th o twice, k 2 together twice, k 1, wrap thread once around the needle, purl 3, th o, purl 2 together, purl 3, purl 2 together, wrap thread once around the needle, purl 3, th o, k 1, k 2 together twice, th o twice, k 2 together 3 times, th o, * k 2 together, th o, and repeat once more from last *. K 5.

Twenty-first row.—K 2, * k 2 together, th o, and repeat twice more from *. K 3, th o twice, k 2 together twice, th o twice, k 2 together, wrap thread around the needle once, purl 2, k 1, purl 2, th o, purl 2 together, purl 1, purl 2 together, wrap thread once around the needle, purl 2, k 1, purl 2, th o, k 2 together, th o twice, k 2 together twice, th o twice, k 3; * th o, slip 1, k 1, pass slipped stitch over and repeat twice more from last *. K 3.

Twenty-third row.—K 1, * k 2 together, thread over and repeat twice more from *; k 3, k 2 together twice, th o twice, k 2 together twice, wrap thread around the needle once, purl 3, k 1, purl 3, wrap thread around the needle once, purl 3 together.

wrap thread once around the needle, purl 3, k 1, purl 3, th o, k 2 together twice, th o twice, k 2 together twice, k 3, * th o, slip 1, k 1, pass slipped stitch over, and repeat twice more from last *. K 2.

Twenty-fifth row.—* K 2 together, th o, and repeat twice more from *. K 5, th o twice, k 2 together twice, th o twice, k 2 together, wrap the thread once around the needle, purl 2 together, purl 3, purl 2 together, purl 3, purl 2 together, th o, k 2 together, th o twice, k 2 together twice, th o twice, k 5, * th o, slip 1, k 1, pass slipped stitch over, repeat twice more from last *. K 1.

Twenty-seventh row.—K 2, * th o, slip 1, k 1, pass slipped stitch over and repeat twice more from last *. K 2, k 2 together twice, th o twice, k 2 together twice, k 1, th o, purl 2 together, purl 1, purl 2 together, wrap thread once around the needle, purl 2, k 1, purl 2, th o, purl 2 together, purl 1, purl 2 together, th o, k1, k 2 together twice, th o twice, k 2 together twice, k 2, * k 2 together, th o, and repeat twice more from last *. K 3.

Twenty-ninth row.—Knit 3, * th o, slip 1, k 1, pass slipped stitch over and repeat twice more from *. K 2, th o twice, k 2 together twice, th o twice, k 2 together, k 1, wrap thread around the needle once, purl 3 together, wrap thread around the needle once, p 2, k 3, p 2, wrap thread around the needle once, p 3 together, th o, k 1, k 2 together, th o twice, k 2 together twice, th o twice, k 2, * k 2 together, th o, repeat twice more from last *. K 4.

Thirty-first row.—Knit 4, * th o, sl 1, k 1, pass slipped stitch over, and repeat twice more from *. * K 2 together twice, th o

NO. 13.—SIDE STRIPE FOR CASE.

(For Description see following Page.)

twice, and repeat once more from last *. K 2 together, th o, p 2 together, p 2, k 3, p 2, p 2 together, th o, k 2 together, th o twice, k 2 together twice, th o twice, k 2 together 3 times, th o, * k 2 together, th o and repeat once more from from last *. K 5.

Thirty-third row.—Knit 2, * k 2 together, th o

and repeat twice more from *. K 3, * th o twice, k 2 together twice and repeat once more from last *. K 1, th o, p 2 together, p 2, k 1, p 2, p 2 together, th o, k 1, * k 2 together twice, th o twice and repeat once more from last *; k 3, * th o, sl 1, k 1, pass slipped stitch over and repeat twice more from last *. K 3.

Thirty-fifth row.—Knit 1, * k 2 together, th o and repeat twice more from *; k 3, * k 2 together twice, th o twice, and repeat once more from last *; k 2 together; k 1, th o, p 2 together, p 3, p 2 together, th o, k 1, k 2 together, * th o twice, k 2 together twice and repeat once more from last *. K 3, * th o, sl 1, k 1, pass slipped stitch over and repeat twice more from last *. K 2.

Thirty-seventh row.—* K 2 together, th o and repeat twice more from *. K 5, * th o twice, k 2 together twice, and repeat once more from last *; th o twice and k 2 together, th o, p 2 together, p 1, p 2 together, th o, k 2 together, * th o twice, k 2 together twice and repeat once more from last *. Th o twice, k 5, * th o, sl 1, k 1, pass slipped stitch over and repeat twice more from last *. K 1.

Thirty-ninth row.—Knit 2, * th o, sl 1, k 1 pass slipped stitch over and repeat twice more from * K 2, * k 2 together twice, th o twice and repeat once more from last *. K 2 together twice, k 1, wrap thread around the needle, p 3 together, th o, k 1, * k 2 together twice, th o twice and repeat once more from last *. K 2 together twice, k 2, * k 2 together, th o and repeat twice more from last *. K 3.

Forty-first row.—Knit 3, * th o, sl 1, k 1, pass slipped stitch over, and repeat twice more from *. K 2 * th o twice, k 2 together twice and repeat once more from last *. Th o twice, k 2 together, k 1, th o, * k 2 together twice, th o twice and repeat twice more from last *. K 2, * k 2 together, th o, and repeat twice more from last *. K 4.

Forty-third row.—Knit 4, * th o, sl 1, k 1, pass slipped stitch over and repeat twice more from *. * K 2 together twice, th o twice and repeat twice more from last *. K 2 together, k 1, * th o twice, k 2 together twice and repeat once more from last *. Th o twice, k 2 together 3 times, th o, * k 2 together, th o, and repeat once more from last *. K 5.

Forty-fifth row.—Knit 4, * th o, sl 1, k 1, pass slipped stitch over and repeat twice more from *. K 1, * th o twice, k 2 together twice, and repeat 5 times more from last *; th o, k 2, th o, k 2 together, th o, k 2 together, th o, k 5.

Repeat all these details, beginning with the 7th row for the next section in the stripe, and work in this way until the stripe is 29 or 30 inches long.

To Knit the Side Stripe (see No. 13).—Pick up the stitches along each edge of the middle stripe. Make 12 rows, knitting alternately as follows: 1 plain row, 2 purled rows.

Thirteenth row.—Knit 1, th o, p 3 together, th o, and repeat to the end of the row.

Fourteenth row.—Purl.

Next 2 rows like the last 2.

Seventeenth row.—Purl.

Eighteenth row.—Knit plain.

Nineteenth and Twentieth rows.—Purl.

Twenty-first row.—Knit plain.

Repeat twice more beginning with the nineteenth row. This completes the edge pattern and brings you to the fancy pattern.

First row.—Purl 3, k 1, * p 5, k 1, and repeat from * across the row. Knit back plain.

Third row.—Purl 2, * k 3, p 3 and repeat from * across the row. Knit back plain.

Fifth row.—Purl 1, k 5; repeat across the row. Knit back plain. This completes one section of the design.

Seventh row.—Knit 1, purl 5 and repeat across the row. Knit back plain.

Ninth row.—Knit 2 * purl 3, knit 3 and repeat from * across the row. Knit back plain.

Eleventh row.—Knit 3, * purl 1, knit 5 and repeat from * across the row. Knit back plain. This completes the second section of the design. Repeat these two sections until there 7 of them in all. Then repeat the edge pattern, knitting it so as to correspond with the one at the other side of the fancy pattern. In completing these side stripes they may be sloped off in knitting them, or they may be finished squarely and turned under when the case is being made. When all the stripes are knitted, join them together in the order seen in the engraving at No. 10, and doubling the sides together for 12½ inches, join them by an over-and-over stitch. This will leave a lap 4 or 5 inches long to fold over the opening of the case. Next crochet a row of cross-trebles around the outer edges of the case, to provide openings for the insertion of ribbon.

Then add the border to the edges and along the center stripe, crocheting it as represented by No. 11. If preferred, a knitted edging may be used in place of the one illustrated.

In lining the case, color may be laid under the middle stripe only.

KNITTED AFGHAN.
(No Illustration.)

A knitted, striped afghan may be made in three colors—dark-red, pale-blue and tan color being pretty shades to select for the stripes—and consist of five stripes which include three patterns. Each stripe should be about a-quarter of a yard wide and should be knitted of Germantown wool on coarse steel, wooden or ivory needles.

CENTER STRIPE.

The center stripe is made of dark-red by the design illustrated at No. 8, on page 21, and is knitted according to the directions also found on page 21.

REMAINING STRIPES.

For the stripe at each side of the middle stripe, knit as follows:

Cast on 50 stitches with the blue yarn. Knit across and purl back, repeating in this order the whole length of the stripe. This will make a right and wrong side the same as in a stocking.

For each outer stripe knit as follows:

Cast on 50 stitches of tan-colored yarn and knit across plain.

First row.—Purl 1 and knit 1 out of every stitch.

Second row.—* Slip 1, knit 1, pass slipped stitch over and repeat from * across the row.

Repeat these two rows until the stripe is as long as required.

Then crochet the stripes together in cable-cord style with black and yellow, after the following method:

Catch one color at a corner of the work and make a chain of 3; slip the hook out, fasten the other color in the next stitch and make another chain of 3, and also slip the hook out; now fasten the first chain with a single crochet in the 3rd stitch, and crochet another chain of 3; slip the hook out and fasten the chain of the other color in the 4th stitch and make another chain of 3; then fasten the last chain of the first color in the next stitch, and repeat these details, always keeping the unfastened chains in front of the hook.

Finish the edges with a crocheted border made of black and edged with yellow, making 5 rows of shells with the black wool, with 6 double crochets in each shell, and each shell made in the middle of the shell underneath. Then take the yellow wool, fasten it in the corner of a shell, and make chains of 3 caught with single crochets in every other stitch of the shell; next make similar chains down the sides of the shells and back again, catching them around the stitches in the spaces between the shells. Repeat these details around all the shells.

KNITTED PURSE.

No. 14.—The purse shown at No. 14 requires black and red purse silk, jet beads, a steel clasp with chain, and 5 steel needles in making it. Begin the purse with the black silk in the center of the bottom part, and cast on for one block 7 stitches. K 14 rows on these back and forth in such a manner that the work is knitted on one side and purled on the other. The 1st stitch of every row is slipped and the 1st row of the block is purled.

No. 14.—KNITTED PURSE.

* On that side where hangs the thread with which you work, take the side chain of the 7 selvedge stitches of the part you have just knitted, on a separate needle, and knit another block, which must have 15 rows, and the 1st row of which is knitted. Repeat 10 times more from *. The stitches of several parts can be taken on the same needle, so as not to be hindered, in working, by too many needles. A reference to the engraving will make clear to the knitter how the stitches are taken up so that the rows of every 2 blocks will run at right angles with each other.

When the 12th block is completed, take the selvedge stitches on the left-hand needle on another needle, cast them off together with the cast-on stitches of the 1st block, and fasten the silk. Then take the 7 right-hand selvedge stitches of one black block on a needle; take the red silk on which the beads have been strung, and work 15 rows on these stitches, working the 1st row from the wrong side, and therefore purled. In the 1st, as well as in all the other purled rows, the last stitch must be purled together with the next stitch of the next black block.

In the purled rows, moreover, excepting in the first and last ones, a bead must be worked in after casting off the 2nd, 4th and 6th stitches. The stitch must be worked by inserting the needle into the back part, and in drawing through the silk which has been thrown forward, let the bead slide through stitch so that it is on the right side of the work.

In the following knitted row, the needle must also be inserted into the back part of the bead stitch. When 12 such red blocks have been completed, work again 12 black blocks on the selvedge stitches of the same, in which the beads are not knitted in, but sewn afterwards, when the purse is completed. Then work 3 times more alternately, 12 red and 12 black blocks. When the last 12 black blocks have been completed, cast off the stitches of the last black block together with the selvedge stitches, the 1st on the wrong side; the stitches of the 6th part are cast off in the same manner, together with the selvedge stitches of the 7th part.

The red blocks which remain to be worked on

No. 15.—Knitted Cloth for Polishing Floors.

the black blocks are thus lessened by 2; the 2nd, 3rd, 4th, 7th, 8th and 9th of these blocks must be 6 rows longer. Then gather all of the stitches and selvedge stitches of the 10 parts on 2 needles, in such a manner that the 2 black blocks, the stitches and selvedge stitches of which have been cast off together, are placed on the sides of the purse, and knit off as follows with black, first on the stitches of the one needle, and then on those of the other:

1 row knitted, knitting together every 3rd and 4th stitch; then work 3 rows back and forward on the same number of stitches, which must be knitted on the right side; then work 8 rows more in the same manner, casting off the first 2 stitches of the 8 rows. Then cast off all the remaining stitches, sew the beads on the black parts from the illustration, also the clasp and bead tassel.

Knitted Cloth for Polishing Floors.

No. 15.—This cloth is made of unbleached wick cotton (see picture) and is knitted back and forth on very large wooden needles. About 90 stitches are cast on by the "First Method" (see page 7). Knit 60 of these stitches, then slip the rest off the needle and pull them into a chain for the loop. In knitting back, pick up the end of the chain and knit it off with the first stitch to form the loop. Knit until the article is square in shape and then bind off. Dusters may be knitted of the cotton illustrated by splitting it. A ball of cotton will knit a polishing cloth about 20 inches square.

Knitted Blue-Bag.

No. 16.—The materials required are Scotch wool, and four needles, No. 16.

The bag is commenced at the top; cast 148 stitches on 3 needles—that is, 49 on 2 needles, and 50 on 1.

First round.—Purl.

Second to Eleventh rounds.—Knit 1, purl 1, alternately, all round.

Twelfth to Fifteenth rounds.—Purl.

Sixteenth to Twentieth rounds.—Knit.

Twenty-first round.—Th o, knit 2 together throughout the round.

Twenty-second to Twenty-sixth rounds.—Knit.

Twenty-seventh to Thirtieth rounds.—Purl.

Thirty-first to Thirty-fourth rounds.—Knit 1, purl 1 throughout.

Thirty-fifth to Thirty-ninth rounds.—Purl 1, knit 1 throughout.

Continue to repeat these last 4 rounds alternately, 4 times throughout the work. In each alternate round decrease by knitting 2 stitches together at the beginning of each needle. (4 rounds form a pattern.) In the fifth pattern, knit 3 stitches together at the beginning of each needle in the last round. Repeat the alternate 4 rows 5 times more without decrease, to give the bag a better shape. You now, in the next pattern, knit 2 stitches together at the beginning and end of each needle in all 4 rows. In the next 4 rows, decrease the same. In the next 4 rows, knit 3 stitches together at the beginning of each needle. Now knit 4 rows, decreasing in each row until no stitches are left. A cord of chain-crochet is run through the holes at the top of the bag and its ends are completed with full tassels of the same wool.

No. 16.—Knitted Blue-Bag.

Knitted Coffee Strainer.

No. 17.—This strainer is made of knitting cotton.

Cast 124 stitches on three needles—that is, 41 on 2 needles and 42 on the other.

First to Tenth rounds.—Knit.

Eleventh round.—M 1, k 2 together; repeat.

Twelfth to Twenty-second rounds.—Knit.

To shape the strainer, knit as for the toe of a stocking—that is, knit 2 together at the end of each needle in every 4th round, until there are no stitches left. Turn the top of the strainer down to the 11th row to form the hem, and sew it to the metal ring which fits the top of the coffee pot.

No. 17.—Knitted Coffee-Strainer.

KNITTED TOWEL.

No. 18.—This towel may be knitted with white

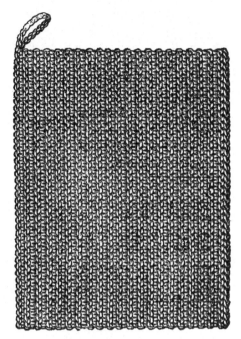

NO. 18.—KNITTED TOWEL.

or unbleached braid or with No. 2 knitting cotton, which is as thick as fleecy wool. Use No. 3 needles.

Cast on 43 stitches, knit back and forth for 42 rows, and then cast off.

The loop may be crocheted before the stitches are cast on, the last stitch of the loop being slipped upon the needle as the first knitting stitch; and when knitting back the end of the loop may be taken up and knitted in the next time across. Or, a long piece of the cotton may be left at the beginning of the casting-on, and the loop crocheted from it afterward and fastened with a large needle. Either method is better than a loop made separately and sewed on. The towel may be made as large or as small as desired, according to the number of stitches cast on.

KNITTED EGG HOLDER.

No. 19.—This is a useful article for keeping boiled eggs warm, and is made of a pretty shade of Berlin wool as follows:

Cast 81 stitches onto a No. 15 knitting needle.

First row.—K 3 and p 3 alternately.

Second row.—P 3 and k 3 alternately.

Third and Fourth rows.—Like 1st row.

Fifth row.—Like 2nd row.

Sixth row.—Like 1st row ; then repeat from the

first row. This forms a basket pattern. Knit in this manner until you have the foundation the length required.

There are 6 pockets. For each cast on 28 stitches ; decrease in every 3rd row by knitting 2 together at the end. Work as follows :

First row.—Knit.

Second row.—Purl.

Third row.—Knit.

Fourth row.—Purl.

Fifth and Sixth rows.—Knit. Repeat from 1st row until no stitches remain.

Crochet an edge around the foundation and each pocket as follows : * 1 double crochet into a stitch, 4 chain, 1 treble into the 1st chain stitch, skip 2 stitches and repeat from *.

Sew the pockets on as seen in the engraving, with a needle and some of the wool.

FRICTION MITTEN.

No. 20.—At No. 20 is seen a friction mitten— a commendable article to use after a bath or, indeed, at any time to promote the circulation of the blood. It is easily made as follows:

Use fine twine or cord for the foundation and hemp packing-twine for the rough outside surface. Knit it in two halves, and sew them together with an over-and-over stitch.

Use steel needles, and cast on 30 stitches. Knit back and forth 80 rows of plain knitting, but in every second row knit the coarse twine in loops, which are cut open after the mitten is finished.

The loops are made thus:

Slip the first stitch, and before knitting the next stitch, lay the thick twine across the working thread; * knit a stitch with the fine twine; bring the coarse twine from the front to the back across the stitch just knitted, and over the working thread; knit a stitch with the fine twine; carry the thick twine around a mesh or rod an inch in circumference which is to be held at the back of the work, and then bring it to the front before the next stitch; repeat from * In the last 26 of the 80 rows, narrow 1 stitch at both ends

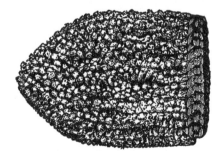

NO. 20.—FRICTION MITTEN.

of every plain row. The edge is finished with a chain crocheted with red cotton and sewed on.

NO. 19.—KNITTED EGG HOLDER.

KNITTED PURSE.

No. 21.—This purse is made of knitting silk, and worked in rounds with four needles.

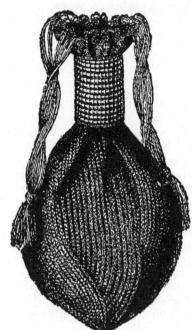

No. 21.—KNITTED PURSE.

Cast on 64 stitches, that is 22 on each of two needles and 20 on the third needle.

First round.—Purl.

Knit for 2½ inches.

Now commence the decrease as follows:

First Round.—K 4, sl 1, k 1, pass the slipped stitch over. Repeat three times more.

Second to Fourth rounds.—Knit without decrease

Fifth round.—K 4, sl 1, k 1, pass the slipped stitch over, k 9.

Sixth to Eighth rounds.—Knit.

Ninth round.—K 4, sl 1, k 1, pass the slipped stitch over, k 8.

Tenth to Twelfth rounds.—Knit.

Thirteenth round.—K 4, sl 1, k 1, pass the slipped stitch over, k 7. Repeat.

Fourteenth and Fifteenth rounds.—Knit.

Sixteenth round.—K 4, sl 1, k 1, pass the slipped stitch over, k 6. Repeat.

Seventeenth and Eighteenth rounds.—Knit.

Nineteenth round.—K 4, sl 1, k 1, pass the slipped stitch over, k 5. Repeat.

Twentieth and Twenty-first rounds.—Knit.

Twenty-second round.—K 4, sl 1, k 1, pass the slipped stitch over, knit 4. Repeat.

Twenty-third round.—Knit.

Twenty-fourth round.—K 4, sl 1, k 1, pass the slipped stitch over, k 3. Repeat.

Twenty-fifth round.—Knit.

Twenty-sixth round.—K 4, sl 1, k 1, pass the slipped stitch over, k 2. Repeat.

Twenty-seventh round.—Knit.

Twenty-eighth round.—K 4, sl 1, k 1, pass the slipped stitch over, k 1. Repeat.

Twenty-ninth round.—Knit.

Thirtieth round.—K 4, sl 1, k 1, pass the slipped stitch over. Repeat.

Thirty-first round.—* K 4, sl 1, k 1, pass the slipped stitch over. Repeat from * three times.

After this, decrease in each round by knitting 1 stitch less between the decreasings, until there are only 4 stitches remaining. Take a coarse needle, thread it with silk, and draw the remaining 4 stitches together.

The top is finished by a narrow crocheted edge made as follows: 1 double into a stitch; 4 chain, skip 2 stitches, 1 double into the next. Repeat all round. Lengths of fine cord or of knitting silk are run through the work about 1 inch from the top, the ends of which are drawn from the inside of the purse. They are finished by being tightly knotted together at the ends to form small tassels. A ring of gilt or steel is slipped over the top.

HOW TO MAKE BALLS FOR THE ENDS OF CORDS.

Nos. 22, 23 AND 24.—Cut from card-board a circular piece about one inch in diameter, and make a large hole in the center (see No. 22); run the worsted in and out through the hole, about the solid portion of the section, as shown by the picture, until the section is thickly and uniformly covered. Then run a thread of the worsted under the worsted on the section, as shown by No. 23, being careful to put the needle back in the place where it comes through till the thread comes out at the starting point; then cut the worsted all around the edge of the section, and tie the thread run round the hole as tightly as possible. The manner

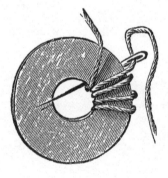

No. 22.

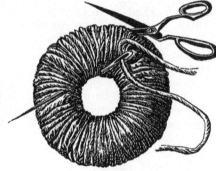

No. 23.

of tying the thread when the worsted is cut is shown at No. 24. After cutting the worsted pull it through the hole, clip the threads evenly and closely with sharp scissors, and roll the ball between the palms of the hands to shape it; then shake it well.

The balls may be made any size desired by increasing or decreasing the size of the card-board section.

Another method is as follows: Cut the wool into lengths of an inch and a-half; take a bunch twice the thickness of a full skein of the wool for each ball, and tie it very tightly through the middle with twine; then with the scissors clip it into shape and sew to a cord.

No. 24.

NOS. 22, 23 AND 24.—DETAILS FOR MAKING BALLS FOR THE ENDS OF CORDS.

Needle-Craft:

ARTISTIC and PRACTICAL.

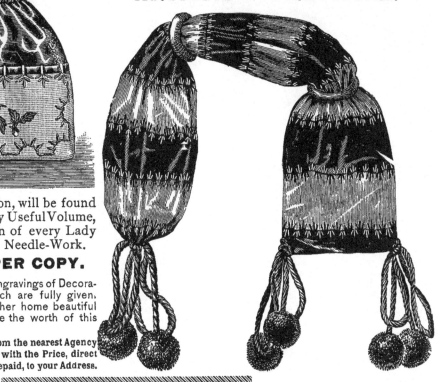

In the Second, Revised, Edition, will be found a Comprehensive and Eminently Useful Volume, that should be in the possession of every Lady who devotes any of her time to Needle-Work.

PRICE, 4s. or $1.00 PER COPY.

THE Book is replete with accurate Engravings of Decorative Work, instructions for which are fully given. Every Lady who delights in making her home beautiful by her own handiwork will appreciate the worth of this handsome volume.

If "Needle-Craft" cannot be procured from the nearest Agency for the Sale of our Goods, send your Order, with the Price, direct to us, and the Work will be forwarded, prepaid, to your Address.

Needle and Brush:

Useful and Decorative,

IS THE LATEST AND MOST COMPLETE WORK ISSUED IN THE INTEREST OF DECORATIVE ART.

A Book of Original, Artistic and Graceful Designs, and one that should be seen in every Boudoir and Studio.

Price, 4s. or $1.00 Per Copy.

In this Volume will be found innumerable Artistic Designs for the decoration of a home, all of them to be developed by the Needle or Brush and the dainty fingers of either the novice or the experienced artist.

The instructions are clear and comprehensive, and fully

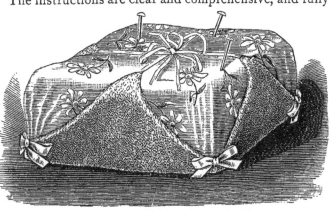

carry out the author's intention of rendering invaluable aid alike to beginners and graduates in the pretty art of decoration.

If "Needle and Brush" cannot be obtained from the nearest Agency for the sale of our goods mail your Order, with the Price, direct to us, and the work will be sent, prepaid, to your Address.

THE BUTTERICK PUBLISHING CO. [Limited],

*171 to 175 Regent St., London, W.; or
7, 9 and 11 West Thirteenth St., New York.*

The Art of Crocheting.

Price, 2s. or 50 Cents.

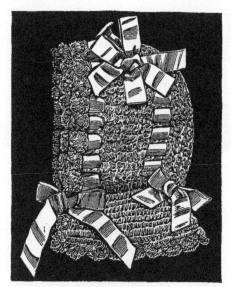

This Beautiful Work is replete with illustrations of *Fancy Stitches, Edgings, Insertions, Garments of various kinds and Articles of Usefulness and Ornament, with Correct Instructions for making them.* In addition to this, it also contains many Specially Prepared and Perfectly Clear Directions, unaccompanied by illustrations, for the Various Kinds of Crochet-Work mentioned.

The Book also contains many valuable Hints and Suggestions as to various applications of the designs illustrated. A Unique Feature is the addition of a Department called "PRETTY WORK FOR LITTLE FOLK," whereby the Younger Members of the Family may be instructed and amused at the same time.

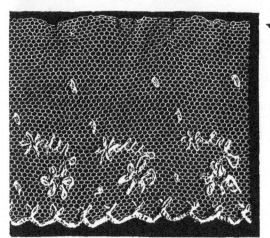

The Work in **Every Respect Excels any other Book upon Crocheting ever issued.** The instructions are so simplified and arranged that any child who can read may learn to crochet from them, while adults who have heretofore found printed instructions generally unintelligible will be able, from the pages of this Manual, to crochet any Article illustrated or described therein. It is printed upon elegant paper, with a handsome, flexible cover.

If this Work cannot be obtained from the nearest Agency for the sale of our goods, send your Order, with the Price, direct to Us, and the Pamphlet will be forwarded, prepaid, to your Address.

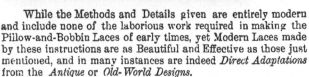

The Art of Modern Lace-Making.

Price, 2s. or 50 Cents.

A BEAUTIFUL Manual of this Fascinating Art, bearing the *above Title* and *containing* over **One Hundred Illustrations** of Modern Lace and Designs, together with Full Instructions for the work, from the *Primary Stitches* to the *Final Details.*

While the Methods and Details given are entirely modern and include none of the laborious work required in making the Pillow-and-Bobbin Laces of early times, yet Modern Laces made by these instructions are as Beautiful and Effective as those just mentioned, and in many instances are indeed *Direct Adaptations* from the *Antique* or *Old-World Designs.*

The Collection Includes **Needle-Point, Honiton, Princess** and **Royal Battenburg** Laces, the new "**Ideal Honiton,**" the popular **Louis XIV. Curtain Lace,** and a variety of **Designs** in **Darned Net.**

Printed upon *Elegant Paper*, with an Attractive, *Flexible Cover*, the Pamphlet is a convenient addition to the Fancy-Work supply selected to employ the idle hours.

Every possessor of a taste for fine fancy-work should send for this beautiful Pamphlet. It will provide a new and dainty field for the genius of her fingers, and charming possibilities for her artistic tendencies.

If this Work cannot be obtained from the nearest Agency for the sale of our goods, send your Order, with the Price, direct to us, and the Pamphlet will be forwarded post-paid, to your Address.

THE BUTTERICK PUBLISHING CO. [Limited],

171 to 175, Regent St., London, W.;
or 7, 9 and 11 West 13th St., New York.

DRAWN-WORK: STANDARD AND NOVEL METHODS

Price, 2s. or 50 Cents.

EVERY step of the Work, from the drawing of the threads to the completion of intricate work is fully illustrated and described.

The Book includes Engravings of SPANISH, MEXICAN, DANISH AND BULGARIAN DRAWN-WORK, in *Borders, Laces, Handkerchiefs, Doilies, Towels, Tray-Cloths, Tidies, Infants' Garments,* etc., etc., together with *Instructions* for Making the Work and Decorating the articles mentioned, and also Innumerable Suggestions as to Fabrics, Knotting Materials, the Selection of Colors, etc., etc.

With the above are also included Twelve Full-Page Engravings of Magnificent Specimens of Drawn-Work which make the Book a Work of Art, that will not be out of place on the drawing-room table, while also affording the Student of the Work the FINEST DESIGNS to be obtained.

If this Work cannot be obtained from the nearest Agency for the sale of our Goods, send your Order, with the Price, direct to Us, and the Pamphlet will be forwarded, prepaid, to your address.

Masquerade and Carnival: THEIR CUSTOMS AND COSTUMES.

Price, 2s. or 50 cents.

A NEW, LARGE AND HANDSOMELY ILLUSTRATED WORK, containing all the Important Points concerning Festivities of this class, as well as those of a kindred variety, and displaying between Two and Three Hundred Illustrations of Historical, Legendary Traditional, Shakespearean, National and original Costumes, with Descriptions of them, especially in reference to Colors and Fabrics. These Costumes are for Ladies, Gentlemen, Young Folks and Children, and have been selected with Great Care as to their Effectiveness and Practicality, as well as to their Correctness of Detail. The Book will be Invaluable in Arranging Amateur, School and Church Entertainments, and should be ordered at once. Many varieties of Fancy-Dress Entertainments are suggested, *Tableaux, Bals Masque, Carnival Sessions,* and *Fashionable Fancy-Dress Parties* for adults and children being fully described.

If this Work cannot be obtained from the nearest Agency for the sale of our Goods, send your Order, with the Price direct to Us, and the Pamphlet will be forwarded, prepaid, to your Address.

THE BUTTERICK PUBLISHING CO. [Limited],   171 to 175 Regent Street, LONDON, W.; or 7, 9 and 11 West 13th Street, NEW YORK.

Metropolitan Culture Series.

GOOD MANNERS: This Book explains in extremely interesting fashion the most approved methods of deportment in every circumstance of Polite Society. It is a comprehensive work, replete with valuable hints and suggestions for the guidance, not only of young people desirous of acquiring refined manners, but of persons of maturer age in regard to those nicer or more rare points of etiquette about which even the best informed sometimes wish information.

SOCIAL LIFE: This Book sets forth in the form of a friendly correspondence, those points of Practical Etiquette regarding which the Novice in polite society desires to be fully instructed. It also contains an Appendix of Approved Styles of Invitations and Replies. Those who acquaint themselves fully with the rules laid down in "Good Manners" will find how they may be applied in "Social Life."

HOME-MAKING AND HOUSE-KEEPING: This is a Hand-Book of Household Affairs, convenient for guidance in all those matters a knowledge of which constitutes that pearl among women—the good housekeeper. It is equally valuable to prospective brides, youthful housekeepers and those whom experience has versed in economic and methodical home-making and house-keeping.

THE PATTERN COOK BOOK: This is a complete, practical and reliable work on the Culinary Science: embracing the Chemistry of Food; the Furnishing of the Kitchen; how to choose good Food; a choice selection of Standard Recipes; Meats, Vegetables, Bread, Cakes, Pies, Desserts; Proper Food for the Sick; Items of Interest in the Kitchen, etc., etc.

BEAUTY, ITS ATTAINMENT AND PRESERVATION: No effort has been spared to make this the most complete and reliable work ever offered to Those Who Desire to Be Beautiful in Mind, Manner, Feature and Form. Defects in each direction are philosophically and scientifically discussed, in connection with suggestions and remedies concerning the same.

STYLE OF THE "CULTURE" SERIES.

These Books are octavo in size and are uniform in type and style of binding. Each contains from 350 to 600 pages of reading matter, neatly printed in clear type on handsome paper, and is elegantly bound in cloth, with gilt title.

PLEASE REMEMBER:

The Price of ANY ONE of the above Books is FOUR SHILLINGS or ONE DOLLAR, prepaid by us to any Address. If the Books cannot be obtained from the nearest Agency for the sale of our Goods, mail your Order direct to Us, sending funds by Draft, Post-Office or Express Money-Order or Registered Letter.

THE BUTTERICK PUBLISHING CO. [LIMITED],

171 to 175 Regent Street, London, W.; or

7, 9 and 11 West Thirteenth Street, New York.

The Metropolitan Pamphlet Series,

SMOCKING AND FANCY STITCHES FOR THE DECORATION OF GARMENTS:

An Illustrated Treatise on the Manner of Making Smocking or Honeycombing by both the American and English Methods, together with suggestions for its Application to Various Garments. This pamphlet also contains Illustrations of Decorative Stitches of Various Kinds, any of which may be used in Connection with Smocking, although they are also Suitable for Decorating Garments which are not Smocked. Among the Stitches are Plain and Fancy Feather-Stitching, Cat-Stitching, Herring-Bone, Briar, Chain and Loop Stitches. Also a Separate Department devoted to the Illustration and Description of NUMEROUS POPULAR DESIGNS IN CROSS-STITCH for Embroidering Garments made of Checked Ginghams and Shepherd's Check Woolen Fabrics, all well as those of Plain Goods. *Price, 6d. or 15 cents.*

MOTHER AND BABE:

An illustrated 52-page Pamphlet, devoted to the Comfort and Care of Mother and Babe, containing full information concerning the Proper Care of Infants and the Preparation of their Wardrobes, and specifying the Various Articles necessary for a Baby's First Outfit. Also, treats of the Necessities belonging to the Health, Comfort and Care of the Expectant Mother, and contains Hints as to the Proper Clothing for Ladies in Delicate Health. *Price, 6d. or 15 cents.*

THE PERFECT ART OF CANNING AND PRESERVING:

A Convenient and Handsome Pamphlet fully Explanatory of Canning and Preserving. It contains full instructions regarding Jams, Marmalades, Jellies, Preserves, Canning (including Corn, Peas, Beans, Tomatoes, Asparagus, etc., etc.), Pickling, Catsups and Relishes, besides many Hints and Suggestions as to Selecting Fruit, the Easiest and Quickest Methods of Doing Good Work, etc., etc. *Price, 6d. or 15 cents.*

THE CORRECT ART OF CANDY-MAKING AT HOME:

A most attractive 24-page Pamphlet containing reliable instructions for successful Candy-Making at Home. It is divided into Departments, which introduce the Finest as well as the Plainest Candies made by the best Confectioners, and include Cream Candies, Bonbons, Nut and Fruit Candies, Pastes, Drops, Medicated Lozenges, and Candied Fruits, Flowers and Nuts. *Price, 6d. or 15 cents.*

DAINTY DESSERTS:

In this Pamphlet the Housekeeper will find directions for the preparation of Dainties adapted to the palate and means of the epicure or the laborer, and to the digestion of the robust or the feeble; there being also numerous recipes admirably suited to those occasions when unexpected company arrives. With its numberless recipes for Puddings and Sauces, Pies, Creams, Custards, and French, Fancy and Frozen Desserts, it is invaluable to every housekeeper, old or young, experienced or otherwise. *Price, 6d. or 15 cents.*

PASTIMES FOR CHILDREN:

A Large, Finely Illustrated Pamphlet for Children, containing Entertaining and Instructive Amusements for Rainy-Day and other Leisure Hours. It is filled with Drawing Designs and Games; Instructions for Mechanical Toys, Cutting out a Menagerie, Making a Circus of Stuffed animals, and Constructing Dolls and their Houses, Furniture and Costumes; Puzzles, Charades and Conundrums; and much other interesting matter. *Price, 1s. or 25 cents.*

PLEASE NOTICE: We will send any of the above Pamphlets to any Address, on receipt of price.

The Butterick Publishing Co. [Limited],

171 to 175 Regent Street, London, W.; or

7, 9 and 11 West Thirteenth Street, New York.

The DELINEATOR

IS A MONTHLY MAGAZINE OF

FASHION, CULTURE
AND FINE ARTS.

"* * * * * * THESE THINGS TO HEAR,
WOULD DESDEMONA SERIOUSLY INCLINE."—
OTHELLO, *Act* I., *Sc.* 3.

EACH issue contains over One Hundred Pages of Reading Matter on the Prevailing and Incoming Fashions for Ladies, Misses, Girls and Children, Seasonable Living, the Decoration of the Home, the Care of the Person, the Cultivation of the Artistic Faculties, the Newest Books, and a wide range of General Literature designed both to please and instruct.

The Fancy-Work Department is large and filled with novel ideas provided for us by special designers. The Magazine is indispensable to the Housewife and Mother.

SUBSCRIPTION PRICE, 5s. OR $1.00 PER YEAR.

(Post-paid by the Publishers to any Address in Great Britain, Ireland, the United States, Canada or Mexico.)

Extra Rates of Postage on the DELINEATOR when sent from the New York Office to Foreign Countries.

When the DELINEATOR is to be sent to any of the following Countries, **40 cents** for Extra Postage must accompany the Subscription Price:—Africa (British Colonies on West Coast), Abyssinia, Argentine Republic, Asia, Australia (South and West), Austria, Azores, Bahamas, Barbadoes, Belgium, Bermudas, Bolivia, Brazil, British Burmah, British Guiana, British Honduras, British New Guinea, Cape Verde, Ceylon, Chili, China (via Hong Kong or San Francisco), Columbia (U. S. of), Costa Rica, Cuba, Curacoa, Egypt, Fiji Islands, Finland, France, German, Gold Coast, Great Britain, Guatemala, Hawaiian Kingdom, Hayti, India, Ireland, Italy, Jamaica, Japan, Madagascar (St. Mary and Tamatave only), Martinique, Mauritius, Nassau (New Providence), New Caledonia, Newfoundland, New South Wales, New Zealand, Nicaragua, Panama, Paraguay, Persia, Peru, Porto Rico, Queensland, Russia, San Domingo, Servia, Siam, Sierra Leone, Singapore, Spain, Sweden, Switzerland, Tasmania, Trinidad, Turkey, Uruguay, Venezuela, Victoria and Zanzibar.

For the following Countries the Extra Rate to be prepaid with each Subscription is appended:—Accra, West Coast of Africa (except British Colonies), Cape Colony (South Africa), Natal (British Mail), and Orange Free State, $1.00 each; Transvaal, and Madagascar (except St. Mary and Tamatave), $1.32 each.

☞Parties subscribing are requested to specify particularly the Number with which they wish the Subscription to commence. Subscriptions will not be received for a shorter term than One Year, and are always payable in advance. We have no Club Rates, and no Commissions are allowed to any one on Subscriptions sent us.

ADDRESS: **THE BUTTERICK PUBLISHING CO. [LIMITED],**

171 to 175 Regent Street, London, W. ; or
7, 9 and 11 West 13th Street, New York.